T0314236

FORGING GLOBAL FORDISM

AMERICA IN THE WORLD

Sven Beckert and Jeremi Suri, Series Editors

For a full list of titles in the series, go to https://press.princeton.edu/catalogs /series/title/america-in-the-world.html.

Forging Global Fordism

NAZI GERMANY, SOVIET RUSSIA,
AND THE CONTEST OVER
THE INDUSTRIAL ORDER

STEFAN J. LINK

PRINCETON UNIVERSITY PRESS
PRINCETON & OXFORD

Published by Princeton University Press
41 William Street, Princeton, New Jersey 08540
6 Oxford Street, Woodstock, Oxfordshire OX20 1TR

press.princeton.edu

ISBN 9780691177540
ISBN (e-book) 9780691207988

British Library Cataloging-in-Publication Data is available

Editorial: Eric Crahan and Thalia Leaf
Production Editorial: Natalie Baan and Leslie Grundfest
Jacket Design: Layla Mac Rory
Production: Danielle Amatucci
Publicity: Alyssa Sanford and Amy Stewart
Copyeditor: Jennifer McClain

Jacket photo: Workers assembling a T-70 tank at Gorky Automobile Factory, 1942.
Courtesy of Central Regional Archives, Nizhnii Novgorod, Russia

This book has been composed in Arno

Printed on acid-free paper. ∞

Printed in the United States of America

10 9 8 7 6 5 4 3 2 1

To Gaby and Solène, with love

CONTENTS

FORGING GLOBAL FORDISM

Introduction

DETROIT, CAPITAL OF THE TWENTIETH CENTURY

Nineteenth-century civilization has collapsed.
—KARL POLANYI, *THE GREAT TRANSFORMATION*, 1944

WHEN REFORMERS and radicals of the 1930s described the contours of the future, they invoked the twentieth century. In doing so, they meant to repudiate the principles of the preceding era. The nineteenth century had been the age of liberalism, but the twentieth would be a postliberal era; the nineteenth century championed individualism, but the twentieth would be the century of the collective, of the "people" and of "space"; if the nineteenth century was the era of laissez-faire, the twentieth century would be the era of economic dirigisme. In exemplary fashion, Mussolini performed this incantation in his 1932 treatise *The Doctrine of Fascism*, in which he attacked liberalism, individualism, and democracy as "outgrown ideologies of the nineteenth century"—ideologies rejected by the "great experiments in political and social transformation" now everywhere under way. In their place would rise the twentieth, "a century of authority, a century tending to the 'right', a Fascist century."[1]

Not only fascists saw a new century dawning in the Thirties. John Maynard Keynes employed the notion in one of the key texts of his long intellectual transformation from classical liberal to leading theorist of state intervention. In the 1933 essay "National Self-Sufficiency," Keynes wrote:

It is a long business to shuffle out of the mental habits of the prewar nineteenth-century world. . . . But to-day at last, one-third of the way through the twentieth century, we are most of us escaping from the nineteenth; and by the time we reach its mid point, it may be that our habits of mind and what we care about will be as different from nineteenth-century methods and values as each other century's has been from its predecessor's.

Keynes considered in this essay the failure of the old internationalism to preserve peace and confessed his newfound willingness to honor deviations from the principles of economic liberalism and free trade. He also expressed his sympathy with the spirit, if not always with the practice, of the new "politico-economic experiments" that shaped the new international scene.[2]

Exiled in Paris, Walter Benjamin evoked a similar sentiment when he summoned the lost world of the nineteenth century in his "Arcades Project." To Benjamin, Paris was the capital of the nineteenth century. Its architecture reflected the rise of the bourgeoisie and the seductive triumph of the commodity form. The arcades of Paris expressed the culture of circulation, the city's world exhibitions the international sweep of the market, and its opera houses and museums the cultural sensibility of the commercial bourgeoisie. Writing in a dialectical spirit, Benjamin perceived in the bourgeois aesthetics of Paris glimpses of a future collective salvation. But in the 1930s, as Benjamin sensed only too keenly, the aesthetics of the nineteenth century—and with them the hope of salvation—crumbled around him.[3]

As Benjamin walked the streets of Paris, nostalgic for the promises of a bygone era, others turned away from the artifacts of commercial capitalism and trained their sights on the centers of industrial production. Port cities and commercial entrepôts may have been the metropolises of the nineteenth century, but the city most representative of the modern age was landlocked, and its iconic industry was as young as the new century itself. In the smokestacks and assembly lines of Detroit, in the din of the motor factories, where whirring conveyors laced together the bustle of thousands of workers, engineers and travelers from across the world glimpsed an image of the future. Seeking to exorcize the nineteenth century, the activists of Keynes's "politico-economic experiments" converged on the American Midwest and anointed Detroit the capital of the postliberal twentieth century.

When it came to developing fresh principles after the bankruptcy of the old economic order in the global crisis of the 1930s, it was Detroit that drew all modernizers of postliberal persuasion, left and right, Soviets and Nazis, fascists and socialists. To be sure, uncounted engineers and admirers had come to see Ford's factories since the 1910s, when the old Highland Park, forge of the Model T, was first equipped with an assembly line. Yet in the 1930s Ford's new factory—the much expanded, vertically integrated River Rouge—became the destination of engineering delegations bent on wholesale technology transfer.

Italian, German, Russian, and Japanese specialists traveled to Detroit, spent weeks, months, even years at River Rouge to learn the American secret of mass production. With the Gorky Automobile Factory (Gaz) in central Russia, the Soviet Union opened its own "River Rouge" in 1932. In 1938, Hitler laid the cornerstone of the Volkswagen works. Nor were Nazis and Soviets alone. Toyota began operating its Koromo plant in 1938, and Fiat welcomed Mussolini for the opening ceremony of the brand-new Mirafiori facility in 1939. As is easily seen, these Depression-era exchanges laid the groundwork for the infrastructure of global Fordism after World War II.

What triggered this expansion of mass production capacity in the decade marred by the Great Depression? How do we account for these rich exchanges in an age we associate with de-globalization and the breaking of the international economy into isolated blocs? What caused such momentous transfers between societies with such different visions of economics and politics? These are the questions that motivate this book. To answer them, we trace mass production to its beginnings in the United States, where it emerged from the distinctive ideology of Midwestern populism (chapter 1). We see how European postliberals on both the left and the right grasped Fordism as a compass by which to navigate the economic and ideological confusions of the 1920s (chapter 2). We then explore how the Soviet Union and Nazi Germany strove to acquire American mass production technology in order to create their own versions of Fordism in the Thirties (chapters 3 and 4). In chapter 5 we see how both regimes put Fordism to use during World War II. What spurred these transfers, this book suggests, was the political need of both Nazi Germany and the Soviet Union to rectify comparative underdevelopment vis-à-vis the United States. This shared engagement with America situates the Soviet and Nazi regimes within a larger interwar framework in which the economic ascendance of the United States conspired with the global Depression to trigger competitive industrial development across the world. The global context is crucial: by heeding it, this book delivers a new account of the rise and spread of mass production regimes in the first half of the twentieth century and suggests a novel framework to understand the interwar period at large—not as a retreat from globalization, as is commonly held, but as an era of furious and consequential attempts to transform its very structure.

What Was Fordism?

To appreciate what is at stake, we first need to clear a path through the conceptual thicket surrounding Fordism. What was Fordism? Henry Ford in fact never used the term—his global admirers created it, and while many claimed ownership, the honor perhaps belongs to a group of early Belgian car enthusiasts. In October 1923, they founded the "Ford Automobile Club de Belgique" and christened their newspaper, which ran articles on cars, progress, and industry, *Le Fordiste*.[4] After Henry Ford's self-exegesis, *My Life and Work*, appeared abroad in 1923, the term *Fordism* quickly spread. But it came to take on quite different meanings. The doyen of the German historical school of economics, Friedrich von Gottl-Ottlilienfeld, was so impressed by Ford's theorizing that he deemed it worthy of an "ism." What Gottl-Ottlilienfeld saw in *Fordismus* was not just a system of production but a historical shift in the relationship between economy and society, the promise of a reconciliation between industrial efficiency and social community.[5] Soviet commentators eagerly received Ford's technical recommendations but dismissed his philosophizing. In Soviet parlance, *fordizm* meant the "American organization of production" at large, replete with connotations of a cutting-edge technological modernity that Soviet engineers aspired to emulate.[6] In the midst of a protracted and vicious standoff with the Ford Motor Company, in turn, American unions in the 1930s used the term *Fordism* to attack what they saw as a quasifascist regime of shop floor oppression.[7]

The most influential usage of the term *Fordism* as we know it today was coined in an unlikely locale: a prison cell in southern Italy. Here the heterodox Marxist Antonio Gramsci worked out the ideas that he would eventually compile in his famous "prison notebook" number 22, titled "Americanismo e fordismo." To Gramsci, Fordism signified a radically new phase of capitalist development emanating from the United States across the world. The assembly line, Gramsci theorized, wrought a wide-ranging transformation of the social, cultural, and psychophysical constitution of the working class. Gramsci took the paternalist intrusions of Ford's agents into his workers' home lives, Progressive puritanism, and even Prohibition as telltale signs that assembly work required a careful and society-wide recalibration of worker discipline. The power of the assembly line thus extended far beyond the factory, giving rise to an entire system of social and cultural imperatives that Gramsci called "hegemony."[8]

Gramsci's notions echoed a broader reception of Henry Ford's ideas among interwar Communists. But his cherished term *Fordism* quickly fell out of fashion during World War II. It enjoyed a big comeback only decades later: in the 1970s, the European New Left rediscovered Gramsci's writings, and the economists of the French Regulation School resurrected "Fordism." Inspired by Gramsci's "hegemonic" reading of the assembly line, the Regulationists now described the entire political economy of the postwar West as "Fordism," distinguishing it from the "post-Fordism" that followed. Regulationists argued that capitalism went through distinctive "regimes of accumulation," each of which required specific patterns of social and political "regulation" in order to function. Fordism was the archetypical example: as an accumulation strategy, postwar mass production rested on a regulatory mode characterized by strong unions, a demand-stimulating welfare state, and a postwar cultural reformation that turned workers into consumers.[9]

No sooner had the Regulation School delineated its object of analysis than Fordism entered into a deep crisis. Corroded by inflation, industrial decline, and rising unemployment, the political compromise of the postwar West collapsed. Post-Fordism had begun. To some, the crisis appeared to portend a "second industrial divide": Perhaps the future lay in discarding rigid commitments to mass production and embracing a regionally based, technologically sophisticated reinvigoration of craft based on "flexible specialization"?[10] Other critics began to question that mass production had ever been as dominant and pervasive as Regulationists contended. Looking for "historical alternatives to mass production," some social scientists discovered a "world of possibilities"—firms embracing a multiplicity of organizational forms and profit strategies in response to ever-changing and unpredictable market environments.[11] Subtly moving the conversation from political economy to the microeconomic level of firm strategies, these scholars increasingly rejected broad concepts such as Fordism and post-Fordism in favor of a transhistorical diagnosis of "flexibility."[12]

These debates subsided in the new millennium. The Western focus and sequential stage model of Fordism/post-Fordism lost its appeal as the connections between economic restructuring in the West and industrial buildup in the East became clearer. Accordingly, "globalization" is today the concept of choice for explaining industrial change. In any case, what concerns us here is that *Fordism*, in its most common usage, was a term that first originated in the 1970s and then boomed in the 1980s, when social scientists sought ways to theorize the structural crises of the industrialized West.[13] The debates surrounding Fordism and post-Fordism have therefore revolved around presentist concerns, and the term *Fordism* took on a meaning quite removed from the postliberal connotations it carried during the interwar period. At the same time, preoccupied with postwar Fordism's *demise*, both the Regulationists and their critics failed to develop a compelling account of its *emergence*.

Fordism enjoys a second popular usage: as a shorthand for a distinctively American modernity that is said to have spread across the world in the twentieth century, in a process that historians of Europe have called "Americanization."[14] Narratives of Americanization often begin with describing the rise of America's pioneering consumer-based economy during the Roaring Twenties, which was based on high wages and mass production; this offered a seductive economic and cultural model to the world. However, despite fascination with assembly lines, European efforts to fashion their economies in the American consumerist image proved vain in the Twenties and Thirties. Awkward attempts at "command consumption"—such as the "peoples' commodities" of the Nazis or the Soviet invocations of a "socialist culture of consumption"—did not help.[15] Only after World War II did Fordism become part of the spread of American-led capitalism across the globe, a core element of the *Pax Americana* based on embedded liberalism and Cold War internationalism. When it came to Fordism and Americanization, we are told, "the postwar decades continued where the 1920s left off."[16] Or, as a Regulationist-inspired piece put it, "Fordist development was interrupted by depression and war."[17] Regulationist and Americanization narratives of Fordism, then, bracketed the 1930s and 1940s, relegated the 1920s to a period of embryonic anticipation, and thus instilled the lasting sense that postwar Fordism was not born of historical contingency, but was somehow preordained.

Finally, *Fordism* is used in a third way that focuses more narrowly on what goes on inside firms and on shop floors. Business historians have reconstructed the Ford Motor Company's early expansion to all regions across the globe, where it served as a disseminator of various signature practices—assembly lines, the one-product policy, the characteristic mix of high wages and open shop, and so on.[18] Ford shop floor arrangements also exerted enormous attraction on other European carmakers in the interwar period. However, as business historians have amply documented, firms abroad adopted American-style Fordism only in selective and hybrid ways—and that assessment included Ford's own subsidiaries. In particular, Ford's rigid ideas on model policy and labor relations proved impossible to transfer one-to-one into different national contexts.[19] To labor historians, meanwhile, Fordism means the shop regime associated with mass production: a focus on unskilled laborers working monotonous tasks on assembly lines. In this vein, Fordism is often mentioned in the same breath as Taylorism—it is seen as a managerial strategy to subdue unruly shop floors.[20] In this view, managers approved of the assembly line because it was a sublime "exploitation innovation," as one German historian memorably put it.[21]

These uses of the term *Fordism* remain valuable, and in this book we build on all three of them. In particular, Regulation Theory asks us to consider the political economy that surrounds mass production, especially the thorny question of demand management. The "Americanization" vein illustrates the deep entanglement of mass production with the politics of postwar American soft power, consumer capitalism, and embedded liberalism.[22] Viewing Fordism as a firm strategy and shop floor setup, finally, reminds us that assembly lines constitute a very specific way of organizing industrial work—one that requires dedicated efforts to mobilize unskilled laborers into the factories and, once there, to keep them working.

At the same time, however, the existing approaches leave some fundamental questions open. First, how did America arrive at mass production and consumer capitalism in the first place? Our narratives surrounding Fordism seem to take two things for granted: that the Second Industrial Revolution would somehow culminate in automotive mass production and the consumer economy, and that it was naturally the United States that would pioneer this breakthrough. It seems to surprise no one that an emblematic *American* company—Ford—first introduced the mass production of cars. These assumptions unwittingly perpetuate a modernization paradigm long thought discarded, namely, the idea that national economies move in stages set out by the advanced West. That successful modernization would converge toward the American model of "high mass-consumption" was, after all, a proposition first put forth by Walt Rostow.[23] As we discuss, however, the rise of automotive mass production in America was hardly a seamless departure. In many ways, in fact, mass production cut hard *against* the mainstream of American nineteenth-century economic development. Emerging from the middling metal-working shops of the American Midwest, mass production had a social, economic, and political context that put it at odds with the emphasis on extraction and producer goods that characterized America's Second Industrial Revolution; it was subversive of the economic hierarchies that found their expression in the grand alliance of finance and industrial capital signaled by the Great Merger Movement at the turn of the twentieth century. In particular, Henry Ford's own ideas on Fordism projected a political (and moral) economy that hardly anticipated the American consumer modernity that emerged after 1945; it is more accurate to say that the postwar world marked the final defeat of Henry Ford's populist vision of mass production. From the outset, then, Fordism was charged with a contrarian politics, and this fact—entirely overlooked by historians—explains much of Fordism's attraction on the global right of the interwar period. This is the first main argument of this book. We explore it in chapters 1 and 2.

Second, what happened to the global diffusion—intellectual, technological, economic—of Fordism in the years assumed to mark a hiatus: the Thirties and Forties? Did assembly lines no longer seem attractive? Did attempts to build mass production industries simply cease? In fact, quite the contrary. True, "command consumption" was a failure—and it could not have been otherwise in regimes that built up industry by curbing consumption. Mass demand, however, is not the exclusive characteristic of consumer economies. Preparing, and waging, a world war also increases demand, especially for vehicles and weaponry that lend themselves superbly to the production arrangements of Fordism. Fordism was amenable not only to a Keynesian regime of demand management: outside of the United States, it in fact flourished first under state-sponsored regimes of rearmament and war. This history—the military history of Fordism—reveals mass production as an intrinsic "dual use" technology: one that could serve civilian needs just as well as military ones, and one that was attractive precisely because of this property. Nor can the military history of Fordism be safely bracketed from its civilian one, as so many histories seem to assume.[24] How Fordism came to serve the purposes of rearmament and war is an intrinsic chapter of its global history, not least because the very same engineers who adopted Fordism in the Thirties ran arms production during the Forties and transitioned back to civilian industries after the war was over. Rather than interrupt, depression and war actually accelerated and intensified the global spread of Fordism. This is the second main argument of this book. We explore it in chapters 4 and 5.

Third and finally, how do we accommodate Nazi Germany and the Soviet Union into a global history of Fordism? Clearly, this question strains the limits of frameworks that associate Fordism with peacetime liberal capitalism. It sharply highlights a central lacuna in our histories of Fordism: the role that activist states played in orchestrating industrial development and in transferring production technology across borders. Here we need to take a step back and apply a fresh dose of empiricism. As industrializing states turned to mass production in the 1930s, what were their motives? How did they do it? And what were the consequences?

Revolt against America

The answers begin with the two most momentous irruptions of the interwar years: the ascendancy of the United States to global hegemony and the cataclysm of the Great Depression.[25] America's rise was not sudden: by the late nineteenth century, European voices began warning of the "American danger" brewing across the Atlantic.[26] After helping the Allies win World War I, the United States appeared unassailable, both as an industrial powerhouse and in its newfound role as the world's banker. Germany's revival after the inflation of 1923 was fueled by American loans. Italy strained to export lemons, crude textiles, and wine to pay for the (American) grain consumed by its workers; but, chronically in deficit, the country still borrowed on Wall Street to balance its payments.[27] Cut off from access to global capital markets after repudiating the Tsar's debt in 1918, even the Soviet Union engineered a stabilization of the ruble in 1924 in an effort to gain renewed access to American commercial credits.[28] At the same time, American export dominance, especially in the signature industry of the era—automobiles—diminished other nations' chances to secure the foreign exchange to repay those loans. Singularly, the United States seemed able to engage the world on its own terms—restricting immigration while exporting capital, raising tariffs at home while pushing the door open for trade abroad, looming over world politics while keeping its distance from the League of Nations. So the world was torn: Was it worth courting the United States in an effort to patch together a new international order, as British and French liberals thought? Or was American power to be seen with trepidation, even fear?

By the early Thirties, the doubters won the day. During the Great Depression, confidence evaporated that world markets would deliver recovery. The problem was not only slump and unemployment—what lastingly undermined liberal internationalism was the disintegration of global credit relations signaled by the gold standard's fall. The Great Depression arrived in all but the most privileged nations as a Great Balance-of-Payments Crisis. Germany, Eastern Europe, and the raw-material export economies of the Global South shared a characteristic predicament: they were deeply indebted, had dim prospects for exports, and could hope to remain creditworthy only by staying a brutal course of domestic austerity. In this environment, the proposition of maintaining traditional trade and investment relations seemed increasingly dubious.

Across the world, the Depression brought to the fore domestic coalitions bent on reorienting national economies away from Britain and the United States. In particular, the Depression handed radical forces within Germany and Japan strong economic reasons and rich political justification to militate against the international status quo. In doing so, these interwar "insurgents" challenged both the global division of labor of the 1920s and the newly risen hegemon in the Western Hemisphere—the USA.[29] The United States' astonishing growth, they surmised, was the result of a successful westward expansion into a fully valorized hinterland and of the creation of a powerful internal market. America's enviable ability to confront world markets on its own terms appeared to reinforce the lesson that the way forward lay in the creation of similar, externally independent and internally refashioned, economic "spaces."

For the insurgents, the solution was "autarky"—a mixture of economic dirigisme and industrial-military buildup based on a reorientation of trade and investment relations away from the West and toward neoimperial "backyards." Japan struck first, reaching into Manchuria at the very depth of the global collapse in the late summer of 1931. Italy's decisive turn to autarky coincided with the invasion of Ethiopia in 1935. Germany began harnessing South-Eastern Europe into trade dependency even before embarking on an expansionist spree that began with the Austrian *Anschluß* and culminated in the invasion of the Soviet Union.

As proponents insisted, autarky was as much a response to a capsizing international economy as it was an artifact of political nationalism.[30] Why comply with the rules of liberal internationalism when even Britain, erstwhile stalwart of free trade, retreated behind imperial tariffs? Why honor crippling debts when the Bank of England itself jettisoned the gold standard? What good was the sophistry of "comparative costs" when depleted foreign exchange reserves made imports an extravagance?[31] Autarky indulged nationalist rhetoric, but it was also a plausible response to economic emergency and the tightening straitjacket of the balance of payments.

At the same time, autarky decisively served nationalist goals. Severing commercial and financial ties with the West strengthened the state's grip on the structure of the economy. In Germany under Hjalmar Schacht and in Italy under Felice Guarneri, foreign exchange management became a primary means to shift resources from agriculture and light industry to capital investment and rearmament.[32] The results seemed to speak for themselves: countries that turned to autarky registered vigorous industrial growth during the 1930s.[33]

If we step beyond the smoke screen of ideology and Cold War assumptions, it is easy to see that the Soviet Union's path was not categorically different. To be sure, that Russia needed to industrialize had been a core Bolshevik demand since the Revolution—but by the onset of the global Depression the Soviet Union had not made much headway, and now time was running out. Like all grain exporters, the Soviet Union by the late 1920s faced declining export proceeds and dangerously low foreign exchange reserves. In response, the gradualist approach to economic development—a continuation of the Tsarist-era accumulation strategy that built on Russia's comparative advantage as a grain exporter—came into serious question. Moderate, world-market-oriented growth based on grain exports would no longer do. Against the background of world commodity markets mired in protracted deflation, Stalin and the radical industrializers in the politburo won their case: if the Soviet Union was to gain economic independence, it had to *accelerate* industrialization, or be condemned to the status of a peripheral grain exporter at the mercy of prissy creditors and punishing terms of trade.[34]

As a response to the global Depression, then, the "insurgents"—whether fascist or communist—radically shifted resources into industry, built up military capacity, and strove to break the stranglehold of the balance of payments and to gain independence from foreign capital. Those blood-and-soil fascists who dreamed of neoagrarian self-sufficiency remained marginal: in fact, twentieth-century autarkists sought to build industrialized, militarily capable, and technologically sophisticated imperial economies—whether called *Lebensraum, Impero italiano*, Greater East Asia Co-Prosperity Sphere, or Soviet Union. These modernist projects, then, depended on one sensitive element impossible to source at home: cutting-edge foreign technology. To gain the forefront of industrial modernity, all insurgents first had to turn for guidance to the most advanced nation of the era. Interim technological dependency on the United States—such was the wager of autarky—would be the price of

long-term economic independence. In particular, the sector seen as the strategic key to American preponderance—the automobile industry and its mass
production mechanisms—demanded emulation. How to build an American-
style economic juggernaut could be learned, it stood to reason, in Detroit. This
explains why after trade and foreign investment collapsed in the Depression,
by the mid-1930s technology transfers intensified. The spread of Fordism during
the interwar years, then, arose from an antagonistic development competition
that was initially triggered by the rise of the United States and then accelerated
by the Great Depression. This is the third main argument of this book.

Antagonistic Development, Technology Transfers, and the Search for "Economic Independence"

With the technology transfers of the Thirties, the "insurgents" sought to close
the development gap that separated them from the United States. In the Soviet
case, that gap was vast. In the 1920s, Russia was an agrarian country with a
smidgen of industry, which—as the Bolsheviks knew only too well—had
failed the test of World War I. The bleak fact of Russia's comparative
weakness—the Bolsheviks' favored term was "backwardness" (*otstalost'*)—
spurred the political debates of the Twenties and the economic policies of the
Thirties. Overcoming the Soviet Union's backwardness remained an overarching political goal.

Accordingly, in moments of frankness, Marxist vocabulary took a backseat
to a conspicuous rhetoric of catch-up development. As an agrarian country,
Stalin pointed out in 1925, the Soviet Union was forced to export agricultural
goods in order to obtain machinery from abroad. "To remain on this level of
development," Stalin warned, would risk turning the Soviet Union "into an
appendage of the capitalist [world] system." In 1933, when Stalin summarized
the "fundamental tasks" of the First Five-Year Plan, he began with these items:
First, to "direct our country from its backward, sometimes medieval technology onto the rails of new and modern technology," and second, "to transform
the USSR from an agrarian and weak country dependent on the whims of the
capitalist countries into an industrialized and powerful country completely
self-supporting and independent of the whims of world capitalism." In 1941,
Stalin instructed a gathering of economists to stop "string[ing] together quotations" from Marx and Engels and grasp that "the main task of planning" lay in
using the power of the state to push the economy toward industrial buildup,
in order "to reach the point where metal and machines are in our hands and
we are not dependent on the capitalist economy." After World War II, Nikolai
Voznesenskii, Stalin's generalissimo on the war production front, credited

victory over Germany to the "development of socialist industry" that had taken place since Lenin, which—in stark contrast to World War I—had now assured "the independence and military-economic might" of the Soviet Union.[35] Industrialization, then, was not purely a matter of ideological predilections: its significance was at once economic, militarist, and political. These considerations were glued together by a strong sense of national mission ("our country") and an expansive notion of "economic independence" that had strong civilizational connotations.[36]

The grand military-economic strategy of Hitler and his National Socialists, as scholars have recently reminded us, was also a reaction to a self-assessment of comparative weakness in the world economy.[37] Hitler saw the United States as a formidable economic force that at once posed an existential threat and offered a highly instructive model of development. The instructive part lay in America's unique combination of continental territory and mass production capacity, a mix that furnished Americans with a fabulously high "standard of living"—a concept dear to Hitler. "Europeans use, albeit not always consciously, the conditions of American life as a benchmark," Hitler wrote in 1928.[38] In modern world affairs, this was the benchmark to which any nation worth its salt would aspire. However—and this was the existential threat—America's immense economic power was increasingly squeezing other nations from world markets, making it impossible for them to catch up. Especially in the sector most telling of future potential, the automobile industry, Germany's feeble producers were destined to extinction. By the depth of the Depression, Hitler's stump speeches drew the apocalyptic tone of an impending "world catastrophe" in large measure from the overwhelming economic threat of the United States. How could German industry hope to compete against America, that "gigantic state with infinite production capacities"? Had not the Depression fully revealed the folly of relying on world markets? Instead, it was now necessary for Germans to turn their backs on the "phantom of the world economy" and build a state endowed with both economic and military independence, one that was able to "secure through its own strength what it needs from the world."[39]

Evidently, both the Nazi and the Soviet self-diagnosis of underdevelopment vis-à-vis the United States was soaked in existential ideological sweat. This diagnosis, however, prescribed a simple and precise course of action: beat America with American methods. Lest Germany become "America's prey," it was necessary "to study the means and mechanisms of the Americans," said Theodor Lüddecke, one of Fordism's most vocal advocates on the Weimar right.[40] Similarly, Arsenii Mikhailov, one of Fordism's ardent Soviet champions, argued that the goals of the Five-Year Plan required "a swift and complete switch to the most advanced American technology."[41]

The making of Gaz, the Gorky "Auto Giant," resulted from this course of action. Gaz marked an extraordinary attempt to transfer American technology wholesale and to indigenize it in a social and economic environment that seemed hardly ready for it. Soviet workers and engineers indeed struggled mightily to adopt what they took from Detroit. But despite enormous sacrifices and waste, somehow, by decade's end, a capable motor mass production industry had materialized in central Russia. We follow the story in chapter 3. Germany could dip into deep homegrown technological capabilities that the Soviet Union lacked and therefore struggled somewhat less to assimilate Fordism. The result was a double reception. The Volkswagen plant echoed the Soviet strategy of comprehensive copying. But the Nazi regime also tried (and largely succeeded) to harness the industrial acumen of Ford and General Motors, both of which had branches in Germany, to its own ends. Ensnaring the Americans in a web of threats and incentives, the regime achieved pervasive, dollar-subsidized transfers of mass production technology into Germany. The story is laid out in chapter 4. In chapter 5, we see how both the Nazi and Soviet efforts to adopt automotive mass production paid off as the two regimes rained military matériel on each other in World War II.

Contexts: Strategic Industrial Policy and Developmental Regimes

Viewing technology transfer as a strategy of development competition sets the Soviet and Nazi efforts against the backdrop of industrial rivalries across the world, in which nations jockeyed to get their hands on the automobile industry and its mass production techniques. In a characteristic double gesture, statesmen and industrialists sought at once to acquire the American carmakers' technology while curtailing their hold on domestic markets. In Japan, no automobile industry existed after World War I, and during the Twenties both Ford and General Motors built assembly plants that fully covered the needs of the domestic market. By the mid-Thirties, however, the militarist government began to support fledgling attempts by Japanese industrialists to nurture a homegrown auto production. In 1936, the government passed the notorious Automobile Manufacturing Enterprise Law, a measure that discriminated against the American firms, penalized imports of vehicles, and encouraged Nissan and Toyota—weak and inexpert producers compared to the Americans—to expand investments and update their technologies. These measures eventually forced GM and Ford to exit the Japanese market and allowed Nissan and Toyota to acquire the Americans' factory machinery and hire their workers and engineers.[42]

In Italy, too, the regime tolerated the presence of American carmakers only for a brief period after World War I. In 1929, Mussolini personally thwarted an attempt by Ford to expand its presence in Italy, declaring that American competition would devastate the domestic automobile industry. Instead, Mussolini decisively backed the Turin-based carmaker Fiat, which benefited not only from the regime's stifling labor policies but also from its military orders, export promotion schemes, and generous foreign exchange allocations for technology from the United States. Ford and GM eventually left the Italian market, while Fiat built its own brand-new, Rouge-style megaplant.[43] Opened in 1939, Mirafiori was very similar to the Nazi Volkswagen project: a Fascist white elephant, valuable for propaganda purposes but also a monument to how assiduously the regime sought to alter its place in the global industrial pecking order. During the war, Mussolini still prided himself for pushing Ford out of Italy and warned that military defeat would bring "the end of our automobile industry." Italy would be forced to again submit to the nineteenth-century logic of comparative advantage and return "to where its eternal enemies always wanted it: a pure expression of its geography."[44]

A strategic policy vis-à-vis the overbearing American automobile industry, however, was hardly the preserve of dictatorships alone. All capable states strove to strengthen domestic producers while encouraging technology transfers from Detroit, in effect curbing imports of cars while supporting imports of know-how.[45] The arsenal of measures included ever-present tariffs, attempts to organize domestic cartels, and pleas for strategic joint ventures with the Americans. Confronted with tariffs, Ford and GM established full manufacturing plants in Britain, Weimar Germany, France, and Scandinavia, and across Western Europe. In all these contexts, the Americans faced stiff headwinds from an alliance of domestic firms and governments, who compelled them to qualify as "national" producers by increasing national ownership and sourcing a high share of locally produced supplies.[46] Governments in Weimar Germany, Britain, and France repeatedly encouraged domestic firms to merge in a bid to confront the Americans (though most of these initiatives came to naught since rivaling firms found it hard to agree on terms). France, which retained the strongest automobile sector outside of the United States, nevertheless was extremely wary of American competition. Returning in 1931 from a visit to the Rouge, industrialist-nationalist Louis Renault declared that the French auto industry was "gravely menaced" and demanded that "everything must change."[47] Renault lobbied successive governments for protection and promotion of the home industry, all the while sending a succession of engineering delegations to Detroit.[48]

These frantic industrial politics, finally, point to the broadest context within which to locate the Soviet and Nazi bids for a homegrown Fordism. That context is the larger restructuring of the global economy during the 1930s—the ubiquitous efforts of regions, nations, and elites to upend the global division of labor inherited from the nineteenth century. Across the world, the Depression triggered revolts against the "great specialization" that divided the world into raw material exporters in Central Europe, Asia, Latin America, and Africa on the one hand, and the industrial core in northwestern Europe and the North American manufacturing belt on the other.[49] The balance-of-payments squeeze that the Depression imposed on Italy, Japan, Germany, and the Soviet Union was felt with equal agony in the peripheral export economies of the world. Unable to pay for manufactured goods with crops that no longer found markets, nations of the global periphery ditched the gold standard, slashed imports, and began to industrialize.[50] While modern automobile sectors were yet beyond the reach of countries in Latin America, the Middle East, and Asia, they nevertheless worked to build up and bolster domestic industries—usually first textiles, then often steel. When it came to the world at large, the consequence was, as a contemporary economist from New Zealand observed, that "the Depression did not halt the industrial revolution, but actually . . . accelerated it."[51]

Twentieth-Century History beyond Modernization

This context of worldwide development competition allows us to think afresh about the places that the Soviet Union and Nazi Germany inhabited in the global Thirties. Since the demise of Cold War frameworks—of Sovietology, of modernization theory, of "totalitarianism"—two prevailing analytical modes have emerged in dealing with the two regimes. The first mode has posited a "dark" or "illiberal" modernity at the height of the twentieth century. By interpreting Nazism and Stalinism as revealing deep contradictions within the Enlightenment project itself, scholars working in this mode ostentatiously turned sanguine modernization conceits on their ear. They pointed out that both liberal and antiliberal regimes embraced characteristic markers of modernity, such as social engineering, top-down homogenization, biopolitics, and scientism, as well as modernist cultural and intellectual sensibilities.[52] To this critique, other scholars responded vehemently: they emphatically reaffirmed liberal-normative commitments and insisted that Fascists or Communists only ever succeeded in creating mimicry versions of modernity—hollow "dissimulations," as it were, that were bound to fail without the trappings of democracy and liberalism to sustain them.[53]

More recently, scholarship has sought to transcend these debates by expanding the lens to a more global purview. The signature move has been to combine fresh comparative inquiries with close attention to borrowings and interactions that cut across the ideological rivalries of the interwar period. This literature's most compelling locus of comparison has been emboldened states, which everywhere responded to the Depression by abandoning markets for planning, engaging in unprecedented economic management, building labor services, expanding welfare systems, and sponsoring public works. While the violence perpetrated by the Nazi and Soviet states still stands out, the overall effect of this literature has been to muddle the stark dichotomies inherited from modernization theory: we now witness "modernities," sometimes described as "multiple" or "entangled." The Thirties emerge as a laboratory of experimentation in a shared transnational crisis; a kind of global antiglobality, in which states eagerly pursued domestic projects while jealously eyeing across borders. If modernization theory deduced the political choices of the interwar period from national historical trajectories, the new literature sees these choices as constituting competing responses, each inflected with a particular ideology, to the shared challenge of post–World War I dislocations and economic depression.[54]

This book too sees the global Thirties as characterized by vigorous transnational exchanges. It aims, however, to do more than simply add a new layer to now familiar narratives of entanglement. Instead, this book suggests that the interactions it documents should be theorized in a novel way: as occasioned by a precise political-economic logic, that of an antagonistic development competition whose reference point was the United States. Technology transfers were more than cross-ideological flirtations: the very logic of development competition *required* transnational engagements that were at once conflictual and intense. It is a truism of catch-up development that those who pursue it must turn, for capital and technology, to those they seek to emulate and challenge. This truism counsels skepticism toward the impression evoked by the "multiple modernities" literature, namely, that the "interwar conjuncture" can be understood as a generic crisis to which all responses were simply variations on a common theme.

When it came to development competition, the challenges that confronted the United States, the Soviet Union, and Nazi Germany were decidedly *not* the same. Because backwardness was measured by reference to the economic and technological level of the United States, Americans were by definition spared its sting; however, backwardness appeared to pose an existential threat to an ideologically embattled late developer such as the Soviet Union. As an expansionist military-industrial state, Nazi Germany found comparative underdevelopment equally intolerable. Similarly, as a net creditor nation and technological leader, the United States enjoyed freedom from the constraints that a chronic shortage of foreign exchange (most importantly, reserves held in gold, dollars, or pounds sterling) imposed on both Nazi and Soviet industrial projects. As we will see, the foreign exchange squeeze, which haunted all global debtors in the context of deflationary world markets, was one of the most vexing problems confronting both Soviet and Nazi economic policymakers.

By the same token, a wide gulf separated the Soviet development challenge from that faced by Nazi Germany—the gulf measuring the distance between an agrarian exporter and an industrial nation traditionally dependent on foreign trade. Each regime's strategy for appropriating American technology has to be understood in light of these differences.

These reflections evoke an image of the Thirties as an arena of sharp and increasingly violent contests over the question, Global economic relations on whose terms? Who would dictate the shape of industrial and technological development and the distribution of power in the global division of labor? This perspective sees the Thirties as a period of struggle over the making and unmaking of different architectures of globalization, a struggle in which claims on capital, goods, and technology clashed in the arena of worldwide development competition.

Rereading the interwar period in this way, finally, invites us to reconsider some fundamental questions about the twentieth century at large. First, the twentieth century has recently been called a "development century"—an era marked by Western efforts, whether framed as civilizing mission or benevolent bestowal of expertise, to export development to the world.[55] These efforts are easily situated within longer histories of Western imperial designs, and Fordism's spread abroad has sometimes been narrated in this vein.[56] The history of state-sponsored Fordism within interwar development competition, in contrast, allows us to foreground a very different development century: one in which self-initiated industrial upgrading resulted not from the dictates of American empire but from revolts against them; in which development aspirations did not emanate from the core but emerged from the semiperiphery; and whose projects were not a response to the paternalism of imposed modernization, but arose from the policies of states vying over the terms of the global economic order. This perspective allows us to discern a genealogy of industrial politics that connects the activist states of the Thirties backward to the mercantilism of Hamilton, List, and the Meiji Restoration, as well as forward to the "developmental states" of postwar Japan, South Korea, and present-day China. It is a story that yet awaits mapping by historians.[57]

Second, the literature on "multiple modernities" has been unable to dislodge, and perhaps has actually reinforced, what historian Charles Maier in a classic statement identified as "moral" narratives of the twentieth century.[58] In such narratives, the catastrophes of Depression and war feature as a swerve away from, and then back to, the normal course of history. In light of the postwar reconstruction of a liberal international order under American auspices, it remains tempting to narrate the interwar period as a kind of nightmarish detour.[59] Post-1945 Soviet Communism, then, appears as a zombie holdover from the interwar period on which the historical clock was always implacably ticking—an impression seemingly vindicated by the collapse of "actually existing socialism" in the 1990s.[60] The close familial relationship that connects these enduring conceptions of the twentieth century to the metanarratives of modernization theory is obvious.[61]

Maier juxtaposed these narratives, in which history revolves around grand notions of moral progress and regression, to hypothetical "structural" narratives that might focus on "economic development or large-scale institutional change."[62] It is striking in this regard that contemporaries of the 1930s invoked the twentieth century precisely as a marker of profound *structural* reversal. "Nineteenth-century civilization has collapsed"—this was the opening sentence of Karl Polanyi's wartime reckoning with the changes wrought by his era.[63] Polanyi shared with the postliberals of the 1930s the sense that a profound reorientation was under way, a change he considered an "institutional transformation" of historical significance—a *Great Transformation*.[64] Polanyi points toward a different periodization of the twentieth century, in which the interwar years emerge not as an aberration but as the century's very fulcrum: a momentous reversal that reconfigured the architecture of the global economic order, as the vision of an integrated world based on liberal-imperial principles imploded and made way for an era of strategic, competitive industrial upgrading orchestrated by activist states. Seen from our own contemporary perspective, it is possible that the American-sponsored reconstitution of a liberal world order after 1945 only veiled this deeper shift. The mass production plants of postwar Fordism were after all a legacy of the global Thirties. Like a palace built of the rocks and sediments of an earlier age, the postwar order rose on the foundations of the antiliberal era that preceded it.[65] The story told in this book, then, aims to situate the global Thirties in a "structural" narrative of the twentieth century: the type of state-led, competitive economic politics, whose full consequences we are beginning to grasp only today, has its roots in the "great transformation" of the Thirties. Tracing these roots is the concern of this book.

Our story begins at the shrine of modern industrialization, in the capital of the twentieth century: Detroit.

1

The Populist Roots of
Mass Production

The primary object of the corporation is to make money, not just motor cars.

—ALFRED P. SLOAN

The primary object of the manufacturing corporation is to produce, and if that objective is always kept, finance becomes a wholly secondary matter.

—HENRY FORD

THE YEAR IS 1937. Traveling to Detroit by train, you leave New York City northbound and advance along the Hudson, pass through Albany, and cross upstate to Buffalo. See the waterfalls at Niagara, if your schedule allows. On the journey's next leg, book a seat on the right side of your Pullman: this will afford you stunning views of Lake Erie as your train measures the full length of its southern shore. After passing through Cleveland and Toledo, you get your first glimpse of Canada on the far side of the Detroit River to your right, as you finally approach the outskirts of Detroit from the south. Your train crosses the Rouge River on a steel bridge, giving you a view of Ford's smoke-stacks off in the distance to the left, then traverses the neighborhoods of Detroit's West Side, before pulling into Michigan Central Station—today an eviscerated ruin, but then a bustling terminal of art deco beauty, rising high.

From here, take a short cab ride downtown along Michigan Avenue, where neoclassical skyscrapers testify to the youth and vigor of the Motor City. Put up at the Book Cadillac if you have the means, where you can mingle with the many distinguished visitors—engineers, ambassadors, royalty, managers, heads of state—drawn to the Motor City in its prime. Then stroll up a few blocks to Orchestra Hall, home to the Detroit Symphony, sponsored by the city's automotive elite. Or make your way to the close-by bank district and marvel at the modernist splendor of the Penobscot Building, the city's financial center.

Of course, in the twenty-first century, no one boards a train to reach Detroit. But in the city's heyday, it was the train that brought bankers and automotive executives, migrant workers and mobsters, journalists and engineers to Detroit, America's young manufacturing heart. This was the journey also made by William Werner, technical director of the German carmaker Auto-Union, on the occasion of his Detroit visit in October 1937. Werner had crossed the Atlantic on the *Bremen*, alighted at the docks of New York City, and made his way to Detroit by train. He lodged at the Book Cadillac and wrote his letters home to Chemnitz, Saxony, on the hotel's stationery. Werner was the senior figure in a delegation of seven automotive engineers, whose task was to compile an extensive survey of the latest mass production technology used by American automobile makers. Through the connections afforded by automotive trade associations, both German and American, Werner and his group procured introductions to the factories of General Motors and Ford, where, as Werner noted, they were "received with extraordinary friendliness." General Motors provided a chauffeur, and Ford opened its doors for an intensive, three-day inspection, "the likes of which few surely have had the opportunity to enjoy."

Testifying to a remarkably dense traffic across the Atlantic, Werner's sortie overlapped with several other high-profile journeys. In November, the German Federation of Car Dealers traveled to the Automobile Exhibition in New York City. In June, Ferdinand Porsche, designer of the Volkswagen and just-anointed executive of the state-sponsored plant that would bear its name, led his own group of engineers to Detroit. Porsche was on the hunt for ideas, machinery, and skilled technicians to equip his brand-new factory, then in the planning stage. Several of Porsche's engineers stayed on through the fall months, purchasing machinery and recruiting specialists. The German engineering delegations were only the latest to voyage to Detroit. A year earlier, a group of representatives from the Italian carmaker Fiat had paid a visit. That group included chief engineer Rambaldo Bruschi as well as Vittorio Bonadè Bottino, one of the foremost architects of Fascist Italy, who was tasked with designing the expansive Mirafiori manufacturing plant outside of Turin.[1]

Following a tightly packed schedule, Werner and his engineers visited twelve different factories over the course of two weeks. The divisions of General Motors came first. At Pontiac, forty miles north of Detroit, GM had built a factory in 1933 that now employed 20,000 workers. The foundry there left "an extraordinarily good and modern impression," the Germans recorded. In the machine shop, they marveled at the elaborate flow production methods and the intricate subdivision of operations. The final assembly line, they reported matter-of-factly, was "one kilometer in length." Detailed descriptions of GM's modern machine tools made it into the Germans' report. They acknowledged, for example, the sophistication of hydraulic presses that took three punches to convert a sheet of metal into a car's roof, and of the battery of fourteen welding machines that fused a car's body into existence within minutes.

At each factory, the Germans took pictures and extensive technical notes. The final report took weeks to compile and finally ran to hundreds of pages, replete with high-quality photographs of machines and work processes and filled with detailed technical descriptions. The Germans, highly qualified specialists in their own right, were not easily impressed and did not spare critical observations where they felt them appropriate: Packard's factory seemed "downright antiquated"; the forge supplying Chevrolet left the unfavorable impression of "decidedly poor working conditions" and "insufferable noise."

For one plant, however, the Germans had nothing but praise. Visiting River Rouge, Ford's giant factory just west of Detroit's city limits, constituted nothing less than the "climax," they recorded, of their American sojourn. Joe Galamb, one of Ford's closest associates, was assigned as a special guide to Werner and his engineers. Their tour began, as it did for thousands of other visitors in the late Thirties, at the Ford Rotunda. A six-story white structure that resembled a set of gears, the Rotunda was designed by Albert Kahn for Chicago's Century of Progress World's Fair in 1933. In May 1936, Ford moved the Rotunda to Dearborn to serve as a visitors' center. Inside the Rotunda, Werner and his group could marvel at the famous globe that displayed the world-spanning operations of the Ford Motor Company, and take in billboard-sized photomurals of Rouge operations as well as choice Henry Ford quotes embossed on spacious marble plates.

From the Rotunda, it was a short bus ride to the factory premises. Passing through the gates, Werner's group entered an industrial complex of world fame. Since coming to full capacity in the Twenties, the Rouge had drawn engineers and artists, journalists and tourists, pundits and photographers. Extensive press features—in periodicals like *Industrial Management, World's Work,* and *Scientific American*—presented Rouge operations to the public. In 1928, *Vanity Fair* featured a series of high-resolution images of the Rouge by Charles Sheeler—iconic works that were style-defining for an entire generation of industrial photographers. Sponsored by Edsel Ford, Mexican artist Diego Rivera in 1933 immortalized the Rouge in a world-famous set of frescoes at the Detroit Institute of Arts.

By all accounts, the Rouge that welcomed Werner was a remarkable spectacle. Here the myriad operations that went into making an automobile came together in a dazzling "ballet mécanique" (Sheeler's phrase). Ships brought ore and coal across the Great Lakes. At the Rouge slip, they disgorged their freight into hissing blast furnaces, which in turn fed the foundry, where molds—propelled by moving conveyors past cascades of liquid iron—cast the automotive innards: engine blocks, crankshafts, pistons, and brake drums. A separate flow of white-hot iron crept from the furnaces toward the steel mill, where gargantuan presses rolled it into strips that emerged as bodies and fenders. Next, the conveyors marched the raw parts into the screeching jaws of the machine shops, where massive power tools bored, drilled, ground, and polished them into shape. Emerging as pistons, gears, flywheels, and spark plugs, these elements met the engine blocks at the motor assembly shop. Feeding off tributaries from the glass plant, tires, and springs shop, another set of conveyors pushed bodies and engines onto the final assembly line, whence the finished automobile, if the Rouge PR department can be believed, rolled exactly 28 hours after the ore from which it was fashioned arrived by ship.[2]

What most impressed visitors to the Rouge was the precise coordination that synchronized the production process into a system of myriad tributaries feeding into each other and finally issuing onto the finishing assembly line. This was "flow production"—*Fließfertigung,* as the Germans said; *potochnoe proizvodstvo,* in Russian parlance—taken to perfection. The symbol of the Rouge's dazzling prowess was the automatic conveyor. The factory resembled a vast maze of all conceivable propulsion devices: "gravity conveyors, bucket conveyors, spiral conveyors, moving belts, trolleys, electric and gasoline tractors, motor cars, moving platforms, cranes of every type, steam and electric locomotives, cable cars." From this cacophony seemed to emerge, as though by magic, an astonishing harmony, as the myriad operations came together to form "one huge, perfectly timed, smoothly operating industrial machine of almost unbelievable efficiency." Coming away from the Rouge, observers reached for superlatives. This, evidently, was "the largest and surely the most inspiring industrial machine that has ever been created." Here, truly, "Ford ha[d] brought the hand of God and the hand of Man closer together than they have ever been brought in any other industrial undertaking." Or, as Werner concluded his report: "Without doubt the Ford works in Detroit are among the most brilliant technical achievements in the history of the world."[3]

Werner and his group considered River Rouge an apex of industrial achievement because something unprecedented was happening there: a factory of awesome proportions put out a device of great complexity in quantities—thousands, millions—that boggled the mind. Before automotive mass production, factories that required huge capital outlays and employed a large labor force usually turned out goods that were extremely expensive. They produced capital goods that supplied other factories (machine tools, for example) or served transportation (stagecoaches, ships, railroads, or railway cars). To be sure, by the late nineteenth-century America was mass-producing a wide range

FIGURE 1.1. Aerial view of Ford's River Rouge factory, with the Rotunda
in the foreground, 1939. Photo: The Henry Ford.

of consumer goods—things like textiles, stoves, sewing machines, and bicycles. But compared to the automobile, these were simple devices. What set
automotive mass production apart was this achievement: unseen economies
of scale allowed decoupling large inputs from high prices. Even as automotive
technology improved, automobile prices tumbled, while the industry paid the
highest wages that unskilled labor had been able to garner since the dawn of
industrialization.

This, as the Germans well recognized, was a groundbreaking economic
phenomenon. Appreciating the momentous impact of automotive mass production, they recalled just how powerful the industry had become since its
origins at the turn of the twentieth century. In 1899, when Ransom Olds set
up shop in Detroit, America possessed a very different economic makeup.
Here was a country that had industrialized by drawing the bounty of the North
American continent into markets both at home and overseas. Steel built the

railroads on which freight trains, drawn by coal-fueled locomotives, carried hogs and wheat to the cities. The dominant industries reflected this pattern. At the turn of the century, the banking houses of the East were busy orchestrating the mergers of coal and steel corporations, sectors closely associated with the railroads. Meanwhile, some of the biggest industries—mills, stockyards, and breweries—were devoted to processing agricultural products. Wages in these branches were often pitifully low and workweeks punishingly long. This industrial pattern lasted well into the twentieth century. In 1914, the US census listed "slaughtering and meatpacking" as the largest industry by value of product, followed by steel and flour milling. Eastern regions—New England with its textile mills, Pennsylvania with its steel and oil, New Jersey with its metalworking, New York City with its manufactures, trading houses, and banks—dominated the economic geography of the USA.[4]

In contrast, by 1937, the year of Werner's visit, the center of gravity of the American economy had shifted west. Easily trumping the rest of the country in industrial value added, the Midwest—Ohio, Indiana, Illinois, Michigan, and Wisconsin—had pulled past the steel towns and centers of coal mining, oil rigging, and metalworking in upstate New York, New Jersey, and Pennsylvania. The Midwest still benefited from Chicago's stockyards, but the region's strength was now broadly based on the automobile industry and its suppliers, whose combined value-added surpassed that of America's second largest industry, steel.[5] The Detroit Big Three, who, as the Germans noted, had "recovered very well" from the Depression, recorded their best year since the boom times of the Twenties. The industry's strength radiated into the larger economy, as statistics in Werner's report reflected: the auto industry consumed one-fifth of all steel produced in the USA, more than half of all malleable iron, four-fifths of crude rubber, almost a third of its lead, and a good part of its precious metals. One out of seven Americans relied for employment on the industry and its supply chains.[6]

Detroit was the center of a new American growth regime, one that departed from nineteenth-century patterns. The city's population had grown fivefold since the turn of the century, as the auto industry drew tens of thousands of migrants into its factories. These newcomers settled into a city that, while rife with racial hierarchies and class tensions, was flush with cash. In 1927, the *New York Times* mused that "Detroiters are the most prosperous slice of average humanity that now exists or that has ever existed."[7] In 1937, as employment again soared, the larger Detroit area easily surpassed all other manufacturing agglomerations—New York, Philadelphia, Boston, Chicago—in per capita wages. The contrast was stark, with Detroit ($308.79) displacing Chicago ($158.29).[8] These numbers implied a level of disposable income that would have been quite unimaginable to nineteenth-century industrial workers. The productivity of the automobile industry allowed its workers to become consumers whose purchasing power increasingly rivaled capital investment in shaping the patterns of growth.[9]

As the Germans noted in their report, the automobile industry also contributed substantially to America's economic dominance within the wider world. In 1937, North American carmakers were responsible for roughly 5.1 out of 6.3 million cars and trucks produced around the world. The United States put out nearly ten times as many vehicles as the United Kingdom, the globe's second producer. Exports had recovered from the slump, reaching over 460,000 vehicles in 1937. American motorcars were now a familiar sight in the East Indies, Latin America, Australia, and South Africa.[10] The significance of these figures was obvious to the visitors from Nazi Germany, where the politics of autarky required not only independence from American competitors but also a concerted effort to challenge their export markets.

The rise of automotive mass production in America at the turn of the twentieth century, then, was without doubt a major watershed in economic history. It paved the way for a consumption-based pattern of growth, and it created new imbalances in the international economic order.[11] From a global perspective, this was unexpected: The automobile, after all, was an invention of French and German tinkerers, and the United States was a copycat adopter. Yet by the eve of World War I, the factories of southeastern Michigan were spewing out tens of thousands of automobiles, while European carmakers continued to build expensive and stodgy models by hand. Seen from another angle, the automobile industry decisively set apart the United States from development patterns elsewhere in the Americas. Argentina and Brazil, for example, had expanded into their Western hinterlands over the course of the nineteenth century, just like the United States. But the economic patterns of these countries remained tied to raw materials, resource extraction, and transatlantic commerce. The automobile industry, in short, marked a pivotal shift in the "second great divergence"—the move of the United States away from its Atlantic orientation toward domestically anchored industrial preponderance in the twentieth century.[12]

And yet the annals of American economic history barely register that mass production *was* a momentous departure. Rather, they assimilate mass production into what might be called narratives of natural emergence: halfway between the end of the Civil War and the rise of the New Deal, automotive mass production issues as though by necessity from the forward momentum of capitalist transformation. The two opposing modes in which the history of this era is generally told fully coincide in this regard. One is a sanguine narrative of progress: technological and organizational innovations converged to form large corporations whose professional managers came to preside over a more efficient, more rational, and less rapacious capitalism.[13] The second variant is told in a minor key: here the very same processes of corporate consolidation and rationalization are seen to defeat more emancipatory alternatives of grass-roots populism and labor self-organization.[14] In these latter narratives, mechanized mass production—Fordism—often features as a weaponized strain of Taylorism, as a tool used by management to conquer shop floors and to usher in the bleak open-shop industrial landscape of the 1920s. Both versions are overdetermined: In the first vein, mass production results from the imperatives of modernization. In the second, mass production results from the iron mandate of capital accumulation. To be sure, this second mode narrated the transformation as one of intense conflict. Strikingly, however, these narratives, too, seem unable to imagine the story as ending in anything other than corporate hegemony: struggle there was, but doomed it was too.[15]

What is lost in these perspectives is an idea that contemporaries of the Thirties would have regarded as self-evident: that mass production could be the engine for creating political economies very different from the corporate capitalism that emerged in the American interwar years. The shape that automotive mass production took in America in the first decades of the twentieth century was not preordained: it was the outcome of concrete struggles over the terms of economic development. The economies of scale unleashed by mass production harbored immense potential for growth. What did this imply for the social and economic order at large? Whose norms and values would govern the distribution of material rewards? What was the proper way to run that momentous new institution—the mass-producing corporation? Buried under the familiar narratives, then, is a *political* history of mass production—one that includes, but goes beyond, the familiar analytic of capital and labor. To be sure, mass production occasioned fierce and consequential conflicts between workers and management. Yet the shop floor was only one site of contestation, and there is no reason to overburden it with an ontological primacy that relegates all other conflicts to a secondary or epiphenomenal status. Doing so would mean missing what was a much larger arena of political struggle and class conflict surrounding the rise of mass production, in which skilled mechanics and unskilled migrants, middling proprietors and privileged investors, a new managerial class and old financial elites battled out the terms of a new economic order.

The point of this chapter is a simple one: automotive mass production spawned widely diverging normative views of social order and economic development. These clashes decisively shaped how the industry matured. We need to understand these conflicts if we want to fully appreciate what attracted interwar modernizers like William Werner to Ford, Detroit, and the American Midwest, what they found there, and what they took back home across the Atlantic.

Mechanics and Financiers

The history of automotive mass production begins with a puzzle. Why did Detroit, of all places, pioneer the industry that would shape the twentieth century like no other? Historians and geographers have long picked at this question without pulling out fully satisfactory answers. The question matters because, initially, it seemed that an arc of carmakers from southern Germany to northern France to New England would dominate the new industry. In 1900, European manufacturers as well as those in Connecticut, Massachusetts, and New York were building stately horseless carriages for the leisure class. Yet only five years later, Detroit turned out the greatest number of cars and boasted the greatest number of automotive factories on the globe, with the Ford Motor Company notably among them.[16]

Was this coincidence, as automotive historians blithely maintain?[17] Was Detroit simply lucky, as it were, to count a Henry Ford and a Ransom Olds among its citizens—incarnations of the American genius for innovation and entrepreneurship? Such notions remove the early tinkerers from the historical context that produced them. Figures like Ford and Olds acted within the political economy of the Midwest and shared the characteristic populist commitments that suffused the region. These two factors—political economy and political ideology—go a long way toward explaining why, at the turn of the twentieth century, southeastern Michigan was in an auspicious position to get ahead of rapid technological developments and to spread its fruits widely.

First, the automobile industry benefited from the Midwest's distinctive pattern of industrialization. The larger Great Lakes basin had seen an "agro-industrial revolution" since the mid-nineteenth century, in which the machine shops and foundries of middling cities connected with commercially oriented farms. In such an environment, industry and agriculture were not seen as belonging to successive stages of development; rather, they were regarded as complementary, indeed symbiotic. Midwestern growth, in short, did not conform to the spatial logic by which the global "great specialization" separated agricultural surpluses from industrial production by vast distances. That meant that farmers had the resources and mechanical savvy to buy a moderately priced gadget such as the runabout—"a horseless carriage with an engine mounted underneath"—turned out by Detroit car builders in the early years.[18]

Second, the economic geography of the Midwest occasioned distinctive political sensibilities. Populist farmers famously rallied against the increasing integration of independent producers into the circuits of money and capital dominated by the East. Less well known is the equally pervasive populism espoused by the middling manufacturers and machine-shop proprietors so characteristic of the Midwest. Less concerned with agricultural prices and railroad freight rates than the farmers, the manufacturers nevertheless shared their producerism. That is, they insisted that the ultimate source of the nation's increasing wealth, and of the civilizational progress it engendered, was productive labor. Material affluence was held to be a prerogative of the productively working, whether they be farmers, laborers, or proprietor-mechanics—closely aligned occupations in the worldview of Midwestern producer populists. As Henry Ford said of his profession: "Machinist and engineer—farmer first."[19]

Experts with machines and metal, Midwestern mechanics gave their producerism a characteristic technological spin. Advances in technology, they argued, served as the motor of increasing prosperity. Through technological progress, productive workers would expand the nation's wealth, in turn furnishing them with increasing time and means for self-cultivation. Because it emerged from collaborative work, technology was a collective good. The technical innovations of the era—electricity, gasoline engines, automobiles—did not belong to the privileged few but rightfully should be available to enhance the lives of the producing classes.[20]

This kind of producer populism permeated Detroit politics. Hazen Pingree, Detroit mayor in the 1890s, exemplified a certain type of Midwestern manufacturer—his shoemaking business employed seven hundred workers—whose relative wealth did not prevent him from fiercely contesting financial elites and the powerful corporations they dominated. This pitted Pingree not only against price-gouging railroads. Pingree also alienated the elites of Detroit by bringing the local gas and power utilities into public ownership. The goal was to offer "cheap gas for the masses" and to "take electric lighting out of the luxuries of life, only to be used by the wealthy, and place it within reach of the humblest citizen." When confronted with the charge that he was dragging politics into the market sphere, Pingree countered pithily: "Corporations are in politics."[21]

At the time, Henry Ford was chief engineer of the city's largest electricity provider, Detroit Edison, so he was surely well familiar with the political fights over urban utilities. Was it a coincidence that Ford applied for the position of chief engineer at Pingree's newly inaugurated, municipally owned City Electric Lighting Plant?[22] We cannot know; Ford did not get the job. But it is evident that his milieu—the city's tinkerers, machine builders, and skilled mechanics who soon piled into the fledgling auto industry—were steeped in the kind of populist sentiment expressed by Pingree. Soon Detroit's early carmakers—with Henry Ford in the vanguard—decided to abandon the narrow market of elite purchasers and make, in Ransom Olds's words, "the automobile, the child of luxury, instead the child of necessity."[23]

Such sentiments put the mechanics, who had the know-how, at odds with the local elite, who had the capital. The copper magnates, stove manufacturers,

and city bankers who formed the Michigan upper crust were very keen on
nurturing an automobile industry. They hoped to rival the Northeast with its
pricey, handcrafted luxury vehicles. While Olds and Ford sought out investors
so they could build sturdy runabouts, the local elites hoped to fund outfits that
would flatter their own sense of social standing. Displaying a penchant for
what one automotive historian has cleverly called "conspicuous production,"
the urban elites of Michigan pressured the mechanics they financed to build
status symbols, not utility vehicles. They hoped for, in the words of Detroit
patrician Henry Joy, "a gentlemen's car, built by gentlemen."[24] Ransom Olds
was soon fired by his investors. Henry Ford's early ventures, too, failed amid
conflicts between the tinkerer and his backers. After Ford quit, the investors
recapitalized the Henry Ford Company and changed its name, in honor of
Detroit's founder, to Cadillac.[25]

With access to local capital now blocked, Ford had to pull together a "rag-
tag band of investors"—a group of middling merchants and wheeler-dealers
who were willing to back his next venture. The significance of this new outfit,
the Ford Motor Company, was this: it was the single Detroit startup that managed to survive on a shaky initial capitalization and generate enough profits to
perpetually refinance itself.[26] Ford therefore gained independence from the
city's elites, which allowed him to realize the vision of populist motorization
that other builders, like Olds, had tried but failed to push against the will of
their investors. For more than fifty years, the Ford Motor Company remained
closely held and free of bonded debt. The company only went public in 1956,
almost a decade after Henry Ford's death.

Given the class politics and populist groundswell of the Midwest, imagining a car for commoners was more than a business proposition. It was a social
provocation, whose bite only sharpened with the Ford Motor Company's increasing success. Ford exploited the social distance that separated the thin
economic elite from the farmers and manufacturers populating the Midwest.
In private, as his associates recalled, Ford scoffed at the notion that the automobile should be reserved for "the moneyed people." Instead, he insisted, "the
workingman should have some pleasure out of it." In public, the Ford Motor
Company cultivated the image of a manufacturer engaged in feisty opposition
to corporations and the wealthy. When the Model T was introduced in October 1908, an ad announced: "This car sounds the death knell of high prices and
big profits." In 1913, another ad quipped: "If there were no Fords, automobiling
would be like yachting—the sport of rich men."[27]

These clashes suggest that we should be careful to ascribe automotive mass
production to intrinsic economic necessity or technological imperative. Building luxury vehicles, as the elites wanted, could be solid business. In 1905, for
example, Henry Joy's Packard sold 503 vehicles profitably. Northeastern

carmakers would continue to build high-priced models well into the 1920s. Neither modernization nor capital accumulation compelled the rise of automotive mass production; it took deep-rooted producerist commitments and the sting of mutual class resentments to launch the mass production era. By 1913, riding the success of the Model T, the industrial district of southeastern Michigan commanded 80 percent of American automotive production.[28]

The Elements of Complex Mass Production

Mass production transformed the factories of the Midwest into buzzing behemoths that attracted production engineers from across the globe. The scale of the transformation was dizzying. In the early automobile workshops, manufacturing resembled the practices of carriage makers, in which teams led by skilled mechanics constructed wagons in small numbers by hand. Each car was assembled on a stationary setup, with workers carrying the parts about the shop. Ford, too, began like this: "We simply started to put a car together at a spot on the floor and workmen brought to it the parts that were needed in exactly the same way that one builds a house."[29] As demand for low-cost, no-frills vehicles surged, such arrangements quickly strained against inherent limits. At the Ford Motor Company, which produced behind demand for much of the first two decades of its existence, the problem of massively scaling up output was particularly pressing. In attacking the problem, Ford's shop mechanics adopted three principal strategies. None of them were novel or unique. Rather, the quantum leap in productivity achieved by American carmakers resulted from combining these strategies and pushing them to unprecedented sophistication.

The first strategy was *sequencing*. Putting the myriad tasks that went into making an automobile into logical order, carmakers found, resolved a whole host of layout problems that had vexed the small workshops. The fundamental idea was simple and entirely commonsense. Anyone who has called friends over to help with a move and organized a line in which everyone stays in place and passes box by box from hand to hand has enacted the core logic of the assembly line. In one swoop, you have eliminated the need for any of your "workers" to move about: the work moves while the worker is stationary. Said Ford: "Dividing and subdividing operations, keeping the work in motion— those are the keynotes of production."[30] Subdividing and sequencing operations resulted in the first assembly lines. Because of their commonsense nature, such layouts were nothing inherently new, and in fact widespread in American industry. Foundry work, can making, flour milling, and the disassembly line of the Chicago stockyards were well known among production engineers. Ford indeed claimed no originality for the idea, recalling that it "came in a general way from the overhead trolley that the Chicago packers use in dressing beef."[31]

Ford's true innovation lay in comprehensively implementing assembly line principles across all operations within the factory. Encouraged by the success of nonmoving lines (tilted scales along which parts and subparts would travel by the pull of gravity), Ford's production staff successively put the making of the engine, of the chassis, and finally of the finished automobile on assembly lines. This process took Ford's staff the greater part of 1913. After "patient timing and re-arrangement," the final step was achieved once "the flow of parts and the speed and intervals along the assembly line meshed into a perfectly synchronized operation."[32] The core innovation was pushing the idea of sequencing to its logical extreme. Industrial experts visiting Ford's plants thus consistently marveled not so much at the novelty but at the perfection of the flow processes they found at play there.[33]

The second element involved the *machines*, the inanimate heroes of mass production, whose awesome power and preternatural precision could move engineers like Werner to exultation. Milling and drilling machines, lathes, presses, and grinders transformed raw metal castings and forgings into recognizable automotive hardware, such as pistons, camshafts, axles, and gears. Mass-producing automobiles demanded tools more sophisticated than the desk-sized lathes populating the shops where bicycles and farm implements used to be made. It required presses that could, for example, stamp entire fenders from sheet metal in one operation. Such presses were massive hulks of steel, weighing tons. These new machines sat next to grinders whose multiple wheels, spinning at speeds unfathomable to the eye, carved metal parts into gleaming shape within seconds. Tool builders customized multifingered drills whose diamond-headed spindles could dip into solid castings with both ease and precision. In 1913, Ford showed off a machine with forty-five spindles, which drilled holes into a cylinder block from four different angles and finished the job in ninety seconds. These new machines were extremely expensive, and only massive throughput could justify their cost. Hence the Ford Motor Company led the way: in 1913, an industry expert observed that "Ford machinery was the best in the world [and] everybody knew it."[34]

These two fundamental elements—sequencing and mechanization—presupposed, and in turn sharpened, the need for other elements of complex mass production, much commented on both by contemporaries and by later historians of technology. Interchangeability of parts was a prerequisite for laying out the flow of production in a minutely subdivided way. Single-purpose machine tools, powerful instruments dedicated to a specific operation, supplanted standard tools that could accomplish many tasks but with less efficiency. The synchronization of the production process required calculating with precision the time and space needed for a given operation. Heaps of inventory that used to clutter the workshops disappeared, allowing for floor layouts that tightly packed machine next to machine. While workers stopped moving about the shop, the lines, parts, and pieces sprang to life. Continuous flow eventually changed the architecture of factories, with immense ground-floor and single-plane layouts replacing multistory buildings. None of these interdependent elements remained fixed—rather, machinists and production engineers continually revised and improved the process.[35]

The third element that made up modern mass production was surely the most momentous: sequencing and mechanization—flow production—allowed factories to *mobilize unskilled labor* in unprecedented numbers into the factories. The rise of unskilled labor can be seen from two perspectives. First, from the narrow perspective of the production process, the advantage was obvious: Building an automobile by hand was a time-consuming and laborious process that required high levels of skill. By disaggregating the process into myriad simple tasks, however, the mass production factory could turn out specimens of equal or better quality in much higher numbers and much more quickly. The essence of complex mass production was this: it allowed inexperienced workers to manufacture highly articulate goods. It meant "utilizing unskilled labor in skilled repetition-production."[36] In fact, as the American automobile industry discovered, the more labor- and material-intensive the original good, the more spectacular the economies of scale that resulted from mass production. This, along with greater spillovers into neighboring sectors and vastly diversified supply chains, is what truly set apart mass-producing automobiles from, say, mass-producing textiles: in putting together a highly intricate good like the automobile, deepening the division of labor both inside and outside the factory tapped into incommensurably larger potential for savings.[37]

Second, seen from a sociopolitical perspective, the arrival of unprecedented numbers of unskilled workers wrought a tremendous transformation of shop floors. Detroit's factories attracted migrants from the Midwestern countryside and eastern and southern European immigrants of peasant backgrounds; with World War I, African Americans leaving the rural South began streaming in increasing numbers into Midwestern factories. As mass production factories proliferated across the world, they would similarly draw in unprecedented numbers of agricultural laborers and peasant migrants—men and women who possessed scant education or factory experience. To the engineers flocking to Detroit from abroad in the Thirties, the capacity of flow production to mobilize this new unskilled workforce was of principal importance. It was telling that Werner's engineers commented within a single sentence on the "extraordinarily high division of labor" and the presence of "a lot of female workers" at one of GM's factories: this confirmed to them that combining the disaggregation of work tasks with specialized machines presented a powerful tool for exploiting the labor of the unskilled.[38]

We will see in later chapters how Soviet and Nazi engineers deployed flow production to mobilize labor when skilled workers were scarce. For our purposes here, it is necessary to understand how complex mass production emerged from the political commitments and social horizons of Detroit's skilled mechanics. Narratives of American industrialization often portray Fordism and Taylorism as siblings: two strategies in a single managerial attack on craft traditions and labor self-organization, which ushered in a lasting and irreversible process of de-skilling work. There are, however, good reasons to carefully distinguish between Taylorism and Fordism. For one, as historians of technology have repeatedly pointed out, there were stark functional differences between the two. Taylorism focused on manipulating the physiological capacities and psychological incentives of the individual worker, offering a kind of biopolitical radicalization of the piece rate system. Fordism focused on the factory process and the machines, thereby transforming the entire industrial metabolism.[39] The former sought to "train" the unskilled; the second devised a system that turned lack of skill into a productive resource. Fordism's consequences, therefore, were more far-reaching and pervasive.

There is a second reason to separate Taylorism and Fordism that historians have overlooked. These two visions of industrial renovation emerged from sharply divergent socioeconomic milieus, which in turn explains much of the practical and philosophical differences between them. The pioneers of mass production were not the type of college-educated engineers championed by Taylor: men with white collars and clean fingernails ensconced in planning offices. Rather, they were mechanics with little formal schooling, who had often apprenticed with the craft aristocrats of the old workshops. They grasped onto automotive mass production with vigor, since this new industry awarded them professional opportunities and avenues of upward social mobility that, as it eventually transpired, exceeded the hopes of even the most accomplished nineteenth-century skilled workers.

Charles Sorensen was a typical example. The son of a Danish immigrant, he quit school at sixteen and started as a patternmaker's apprentice, moving from shop to shop until settling in Detroit. At the Ford Motor Company, he worked his way up to foundry superintendent. By 1921, he was in charge of production at the Rouge, a position he held for more than twenty years. Sorensen's best-known feat, the layout of Ford's mile-long bomber assembly plant at Willow Run, came at the apex of his career in 1941. P. E. Martin, Ford's second longtime production chief, also came from an immigrant working-class background—he was the son of a French-Canadian carpenter. He left school at the age of twelve to work as a machine tender in Detroit. One of the very first machinists to join the Ford Motor Company, Martin quickly rose to foreman positions and was directly involved in setting up mass production at Highland Park. In duumvirate with Sorensen, Martin remained in command of Ford's shop floors until his retirement in 1941. Martin's proficiency with machines and expertise with production stemmed entirely from on-the-job experience. Mass production made him wealthy, but he retained the outlook of the shop.[40]

Besides Sorensen and Martin, who belonged to Ford's inner circle, many skilled mechanics whose names are forgotten today contributed to the creation of modern mass production. Their recollections, which survive in the Ford archives, show that mass production was not imposed from the planning office but emerged from the shop. The technological quantum leap that materialized at Highland Park resulted not from the theoretical distillation of "one best way" but from a continuous process of trial-and-error. Uniformly, those involved recalled the emergence of the assembly line as a sequence of attempts, mishaps, revisions, and renewed attempts. "We fixed our mistakes as we went along," Bill Klann recalled. Klann, a machinist who had first learned his trade in the Detroit shipyards, related how operation after operation was put in sequential order, a process that continued until "we had the job licked."[41] Decades after the fact, floor-level machinists recalled the process with a vividness that betrayed deep intellectual investment. Assembly line foreman James O'Connor was able to retrieve from memory the detailed sequence of experimental steps that led to the first assembly lines.[42] "Mass production," recalled assembly foreman Arthur Renner, "came from men like myself who were thinking on the job."[43] Highland Park involved the skilled mechanics in something they recalled as a momentous collaborative achievement with irresistible professional rewards. Alex Lumsden, a young immigrant metalworker from Scotland, recalled his involvement in mass production at Highland Park as imbued with "the sheer thrill of being a person and trying to project ideas." Working at Highland Park, "you felt that you were somebody. You didn't feel that your service was a bondage."[44]

Ford's production engineers, then, were a very different crowd from the white-collar efficiency engineers who began to intrude on American shop floors during the same period.[45] Taylor liked to advertise his personal distance from the milieu of the shop; as he emphasized in his *Principles of Scientific Management*, he was "not the son of a working man," and he felt that it was precisely this fact that allowed him to embrace the view of management.[46] It is hard to imagine Sorensen or Martin, who took great pride in their immersion in the shop, saying such a thing. Unsurprisingly, Sorensen claimed that "no one at Ford . . . was acquainted" with Taylor's prescriptions.[47] The mechanics who built the Ford Motor Company, in short, remained vested in the traditions of the shop even as their factories expanded to house tens of thousands of workers. They came from the old milieu of the skilled mechanics, but to them, mass production did not imply de-skilling or loss of status. Quite the contrary: in building the automobile industry, a generation of Midwestern mechanics scaled up the workshops of old and reinvented what it meant to be in possession of a craft.[48]

As the recollections of Ford's production engineers show, complex mass production came to be characterized by a stark *bifurcation of skill levels*. Mass production is rightly associated with the unskilled operatives who worked the lines and tended the machines. Equally important, however, was a group of experienced production engineers that formed what can be called the "skilled core," which, depending on the factory, might consist of anywhere between 12 and 20 percent of the workforce. This group comprised the superintendents who prepared and supervised the shop; the toolmakers who built, modified, and installed machines, jigs, and dies; the engineers who devised and revised work procedures; and the purchasing technicians who communicated with outside suppliers. All of these tasks demanded deep practical know-how and immersion in the routines of the shop. Though many of the engineers who ran twentieth-century mass production factories enjoyed some theoretical education, they necessarily acquired the bulk of their qualifications in long years of shop experience.

Another fact springs from the recollections of Ford's staffers: mass production setups were never finished. Instead, they relied on constant microinnovations that emerged from continuous learning by doing. Long before American economists formalized so-called economies of learning into hyperbolic functions based on World War II aircraft production data, the potential of constant process innovations was intuited and put into practice by the skilled mechanics of Midwestern automobile makers. These economies of learning constituted an intrinsic part of complex mass production—like in the better-known economies of scale, the more intricate the initial task, the greater the potential for revisions, adaptations, and improvements. Unskilled operatives contributed to this process of collective learning—a fact honored by the suggestion systems that proliferated in twentieth-century mass production factories.[49] By necessity, however, the accumulated production experience—what might be called the institutional memory of the mass production shop—resided in the skilled core. As the Soviet and Nazi adopters of Fordism knew well, these skilled technicians furnished the key to transferring mass production technology abroad; as we will see, they hired them in the hundreds.

East and Midwest

If conflicts between local magnates and populist mechanics dotted the early Michigan automobile industry and helped carmakers like Ford sharpen their sense of mission, how the new industry would fit into the larger American political economy took longer to determine. Broadly speaking, the contest involved two parties: Midwestern manufacturers, with their production orientation and populist leanings, and Eastern financial elites, who had a hard time attaching much significance to the upstart automobile industry at first but eventually had to reckon with its success. Within the Midwestern automobile industry, two strategies vis-à-vis the East emerged. One was to avoid outside capital and self-finance through reinvestment. That was Ford's strategy. The other was to court Eastern investors and make the raucous new industry palatable to the world of securities markets. That was the idea of William "Billy" Crapo Durant, the founder of General Motors.

Durant hailed from Flint, Michigan, and began his career as a manufacturer of horse-drawn carts. Though he grew up modestly, Durant came from pedigree—he was a grandson of Henry H. Crapo, lumber magnate and erstwhile governor of Michigan. He was no mechanic: in contrast to the likes of Henry Ford, Durant built his business not from the shop floor upward but from behind a desk weighed down by securities ledgers. He subcontracted production to established local factories, acquired suppliers and competitors, and combined them into complex edifices of interlocking shares. By the turn of the new century, Durant was one of Michigan's most successful businesspeople: Durant-Dort was the largest carriage maker of the day.[50] In 1908, Durant geared up to repeat in the automobile business the combination strategy that had made his carriage fortune. He founded General Motors as a New Jersey holding company and folded into it Buick, Cadillac, Olds, and more than twenty other manufacturers and suppliers. Durant lacked the tinkerer's delight in the automobile and, as a later commentator quipped, could not tell "the difference between a crankshaft and a differential." What piqued Durant about the fledgling auto industry were prospects of financial conquest. "What he desired, most of all," an associate recalled, "were large stock issues in which he, from an inside position, could dicker and trade."[51]

With General Motors, accordingly, Durant aspired to involve Eastern capital in the Midwestern car business. As a fellow promoter later put it, the goal was to combine carmakers into "one big concern" on the model of "the United States Steel Corporation"—to mimic, that is, the Great Merger Movement in the automobile industry.[52] Eastern financiers, however, were skeptical: they associated the new industry with high-priced electric vehicles and not the noisy gasoline engines of the Midwest; they failed to see an economic future in a consumer product with pronounced plebeian connotations. They continued to regard large-scale investments in capital-goods industries and utilities— coal, steel, oil, railroads, electricity—as the primary drivers of growth. Not attuned to the possibility of consumption-driven growth, they worried that farmers buying automobiles engaged in wasteful spending. From the East, it appeared that "the craze for automobiles" was creating dangerous bubbles. "Autos have led to extravagances and to people living beyond their means," the *Wall Street Journal* opined.[53]

Durant's courting of Eastern money, therefore, was a drawn-out and complicated dance. In 1908, the House of Morgan declined to get involved in General Motors. In 1910, flagging sales threatened to take down Durant's car combine, and he again turned East. This time the Boston investment house Lee & Higginson agreed on a bailout but demoted Durant from GM's presidency. Over the next few years, Durant organized a successful new car business, Chevrolet, and prepared a remarkable comeback. He persuaded the du Pont family—owners of the chemical giant du Pont de Nemours and, even by Eastern standards, very much representatives of "old money"—to invest substantial sums in GM stock. With the du Ponts as allies, Durant convinced the Boston bankers to relinquish control of GM when their loan expired. In 1916, Durant reacquired GM's presidency, and Pierre du Pont took a seat as the chair of the board.[54]

Durant's second tenure at GM's helm was short-lived, too. As powerful new co-owners, the du Ponts objected to what they saw as cavalier accounting and perilous stock maneuvering on the part of Durant. As the du Ponts channeled more capital into GM, this reflected not only confidence about the future prospects of the automobile industry but also anxiety about the safety of their original investments. Hit hard by the postwar recession, GM needed tens of millions of dollars in fresh capital in the winter of 1920–1921—a sum only a major investment house could raise on short notice. After personal mediation by Pierre du Pont, J. P. Morgan got involved. In short order, Morgan was called upon to bail out Durant's personal accounts. The bankers, who considered Durant "totally incompetent to manage the corporation," forced him to resign.[55]

For the second time in ten years, then, Eastern backers of a GM bailout fired Durant, earning him a lasting mercurial reputation in the annals of automotive history. Durant's significance for the history of mass production, however, lies elsewhere: he succeeded in making the Midwestern automobile an investment proposition for the financial big leagues of the East. It took a Michigander of relative pedigree to make the proposition palatable. Aspiring to join the echelons of Wall Street, Durant assiduously cultivated the personal relationships so indispensable for garnering the trust of investors; precisely the kind of relationships that Midwestern mechanics like Ford would have found both impossible and inconceivable to forge. The consequences were profound. With the 1921 takeover, General Motors had become a corporation whose executive brains and financial muscle resided in New York City, even as its most prolific factories—Buick and Chevrolet—remained in Flint and Detroit. Control of the new industry was now split between Eastern interests and a populist maverick from Michigan.

Contrast, then, GM's rise to the trajectory of the Ford Motor Company. In 1908, in fact, Durant had prodded Ford and Olds to join General Motors. In a telling rebuke, however, both mechanics rejected payment in stock and insisted on cash instead—a demand that Durant could not meet. Over subsequent years, while Durant tangled with his investors, a series of very different conflicts honed Henry Ford's conviction that automotive mass production should reflect a producer-populist orientation.

The first conflict was a remarkable courtroom battle over the nature of intellectual property. It concerned the Selden patent—a dubious license that laid claim to the gasoline-powered automobile, acquired in 1903 by a coalition of Detroit magnates and New York banks. While most Michigan carmakers in the early years grudgingly payed royalties to the patent holders, the Ford Motor Company demurred and dragged the matter into protracted litigation. The case garnered considerable public attention: it pitted a carmaker with grassroots appeal against an organization that acted like a monopolistic bully. In 1911, the courts ruled in favor of Ford and adopted the company's logic, arguing that "from the point of view of the public interest," it would have been better "if the patent had never been granted."[56]

Ford drew his own conclusions. Calling the idea that patents "stimulate invention" an "exploded theory," he eventually called for "the abolition of all patent laws." More remarkably, after the Selden affair the Ford Motor Company adopted an open-source stance that was in keeping with the producerist idea that technological progress should contribute to the common repertoire of human ingenuity. The company stopped enforcing its own patents and began furnishing blueprints to interested parties upon request.[57] Such practices eventually came to benefit William Werner and many other would-be mass producers streaming to the Rouge. In particular, as we will see, the Soviet delegation took full advantage of Ford's open-door policy in the early Thirties.

The second conflict that connected automotive mass production to producer-populist tenets was the five-dollar day. As is well known, in 1914 the Ford Motor Company more than doubled its going wage rate for unskilled workers while cutting the workday to eight hours. The raise was tied to stiff expectations: it applied only to workers who had been on the company's rolls for at least six months, barring so-called floaters from qualifying. A "Sociological Department" made sure that five-dollar workers did not accommodate boarders, were married, and renounced smoke and drink. The scheme also involved an effort to assimilate immigrant workers to presumed American ways of life. A Ford School was set up to teach workers English and American customs. Famously, the school's graduation ceremony featured a gigantic "melting pot" into which immigrant workers descended "with their foreign clothes" and from which they emerged in "the best American clothes and waving American flags."[58]

In master narratives of Fordism, the five-dollar day is often seen as the clearest anticipation of postwar demand-side dispensations: Ford allegedly raised wages so his workers could afford the cars they built. In fact, Ford made no such claim at the time (though he would adopt purchasing-power arguments some years later). Instead, the main problem that the Ford Motor Company said it hoped to solve with the five-dollar day was labor turnover. (Mass production managers across the globe would soon approach the same question with varying combinations of enticement and coercion: Once large numbers of unskilled migrants arrived in the factory, what would keep them at their stultifying jobs?) In the context of early twentieth-century Detroit, it was difficult to retain workers, who routinely sampled jobs and factories in search of better conditions. In 1913, the Ford Motor Company reportedly had to hire "between 50,000 and 60,000 people" to maintain an average workforce of 13,000.[59] There was also the sheer diversity of the Highland Park workforce: in 1914, 71 percent of workers had been born outside of the US, the majority of them southern and eastern Europeans. Klann recalled being in charge of a group that comprised fourteen different nationalities. Communication was difficult; he scrambled to find "subforemen who could speak several languages."[60]

If company publications can be believed, the five-dollar scheme achieved its purpose. In the first two years, labor turnover fell from the enormous rate of 370 percent to 16 percent. Absenteeism declined and productivity went up. Some 16,000 laborers came through the Ford School. Allegedly, Ford workers saved more, and more got married.[61] Because of these results, the five-dollar day galvanized Progressive Era reformers. Later, labor historians described it as a strategy of capitalist "social control"; economists theorized about "efficiency wages".[62]

And yet, if one listens closely, the five-dollar day eloquently spoke the language of producer populism. In a statement before Congress, Ford made no mention of purchasing-power arguments, but said that the "first purpose" of the five-dollar day was "substantial justice to our coworkers." The scheme was devised in the "knowledge that market rates were not sufficient" for workers to live decently, and the "object was simply to better the financial and moral status of the men."[63] Announcing the raise to the press, the company justified it in these terms:

Social justice begins at home. We want those who have helped us to produce this great institution and are helping to maintain it to share our prosperity. We want them to have present profits and future prospects. Thrift
and good service and sobriety will all be enforced and recognized. Believ-
ing as we do, that a division of our earnings between capital and labor is
unequal, we have sought a plan of relief suitable for our business.[64]

Puffy rhetoric, no doubt—but what kind of rhetoric? With its emphasis on
justice, economic cooperation, and the cultivation of virtues, this language did
not quite match familiar paternalist nostrums or the prescriptions of progressive social engineering. Take the "division of earnings between capital and
labor." If the sole purpose was to provide monetary incentives for efficient
conduct, the company would have had little reason to insist, as it did obsessively, that the point was not to raise wages but to share profits. In the telling
of Charles Sorensen, the idea initially resulted from a chalkboard exercise by
which the company's directors tried to determine how future pay envelopes
could more adequately reflect the company's astonishing growth. They eventually allotted $10 million of anticipated 1914 profits toward increasing pay (or
roughly one-third of that expected sum: 1913 had delivered a good $27 million
in net income).[65] To the press, Ford said, "I wish you would lay stress on the
fact that it is not higher wages we are paying our employees, but profits." In
what was "distinctly a sort of dividend," up to half of future profits would be
passed on to workers. This was neither socialism nor paternalism, Ford told a
befuddled *Times* reporter, but a recognition of workers' contribution to the
company.[66] Or take the notion of thrift, which the Sociological Department
purported to instill in five-dollar beneficiaries. Thrift, as a company pamphlet
explained, was "an index of character. It indicates self-control, self-respect, and
some plan and purpose in life looking to the future." Thrift was incompatible
with attachment to alcohol or with the strictures of debt.[67]

Far from foreshadowing the consumerism of the mid-twentieth century,
then, the Ford Motor Company's five-dollar rhetoric reasserted labor-
republican notions of the nineteenth century. In fusing industrial cooperation
with the expectation of virtue and self-ownership, it echoed the moral economy of the Knights of Labor. Recall that the Knights had sought not to overcome capitalism through class struggle but to harness corporate organization
and financial accumulation for the benefit of the laboring producers, with the
goal, as the preamble to the Knights' 1878 constitution had put it, "to secure to
the toilers a proper share of the wealth that they create."[68] The Knights proposed cooperative industrial organizations that would pass on proceeds to
their participants: profit shares should supplant wages.[69] In this vision, production was not a contractual affair but tied individual rewards to collective

expectations: economic betterment implied not only greater disposable income and more leisure time but also moral improvement. For all its impracticality, then, the Sociological Department conveyed a "demanding conception of virtue"[70]—mass production put moral demands on its participants, and the company would see to it that its members held up their end of the compact. Fully in keeping with this tradition was also the evidently patronizing idea that recent immigrants, while deemed capable of advancing themselves to citizenship through work, required some nudging and pushing along the way—which the Sociological Department would provide.[71]

If such notions seem decidedly stodgy today, at the time they caused a stir. The five-dollar day dragged into the daylight central questions about the industrial order: To whom would accrue the benefits of technological and economic progress? How should the material rewards of mass production be distributed? Those were questions that many industrial elites at the time would have preferred not to discuss—that, in any case, is what their dismayed reactions indicated. "The plan contravenes all economic laws," the vice president of Studebaker submitted on the five-dollar day. The *New York Times* editorialized that the scheme was "distinctly Utopian and dead against experience." The *Wall Street Journal* spoke of "economic blunders if not crimes" and warned of "material, financial, and factory disorganization." A Pittsburgh industrialist feared the "ruin of all business in this country." John D. Rockefeller Jr. claimed that most businesses lacked the means to pursue such generous wage policies, and he implausibly included his own.[72] Given such alarmed reactions, it is clear that the Ford five-dollar day touched a nerve that other so-called profit-sharing plans of the era did not. The scheme raised the awkward possibility that employers who paid skimpy wages were veiling a policy decision behind appeals to economic "laws."

To be sure, the consequences of the five-dollar day did not live up to the initial uproar. Workers predictably resented and resisted the intrusive investigations. The distinction between wages and profit shares, so dear to the scheme's designers, made little practical difference to those who received the pay envelopes. The inflation triggered by World War I, meanwhile, rendered the five-dollar figure much less impressive, and Ford's competitors soon caught up with raises of their own. In addition, disagreements within the company roiled the scheme: foremen and the skilled elite saw the Sociological Department as meddling with shop procedures and began working against it. In 1921, during the postwar recession, the department was unceremoniously scrapped.[73] Nevertheless, the five-dollar episode allows us to see Henry Ford's social and political imaginary in a new light. Though this is counterintuitive to our own impoverished economic sensibilities, the scheme suggests that Ford and his skilled mechanics liked to think of their company as an industrial cooperative of unprecedented scale and power, one in which social obligations were inseparable from work commitments.[74]

The *third* conflict that solidified Ford's producer-populist convictions also concerned the question of what the Ford Motor Company should do with its profits. The period from 1914 to 1917 brought unprecedented income; Ford used the windfall to acquire large tracts of land along the Rouge River in Dearborn, just west of Detroit's city limits. The idea was to build a factory that would surpass even Highland Park and mass-produce tractors just like Model Ts. Several of the Ford Motor Company's stockholders—holdovers from the group of backers from 1903—objected to these plans. In 1916, John and Horace Dodge, who together held 10 percent of Ford Motor Company stock, filed suit against Henry Ford and the company. Instead of using profits to expand production, the Dodges held, the company should distribute them to the stockholders.[75]

The suit revealed that Ford and his stockholders held conflicting views on the purpose of corporate profits. The Dodges adopted an investor's standpoint. They argued that company profits represented a return on their investment, due to them as a reward for the initial capital advanced and the risk assumed. Calling the Rouge expansion plans "reckless in the extreme," they demanded that "a large part of the cash accumulation" should be "distributed by way of dividends to the stockholders to whom it belongs."[76] Ford, in contrast, argued that profits constituted a fund for the continued expansion of operations. It had been a matter of principle at the Ford Motor Company not to chase profits but to focus on production; future growth would similarly require doing so. "To spread the benefits of the industrial system," Ford said, it was necessary to put "the greatest share of our profits back into the business." Ford also added a moral dimension to the issue. He "did not believe we should make such an awful profit on our cars," Ford told the press. "A reasonable profit is right, but not too much." Ford said that the Dodges had initially put $10,000 into the company. On this amount they had to date reaped $5,517,500 in dividends, Ford explained, clearly implying that he regarded the 55,000 percent return as ample enough.[77]

The Michigan Supreme Court eventually sided with the Dodges, arguing that "a business corporation is organized and carried on primarily for the profit of stockholders."[78] In 1919, the company complied with the verdict and dispensed a special dividend of roughly $19 million plus accrued interest. Having lost in court, however, Ford found a different way to prevent future conflicts over the course of the company: he moved aggressively to buy out the remaining minority stockholders. As a result, by 1920, the number of owners had dwindled to three: Henry Ford, his wife, Clara, and their son, Edsel. In short, at the same time that Eastern investors took control of General Motors, Henry Ford moved his company in the opposite direction by taking it private. Billy

Durant lost control of his corporation to powerful stockholders, while Ford reacted to a challenge by his stockholders by removing them from control.

Ford versus GM

In the 1920s, the automobile industry led the American economy into a boom. The wellspring of the boom was the enormous productivity gains delivered by mass production. Over the course of the decade, consumption as a share of national income increased by one-third, but the impact of this shift varied substantially across regions. In the automotive hotbed of southeastern Michigan, wages rose along with productivity: over the course of the 1920s, average yearly employee earnings at Ford were between 23 and 47 percent higher than the manufacturing average, and wages at GM had caught up with Ford's by 1926. Hours were shorter, too. While Detroit workers were at least able to trade a grueling eight-hour workday for generous compensation, many workers in steel, coal, or textiles continued to toil sixty-hour weeks or more for poverty wages. Not all workers, therefore, benefited from new consumption opportunities. Across American industry as a whole, wages failed to keep up with productivity, and profits went into corporate coffers, or to shareholders, and from there to the burgeoning securities markets. The Roaring Twenties, then, engendered new patterns of inequality. Not all regions shared in the growth, and many of its gains ended up at the very top of the income stratification.[79]

As the two dominant concerns of the automobile industry, General Motors and the Ford Motor Company stood at the very center of these economic transformations. Both corporations built their power on the formula of complex mass production pioneered by Midwestern mechanics. Ford celebrated the Model T's most successful years in 1923–1925; the successor Model A clinched another sales record in 1929. Of GM's divisions, it was the low-price make, Chevrolet, that carried the corporation on its eminent ascent. At Chevrolet, William Knudsen, who was a Ford veteran, took his former employer's key idea—economies of scale in the low-price segment—and added the annual model change, developing a more flexible style of mass production. Beginning in 1922, and for most years after that, Chevrolet produced and sold more vehicles than all other GM divisions combined. Single-handedly, Chevrolet overtook Ford in sales for the first time in 1927, marking the beginning of GM's erosion of Ford's erstwhile market dominance.[80]

The story of GM passing Ford has often been told as a narrative of rationalization: the managerial model and the marketing strategies of the New York–owned corporation, it is said, were simply more modern than Ford's outdated ways.[81] In a less overdetermined view, it is plain that market share was only one issue in what was a much larger contest over the social and ideological implications of automotive mass production. Both corporations remained obliged to their distinctive histories and loyal to the dominant values of their leading men. Henry Ford, no longer beholden to stockholder interference, shaped his company into an organization that continued to elaborate, albeit idiosyncratically, on the tradition of producer populism. GM, meanwhile, harnessed automotive mass production to the ways of investor capitalism. The two corporations, therefore, not only developed starkly diverging business practices, they also engaged in a fierce ideological rivalry over the role of the large, mass-producing corporation in the new era of consumption-based growth.

When it came to management, the task facing GM's new owners was how to turn the assemblage of Midwestern manufacturers, from Chevrolet to Cadillac to suppliers and parts makers, into a group of corporate "divisions" legible to the investors and accountable to the metric of returns. (Or, as one of GM's new managers later put it, it was necessary to "bring the operating people around to accepting the principle that their individual affairs must be aimed at serving the interests of [GM's] stockholders.")[82] To do so, the du Ponts appointed a group of professional managers under president Alfred P. Sloan. By skillfully brokering between the owners and the divisions, Sloan succeeded over time in co-opting a set of fiercely independent carmakers into a corporate-wide identity. In the process, GM changed its image: long seen to have "a financial rather than industrial character," it now became associated with a supposedly new type of rational management.[83] The high-level executive—as opposed to the financier or the engineer—now assumed the starring role in corporate activity.[84] Ford's staffers, meanwhile, rejected the trappings of managerial bureaucracy and perpetuated a culture in which "the manufacturing and production people were in the saddle" while "the book-keepers were merely tolerated as necessary evil."[85] Organization charts and committee meetings were disallowed; instead, administration drew on the institutional memory—implicit protocols and informal routines—vested in a tight-knit group of blue-collar staffers who (like Sorensen and Martin) had been with the company for many years. Ford rarely got involved in day-to-day business; he presided over the company as a distant charismatic leader.[86]

The two corporations also adopted very different stances vis-à-vis the market. General Motors regarded the automobile market as a sphere that had to be created: customers had to be made, consumption appetites stimulated. To this end GM launched market research, offered installment financing, and developed elaborate advertising and image campaigns. Famously offering "a car for every purse and purpose," General Motors not only began targeting customers up and down the income ladder, the corporation also sold the prospect of price-bracket upward mobility (start with a Chevy, move up to a Cadillac). To further stimulate turnover, GM began changing its models every year.[87] The Ford Motor Company, meanwhile, rejected such tactics. The company embraced installment financing only half-heartedly and resisted for many years the planned obsolescence of annual model changes by holding on to the one-size-fits-all Model T.[88]

Less well known but equally revealing were starkly diverging financial practices. General Motors took full advantage of—and substantially contributed to—the deepening of securities markets during the 1920s. Durant's combine had early attracted elite investors; in 1917, their number stood at 2,920. As a result of Morgan's involvement, the number of GM shareholders rose to 66,837; by 1937, more than 375,000 individuals owned GM stock. During the same period, the number of Ford stockholders remained at 3. GM used the blue-chip status of its stock to finance investment. Between 1917 and 1937, the corporation issued some $724 million in shares to raise cash or to acquire plants and property.[89] During the same period, not a single Ford share crossed the desks of New York City brokers. The Ford Motor Company financed expansions and acquisitions exclusively out of retained earnings: the Rouge that William Werner toured in 1937 was built with Model T profits. The Ford Motor Company reinvested more than 75 percent of its net income in the 1920s and 1930s. The reinvestment figure for General Motors stood at 23 percent, with the remainder of earnings paid out as dividends to stockholders.[90] GM's management explicitly embraced "return on investment" as the metric by which to assess industrial performance; Ford's staffers continued to regard low production costs as the key criterion.[91] Each in their own way, Ford's bare-bones tax statements and GM's elaborate annual reports conveyed financial information as much as they reflected corporate philosophy.

In an era in which business elites felt increasingly authorized to assume public leadership, both Henry Ford and his circle, as well as the new executives running General Motors, expounded on their respective belief systems. Collaborating with various ghostwriters and congenial journalists, Ford attained a particularly high public profile.[92] Sloan and his group of manager-savants were less visible, but their ideological work was no less assiduous: their outlets were the venues of business interest politics, public speeches, and periodicals like *Management and Administration*.[93]

Both Ford and Sloan countered traditional anxieties about economic concentration by claiming that the large corporation was now an unmitigated force for good. To Ford, the justification of the big corporation lay in its wealth-generating efficiency. The large corporation, properly understood, was a "productive organization"—a place where the collective labor of thousands of workers converted raw materials into prolific output. Higher living standards flowed exclusively from this source. It was an error to "confuse big business with big money power": the Ford Motor Company had demonstrated

FIGURE 1.2. Henry Ford and close associates, 1933. Left to right: P. E. Martin, B. J. Craig (treasurer), Charles Sorensen, Henry Ford, Ray Dahlinger, Edsel Ford, A. M. Wibel (accounting and purchasing). Photo: The Henry Ford.

that industry, released from the yoke of finance capital, could channel productivity increases into lower prices and higher wages. Once profits were uncoupled from private rents, Ford began to argue, they could serve as a trust fund in the virtuous cycle of accumulation. Capital was "a working surplus held in trust and daily use for the benefit of all," Ford indeed claimed, since it represented "the joint product of [the] whole organization." Ford's ghostwriter packaged this conceit into the formula that truly modern business would increasingly replace the "profit motive" with the "wage motive."[94]

Sloan, in contrast, developed what might be termed a consensus view of the modern corporation. The large corporation was justified because it bridged the antagonisms that had cleaved society in the past. Unlike its muckraking-era predecessors, a corporation like General Motors provided equal stakes to employees, stockholders, management, and the consuming public. The public and the corporation shared the same aims; after all, "the economic welfare of millions" was linked "with the welfare of GM." Prolific, transparent, and keenly sensitive to the public interest, the modern corporation had revealed that at bottom there was no contradiction between the interests of consumers and producers, the corporation and the public, investors and the firm, finance and production, or labor and capital.[95]

The ideological contrast should be properly appreciated. In the producerist lexicon, finance and industry worked at cross-purposes. As Ford put it, "the function of business" was "to produce for consumption and not for money and speculation." The GM view, in contrast, treated investment capital as a coequal contributor to economic progress. Investors, Sloan said, were "entitled to a return," and it was the task of management to ensure that this return was "fair and equitable."[96] Different corporate ideologies also implied diverging roles for management. Ford insisted that industrial leadership was properly directed inward, toward the sphere of production, and that its supreme task was to improve the metamorphosis of labor power and materials into consumption and utility: "True management begins with the product and its making." Sloan, in contrast, saw corporate management naturally gravitating toward a more expansive leadership role. Technical knowledge and production expertise were necessary; but it was financial and managerial skills that conferred authority in steering the political economy at large. Business elites, rather than government officials or labor representatives, were best equipped to serve as the arbiters of conflict. "Those charged with great industrial responsibility must become industrial statesmen," Sloan said.[97]

The final issue raised by mass production involved the new status of consumption in economic progress. Here Ford energetically adopted an argument that emphasized consumption (not investment, as classical economists insisted) as the engine of growth. Though Ford perhaps did more than anyone to popularize the idea, it was by no means his own; rather, it emerged from among a coalition of progressive thinkers and moderate labor leaders.[98] The argument implied that high wages were not just morally desirable but systemically necessary to sustain growth in the mass production era. At this point, however, Ford and purchasing-power progressives diverged. Labor leaders framed wages as a matter of rights and entitlements; progressives suggested that stimulating demand should become a goal of state policy. Ford would have none of that: wages flowed solely from productivity gains, he said, and if employers consistently channeled productivity gains into high wages and low prices, slumps were an impossibility, and there was no need for state intervention. "The cure of business depression is through purchasing power, and the source of purchasing power is wages."[99]

The GM view found different answers to the problem of demand. Sloan, to be sure, publicly conceded that the productivity-wage cycle propelled by mass production was a lesson imparted to him by Henry Ford. Sloan also embraced a vision of economic progress based on constant technological innovation and prolific productivity increases—an "industrial scheme of things that is constantly turning luxuries into everyday conveniences for more people." However, market saturation was a real danger that could not ultimately be overcome by higher wages and lower prices. GM's consumer market-making, then, amounted to a genuinely new apparatus of qualitative demand management.[100]

Conclusion

American "high mass-consumption," then, did not arise fully fledged from the Roaring Twenties. On the contrary, what mass production implied for America's economy and society remained a sharply contested question as the 1920s drew to a close. The dominant historical perception of Henry Ford as a zany folk hero increasingly left behind by the progress of his times has made it exceedingly difficult to appreciate the political valence of the mass production ideology he propounded. Ford, to be sure, was enthralled to absurd conspiracy theories, and felt that broad popular acclaim absolved him of the need for compromise and coalition building. There were also obvious contradictions between the righteous Ford rhetoric and the harsh reality of his factories. The Ford Motor Company dismissed the idea that Rouge work routines were overly arduous; and unskilled workers, allegedly respected members of the "productive organization," suffered extreme hostility toward their schemes of self-organization. Nevertheless, the company creatively rearticulated, both in practice and ideology, a producer populist tradition that is generally presumed to have expired along with the workshops of nineteenth-century artisans. The Ford Motor Company, then, remained a visible reminder that mass production initially arose by challenging liberal conceits about economic development. As we discuss in chapter 2, interwar postliberals from around the globe intuited this sharply.

The GM view of mass production should be against this foil. Business historians have been taken in a tad too far by Sloan's own presentation of the matter, which suggested that the actions of General Motors were coterminous with capitalism's march into efficiency, rationality, and modern purpose. Financialization, consumer market-making, and "managerial revolution," however, constituted not so much an inevitable rationalization of older production conceits but a potent rival tradition with its own ideological charge. GM's version, by putting the enlightened executive in front of the bogey of the absentee owner, refurbished investor capitalism and removed the populist sting that had attached to mass production since its origins. Against producerist tenets, the GM vision first established, and then naturalized, the view that mass production worked best, and to everyone's advantage, when it was submitted to the logic of capitalization—to the proposition, that is, that industrial resources constituted assets meant to furnish investment returns.[101]

As it turned out, the Depression challenged both visions, though GM found it easier to adapt than Ford. Ford's problem was, for one, philosophical: a modernist theory of continual growth and technological advancement was unequipped to deal with the Depression. The Ford formula—high wages, paid out of constantly increasing productivity gains—had few answers to evaporating demand. In the fall of 1929, Henry Ford defiantly announced the seven-dollar day. By 1932, however, his company had sent half of its workforce into unemployment and was operating steeply below capacity.[102] The optimistic notion of an ever-expandable productivity-wage cycle looked distinctly battered as the boosterism of the Twenties gave way to deeply pessimistic notions: technology caused not abundance but "overproduction," growth had come to a permanent stop, and times no longer required improving production but organizing equitable distribution and combating unemployment. Such views were difficult to assimilate to producerist principles.

A new political economy emerged whose pillars—an empowered regulatory state and a labor movement of unskilled, mass production workers that had the state's backing—were inimical to Ford's vision. In the Twenties, automobile workers had accepted the mass production bargain that traded degrading factory conditions and mindless tasks against modest opportunities for consumption. In the Depression, that bargain unraveled.[103] Now workers organized for dignity, job security, grievance procedures, and against the assembly line speedup. GM was hardly accommodating: only sit-down strikes eventually forced the corporation to the table in 1937. The Ford Motor Company refused to recognize the unions before 1941. Ominously, Ford remained unable to see why workers would self-organize in the first place. "The unions," Ford submitted, "were created by Wall Street—by capital." Such talk was a stark admission of helplessness, even if Ford surely believed it.[104]

The Depression also revealed the institutional weakness of producerism. The Ford Motor Company inhabited a profound outsider position to the thickening interest politics of the Thirties. If it had been adopted early and broadly, Ford's anticyclical wage policy might have served to mitigate the deflationary collapse of the Depression. But unlike his competitors at GM, Ford was notoriously indisposed toward political advocacy and effective coalition building. Personally, Ford refused to join the social circles of the industrial elite and consistently avoided their gatherings.[105] He declined to join the anti-Roosevelt Liberty League sponsored by Sloan and other magnates of the du Pont–GM alliance.[106] On the institutional level, the Ford Motor Company abstained from the busy associational activity pursued by GM's executives.

Alfred Sloan built the National Manufacturers Association into an effective vehicle of political advocacy against the New Deal. The Ford Motor Company never joined the NAM or the Automobile Manufacturers Association.[107] By the late Thirties, instead, Henry Ford sought desultory alliances on the isolationist right—Coughlinites, America Firsters, Charles Lindbergh.[108] The company thus remained isolated from the emerging corporatist compromises of the New Deal era.

At the same time, however, River Rouge remained a paean to Ford's erstwhile producerism. The large cash cushions accumulated in the Twenties allowed the Ford Motor Company to recover from the Depression with new rounds of investment. In 1935, the company embarked on a $35 million modernization program of the Rouge; establishing the extravagant Ford Rotunda in Dearborn was part of this package.[109] The thousands of visitors flocking to the Rouge in the Thirties testified to the fact that the spectacle of mass production continued to exert a magnetic pull on the era's imagination.

The day after concluding his tour of the Rouge, William Werner boarded the train back to New York, where he spent the final day of his American sojourn—November 2, 1937—with a visit to the American Automobile Exhibition. Here Werner checked in with engineers sent by German carmakers BMW and Opel, about to embark on their own tour of the Midwest. After Werner's return to Chemnitz, his office sent out a series of thank-you notes to officials at the various American firms he had visited, commending the spirit of cooperation that prevailed in the international car industry, and offering to open the doors of Auto-Union to American visitors in return.[110]

Such exchanges, so characteristic of the 1930s, were already reshaping the global landscape of mass production. In May 1937, Ferdinand Porsche received the Nazi regime's assurances that construction of the Volkswagen plant would be sponsored by the deep pockets of the German Labor Front. Porsche immediately left for the USA. During three weeks over the summer of 1937, Porsche was "all over the Ford plant" and "walked through the most wonderful factory I have ever seen," as he wrote to Henry Ford in a thank-you note jotted on Book Cadillac stationery.[111] In October, a group of German-American engineers set up shop in the Volkswagen planning office in Stuttgart, Germany. They were mass production specialists that Porsche had hired away from Ford. That fall, the man responsible for bringing Rouge techniques to Russia, Stepan Dybets, was arrested by the NKVD in Moscow, as Stalin's purges began ensnaring industrial managers. In a mordant irony, the automobile plant in Gorky (which Dybets helped launch) was just hitting stride, surpassing in output for 1937 the largest plants in Germany and Britain. These biographical notes point to the deepest and most counterintuitive legacy of Midwestern producerism for the twentieth century at large.

2

Ford's Bible of the Modern Age

Ford's name will be remembered many years after capitalism has disappeared
from the face of the earth.

—N. BELIAEV, *GENRI FORD*, 1935

ON OCTOBER 22, 1937, five days before William Werner's investigation of the
Rouge, the Ford Motor Company welcomed a separate group of German visitors. Like Werner and his entourage, they had crossed the Atlantic by ship and
used the train to reach the Midwest. But their purpose was a different one. This
group, comprising some twenty academics, diplomats, and businessmen, traveled under the sponsorship of the Carl Schurz Society, an organization
founded in 1926 to foster German-American cultural exchanges. By the mid-
Thirties, the Society had become an important vehicle of Nazi cultural diplomacy in America. Carl Schurz groups were known to visit Dearborn; this reflected the special place that Henry Ford had in the Nazi imagination of
America: genius of production, opponent of finance capital, and herald of a
motorized *Volk*. After enjoying the requisite two-hour tour of the Rouge, the
group retired to company premises for a luncheon. Ernest Liebold, Ford's personal secretary, invited an exchange of friendly words in German.[1]

Most prominent among the travelers was Gottfried Feder, formerly a secretary in the German Ministry of Economics, *Reichstag* member since 1926,
and cofounder of the National Socialist German Workers' Party. During the
Twenties, Feder had acted as the party's ideological steward in economic
matters, contributing popular slogans, such as "common good precedes self-
interest" and "breaking the bondage of interest." Like others from the Nazi
founding circle, Feder fell casualty to Hitler's post-1933 turn to realpolitik.
Eased out of political influence into an honorary professorship, Feder was, on
that October day in 1937, visiting in the Ford Motor Company a source of inspiration from the early days.[2]

As a member of the sprawling radical right of early Weimar, Feder first learned of Henry Ford as a purveyor of anti-Semitic conspiracy theories. The wild mash-up of the "Protocols of Zion" that Ford disseminated under the title *The International Jew* was a mainstay among members of the *völkisch* fringe.[3] At least as much as Ford's anti-Semitism, however, it was the American's self-exegesis, *My Life and Work*, that drew a discernible trail across Feder's ideological orbit. As Feder elaborated it, Nazi economic doctrine rejected both liberalism and Marxism; unfettered private gain would lead to exploitation, collectivized property to decay. The correct view lay in an economy that allowed "true" entrepreneurs to harness their efforts to an overarching collective purpose. Such leaders scoped out "the best and cheapest methods of production," pushed "prices to their lowest limit," paid workers well, and constantly worked on production and distribution. "The most eminent and world-renowned example" of this kind of entrepreneur, Feder wrote, was Henry Ford.[4]

That a Nazi ideologue extolled Ford as a political inspiration points to how widely the American auto king's ideas resonated in the 1920s. In Germany, the translation of Ford's *My Life and Work* induced a remarkable fixation that affected readers far beyond the Nazi fringe. In the thrall of a veritable "Ford psychosis," many Germans greeted the book like the savior of a millenarian cult. It offered "revelation and redemption," said one engineer; it spelled a "doctrine of salvation," offered a journalist. Another commentator saw Ford revealed in the book as "an optimistic, muscular, and crystal-clear thinker," a veritable Nietzsche of the twentieth century.[5] An opponent called it "one of the most frightful and ghastly books in world literature." *My Life and Work* saw a run of 200,000 copies in Germany.[6]

Nor were the Germans alone in their obsession. Over the course of 1924, *My Life and Work* cropped up in at least a dozen languages. French, Danish, Finnish, Dutch, Polish, Spanish, Swedish, Serbo-Croatian editions came out, even one set in Braille. A Japanese translation was under way. The first Russian translation appeared in the Leningrad publishing cooperative *Vremia* in 1924. It enjoyed spectacular resonance in the Soviet Union, going through ten printings comprising some 80,000 copies. *My Life and Work* was "attractive to the stern Soviet reader," an editor opined, "despite its evident capitalist bias." To Soviet ears, the book intoned "the hymn of industrialization, the hymn of the highest and fullest development of the productive forces, boundless creation and energy, the hymn to the victory of the human intellect over the inertia and blind power of nature."[7]

Remarkably, Ford's successor volume, *Today and Tomorrow*, published in the United States in April 1926, matched the sensation of the earlier book. It received translations into all major European languages; three competing editions circulated in the Soviet Union. To both volumes, readers reacted with exuberance; many spoke in terms of an epiphany. To French economist Yves Guyot, Henry Ford was "the *homo economicus* of the twentieth century." British journalist Albert Kinross considered Ford "the greatest revolutionary of the present day." José Monteiro Lobato, Brazilian man of letters, crowned Henry Ford as "the most lucid and penetrating intellect of modern times." Lobato asserted that "no conscientious man reading *My Life and Work*" could "fail to discern in it the Messianic Gospel of the Future." Half a globe away, Kato Saburo, an executive at a Tokyo-based trading firm, read *My Life and Work* and professed that it made him "a worshipper of Henry Ford." Kato worked in the wee hours before his day job to produce not one but two full translations of the book into Japanese (the first fell victim to fire). *Henrī Fōdo jijoden* finally appeared in 1927. In 1926, the banker and economist T. Nakamura addressed Henry Ford from Tokyo, volunteering his own services for the translation of *Today and Tomorrow*. Japan, Nakamura said, was much in need of Ford's instruction. The country desired "neither socialism nor capitalism," but rather Ford's ideas, which would bring about "the general welfare of the Japanese community." *Today and Tomorrow*, Nakamura asserted, was "the Bible of the Modern Age."[8]

My Life and Work tore across the postwar world like a comet. What accounts for the book's astonishing impact? Part of the answer lies, as historians have long recognized, in the fascination that all things American exerted upon the world after the Great War. Dazed and diminished by the war, Europeans squinted across the Atlantic and saw an image of the future: a new type of civilization, characterized by mass production and mass consumption, skyscrapers and Hollywood, assembly lines and flapper dresses. Like no other phenomenon, Henry Ford's factories seemed to exemplify this new American modernity: here the machinelike uniformity of modern industrial production begot a high standard of living and new possibilities for extravagant consumption and cultural expression. In this perspective, Ford's interwar popularity was a chapter in the *longue durée* of Europe's twentieth-century infatuation with America.[9]

But the groundswell of economic envy and cultural fascination cannot quite explain the histrionic intensity with which contemporaries reacted to *My Life and Work*. What about this book, as a German author put it, "answered to a spiritual need"?[10] Why was it political radicals who seemed to offer it the highest praise? How come the book kindled the most combustible disagreements simultaneously in Weimar Germany and the Soviet Union? Explaining this requires shifting the focus from cultural obsessions to politics and economics, from "Jazz Age" tropes to the realities of a profoundly destabilized global order.

Of the many contradictions that World War I had left in its wake, the most vexing was the "absent presence" of the new hegemon, the United States.[11] America had replaced Germany as the world's leading manufacturing power and had wrested the baton of world creditor from Britain. Though abundant, American credit only precariously propped up an off-kilter global division of labor: a deluge of primary products inundating world markets, and feeble European industries unable to compete. Insulated behind high tariffs and refusing to negotiate war obligations, America at the same time offered ample loans to Europe, only accelerating the vortex of reparations and debts that sucked international finance underwater. Seen in this light, the salience of America for Europeans lay less in its cultural provocations than in a challenge that not a few observers likened to an existential threat, and the reception of Ford's books thus looks more like a chapter in the panic and apprehension that the "American danger" had been arousing among Europeans since the late nineteenth century.[12]

How to respond to America's challenge cleaved the Twenties' political landscape in two opposing camps. There were those who sought to accommodate America's new prominence, revive liberal internationalism, restore trade and the gold standard, and give faith to the League of Nations. On the other end loomed an increasingly restive camp of "insurgents" (Adam Tooze) who sought the opposite: to repudiate prewar precepts and challenge America's power by fundamentally altering the political architecture of the global order. The first to rebel was the Soviet Union, which banished world market forces from Russia by submitting foreign trade to the state. But an equally remarkable transformation occurred on the right, as conservatives turned against liberalism, nationalists pressed to overthrow the Paris peace settlement, and the völkisch-inclined began to mix fantasies of racial purification with notions of world-economic reversal. A newly invigorated postliberal right reared its head in Germany, Italy, and Japan, throughout Central Europe, and across Latin America. With a vigor and conviction that increased as the Twenties wore on, the postliberal right railed against the international system of finance and trade, which they argued was held together by chains of debt and dominated by the United States, Britain, and France.[13] These postliberal rebels felt America's challenge most keenly, and urged most vocally to scrutinize the sources of America's rise, in order to emulate, rival, and overcome it. Little wonder that *My Life and Work* spoke with particular force not to the voices of stability but to the insurgents; not to the forces of restoration but to their opponents.

The career of *My Life and Work* reveals that the global reception of mass production began with furnishing a development model not to the forces of liberal restoration but to the voices of postliberal reversal. There were other books that electrified contemporaries because they encapsulated the tensions of the postwar world. Keynes's *Economic Consequences of the Peace* delivered a bleak indictment of the Versailles settlement; Coudenhove-Kalergi's *Pan-Europa* expressed widespread sentiments that Europeans should join forces to confront America.[14] Only *My Life and Work*, however, spoke with equal force to the insurgent left and the postliberal right. As we shall see, Ford's book went straight to the heart of the fierce Soviet debates about socialist industrial development. To the right, Ford's ideas suggested how to insert modern industry into postliberal social orders. These readings were, to be sure, creative misprisions: virtually none of Ford's readers accurately discerned in *My Life and Work* the local history and political context of Midwestern populism. This misrecognition, however, did not make the book's reception any less potent. Given its remarkable range of readership and ideologically promiscuous impact, one may without exaggeration call *My Life and Work* one of the quintessential books of the global Twenties.

In short, we have to perform an analytical move that, remarkably, none of the previous accounts of Fordism's international reception have considered necessary: we have to subject *My Life and Work* to a careful reading.

My Life and Work

In essence, *My Life and Work* and its successor volumes elaborated a producerist agenda for the twentieth century. Contrary to what many suspected, *My Life and Work* was not the product of a carefully conceived public relations strategy. Rather, the book materialized from the widespread publicity that Ford enjoyed among Americans in the early 1920s. Samuel Crowther, the book's ghostwriter, was one of many journalists who converged on Dearborn in those years to interview Ford. As he did with select visitors, Ford made himself available for conversations with Crowther and granted him access to company premises. Reportedly, however, Ford declined to read the finished manuscript of *My Life and Work*. "It was definitely understood that it was Crowther's book," recalled Ford's secretary, Ernest Liebold. Upon publication, the company initially declined to aid the book's distribution through its dealer network, citing the principle that "our dealers handle Ford products only" and because the company wanted to avoid the impression "that Mr. Ford was endeavoring to advertise himself." Only as the astounding success of the book transpired, and Ford's associates assured him on good faith that it indeed represented his ideas remarkably well, did the industrialist prove increasingly willing to adopt the work as his own.[15]

The origins of *My Life and Work* go back to the recession of 1920–1921. The crisis hit Detroit's automakers hard—as we saw in chapter 1, it resulted in the momentous du Pont/Morgan takeover of General Motors. The Ford Motor

Company, too, found itself in stark financial trouble, and solicitous New York bankers tendered their services. But Ford rejected such entreaties: instead of resorting to a loan, his company shut down operations, strong-armed dealers into accepting a backlog of Model Ts, liquidated by-products, and permanently retired a large chunk of clerical functions. (The Sociological Department, too, was a casualty of this housecleaning.) To the trade press, these measures smacked of desperation. But predictions that the Ford Motor Company would falter proved premature as business recovered in the spring of 1921. Ford lived to tell the tale of how he "foiled Wall Street."[16]

Russell Doubleday, chief editor of the New York publishing house that bore his name, closely followed the well-publicized standoff. He wrote to Dearborn, doffed his hat to Ford's "financial triumph," and suggested an idea: How would Henry Ford feel about compiling a book about his "business life"? Doubleday offered to send a seasoned writer to facilitate the task.[17] That writer was Samuel Crowther, a veteran of European war reporting. Crowther was at the time emerging as a major figure in the rise of a new genre: a boosterish business journalism that fashioned entrepreneurs as popular icons of democratic affluence and opportunity, thus helping the Twenties acquire their "roaring" sound. Beyond the collaboration with Henry Ford, which spawned three books and numerous articles, Crowther authored portraits and "autobiographies" of other business elites (among them John H. Patterson, the National Cash Register king, and the tire tycoon Harvey S. Firestone). Just before he first met Ford, in fact, Crowther had published an effusive portrait of John J. Raskob, which praised the du Pont executive for his role in orchestrating the merger with General Motors.[18]

That Crowther managed in close order to draw up equally compelling portraits of an Eastern financier (Raskob) and an enemy of Eastern finance (Ford) revealed Crowther's unique talent: he was a brilliant ghostwriter endowed with an uncanny ability to give expression to the views of his interlocutors. This talent allowed Crowther to use the first-person voice in *My Life and Work* and convince countless readers that Henry Ford was speaking to them directly. Crowther's contribution to the phenomenon that was *My Life and Work* should then be properly appreciated: Ford, who was by all accounts an impulsive and difficult interlocutor, found in Crowther a congenial interpreter capable of amplifying Ford's political program to great effect. Thanks to Crowther, the radiant modernism of *My Life and Work* began to eclipse the association of Ford's authorship with the lashing cynicism of *The International Jew*.

Crowther constructed *My Life and Work* so that its producerist agenda flowed naturally from the lessons that the Ford Motor Company had to impart. These lessons had "nothing peculiarly to do with motor cars or tractors," the book said, but were "capable of the largest application." From its opening pages, the book made clear that it was not interested in dispensing business advice, but rather intended to expound on a program of social and economic reform. Hence the book's core agenda was ambitiously comprehensive: namely, to "criticize the prevailing system of industry and the organization of money and society."[19]

The first half of the book told the story of Ford's beginnings as a Detroit mechanic and described how mass production took hold at the Ford Motor Company. These chapters recounted Ford's tinkering with machines and his early clashes with investors, and re-created, with a palpable sense of achievement, the heady days of experimentation that resulted in flow production at Highland Park. More alarming was the second half of the book. Here Crowther began to elaborate on the larger political and economic lessons that the Ford Motor Company's successes had to impart.

These lessons were fourfold. For one, mass production could not succeed unless it shed the yoke of finance capital. Only strict independence from capital markets and investment banks had allowed the Ford Motor Company to become what it was. Experience had shown that the mass-producing firm and investment capital operated at cross-purposes and could not be reconciled. Under the direction of finance capital, all production was necessarily subjected to the metric of financial returns—but this was the wrong criterion to measure industrial success. "It has been said that business existed for profit," *My Life and Work* said. "That is wrong. It exists for service." Since the "primary object of the manufacturing corporation" was "to produce," allowing financial executives to dominate corporate affairs meant "courting disaster." Accustomed to treating "a factory as making money not goods," bankers were unfit to guide any business whose creative center was the shop floor.[20]

The book gave concrete examples of how eschewing banker control had allowed the Ford Motor Company to stay the producerist course. Sharp pricing regardless of competition was a company axiom—since introducing the Model T, the company had consistently reduced its price, even in an otherwise inflationary environment. Ambitiously low prices exerted constant pressure on the shop floor to improve methods and raise productivity. But this was a point that "bankers and lawyers" failed to appreciate: it was "beyond their comprehension that the price should ever voluntarily be reduced." Ignorant of the shop, investors would instead attempt to raise revenue by cutting wages. But doing so amounted to "throwing upon labor the incompetency of the managers." Squeezing wages was also shortsighted and purpose-defeating: only plentiful wages guaranteed broad purchasing power. Finally, the company had been built up from a backyard workshop to a giant enterprise strictly by reinvesting its proceeds into production. But the principle of reinvestment conflicted with investor demands for dividends. The question was a simple one: Would proceeds redound to the shop to enhance production, or would they migrate into the pockets of "non-working stockholders"? The "banker-legal mortmain" would assure the latter, rendering business not only unethical but unstable.[21]

And here lay the second lesson. Instead of a business system run with the primary purpose of capital accumulation, *My Life and Work* presented a vision of large-scale production as a collective endeavor, enhanced by the liberating forces of technology and subject to a moral economy of contributions and rewards. At the center of this vision stood the "productive organization"—an association of "men and machines" from which issued tangible material wealth. Workers should receive the "maximum wage," but the lion's share of the profits should be "put back into productive enterprise." The focus on reinvestment was programmatic: it reflected an understanding of surplus as a social product. Profits were not to be considered investment returns, to be privately appropriated, but constituted a "trust fund" for future production and employment. "No man," *My Life and Work* said, "can view such a surplus as his own, for he did not create it alone. It is the joint product of his whole organization."[22]

Production was a collective endeavor, but—this was the third lesson—it brooked no vain egalitarianism. Regarding the shop floor, *My Life and Work* channeled a skill-aristocratic ideology in which machining expertise and production organization constituted the highest art. In response to the charge made by "parlor experts" that the Ford factories had removed skill from work and made it crushingly monotonous, the book replied that mechanized mass production had for the first time allowed the employment of thousands of unskilled workers at good wages. If a worker was otherwise unemployed and destitute, was it befitting to withhold machinery "because attendance upon it may be monotonous?" Conversely, mass production actually increased the possibility for skilled work. The Company had "skilled men in plenty," and they were the ones planning the work and building the machines. Regarding old handicraft skills, there was nothing worth preserving about their inefficient and outdated ways: "A million men working by hand could not even approximate our present daily output."[23]

The principles that had made Ford's company the world's largest auto builder—separation from capital markets, reinvestment of surplus, the doctrine of low prices and high wages, the collective vision of production, and the modernist reinvention of craft—unveiled sweeping new vistas of development. This was the fourth lesson. With private control over credit ended and money reduced to the proper task of intermediation, the technology-fueled spiral of high wages and low prices would unleash a civilization of material comfort, "widely and fairly distributed." In this vision, nature and technology would be thoroughly reconciled, indeed mutually enhancing. A widely dispersed web of high-tech manufacturing would dot a landscape of bountiful power farming. With both manufacturing and raw materials sourced locally, specialized trade patterns were dispensable. Foreign trade would cease to be an instrument of "exploitation," and "backward nations" would "learn to manufacture themselves and build up a solidly founded civilization." On the social level, this vision certainly retained a hard edge. Everyone was entitled to a "share of the luxuries," but the "economic fundamental" was labor. Those who did not contribute to production should "have the freedom of starvation." There was "no place in civilization for the idler."[24]

These sociopolitical prescriptions clearly displayed their populist lineage. Conjuring a future beyond scarcity, *My Life and Work* evoked Bellamy's *Looking Backwards*. In its uncompromising condemnation of finance capital, the book was reminiscent of nineteenth-century labor radicals like William Sylvis and Ira Steward. Echoes of the Knights of Labor could be discerned in the case for merging technology and the corporate form into a "productive organization" that would serve as a vehicle for progress and civilization. More subtly, *My Life and Work* sketched the contours of an illiberal moral economy that reaffirmed the producer-populist critique of liberalism. The book conceived of production relationships not as contractual but as social (wages were "partnership distributions," not subject to supply and demand); it subjected property to collective responsibilities, not to the absolutism of private disposal; made certain notions of justice central, rather than irrelevant, to a well-ordered economy; and cast production as the accomplishment of collective creativity, not the by-product of self-interested market transactions. Selfishness, Ford conceded, was a deep human impulse, but it should be "robbed of its power to work serious economic injustice" rather than exaggerated into the single human proclivity to which the economy answered.[25] To top it off, this dispensation was couched in a strident modernism that portrayed Ford's principles as part of a powerful groundswell of ineluctable change that was gripping the entire world. This gave the book a visionary sensibility that exhilarated readers.

Not all readers, to be sure. *My Life and Work* wore its populism on its sleeve; it built its appeal not on displays of erudition but on a pose of practical accomplishment, straight talk, and common sense. The book eschewed conventions of linear reasoning, it meandered, it was more evocative than detailed, it flirted with platitude. This exasperated many reviewers, who sensed the book's radiance but struggled to capture it, and often fought simply to summarize its contents. To say that the book evoked "a man sitting near you at his ease and talking earnestly with a curious sort of impersonal objective attitude," as the

New York Times did, was a generous way of putting it. Others were harsher. Reviewing *Today and Tomorrow*, Rexford Tugwell—future New Deal brain truster—found that much of what Ford had to say was "sound, and some of it illuminating." But, he added, "some of it is nonsense." Sound social theorizing tragically eluded Ford's grasp, Tugwell said. The book indeed betrayed "a kind of illiteracy" and "unconscious resistance to the written word," which prevented the author from engaging with "scholars" and "economists." The German economist Gustav Faldix dismissed *My Life and Work* as delivering "not really a system" but rather "an aphoristic collection of disconnected thoughts" held together only by "their contradictions, incoherence and superficiality." Antonio Gramsci felt that Ford was certainly "a great industrialist" but, indeed, "quite comical as a theoretician." Gramsci's response echoed Soviet voices, who argued that Ford had much to impart when it came to industrial organization but mocked the politics on display in his books. Where Ford digressed into social philosophizing, "the lively and fascinating engineer-organizer" turned into "an extraordinary type of hypocrite," noted the preface to the Leningrad edition of *Today and Tomorrow*.[26]

If we step back and venture an overview of how different readers around the globe responded to the Ford books, we would find Progressives, economists of classical persuasion, and theory-versed Marxists rather unimpressed; but engineers, those inclined toward heterodox economic thought, and antiliberal intellectuals loved it. Readers steeped in economic and social theory were immune to the book's charms. But a whole legion of middling intellectuals and theory autodidacts relished the book's commonsense appeal. What gave Henry Ford's ideas that "strange tang of newness?" asked José Monteiro Lobato, Ford's Brazilian advocate. "Simply the element of good sense." To Lobato, Henry Ford was a "shatterer" of the ossified preconceptions of theory— "and that is why when we read him we find ourselves punctuating the whole series of his conclusions with 'That's perfectly true! He's right!'"[27]

White Socialism: The Weimar Right Reads Ford

My Life and Work hit German bookshelves in November 1923, at a time of heightened unrest. That month hyperinflation reached its apex, and Bavarian brownshirts attempted a putsch that familiarized the world with the name of the *hazardeur* who led them, Adolf Hitler. The German romance with Fordism thus coincided with the period that began with the currency cut of 1924 and lasted until tensions over reparations brought down the last Weimar Coalition in 1930. These were the years known as "stabilization"—though the case for stability looks strong only in comparison with what came before and after.

During these years, Weimar's economy expanded but remained haunted by deep-seated weaknesses, such as an agricultural sector battling sagging grain prices and depleted public coffers. At the center of Weimar's troubles was an industrial landscape that was traditionally highly dependent on exports, but whose weak capital base, dated technology, and uncompetitive costs gave it dim prospects on world markets—especially in contrast to America's exporters. Hoping to make up for lost time, corporations and public governments began a borrowing binge that eventually involved over 7 billion marks, more than three-fifths of which came from America. By decade's end, the burden of reparations and debt, amounting to 90 percent of national income, ignited the financial and fiscal crisis that was Germany's contribution to the global Great Depression.[28]

From *My Life and Work* Weimar readers sought answers: What were the secrets of America's overweening industrial might, and how was Germany to respond? Weimar industrialists took a close look at Ford and found little that they liked. The high-wage, high-productivity formula applied only to America's serendipitously large economy, they reasoned; in Germany, in contrast, the capital outlays required for mechanization were not justified by market prospects. Industrialists instead proposed that wage retrenchment and long workweeks were required to build up investment funds and boost Germany's competitiveness on world markets. ("What is needed to replenish capital to prewar levels," offered Siemens president Carl Köttgen, "is harder work."). Social Democrats and their allied unions, in contrast, fell hard for Ford, especially the dispensation of high wages and low prices. Just like Progressives in America, German Social Democrats began to project a consumption-based development path: high wages would increase domestic purchasing power, and this would furnish the key to recovery and growth. The lure of high wages even allowed shrugging off concerns about the exploitative working conditions in Ford's factories. Social Democrats, then, fully embraced the bargain that they took to be the core of *My Life and Work*: surrender shop floor control in return for new opportunities of consumption.[29]

Beyond the orthodoxy of the industrialists and the purchasing-power reformism of Social Democrats, Weimar's raucous right contributed a third reading of Ford. Readers like Gottfried Feder took *My Life and Work* not primarily as an instruction manual on assembly lines and high wages. Rather, to them the book signaled a profound shift of mentality—a "new thinking," a "new economic spirit"—from which arose, as one engineer put it, "the possibility of our resurgence."[30] Here was a practical example of a modern community of producers—a veritable *Gemeinwirtschaft* of the type invoked since the world war. Ford's triumph over Wall Street seemed to demonstrate that American finance capital was not invincible. Ford showed how to reconcile leadership and common purpose. ("Capital is for the service of all," as *My Life and Work* said, "though it may be under the direction of one.")[31] To those on the right, there was a clear (and ominous) attraction in how *My Life and Work* policed the boundaries of the producing community: those who failed to contribute—or were deemed to be incapable of doing so in the first place—faced hostility, ostracism, and worse. Read in this way, the book reveals central elements of the postliberal right's economic ideology: critiques of finance that shaded into anti-Semitism; populist demands to put credit and technology in the service of "producers"; a theory of "socialism" built around notions of leadership, duty, and service; and the conviction that economic incentives should be yoked to the obligations of hierarchically structured, "organic" communities— be they factory, nation, or *Volk*.

In short, readers like Feder recognized that Henry Ford strove to put mass production at the core of a political theory, and they correctly sensed the book's modernist aspirations and antiliberal thrust. The broad appeal that *My Life and Work* had on assorted postliberals across the world shows that these notions formed part of a larger discourse. To reconstruct how the Weimar right read Ford, then, means mapping a global zeitgeist.[32] In the Thirties, post-liberals in Germany, Italy, and Japan would oversee large-scale technology transfers aimed at harnessing Fordism to momentous projects of social and industrial transformation. The ideological horizon against which these trans-fers took place acquired sharp definition during the Twenties.

The Weimar right found a *first* affinity in Ford's stance on finance. In *My Life and Work*, the denunciations of finance capital opened up to a larger monetary critique. There was "something wrong" with a financial system that gave bank-ers disproportionate power over industrial affairs, the book said. Money, credit, and capital accumulation certainly were essential for industrial pro-gress. As it stood, however, control over capital was too tightly concentrated among the most powerful banks. The bankers' dubious dogma, the gold stan-dard, was simply an ingenious tool to keep money scarce and dear. Financial elites routinely threatened "credit curtailment" and played "fantastical tricks," which they would then "cover up with high technical terms." To change this "faulty system," it was necessary to enlighten people about monetary affairs and to demystify gold.[33]

During the very period that Crowther compiled *My Life and Work*, Ford was in fact waging a campaign for an object lesson in monetary reform. At Muscle Shoals on the Tennessee River in Alabama, an agglomeration of half-built dams and defunct nitrate plants remained from a federal World War I project. In an idea Ford developed with Thomas Edison, he offered to lease and operate the facilities if Congress would fund the completion of Muscle Shoals by issuing—not borrowing!—the sum of $30 million of designated currency. Why, Ford and Edison asked, should reconstruction depend on the capital markets of New York and London? Was not the authority over currency vested in Congress, as a representative of the people? Instead of saddling the federal purse with interest-bearing obligations, the Muscle Shoals "energy dollars" would pay for themselves, Ford and Edison claimed. Bypassing Wall Street and untethered from gold, these bills would finance wages and material, circulate freely, and eventually "be retired by the earnings of the power dam."[34] The proposal bore a purpose more ambitious than simply rebuilding Muscle Shoals. If successful, the scheme would prove the hollowness of the gold standard, embarrass the international bankers who controlled it, and end "generations of financial slavery."[35] (As it turned out, the plan came to naught. Opposed by a powerful coalition in Congress, Muscle Shoals languished in federal hands until the New Deal built the TVA on its foundations.)

Gottfried Feder's most deeply cherished slogan—the "breaking of interest bondage"—echoed the sentiments expressed by Edison and Ford. Feder's 1923 tract, *The German State on National and Social Foundations*, similarly combined anti-Semitic conceits with heterodox monetary proposals. Orchestrated by "global finance," Feder argued, the reparations declared at Versailles were pushing Germany into a perpetual state of indebtedness. Reparations would never be repaid, Feder predicted, but rather would result in a permanent drain on Germany's productive resources. A remedy, Feder submitted, lay in "productive credit creation," a sovereign self-financing very similar to Ford's scheme. "Money is what the state declares it to be," Feder pronounced, and provided a cautionary example. In 1920, funds were needed for a water power plant at the famous Walchensee in the Alps. Feder had then proposed that the Bavarian state should emit interest-free "construction bills" to finance the development; instead, the state tapped capital markets for 800 million marks, at interest. In Feder's view, Bavarian power had been "pawned" to the powers of capital.[36]

Ford's and Feder's efforts reflected a groundswell of monetary critiques that gained momentum after the Great War. In America, Ford was in the company of finance skeptics such as Thorstein Veblen, the Wisconsin economist who argued that industry and financiers worked at cross-purposes, and proposed that "a Soviet of engineers" was best equipped to guide the economic future of the American nation (though Veblen's technocratic vision clashed with Ford's populism). Feder in turn was well acquainted with Silvio Gesell, finance minister of the short-lived Bavarian Soviet Republic of 1919, who made a name for himself as a proponent of a grassroots-issued, self-depreciating "free money." In Britain, New Zealand, and Canada, the engineer C. H. Douglas was beginning to receive attention for his "social credit" theories. Heterogeneous as these schemes were, they converged on a common set of ideas. These critiques rejected the gold standard and argued that authority over credit should be taken out of private hands and subjected to popular control. They proposed "productive credit expansion"—a kind of populist fiscal policy by which governments, instead of resorting to credit markets, issued new money to finance the construction of utilities, dams, or housing. (Such money was not inflationary, proponents argued, because it was "backed" by the productive assets thereby created.) More often than not, the money reformers spun anti-Semitic conspiracy theories.[37]

This proliferation of money critiques, including their delusional elements, is best understood against the backdrop of postwar economic dislocations. In North America's rural West, the opposition against the "money trust" had never quite abated; it was simply muted by an era of rising farm prices and relative prosperity that peaked during the Great War. The postwar recession, amplified by the Federal Reserve, marked a turning point: in the early Twenties, the vast agricultural region stretching from the Gulf Coast cotton fields to the wheat plains of Alberta descended anew into prolonged and catastrophic deflation. The "money question" resurfaced. In Europe, meanwhile, money gyrated in the opposite direction. The immense debts that governments had accumulated to pay for the war implied that the costs of the carnage would continue to be borne unevenly: taxes imposed on the masses would accrue to bondholders, rentiers, and *Kriegsgewinnler*, who stood to profit from the destruction. Striking a grim compromise, the political leaders of Germany, Poland, Hungary, and Austria let rip hyperinflations that wiped out domestic government obligations along with the petty savings of the masses. But heavy bills of external debt, for which creditors would surely not accept devalued currencies, were left unaffected. Unless a government was prepared to resort to the methods of the Bolsheviks, who declared the Tsar's bonds "odious" and ended repayments for good, such debts would prove a lingering burden. As central banks returned to the gold standard, the standard's deflationary bias magnified these external burdens, effectively privileging the security of cross-border obligations over the health of domestic industries and farm incomes.[38]

In the Twenties, then, Henry Ford was not only hailed as a production wizard. Through his anti-Semitic tracts, the critique of finance capital offered in *My Life and Work*, and his engagements in Muscle Shoals, he also gained an unlikely global reputation as a financial reformer. In March 1923, the Banking and Commerce Committee of the Canadian House of Commons requested Ford's testimony "on the question of credit and finance." Initiated by representatives from Canada's western farm regions, the hearing investigated why farm prices languished and credit was tight. Ford had "made a study of finance" and who was in a position "to speak without fear." Would he come to Ottawa? Ford declined, but the representatives got to hear "social credit" promoter C. H. Douglas instead. Douglas used the occasion to argue for a publicly administered credit system. It was a recommendation that echoed the schemes of Feder and Ford.[39]

A *second* source of inspiration for the right issued from how Ford described the collective ethos animating mass production in terms that were both communitarian and antiegalitarian. Not a few German readers, grappling with how to classify the moral economy on display in *My Life and Work*, likened it to "a kind of socialism."[40] This has baffled historians—how could one so spectacularly misconstrue that presumed herald of American capitalism, Henry Ford? The confusion is unwarranted, however. As right-wing critics marshaled "organic" notions of community against liberalism during the Twenties, they began to challenge Marxism's monopoly over the term *socialism* on a broad front. True socialism, the right said, was not proletarian or egalitarian; instead, it reflected the duties, responsibilities, and hierarchies that bound individuals to their communities—whether factory, family, nation, or *Volk*. Walter Rathenau, Germany's wartime resource impresario, predicted that from the "socialism of war" would arise a "new economy," which would subject Germans to a strict collective production regime. Oswald Spengler polemicized against the German revolution of 1918 by casting a "Prussian Socialism," in which the duties of officialdom would displace vain differences of status and class. The "conservative socialism" of the engineer Wichard von Moellendorff extolled a technocratic vision of an "economic state" humming with efficiency like one terrific engine.

What these visions had in common was the embrace of a peculiar notion of "service"—*Dienst*. Devoid of latter-day connotations (such as in "service sector" or "customer service"), *Dienst* was meant to invoke an ethos by which individuals cheerfully submitted to a larger purpose or directed their energies to the presumed benefit of the *Volk*. As the champions of right socialism saw it, this ethos distinguished them from the leveling nihilism of the left. In their view, it also made them the better anticapitalists. As Werner Sombart said, "German Socialism," in its rejection of liberalism, was "far more radical" than proletarian socialism. The latter provided no more than the doltish idea that the hierarchy of the current order could be turned upside down. The former projected a broad civilizational and spiritual renewal in the image of *Dienst*.

Proletarian socialism was "capitalism in inverted form; German Socialism is anti-capitalism."[41]

Their commitment to *Dienst* predisposed right-wing readers favorably to Ford's "service" ideology: that the American auto king would claim to put his efforts in the service of production and progress, rather than self-seeking, struck readers like Feder not as preposterous or absurd but as instructive. The most influential among those who read Ford's "service" ideology as a contribution to the socialist imagination of the right was Friedrich von Gottl-Ottlilienfeld, who delivered an early theoretical reflection on *Fordismus*—a concept by which he meant not the introduction of certain factory techniques but a political ideology.[42] Obscure today, Gottl was a leading representative of the German historical school of economics; beyond Germany, he was also avidly read in Japan.[43] Gottl was of the generation of Max Weber and Werner Sombart, and like them, he regarded economics as a discipline of sociology and history, subject to the method of *verstehen*. To Gottl, economic relations were integral expressions of human life, inescapably shaped by history, culture, mentalities, and geographies. The project of neoclassical economics—to deduce economic laws from the choices of abstract individuals who stood outside of history and were free of the bonds of community, state, or people—was quackery to him. While the neoclassical school was reinventing economics as a study of strategic action (How did individuals allocate limited resources to alternative ends?), Gottl maintained that the object of economics was to understand how humans go about the social task of satisfying material wants. Economics was the study of how "human co-existence takes shape in the spirit of perpetual accord between want and its satisfaction." (Here Gottl used the terms *Bedarf und Deckung*, matching Gottfried Feder's vocabulary.)[44]

In the 1920s, Gottl saw modern industry at an impasse. The historical unfolding of what Gottl called "Technical Reason" (a concept of Hegelian vintage) had brought about giant factories that operated at unprecedented efficiency even as they degraded those who toiled in them. Mechanization and Taylorism at once sustained the "existence of the masses" and ruled over them through "coercion and monotony." Was this state of affairs ineluctable? No, Gottl averred, and Ford's system pointed toward the solution. In May 1924, shortly after *My Life and Work* appeared, Gottl dedicated his inaugural lecture as chair of economics at the University of Kiel to make his case.

To show that Ford's system marked an unprecedented advance, Gottl contrasted it to Taylorism. Both, certainly, reflected the assiduous application of Technical Reason to industry. Taylorism, however, only deepened the social divisions that plagued modern production. By obsessing over individual work performance, and by removing the planning staff from the factory floor,

Taylor's practice isolated workers from each other and from the firm. Though Taylorism professed to achieve a "synthesis between economic life and Technical Reason," in reality it utterly failed at this goal. Taylorism reduced the worker to a "mere physical and energetic locus of execution" of the production planner's will. It was an obsessive-compulsive "orgy of organization," which, instead of accomplishing the "soulful infusion of the firm to a true community," achieved only its "parody."[45]

Ford's factories, too, necessarily restricted the workers to the "desperately narrow bounds" required by modern production technique: minuscule subdivision, repetitive tasks, the stopwatch timing of individual operations, and so on. True, the task of the Ford worker remained "miserable piecework." In contrast to Taylorism, however, Fordism found a way to impress on each worker how his or her tiny realm of activity contributed to a formidable collective endeavor. Connected to coworkers by conveyors and moving lines, the Ford operative would look "up- and downstream from his post" and "vividly perceive how, in rational restriction, he takes part in the creation of one awesome totality." What was more, Ford workers understood that their shop floor efforts formed part of a comprehensive system, one that included Ford's pricing policy as well as his stance on wages, capital, and reinvestment.

Gottl maintained that making high wages and low prices a policy priority, rather than submitting them to the calculus of profitability, was a momentous decision. Prioritizing wages released workers from being a mere cost entry in the accounting ledger, constantly subject to reduction, and instead acknowledged that adequately compensating workers was a core goal of the industrial enterprise. Ford's wage policy broke "the sharp pecuniary opposition between worker and employer." Low prices, in turn, provided not only a constant spur to productivity but a complementary boost to real wages. Indeed, Gottl pointed out, the doctrine of low prices embarrassed the very law of supply and demand: in the face of insatiable demand, the Model Ts had registered continuous price reductions. All of this stood in "deathly contradiction" to the dominant spirit of capitalist economies. The "spiritual emergency" of modern factory work was finally alleviated: workers realized that their labor was not complicit in price gouging or serving the self-enrichment of the factory owner. Rather, they took part in an enterprise of larger meaning and purpose. The traditional antagonisms of industry became "reciprocity"; the "will to financial returns" made way for the "will to service"; and self-interested market competition (*Wettbewerb*) turned into the amicable rivalry of excelling in pursuit of a shared cause (*Wetteifer*).

In short, Gottl opined, the reader could distill from *My Life and Work* the contours of a distinctive political-economic ideology. This ideology—"one would have to refer to it as *Fordism*"—pointed to a profound reversal of the entire mental-cultural disposition of modern economic behavior. Indeed, *Fordismus* pointed beyond the "dense web of capitalist obligations" and toward a "white socialism," as Gottl said, a "socialism of leadership" in which the industrialist's bold ethical example would serve to overcome the antagonisms of industry, as it were, from the top.

Gottl's "socialism of leadership" operated on the level of the firm, yet it pointed to a *third* mode by which the right considered Ford: as providing a road map for the producerist reconstruction of the entire German economy. This was the reading put forth by Theodor Lüddecke, a *Freikorps* veteran, student of economics, and aspiring journalist, who toured the United States in the early Twenties (working variously as a miner and a bank clerk) and returned from his sojourn committed to rousing Germans to action.[46]

Lüddecke's premise was that Germany's postwar economic predicament boiled down to the disappearance of export markets. On the one hand, regions of the world that had formerly traded raw materials against European goods were building up their own industries, narrowing the foreign markets on which German industry depended. On the other hand, Germany had to reckon with the rise of America, which was poised to enter "the struggle for export markets endowed with the most modern production apparatus and almost unlimited capital power." If Germany was to prevail, Lüddecke argued, the nation must abandon internecine bickering and social conflict, accept collective sacrifices, and regroup toward production. It was imperative to unite all producers—entrepreneurs, engineers, workers—into one "great vital community" of German industry. There was no alternative: Germany would either "prevail in the export struggle as one unified whole, or it will not prevail."[47]

Lüddecke found a model for the requisite reconstruction of German industry in *My Life and Work*. Central was Ford's lesson that successful mass production depended on personal leadership and the rejection of investor capitalism. This was a vital instruction to German industry, whose embrace of the publicly traded corporation, that "most torpid of enterprise forms," had resulted in bloated, selfish, and indecisive industrial management. Widely dispersed shares, Lüddecke argued, removed stockholders from industry's raison d'être—production. Stockholder capitalism propagated short-term financial results over long-term productive goals and shackled economic progress to the chains of dividends. To all of this, the Ford Motor Company provided a trailblazing counterexample. Liberated from stockholder rents, mass production released immense energy into the economy at large. Here lay the "harmonic resolution" of "capital accumulation and industrial development."[48]

To learn from the Ford Motor Company, then, it was not enough to put up assembly lines: nothing short of a "whole-scale revision of the body economic" was necessary. German industries needed to reorganize along the lines of the Ford Motor Company: as massive and powerful enterprises under unified, personal leadership. Vertical integration would eliminate unnecessary middlemen, ensure stable supply chains, and end market gyrations. Bank capital and securities markets would lose their grip over production. Robust products of universal appeal would make redundant the make-believe of advertising. Germany would no longer tolerate "unproductive professions" whose maintenance "weighed on German export prices." Craft workers, salesmen, and corporate clerks would have to cease their activities and move into mass production. Intellectuals would have to prove their utility. In these ways, the Ford Motor Company portended the "economy of the future."[49]

The anti-Semitic financial critiques articulated by Feder had been Nazi conceits since the earliest days. Gottl's "socialism of leadership" and Lüddecke's nationalist producerism demonstrate how Nazi economic ideology evolved as it soaked up the postliberal right's conversation with America. Gottl and Lüddecke flourished after 1933. Gottl's theories fed into the discourse on Nazi industrial rationalization, and his historicist style came to dominate the Nazi economics profession.[50] Lüddecke joined the party and became a propagandist: he directed a journalism school and was active as a tub-thumper on the Labor Front speech circuit.[51]

The reactions of Feder, Gottl-Ottlilienfeld, and Lüddecke thus provide a revealing ideological context for a *fourth* reading of Ford within the Weimar right, a reading that was surely the most consequential of all: that of Adolf Hitler. In the spring of 1924, as Gottl-Ottlilienfeld was developing his views on *Fordismus*, Hitler was under house arrest in Landsberg, serving a sentence for his role in the abortive Beer Hall putsch. Material evidence that has recently come to light suggests that Hitler read *My Life and Work* in Landsberg: a copy of the German edition was given to him by Ernst Hanfstaengl, his Munich high-society intimate, as a New Year's present for 1924 (see figure 2.1).[52] What impact did the book have on him? On the one hand, it is clear from the letters of Hitler's confidant Rudolf Hess that when conversations in Landsberg turned to economic questions, Ford and America were often invoked.[53] On the other hand, we know that Hitler spent the bulk of his time at Landsberg dictating the monologues that would become *Mein Kampf*—and in that sprawling book, America barely featured. In *Mein Kampf*, Hitler anticipated that an expansive Germany would stand off with other world powers, but he did not include the United States among them, and named instead named Britain, Russia, China, and a French Empire boasting "an immense contiguous settlement territory from the Rhine to the Congo."[54]

What is clear, however, is that over subsequent years America became the bigger threat in Hitler's mind, and his vision of Germany's future empire attained discernibly American features. By 1927, when the future dictator penned his unpublished "second book," America's overbearing economic power had morphed into a central preoccupation. It thus appears that the United States did not have a fixed place in Hitler's worldview from the beginning, but instead took decisive shape between 1924 and 1927. In essence, during the mid-1920s, as Weimar Germany obsessed over *My Life and Work*, Hitler gave the old *Lebensraum* conceit of the *völkisch* tradition an original spin by wresting it from long-standing agrarian connotations and fusing it with Fordism.[55]

As Hitler came to see it in the mid-1920s, the twentieth century's central challenge would be "the threat of the world's subjugation by the American Union."[56] What made the United States mightier than any previous power? A vast contiguous territory, Hitler answered, combined with a burgeoning population and almost complete economic self-sufficiency. Blessed with abundant raw materials and able to supply its own food, America enjoyed two strategic advantages that Germany painfully lacked. A populous nation, America also bred the mass demand that was pushing sectors like the automobile industry toward mass production. "The size of America's internal market, its wealth of purchasing power and raw materials," Hitler reasoned, "alone justify production methods that would be simply impossible in Europe."[57] As Hitler posed the rhetorical question to a party audience in early 1928, how come Ford had received hundreds of thousands of orders before his new Model A was even released? Because in America "the possibilities for production are different. Because there, natural resources abound in quantities unimaginable."[58]

Deep production runs, in turn, assured American dominance in world markets, against which Germany, wedged into the post-Versailles borders, could not hope to compete. Yes, Germany's wages were "ridiculous" and America's "enormous," and this should have given German exports a competitive advantage. But because Americans had mass production, Germans remained "incapable of exporting against the American competition," and even had to watch as American carmakers invaded the German market. Gearing Germany's industry up for exports, as so many urged, was a losing proposition. A much more ambitious goal was needed, a "clear and far-sighted spatial politics" that would acquire territory in the East. The lesson of America's rise was this: if Germany could win a continental space akin to that of the United States, it would solve its food and raw material problems, push toward mass production, and match America's high standard of living.[59]

Hitler remained preoccupied by these themes as he led the Nazi party from the rabble-rousing fringe to the center of Weimar's political crisis. In his speeches to party affiliates, he showed himself sufficiently au courant with all

FIGURE 2.1. A copy of the 1923 German edition of *My Life and Work,* with Ernst Hanfstaengl's dedication: "To my dear Adolph [*sic*] Hitler with all best wishes for 1924." Photo: Granger Historical Picture Archive.

things Ford to repeatedly invoke the American, his cars, and his factories.[60] America's might and its automobile civilization became a standard reference point in Hitler's stump speech in the late Twenties. During the Depression, Hitler's *Lebensraum* conceit absorbed calls from the radical right to withdraw from world markets and move Germany toward autarky. Conservative industrialists and right-wing pundits like Lüddecke had proposed austere visions of export-oriented development in response to Weimar Germany's economic predicament. Hitler, in contrast, intended to break with world markets entirely. As Hitler told his party in the bleak winter of 1931, there was no outlasting America, that "gigantic state with infinite production capacity," unless Germany gained *Lebensraum*. But doing so required "turning our back on the phantom of a global economy."[61]

The future *Lebensraum* never acquired concrete economic elaboration, but that did not distract from its utopian evocativeness. It conjured a vast "space" stretching from Western Europe to the Urals, self-sufficient and independent of world markets, with an industrial, mass-producing core in Germany and an agrarian periphery beyond, with millions of people's cars zipping along the highways and tens of thousands of people's tractors plowing the resettled East. In this vision, mass production had a precise double role: it was necessary to create and sustain the armaments complex that would allow the conquest and control of territory in which industry would supply a vast contiguous market with a standard of living to match America's.[62]

My Life and Work, then, provided promiscuous but fertile inspiration for the conceits of the postliberal right. The "socialism" that Gottl-Ottlilienfeld saw on display in Ford's "productive organization" fed easily into the Nazi ideology of industrial rationalization, which claimed to wrest technical improvements and productivity enhancements from the tyranny of financial proceeds and make them subject to the racial community of the *Volk*. Visions of breaking away from world markets into Eastern *Lebensraum*, in turn, acquired a markedly modernist flavor as they absorbed, in Hitler's vision, mass production, automobiles, and a high standard of living based on standardized goods. Fordism thus became a key element in the insurgency against the world economic system. The right, then, took Ford as demonstrating that America offered the world not only the aspirational ideal of a consumerist modernity, and not only the dubious privilege of dollar loans, but also the means for a postliberal resurgence.

Interlude: The Soviet Context of Gramsci's "Americanism and Fordism"

Picture this scene: a courtyard walled off by massive stone ashlars, in its midst a group of men engaged in debate, guards standing by. They are Communists, political prisoners. One of them is speaking, gesticulating, making a case. Among the listeners is a short bespectacled man, who listens tight-lipped, shakes his head, and then takes his turn to disagree eloquently and vehemently. The topic of debate? Henry Ford and his books. Comrade Ezio Riboldi, formerly of the Socialist Party, has just extolled Fordism as a blueprint for socialism. His opponent is Antonio Gramsci, former head of the Italian Communist Party, whose antagonism with Riboldi goes back to when Socialists and Communists clashed over the correct strategy in the fight against Fascism. Now, Gramsci insists that Riboldi has failed to think dialectically about the issue at hand. Fordism was a revolutionary force, to be sure, but Communists could hardly import it uncritically. The true potential of Ford's methods could not be unlocked before they had been wrested from the bourgeoisie and placed in the hands of a self-improving and self-rationalizing working class. Later Gramsci would sit down in his small cell to write, spilling his disagreement onto the pages.

The recollections of one of Gramsci's fellow inmates allow us to imagine that this scene—or one like it—played out at some point during the early Thirties in the prison fortress located in the Apulian municipality of Turi di Bari. Gramsci's "discussion of problems of Fordism," according to this Turi prisoner, "was in effect a reply to positions adopted by the honorable comrade Riboldi, who after reading a few books by Ford decided that Fordism was tantamount to socialism."[63] The claim is intriguing and almost certainly exaggerated. Riboldi hardly needed to introduce Gramsci to Fordism, a topic that had been very much on Gramsci's mind since the mid-Twenties. In his cell at Turi, Gramsci kept a French edition of *My Life and Work*, which he reported reading in 1927. He also owned a copy of *Today and Tomorrow*, in French, and eventually acquired an Italian translation of *Moving Forward*. When Gramsci, in 1929, jotted down some problems he intended to investigate—an outline of what would become the *Prison Notebooks*—he added "Americanism and Fordism" to the list (see figure 2.2). Shortly after, he confirmed that this theme was to be one of his three core occupations in prison (along with the theory of history, and the history of nineteenth-century Italy). In 1934, Gramsci finally came around to compiling his famous notebook 22, under the title "Americanismo e fordismo."[64]

Little illustrates more vividly how widespread Henry Ford's ideas were on the interwar left, and how urgent they seemed, than the fact that Italian Communists would debate them as prisoners of Mussolini's regime. The disagreement between Riboldi and Gramsci encapsulated the differences between a Social Democratic reading of Ford and a Communist one. German Social Democrats had demonstrated that it was possible for working-class voices to wax enthusiastic about Fordism and espouse it as the surest path toward a socialism of affluence: rationalize production, cut prices, raise wages, and

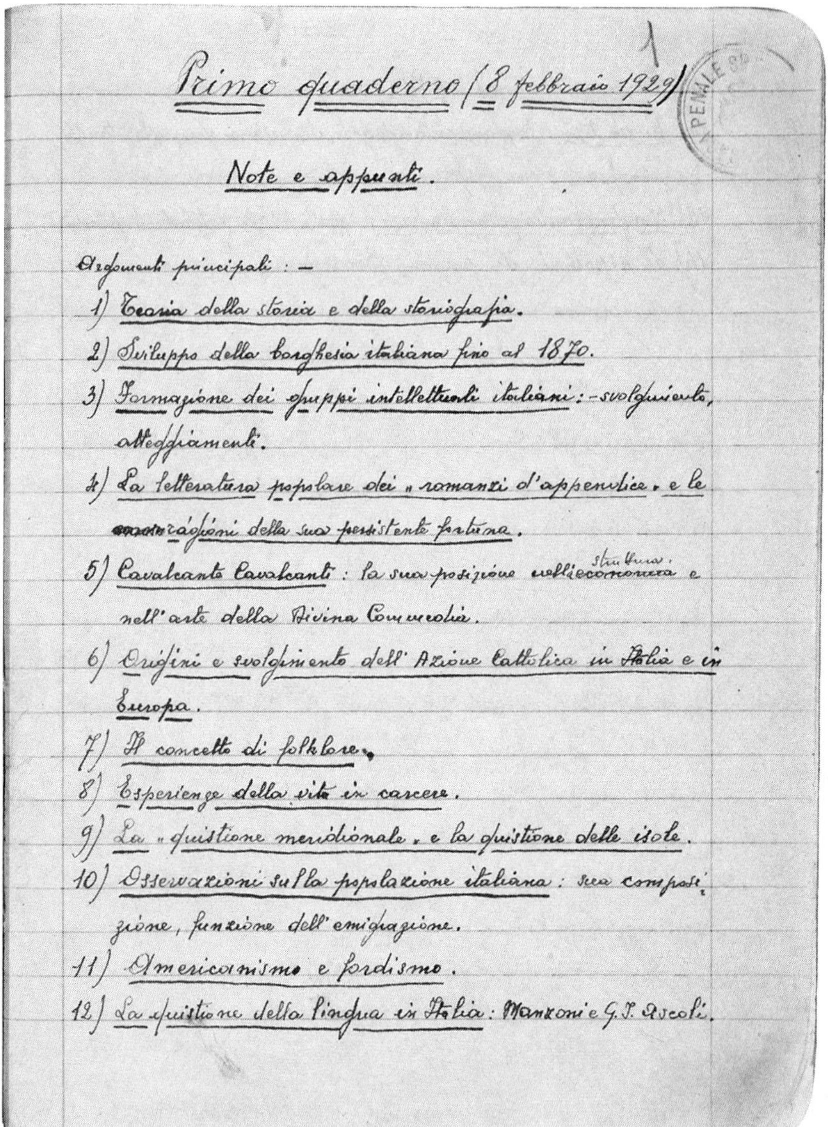

Primo quaderno (8 febbraio 1929)

Note e appunti.

Argomenti principali : —

1) Teoria della storia e della storiografia.

2) Sviluppo della borghesia italiana fino al 1870.

3) Formazione dei gruppi intellettuali italiani: – svolgimento, atteggiamenti.

4) La letteratura popolare dei « romanzi d'appendice » e le ~~ragioni~~ ragioni della sua persistente fortuna.

5) Cavalcante Cavalcanti: la sua posizione nell'economia e nell'arte della Divina Commedia.

6) Origini e svolgimento dell'Azione Cattolica in Italia e in Europa.

7) Il concetto di folklore.

8) Esperienze della vita in carcere.

9) La « quistione meridionale » e la quistione delle isole.

10) Osservazioni sulla popolazione italiana: sua composizione, funzione dell'emigrazione.

11) Americanismo e fordismo.

12) La quistione della lingua in Italia: Manzoni e G. I. Ascoli.

FIGURE 2.2. The opening page of the first *Prison Notebooks* from February 1929, where Gramsci outlined principal themes to be investigated. Number 11 reads "Americanismo e fordismo." Photo: Fondazione Gramsci, Rome.

watch living standards take wing. To Communists, however, such sentiments smacked of reformism. As they saw it, the proposition was rather more delicate: before Fordism could be marshaled for the building of socialism, it first needed to be cleansed of its capitalist accretions. It was necessary, as Trotsky put it in 1926, "to separate Fordism from Ford" and to "socialize and purge it."[65] In essence, Gramsci's reflections in notebook 22 explored this very question: What was Fordism's emancipatory potential, and how could it be wrested from its American capitalist entanglements?

Like his other prison writings, "Americanism and Fordism" is not a fully formed essay but a sequence of sketches whose loose associative character reflected the reality of censorship and confinement. Among the prison writings, notebook 22 forms a culmination point: it assembles the major themes that preoccupied Gramsci over the years of his imprisonment—the theory of hegemony, the challenge of "Americanism," civil society and the state, and the role of "organic intellectuals" in the emancipation of the working and peasant classes.[66] Notebook 22 is also the sealed bottle in which the term *Fordism* traversed the ocean that separates the 1930s from the 1970s. Smuggled out of Turi, stowed in Moscow, and returned to Italy after World War II, the notebook first received renewed attention in the debates of the New Left. From there, the term *Fordism* entered the canon of Western Marxism and handed the Regulationists a concept for theorizing the accumulation crises of the late twentieth century.[67]

The prominence that Gramsci's work has enjoyed in late-twentieth-century debates has mostly eclipsed the awareness that notebook 22 is, first and foremost, a period piece: a work that refracts the preoccupations of its time. In "Americanismo e fordismo," Gramsci was meditating on the challenge that the American industrial modernity of his time was putting to an agrarian country with an underdeveloped industry, in which a large and poor peasant population dwarfed the urban proletariat. Writing in 1934, Gramsci clearly had his own country in mind, Italy. At the same time, "Americanism and Fordism" drew its problems and ruminations from the experience of Russia, a country with which Gramsci was intimately familiar and in whose social and economic underdevelopment he saw a reflection of the challenges that a proletarian revolution would face in Italy. Gramsci's reflections, then, provide an introduction as good as any for the feverish debates on "Americanism"—Taylorism, Fordism, technology—that consumed the Soviet Union during the 1920s. In yet another prison anecdote, Gramsci is said to have admonished his fellow Communists to "remember that the coming of Americanism has changed everything." Doing so, he said, was imperative if Communists cared to "establish socialism in the West" and "avoid the mistakes made in Russia."[68]

Gramsci's experiences of Russian realities were personal and deep. As a delegate of the Communist International, Gramsci sojourned in and around

Moscow between June 1922 and November 1923. He returned for two months in early 1925. On these trips, Gramsci hobnobbed with the Bolshevik elite: he gave a speech at the 12th Party Conference in August 1922, and he counted Bukharin, Zinoviev, and Trotsky among his interlocutors.[69] On the first of these trips, Gramsci met his wife, the Russian violinist Julia Schucht, with whom he had two sons; Julia's sister Tania, who moved to Italy, remained Gramsci's closest personal correspondent during his prison years.[70] In Russia, Gramsci soaked up the debates about development and industrialization riveting the "NEP" years, the New Economic Policy interlude between the ravages of postrevolutionary "war communism" and the onset of Stalin's crash industrialization in 1928. Among the abiding preoccupations of this period was the question of "socialist rationalization" and the role that American technology would play in it—a question that continued to resonate in Gramsci's writings throughout his years of confinement.

NEP, as Lenin had decreed, was thought to be a transitional period. Based on the limited reintroduction of market relations, the New Economic Policy was an acknowledgment that socialism had not emerged from the Revolution fully fledged, and that building it would require continuous work. In particular, socialism would not be complete unless Russia overcame its low level of development, which was visible not just in the overwhelmingly agrarian nature of the economy—in the mid-Twenties, 82 percent of Russians were peasants, 10 percent more than on the eve of World War I. Perhaps more worrying for the workers' state, underdevelopment was also visible in the weak productivity and technological depletion of the factories, which had suffered severely since the Revolution. Between 1917 and 1920, the industrial workforce more than halved (from 2.6 million to 1.2 million) as workers fled the undersupplied cities. As the guns of the civil war fell silent, production stood at 18 percent of the prewar level. Industrial output would approach that benchmark again by mid-decade. But, to the vexation of Soviet planners, inefficient work methods, high labor turnover, absenteeism, soldiering, and alcoholism among the workers stubbornly lingered.[71] "The regime of proletarian dictatorship," as Trotsky formulated the widespread lament, "has been established first in a country with a monstrous inheritance of backwardness and barbarity." He continued:

> Our social forms are transitional to socialism and consequently are incomparably higher than capitalist forms. In this sense we rightly consider ourselves the most advanced country in the world. But technology, which lies at the basis of material and every other kind of culture, is extremely backward in our country in comparison with the advanced capitalist countries. This constitutes the fundamental contradiction of our present reality. The

historical task that follows is to raise our technology to the height of our social formation.[72]

How might Soviets tackle this historical task? This is where "Americanism" came in. NEP was to mark a way station between a Russian backwardness that Bolsheviks liked to call "Asiatic" and an industrial modernity that they associated with "America." A common trope in the NEP ideological arsenal held that socialism equaled Soviet revolution plus American technology. "We need Marxism plus Americanism," was one of Bukharin's favorite expressions; indeed, the construction of socialism demanded "merging Marxist theory with American practicality and 'business know-how.'"[73] "American technology," Trotsky said, "will transform our order, liberating it from the heritage of backwardness, primitiveness and barbarism."[74] It was in this context that Stalin could claim, after Lenin's death in 1924, that "the essence of Leninism" was "the combination of Soviet revolutionary sweep and American efficiency."[75]

Like the Revolution itself, "Americanism" elicited utopian expectations. The transformative power of modern machinery and cutting-edge production methods, it seemed, would extend far beyond the benefits of increased output and higher efficiency: it constituted a cultural and educational force of first order, a school through which barely literate peasant-workers would pass on their way toward socialist civilization. In the debates about "proletarian culture," some Bolsheviks openly relegated revolutionary art to a supporting role. Rather, "culture" implied an encompassing mix of technological expertise, organizational maturity, rationalized habits, efficient work discipline, and a collective consciousness cleansed of bourgeois fetishes and superstitions. Machines, not poems, would change obsolete patterns of work, elevate the cultural level of the masses, and cultivate their habits, attitudes, and morals; modern technology and production methods provided refinement and instruction that no longer required the mediation of art.[76]

The effects would extend into the molecular level: the worker's very physiological fiber and deep psychological dispositions were at stake. As Aleksei Gastev, an outspoken champion of Soviet Americanism, noted: "The motor car and aeroplane factories of America" constituted "new, gigantic laboratories where the psychology of the proletariat is being created, where the culture of the proletariat is being manufactured." Demanding heightened precision and superior discipline, standardized production methods and rationalized work organization would transform the worker's very being, "even his intimate life, including his aesthetic, intellectual, and sexual values."[77] Matched with Soviet power, American-style industrial rationalization would birth a "new man."[78] The slogan that the Soviet Union needed, like a runner, to "catch up and overtake" the capitalist West, came later, during the crash industrialization of the

First Five-Year Plan; in the NEP years, it seemed that the new workers' state first had to virtually pass through America, like a metamorphosis, in order to reach modernity's shores and start running.

From a distance, notebook 22 echoed these themes. Gramsci shared the Soviet conceit that modern factory methods, cleansed of their capitalist accretions, would serve as a source of acculturation of the working class to greater self-consciousness, self-mastery, and rationality. American industrial forms were creating "a new type of worker and man," Gramsci wrote, whose very "psycho-physical nexus" was being remade, and who would turn out to be "undoubtedly *superior*" to his or her predecessors. There was fundamentally "nothing originally new" about this process, Gramsci averred: American-style rationalization marked only the latest stage in the long and bloody history of industrial progress, in which ever more complex production arrangements required a continuous disciplining of mental and bodily impulses: rationalizing production had always implied rationalizing humans. Like the Soviets before him, Gramsci viewed rationalization from a perspective of historical totality, in which industrial progress and cultural progress coincided on the ascent toward a "new civilization" that was fully "rational" because it was based on reason: freed, that is, from the fetishes and brutality of previous epochs, including those of bourgeois capitalism. [79]

The question, then, was not *if* Fordism would spread from America to Europe, but *how*. In Italy, Gramsci said, Fascism had preserved an atavistic social and economic structure under which it was impossible to advance a genuine program of industrial progress with broad worker support. The result was a mimicry of rationalization, which "changes the vocabulary but not the facts, the external gestures but not the human interior."[80]

More troubling was the Soviet experience. Trotsky, Gramsci acknowledged, had understood that the new work methods were "inextricably connected to a certain way of living, thinking, and feeling." (Indeed, Trotsky had said in 1923 that "morals cannot be rationalized . . . unless production is rationalized at the same time.") In practice, however, Soviet industrial development had largely bypassed the spontaneous intellectual capacities of the masses. The Soviet leadership had failed to convince workers that they had a stake in their own "psycho-physical" adaptation; instead of collective mobilization and ideological persuasion—"hegemony," that is—industrial rationalization had degenerated into unqualified coercion. In a striking passage, Gramsci invoked "a state" where "the working masses are no longer subject to the coercive force of a higher class." In this state—was Gramsci referring to a future Italy or the squandered possibilities of the Soviet Union?—"the new habits and psycho-physical attitudes connected to the new production methods have to be acquired by way of mutual persuasion or individually proposed and accepted conviction." Rationalization would then amount to a collective act of "self-imposition and self-discipline," which required organic leadership: a "new type of coercion" exerted by "an elite of a class against its own class." Developing such an elite was a task of historical significance.[81]

In wondering about the role that elites would play in the painful but necessary process of industrial modernization, Gramsci dipped his probing finger into an ideological contradiction that the Soviet Union indeed had never quite been able to resolve.[82] The Revolution promised worker control; industrialization, however, required engineers, planners, and technical experts—in short, elites—who by virtue of their expertise commanded positions of authority that contradicted the egalitarian promise of Communist society. The Bolshevik leadership was torn between two conflicting imperatives. On the one hand, it was necessary to raise productivity and establish the planned allocation of resources, and this implied backing the engineers and strengthening managerial authority and labor discipline. On the other hand, political mobilization required backing the rank-and-file workforce against the technocratic pretensions of managers and experts. In consequence, the Soviet interwar period was marked by a fierce struggle over who would lead the construction of industrialized socialism: the engineers and technical experts (in Soviet parlance, the "specialists") or the workers and the party faithful. Trapped in this tension, the Soviet Union alternately courted and harassed, pampered and imprisoned the specialists who supervised industry during the NEP years.

That was because those who ran industry and staffed the planning organs throughout the 1920s were managers and engineers who had received their training during the Tsarist period. Many of these "bourgeois specialists" sympathized with the modernizing agenda of the Bolsheviks, but they were not Communists. Rank-and-file workers resented their authority in the factories and did what they could to challenge it. (As trade union leader Mikhail Tomsky put it sharply, "the specialists did not make the Revolution."[83]) During the cultural revolution that accompanied Soviet industrialization after 1928, the bourgeois specialists were subjected to harassment and persecution. Meanwhile, a younger generation of workers flooded into technical higher education. Those who graduated from the technical schools in the late 1920s and early 1930s took over the managing positions of Soviet industry after the purges of 1937–1938. These new types of worker-engineers, beneficiaries of Stalin's social revolution (they were called *vydvizhentsy*—or "the promotees"), finally squared the circle of egalitarian promise and industrial advancement. As the promotees arrogated the key posts of the Soviet production sphere, they often benefited from the forcible removal of their superiors. At the same time, their proletarian roots testified to the social and generational revolution that had swept Soviet industry. It was from the generation of Stalin's promotees—Leonid Brezhnev being one—that the Communist Party would draw its leadership personnel for decades to come. When they first came to power, quite ironically, the promotees lost no time in putting into practice the demands that the "bourgeois" specialists had put forth only a few years earlier.[84]

The Soviet debate over Fordism unfolded amid these struggles. First, Ford garnered attention among engineers of the older generation, who became interested in American mass production techniques even before the Revolution of 1917. This camp was exemplified by N. S. Lavrov, Petrograd professor of engineering, who traveled to Detroit in 1916 just as the assembly lines at Highland Park were hitting full stride. A fervent advocate of Fordism, Lavrov illustrates how enthusiasm for American technology allowed a generation of Tsarist-educated engineers and specialists to align themselves with the Bolshevik modernization agenda.[85] Second, a group of avant-garde rationalizers like Aleksei Gastev embraced Fordism in the mid-Twenties, just as they had Taylorism immediately after the Revolution. In their vision, American technology would forge a disciplined and culturally sophisticated cohort of "living labor machines."[86] Third, the Soviet rationalization debate had a populist camp, whose members opposed the intensification of labor under Taylorism and Fordism and dissented from their colleagues' uncritical embrace of American production methods. This camp was exemplified by Osip Arkad'evich Ermanskii, a first-generation Menshevik who spent the 1920s as a professor of labor science at Moscow State University. His criticisms echoed the voices of rank-and-file workers and party stalwarts, who mixed grassroots demands for shop floor control with deep suspicions of "specialists" and their uncritical embrace of capitalist technology.[87] Finally, a faction of radical Bolshevik modernizers emphatically embraced Fordism and recommended its comprehensive transfer to Soviet industry. To this maximalist camp belonged Arsenii Mikhailov, who in 1929 joined the staff of the newly created Soviet Automobile and Tractor Department. To Mikhailov, Fordism ranked among humanity's highest technological achievements, and Soviet industry would do with no less.[88]

The members of these four camps followed the fate of the Soviet technical intelligentsia. By the late 1920s, Lavrov suffered professional and personal persecution in the radicalized environment of accelerated industrialization. As demands for tangible economic results became more pressing, Gastev's dream of creating "new men" by fusing human bodies and modern machines had equally lost its appeal. During the First Five-Year Plan, the modernizers won out, as the humanists, too, lost their influence and academic posts. But even for the modernizers, it was a Pyrrhic victory. It is testimony to the perilous realities of Soviet industrialization that even as American technology arrived in scale in the Soviet Union during the Thirties, Americanism's erstwhile boosters fell victim to the period's purges. Both Gastev, the avant-garde Taylorist, and Mikhailov, the radical proponent of *fordizatsiia*, perished in the Great Terror of 1937–1938.

Socialist Rationalization: Soviets Read Ford

The debate over socialist rationalization began with Taylorism. To ensure factory discipline after the Revolution, the Bolshevik leadership sharply reversed its negative attitude toward Taylorism and began to embrace its core elements, such as stopwatching, motion studies, norm setting, and piece rates. With Lenin's backing, the Central Institute of Labor was founded in 1920 as the principal conduit for research and training in Taylorism. The Institute was the creation of Aleksei Gastev, a first-generation Bolshevik and proselytizer for Taylor's prescriptions ever since he experienced them firsthand as a metalworker in prewar St. Petersburg. His proximity to the avantgarde circles of *Proletkult* gave his embrace of Taylorism a distinctively futurist flavor, and he regarded his activity as a poet-propagandist and as a labor scientist as a unified whole. Gastev had transformative ambitions. In an effort at knowledge transfer, the Institute acquired and translated a comprehensive set of German, British, and American publications on Taylorism and labor science—a library comprising thousands of titles. Time-and-motion studies at the Institute's Moscow laboratory filmed and photographed volunteers in order to document, and then optimize, their workplace movements. Most consequentially, the Institute trained hundreds of technicians, who fanned out across industry tasked with classifying operations and setting work norms.[89]

The tension in the Bolshevik leadership's simultaneous commitment to high productivity and worker empowerment haunted these efforts from the start. In the mines and on the shop floors, norm setting met with enormous resistance from the rank and file; proletarian managers and the trade unions criticized it sharply, sparking a fierce debate. Could Soviet workers raise productivity on their own in collective initiative, as the trade unions argued, or did they require the instruction of specialists schooled in "scientific" best practices, as the Labor Institute averred? Was Taylorism pointing toward socialist rationalization, or was it a "vulgar-bourgeois doctrine" unfit for Soviet conditions? Did time-and-motion studies elevate workers, as Gastev said, or did these methods turn them into "unreasoning and stupid instrument[s]" robbed of creative faculties? Did the Labor Institute's norm setters raise the sophistication of Soviet industry, or did they subjugate shop floors to the rule of "aristocrats of the working class, priests of scientific management"? Confronted with these questions, the party leadership and the highest economic organs reacted with unswerving equivocation. They roundly acknowledged that worker demands were valid. But they also backed the Labor Institute against its sharpest critics and decisively reaffirmed their support at a high-profile conference on Soviet labor science in early 1924.[90]

Into this impasse exploded the first Russian translation of *My Life and Work*. Suddenly, as Osip Ermanskii noted, "the nimbus surrounding the name of Taylor disappeared" and "another name—Ford—began to move to the center of public attention."[91] A Leningrad publishing house put out the first edition of *My Life and Work* in early 1924; it reached a second edition within months. By the end of the decade, ten editions exceeding 80,000 copies were circulating. In 1926, three competing translations of *Today and Tomorrow* appeared in Soviet Russia, at least one of which was subsequently republished in several editions. Taylor's joyless manuals had certainly never achieved such broad popularity. Like in Germany, Ford's books appeared to crash the Soviet scene at a moment when it was unexpectedly ripe for them.[92]

Fundamentally, the Ford-Crowther manifestos confirmed the ambiguity at the heart of the Soviet obsession with America: *My Life and Work* seemed to reveal at once the stunning technological development, and the woeful social inferiority, of American capitalism. Armed with the scalpel of dialectical materialism, Soviet commentators set about separating Ford's production achievements from his political philosophy. Ford, said N. S. Lavrov in his preface to *My Life and Work*, had "splendidly" put into practice laws of production whose "economic essence" nevertheless eluded him. Invoking the sections of Marx's *Capital* that dealt with the division of labor and the organic composition of capital, Lavrov submitted that Ford "does not understand Fordism," which was "a system whose principles had long ago been laid out by Marx."[93] The work *Ford or Marx* by the German Communist Jakob Walcher, who resided in Moscow as a Comintern functionary, was syndicated in the Russian and German press. Walcher subjected *My Life and Work* to a blow-by-blow refutation with quotations from *Capital*. His book echoed the argument that Ford had created, as though blindly, a system of production that pointed beyond boundaries that Ford himself was incapable of transcending. Where Ford spoke of economic justice and the common good based on affluence and dynamic production, he advocated "much that is not only rational but indeed necessary," Walcher said. But Ford ultimately foundered on "the unyielding truth that carrying out [his] recommendations requires abolishing the capitalist system."[94]

The producer populism that so excited the postliberal right was equally lost on Soviet readers, who consistently took it as a particularly risible form of capitalist apologia. There was hardly a page in *Today and Tomorrow* that did

ГЕНРИ
ФОРД

МОЯ ЖИЗНЬ
МОИ ДОСТИЖЕНИЯ

ВТОРОЕ ИЗДАНИЕ

«ВРЕМЯ»
1924

FIGURE 2.3. The title page of the second Leningrad edition of *My Life and Work*.
Photo by author.

not "require rebuke, clarification, and debunking," groaned Bolshevik labor scientist I. V. Rabchinskii. Ford's shibboleths—high wages, the dismissal of finance capital, the romantic invocations of a single class of producers—drew impassioned denunciations. Ford displayed "colossal cynicism" when calling the wages of his workers "high" while remaining silent about how productivity in his factories far outstripped wage growth. Where Ford rejected the label of capitalist, he gave away his failure to grasp "the basic part of political economy known to every worker," which defined a capitalist as an owner of the means of production.[95] The talk about high wages, added Osip Ermanskii, neglected the intensity of exploitation in Ford's factories. When Ford "lobs some critical remarks at capitalism," this was a feeble attempt to veil the contradictions of capitalism that Ford's factories themselves most brilliantly expressed. Amid the most advanced achievements of machinery and technology, Ford workers toiled in reactionary conditions—spies, invasive paternalism, the open shop—that amounted to nothing short of "industrial feudalism."[96]

Under capitalism, as Soviet commentators saw it, technological advances necessarily deepened the barbarity of labor relations. By the same token, the extreme exploitation of workers in Ford's factories suggested the immense potential his production system might unleash once it had been adapted to socialist conditions. When it came to modernizing production, then, Fordism struck Soviet commentators as harboring possibilities that far exceeded anything Taylor had been able to offer. Fordism revealed that the future of rational production lay in moving from the animate elements to the inanimate, from the workers to the machines, from rationalizing people to perfecting the production system as a whole. Taylor's obsession over individual worker performance seemed quaint next to Ford's mastery of machinery and coordination. In Ford's factories, "the fundamental labor force are the machines," wrote N. S. Rozenblit, a colleague of Ermanskii's in the humanist camp of Soviet labor sciences. Taylor may have succeeded in making laborers toil like oxen, but even the sharpest economy of movements and the most exacting work norms would eventually encounter the limits of human physiology. Hence Taylorism would sooner or later "arrest" the development of the productive forces. Ford's innovations, in contrast, suggested that the possibilities for technological and organizational improvements, for mechanization and coordination, were essentially "limitless." In this sense, Rozenblit said, "Ford represents the 20th century, while Taylor remains stuck in the 18th."[97]

What practical lessons, then, could Soviet modernizers learn from Ford's system? Commentators pointed to several issues: first was the standardization of products like the Model T, which lent themselves to deep mass production runs and allowed reconciling quantity with quality. The flow principle, supported by mechanization and special-purpose machine tools, seemed equally worthy of emulation. Adopting the conveyor system promised not only efficient transportation but also the "automatic regulation" of the entire production process, including its speed. Continuous testing, control, and inspection would accompany the production process, as well as efficient use of raw materials and energy. Equally instructive was the maximal division of labor and the bifurcation of skill levels that came with it: a newly empowered technical staff guided and controlled an army of low-skilled operatives.[98] These measures struck Soviet technocrats as immensely attractive, since they seemed to portend "the decisive repudiation of craft-based principles" and the replacement of "subjectivism, traditions, routines, and secrecy" with "rational work methods."[99]

The precise coordination under Fordism appealed to the Bolshevik instinct for top-down planning and administrative fine-tuning. Of all elements of Fordism, Soviet commentators were particularly enamored of the conveyor, which encapsulated the smooth synchronization of complex supply chains and myriad production processes. The moving belt, submitted Gastev, was not inherently a system of "pushing and driving"; saying so amounted to adopting an "overly Asiatic notion of labor organization." Rather, the conveyor expressed "the principle of harmonic coordination" of men and material; it was less "an accelerator" than "an organizer."[100] Trotsky went so far as to speak of the "conveyor principle of socialist economy": what Ford had achieved for one branch of industry, Soviet rationalization would achieve for the entire economy. From the sources of raw materials to the churning factories themselves, all elements of the production process would be coordinated as though by "a mighty conveyor." Smoothly connecting all economic spheres, the conveyor principle would decentralize industry and eventually abolish the very distinction between city and countryside. If capitalism was an anarchic system of jealous partitions, cross-purposes, and collective blindness, Soviet socialism would be a system of total and harmonic coordination.[101]

Unsurprisingly, however, efforts to introduce flow production in the factories—there were attempts in the textile, metallurgical, and electrical sectors—encountered the same headwinds as norm setting. Gastev deplored that workers stubbornly refused to relinquish anachronistic craft practices: they jealously guarded their expertise, refused to submit to a rational division of labor, and showed themselves incapable of considering their work from the vantage point of the entire production process. Such attitudes were "extremely conservative, individualistic, and anti-social," Gastev held, but they were hard to break.[102] Mikhailov submitted that combating the "conservatism and backwardness" of older skilled workers required "psychological preparation": educational campaigns that would raise awareness among the workforce of the highly cooperative nature of flow production. Generous breaks, sitting, and sporadic switching of tasks should be a matter of course, but "heightened labor discipline" was indispensable, since one operative's error could upset the entire work flow.[103]

With the onset of accelerated industrialization in 1928, public rhetoric swung decisively toward class war and against the technocratic rationalizers. Emboldened by a party-backed show trial against "bourgeois specialists"— some of them British engineers—Communist youth and rank-and-file workers attacked the rationalization establishment, whose sanguine assessments of American technology could now spell political peril. Grassroots radicals felt emboldened to attack technocrats like Gastev for attempting "to transfer

Fordism and methods of capitalist rationalization to Soviet soil," or to "build the house of proletarian culture on the practice of Ford and Taylor."[104] The furor brought down N. S. Lavrov, whose last pamphlet, *Fordism—A Study on the Production of Things*, was denounced as "a professor's utterly confused closet ruminations" and "nonsense."[105] Lavrov was removed from the helm of the Moscow-based Scientific Automotive Institute in 1928 after a campaign against his "reactionary professorship."[106] In the summer of 1930, even Ermanskii was expelled from the academy.[107]

Gastev, however, survived the "specialist baiting" since his Labor Institute continued to enjoy the support of the Soviet leadership. Just as Stalin famously embraced radical industrialization promptly after demoting its erstwhile proponents among the party's "left opposition," a new political coalition embraced mass production even as the old guard of Ford champions lost public influence. This coalition united young, party-affiliated "red engineers," active in the factories, with a group of radical Bolshevik modernizers, who in 1930 took control of the highest economic organs and decisively reasserted a vision of industrial modernization based on mass production and Western technological transfers.[108]

In this coalition, a group of Bolsheviks formerly associated with the left opposition—the likes of Iurii Piatakov, Arkadii Rozengol'ts, and Nikolai Osinskii—played the decisive ideological role. Their cherished vision now had Stalin's backing. They imagined a future in which the Soviet party-state orchestrated the modernization of Russia by radically altering the agricultural makeup of the country. Instead of the slow transformation of Russia's factories, an entirely new industrial system based on the latest Western technology would be grafted on top of the old. A new landscape of production giants—tractor and automobile plants, chemical works and steel factories—would stretch from Siberia to the Caucasus. Tightly administered from the center, this new economic geography would supplant the wasteful regional competition of existing Soviet industry. In the factories, authority would be centralized in capable and experienced hands—those of specialists, if necessary. There was no room for the "Communist arrogance" (*komchvanstvo*) of those who objected to working with Western specialists and opposed the top-down rationalization of industry.[109]

In this developmental vision, Fordism had a threefold significance. First, automotive mass production would create a supple system of motorized transport that complemented the overburdened train system and eased the coordination of industries and the allocation of resources between them.[110] Second, the new industrial clusters did not require compromises with an established labor force. Stomped out of the ground, these new megaplants could instantly start up mass production and thus mobilize vast new reservoirs of unskilled labor. Third, gradual agricultural accumulation—the favored strategy of the "right deviation"—was rejected in favor of massive imports of capital goods and knowledge transfer from the West, with mass production at the core. Making "maximal use" of Western technical experience was "essential," said Rozengol'ts: this applied to importing Western machinery, attracting European and American specialists, and sending young Soviet engineers abroad.[111] Mikhailov expressed the new maximalist stance on Western inputs with utmost clarity:

> The more grandiose the plans of the Five Year Plan, the more decisive the ongoing social, technological and cultural changes, the more energetic . . . the struggle for the highest possible pace of construction—the more obviously necessary is a swift and complete switch to the most advanced American technology.[112]

Yet the bitter conflict between technocrats and the rank and file hardly abated. It still shone through between the lines of Aleksei Gastev's entry on Fordism in the *Great Soviet Encyclopedia* of 1936. No more mention was there of the Soviet "new man," no invocation of the transformative power of modern American technology. Fordism, Gastev wrote, was "a bourgeois system of organizing production," and Ford's "social conception" was "demagogic propaganda." But the bulk of the piece gave a detailed and appreciative description of the core aspects of Fordism—flow, special-purpose machines, standardized parts, the conveyor system, a sharp division of labor, and the resulting splintering of skill levels. These innovations had to be seen, Gastev submitted, through the lens of Leninism: Had not Lenin recommended Taylorism as a way to raise proletarian culture and combat sloppy work and shirking? Now, under Stalin's directive, the shock workers had taken Taylorism into their own hands. This required, similarly, a "critically interpreted and revised" system of flow production, adapted to Soviet conditions.[113] Even as a curtain of silence was drawn over the vivid Soviet Americanism of the 1920s, Henry Ford enjoyed canonization as one of the bourgeois technicians whose accomplishments pointed beyond their own times. "Ford's name," said a popular biography of the mid-Thirties, "will be remembered many years after capitalism has disappeared from the face of the earth."[114]

Conclusion

My Life and Work became the unlikely best seller it did because it connected like no other artifact of the Twenties the dual challenges of industrial reconstruction and political resurgence. How did modern production technology reshape the social order, what were the political implications of mass production, what were its cultural effects? Could mass production provide the foundation for a normative doctrine of social change? To these questions, Ford gave specific answers—answers that enthused many even as they provoked others to articulate their own counterproposals. Those on the right read Ford as an organic intellectual of the postliberal turn: a genius engineer-philosopher who at once encapsulated America's ascendancy and delivered the tools to surmount it. On the left, *My Life and Work* stirred intellectuals to consider what would distinguish socialist mass production from its capitalist variant. Hence *My Life and Work* spurred a debate of global scale. Not only the book but the prolific commentary that it inspired—interpretations, explications, rebuttals—circulated in multiple languages. The Soviet press avidly translated everything from Louis Lochner's account of Ford's Peace Ship expedition in 1915 to technical manuals on mass production. The German reference work *Flow Production: Contributions to Its Introduction* appeared in Russian translation in 1927; Mikhailov called it "outstanding."[115] Osip Ermanskii's works percolated through the syndicated Communist presses in Vienna and Berlin.[116] Gottl-Ottlilienfeld's works on Ford inspired French and Japanese postliberals.[117] German sociological dissertations resurfaced in the Soviet Union. These included Irene Witte's *Taylor-Gilbreth-Ford* and Hilda Weiss's *Abbe and Ford: Capitalist Utopias*.[118]

Communists mocked Ford's neoproducerism, the very ideology that postliberals on the right found so inspiring. Both camps, however, shared a subtle set of Occidentalist preconceptions: America was a spatialized expression of historical time, the quintessential locus of modernity, and Ford was its avatar. The trope that America lacked the inhibiting cultural traditions and obsolete social structures constraining Europe was widespread across the political spectrum. Gramsci felt that the absence of "historical and cultural traditions" and the nonexistence of "parasitic" social elements had allowed America to "base the country's entire life on production."[119] Theodor Lüddecke suggested that the "economic principle" governed American life because the country suffered fewer "frictions with tradition."[120] Europeans ruminated and hesitated; Americans attacked the practical problems of the world. "That indomitable force which neither knows nor recognizes obstacles; which continues at a task once started until it is finished," was Stalin's definition of Americanism.[121] "Decisive, generous, resolute and coolly calculating," that was the American mentality according to Lüddecke.[122] Fascism flattered itself as a philosophy of the deed, Gramsci chuckled, when in actuality that badge belonged to Americanism.[123]

Though all agreed on the momentous significance of Fordism, its precise assessment depended on the place it inhabited in the insurgents' various economic ideologies. To the right, Fordism provided both a recipe for economic resurgence and an antidote to spiritual degeneration. To Hitler, escaping the existential threat posed by America's rise required emulating the country's core building blocks, which he saw in territory and Fordism. Gramsci hoped that modern industrial production would prepare the working class for a higher level of culture and self-mastery, even if the problem of "hegemony"— that of organic elites—remained intractable. To Soviet commentators, meanwhile, Fordism posed a prolific riddle through which to parse the distinctions between capitalist rationalization and its socialist spawn. To the radical Stalinist modernizers, finally, Fordism promised a cure for the defect that most offended their ideological sensibilities: Russia's grinding economic backwardness and the cultural crudity that enthralled its workers. These diverging development horizons colored the trans-Atlantic technology transfers over which Nazis and Soviets presided in the 1930s.

3

The Soviet Auto Giant

The tempo of industrialization is not something arbitrary but is internationally conditioned.

—LEON TROTSKY, 1926

We must at all costs set out, first, to learn, second, to learn, and third, to learn.

—VLADIMIR LENIN, 1920[1]

Every latecomer must learn from an established master.

—ALICE AMSDEN, 2001[2]

GIANCARLO CAMERANA was secretary of the Fiat board of directors and second in command at the Italian carmaker when he made his first trip to the United States in September 1936. His destination was Detroit, where Charles Sorensen, head of operations at the Ford Motor Company, received him and showed him around River Rouge. At the time of Camerana's voyage, Fiat was planning the construction of a new production complex at Mirafiori. The new factory's layout was to be based on the Rouge.[3] After returning to New York, Camerana paid the obligatory homage to Sorensen ("I am speechless in admiration of the Ford factories and organization") before asking for advice. How could the new plant at Mirafiori best benefit from Ford's experience? Sorensen replied:

> It is my understanding that you want to put in modern methods and reorganize your plant in Italy. . . . To get the benefit of each of the various kinds of machinery, conveyor systems, and plant organization in general that you see around our factory, you first of all have to have a competent engineer who would come over here, establish an office, and then contact with different companies who make a specialty of fitting out plants.[4]

Camerana heeded Sorensen's counsel and in November sent Rambaldo Bruschi, Fiat engineer in chief, to Detroit. What Sorensen did not say was that the procedure he recommended exactly followed a precedent that had been set a few years earlier. In the summer of 1929, a commission headed by Stepan Dybets set up shop at the Ford Motor Company at the behest of the Supreme Economic Council of the Soviet Union (*Vesenkha*). The Soviet commission stayed for the better part of six years, supervising the transfer of blueprints, engineering know-how, and production technology from Detroit to Nizhnii Novgorod, where as part of the First Five-Year Plan the Soviet Union was building its own River Rouge replica.

Stepan Dybets was not an aristocrat like Fiat's Camerana, nor was he a dyed-in-the-wool engineer like Ferdinand Porsche. Dybets was born into a Ukrainian working-class family in 1887 and as a twenty-year-old emigrated to the United States, where he picked up work in New Jersey metalworking plants. Active first as an anarcho-syndicalist, he eventually joined the Wobblies and was deported to a war-torn Ukraine in the wake of the Espionage Act of 1917. Dybets joined the Bolshevik Party in 1918, narrowly escaped death during the Russian civil war, and made his career in the 1920s in the management of the powerful Soviet Southern Steel trust. In 1929, he was appointed to the head of *Avtostroi*, the Soviet agency responsible for the Nizhnii factory. In 1934, he was put in charge of the entire Soviet automobile and tractor industry—a key position in the powerful People's Commissariat of Heavy Industry, the administrative centerpiece of the Soviet industrialization drive.[5]

When Dybets arrived in Detroit in the summer of 1929, he was no longer a radical immigrant laborer but a leading functionary of a Soviet regime engaged in an industrial revolution. Given the prominence that Henry Ford enjoyed in the industrial debates of the 1920s, the contract with his company had a rich symbolic significance for the Soviet side. But engineering delegations such as the one headed by Dybets also scoured many other Western firms in the early Thirties. By 1931, Soviet industry was bound into 124 technical assistance agreements with foreign firms.[6] The list contained many of the most prominent American corporations, such as du Pont, International Harvester, General Electric, and RCA.[7] Equally important were many lesser-known engineering firms and machine tool suppliers, the majority of them American. The Detroit-based architectural firm of Albert Kahn, for example, almost single-handedly designed the striking modernist style so characteristic of the era's Soviet industrial infrastructure.[8] Among the Germans, too, the list represented a veritable who's who of industry: Krupp signed a ten-year treaty with the Soviet machine tool industry and shared the field with big names like Siemens, Borsig, Deitz, AEG, Telefunken, and IG Farben.

The Soviet technical assistance agreements with Western firms are well known, but they are not well understood. The classic accounts of Stalin's industrialization mention them only in passing and make little attempt to integrate them into their narratives.[9] Where Soviet technology transfers elicited focused attention, this was in the context of Cold War security concerns.[10] True, historians have repeatedly been drawn to the Soviet links to Western firms, the Ford agreement prominently among them.[11] While empirically rich, however, this literature has tended to treat these connections as some kind of curiosity, and as a result has often been tempted to belabor the minor irony of Communist state officials cavorting with capitalist businessmen. Surveying the field, one cannot help the impression that the scholarship still labors under received Cold War paradigms, including the assumption that an ontological abyss separated the economics of Soviet Communism from the "capitalist West." In this light, the Soviet engagement of Western firms must necessarily seem incongruous.

Yet the incongruity dissolves once we set Soviet technology transfers in the light of the transnational nature of catch-up development. This perspective reveals the Western technical assistance agreements to be in fact central for Soviet industrialization: it is impossible to pursue domestic economic upgrading without turning abroad. All late developers must turn, for capital and technology, to those they seek to emulate. Scholars of the developmental states of late-twentieth-century East Asia have identified strategic technology transfers as fundamental to catch-up industrialization. They have shown that such transfers involved more than simple imitation: they are difficult processes of indigenizing, diffusing, and adapting to homegrown institutions the prescriptions of technological leaders.[12] In this perspective, Soviet industrialization emerges as one particular type of developmental strategy among many, one whose precise forms were shaped both by the sharp degree of Soviet comparative underdevelopment and by the ruthless dedication of the Bolshevik leadership. During the First Five-Year Plan, the Soviet Union embarked on possibly the most comprehensive and concentrated campaign at state-orchestrated technology transfer in recorded history, and the Bolshevik leadership proved willing to pay almost any price for the effort.

The historical literature has often emphasized the hair-raising inefficiency of Soviet technology transfers and their seemingly quixotic quality—how could the Bolsheviks seriously have hoped to bridge the yawning developmental gap separating the Soviet Union from America in such a short time span?[13] There is indeed little doubt about the brutal inefficiency of Soviet technology transfers and their enormous social and economic cost: precious foreign exchange was first extorted from the populace and then squandered as imported machinery went to waste and expensive foreign specialists were ignored on the construction sites of the Five-Year Plan. Developmental states, however, tend to be interested less in efficiency than in results.[14] By this criterion, Soviet technology transfers could hardly be called a failure. What emerged by the late Thirties was a hybrid industrial system, fragile but operable, that reconciled knowledge and machinery from the West with the demands of Soviet labor mobilization and with the political constraints of the Stalinist social revolution—a system in which cutting-edge machine tools operated among an army of "auxiliary" peasant laborers working by hand, shovel, and wheelbarrow, in which a small skilled core of promotee-engineers mediated between unskilled workers and Stakhanovite heroics; a system that mass-produced steel sheets, machine tools, trucks, and airplanes that were technologically inferior to their Western templates but sturdy enough to uphold Soviet political and military power.

The Soviet transfer of automotive mass production exemplifies this process, and this chapter explores it by following the origin and operation of one of the prestigious objects of the First Five-Year Plan: the automobile factory at Nizhnii Novgorod. After 1933, when the city changed names in honor of its scion Maxim Gorky, the Soviet River Rouge went by the official name of Gaz (*Gor'kovskii Avtomobil'nyi Zavod*); but to the boisterous Soviet press, it was known simply as the "Auto Giant."[15]

Soviet Industrialization and Technology Transfers: From NEP to the First Five-Year Plan

In the global history of catch-up industrialization, the Soviet effort stands out in both ambition and ruthlessness. Within a few short years, a predominantly agrarian economy acquired a massive, capital-intensive industry based on steel and complex mass production. By the end of the Thirties, the Soviet Union possessed sectors that had been weak or nonexistent in the Twenties— widespread electrification, automobiles, airplanes; other sectors, such as machine tool building, had been revolutionized. Brand-new industrial clusters arose in the Urals and Western Siberia, transforming the economic geography inherited from the Russian Empire. The scale and speed of the Soviet industrial revolution remain unmatched in global history; commensurately enormous was the social dislocation and human suffering that accompanied it. Industrial investment was funded by drastic cuts in urban consumption and by sweeping primitive accumulation in the countryside. Collectivization turned out to be a ruinous policy, but it did put the countryside under the control of the state, which ruthlessly siphoned dwindling agricultural surpluses into industry. Some twenty-three million men and women left the countryside and streamed into the new factories.[16] Many millions starved in famines that the Soviet leadership not only tolerated but often punitively exacerbated. Millions more joined the swelling forced-labor camps, where they toiled in construction, lumbering, and mining in support of industrialization.[17] This industrial revolution also ate its own: the generation of engineers who stomped Soviet industry out of the ground during the First Five-Year Plan—Dybets among them—fell victim to Stalin's purges in 1937–1938.

If such monstrosity made Soviet industrialization sui generis, the process nevertheless bore the characteristic traits of state-led development. Bolshevism surely had millenarian traits, but it remained a modernizing ideology that connected social revolution to technological and economic transformation.[18] Emerging from revolution and civil war, the Bolsheviks cast their eyes abroad and found they presided over a state that was weak and underdeveloped, especially in comparison with the United States. They attached utmost political significance to overcoming this predicament. In this effort, however, the Soviet Union found itself constrained, like all late developers, by a stark dearth of capital and technology; like all late-developing regimes, therefore, the Soviet leadership had to come up with a strategy of engaging international markets for goods and capital, as well as devise mechanisms to wrest proprietary know-how and technology from foreign enterprises and multinational corporations.[19] Like all projects of catch-up development, then, the Soviet one was inescapably bound to global economic structures. This is what Trotsky meant when he pointed out that "the tempo of industrialization is not something arbitrary but is internationally conditioned."[20] Stalin, too, understood this: his slogan "socialism in one country" was a political directive, not an economic one. The phrase around which the Bolshevik developmental ideology congealed was not "socialism in one country" but "economic independence"— understood not as isolation or self-sufficiency but as control over strategic supply chains, as the potential to withstand a hostile blockade, and as the ability to turn Russia's position of weakness vis-à-vis world markets into one of strength.[21]

Why did industrial buildup seem so urgent? With the possible exception of Bukharin, none of the leading Bolsheviks ever grew comfortable with the New Economic Policy—that 1920s dispensation that uneasily combined state direction in foreign trade and heavy industry with market relations in agriculture, petty trade, and consumer goods. As long as hostile elements—*nepmen* profiteers and *kulak* peasants—burrowed through the economic topsoil, the Bolsheviks feared a creeping reintroduction of capitalism from within. Coupled with that came perceived threats from without: what Bolsheviks called "capitalist encirclement" signified a mix of political isolation, fear of renewed military intervention, and an unfavorable position on international capital markets.[22] To survive in a hostile world, the Soviet Union had to unfasten itself from the position in the global division of labor it had inherited from the Russian Empire. On this principle the otherwise fractious Bolshevik leadership agreed, and so it was enshrined by the 1925 Party Congress. Lest the Soviet Union become "an economic appendage of the capitalist world economy," it had to be "converted from a country which imports machines to a country which produces machines."[23]

The ability to produce machines, however, rested on large-scale technological imports from abroad. This fact leads us straight to the core of the Soviet economic policy predicament during the 1920s. Having repudiated Russia's debts in 1918, the Soviet Union's access to international credit markets was precarious; hence the imports needed for industrial buildup had to be paid with exports, especially—or so the Bolsheviks hoped—with grain. The Bolsheviks' industrializing ambitions, then, depended on the cooperation of a vast countryside over which they lacked firm control. Backward Russian agriculture held Soviet industrial development on a tight leash. Or put differently, Soviet power on global markets was constrained by the weak productivity of its agriculture and by its industrial underdevelopment—precisely the condition that Bolsheviks strained to overcome.

It was, then, no coincidence that NEP ended in 1928, a year of miserable grain procurements. That year political crisis came to a head, too: Trotsky and other prominent "left" oppositionists were exiled, and the persecution of "bourgeois specialists" intensified with a highly publicized show trial that portended the radicalization of class war in the factories. But the economic crisis was most visible in the balance of payments. Grain exports fell off a cliff at the very moment when the First Five-Year Plan demanded ever-increasing outlays for imported machinery. As a result, foreign exchange reserves shrank by almost a third, severely curtailing the claims that the Soviet Union could put on resources unavailable within its borders.[24]

A stark choice now confronted the Bolshevik leadership. One course of action was to *cut back imports* and delay the buildup of industry, as Bukharin and Rykov pleaded. Stalin, however, was no longer willing to let agriculture dictate the speed of development. In this he found the support not only of loyalists in the Politburo but also of modernizers formerly associated with the left opposition, and in a cohort of young "red engineers" appalled with what they regarded as foot-dragging and conservatism in the factories.[25] In an atmosphere of ideological radicalization, they succeeded in pushing the other alternative: *expand imports* for industrialization by rounding up all available resources for export. What became known as the policy of "mobilizing the population's funds" most prominently featured the forcible requisitioning of grain, otherwise known as *collectivization*. It also included rationing food and consumer goods, suppressing wages, imposing forced loans on bank balances, and requisitioning convertible assets, such as privately held gold and art-work.[26] The result was a boom in Soviet foreign trade while living standards fell precipitously.[27]

During the First Plan, then, the Soviet leadership threw its weight behind a trade strategy that exchanged grain, lumber, oil, and sundry exportables against high-quality steel and machine tools. Thus the link between the buildup of industry and the lethal logic of collectivization was forged on the ailing world markets of the Depression. The policy was deliberate and explicit. Writing to Molotov in August 1930, Stalin put it bluntly: "The quota for daily [grain] shipments should be raised to 3–4 million poods at a minimum. Other-wise we risk being left without our new iron and steel and machine-building factories (*Avtozavod, Cheliabzavod,* etc.)."[28] In short, the dollars flowing from the Soviet trade agencies into the Depression-hit accounts of the Ford Motor Company were raised on world markets in exchange for grain extorted from a famished peasantry.

The goal of these measures, as Stalin's motto had it, was "to catch up and overtake" the advanced economies of the West. Those who orchestrated the industrial buildup of the early Thirties understood this goal in a specific way. Stalin and those former left oppositionists who came to dominate the ad-ministrative apparatus of industrialization did not refer to their goal in "social-ist" terms. Economic equality, social justice, or the equitable distribution of property were not their concerns. In fact, collectivization countermanded the Revolution's most important redistributive decision, that of turning the land over to the peasants. Neither did Stalin's industrializers anticipate the develop-ment concepts that came to prominence after 1945. At the People's Commis-sariat of Heavy Industry, there was no talk of alleviating poverty, removing malnourishment, or raising income per capita. Rather, these modernizers embraced a vision of development in which a powerful party-state wrested a backward agricultural colossus into the twentieth century—an era when, as they saw it, geopolitical stature and civilizational triumph depended on indus-trial might. What they envisioned was *industrial'naia derzhava*—a formidable power-state whose industrial prowess fortified its military strength and testi-fied to its global preeminence.[29]

This was the context in which the large-scale adaptation of Fordism in the Soviet Union took place. This chapter follows four men who helped the Auto Giant awaken and rise. Nikolai Osinskii, economist, Bolshevik leftist, and USA traveler, vocally advocated mass automobilization during the industrialization debates of 1927–1928. In conflict with a cautious state-planning agency (Gos-plan), Osinskii pushed through an ambitious agenda for Soviet motorization that culminated in the foreign technical assistance contract with the Ford

Motor Company of May 1929. In fulfillment of this agreement, Stepan Dybets traveled to Detroit at the behest of the Chief Economic Council (*Vesenkha*). Dybets led a group of Soviet engineers who were in charge of transferring Ford technology and know-how from the Midwest to central Russia during the years of the First Five-Year Plan. As director of Gaz between 1932 and 1938, Sergei D'iakonov oversaw the uneven and troubled implementation of Fordism during the Second Five-Year Plan. In this period, persistent problems of supply coordination, as well as Soviet policies of labor mobilization, obstructed the smooth functioning of Fordism at Gaz. Finally, Ivan Loskutov ascended to the helm of Gaz after Stalin's purges, and presided over the factory's redoubled embrace of Fordism in the late Thirties and World War II.

Of these four men, only Loskutov never saw River Rouge with his own eyes.

Nikolai Osinskii and the Origins of Soviet Motorization

When it came to automobiles, the Soviet Union was firmly rooted in the lower end of the global periphery in the 1920s. The country possessed a single automobile factory, located in the industrial district of southeastern Moscow. AMO—short for Moscow Automobile Society—had been founded in 1916 to assemble imported trucks for the Tsar's military. During NEP, AMO built armored vehicles and trucks modeled on a Fiat type. Manufacturing was largely nonmechanized, and output did not exceed a few hundred vehicles before 1927. The great majority of Soviet motor vehicles were imports. Between 1925 and 1927, the Soviet motor park hovered at around 18,000 cars, trucks, and buses—one-third of which were reportedly in a state of disrepair. This figure compared favorably with Turkey's estimated 5,500 vehicles (1928) and Poland's 16,000 (1927). During the same period, however, Japan more than doubled its vehicle supply to 30,387, thanks to Ford's assembly plant in Yokohama. Brazil reported 29,084 vehicles in 1924, Argentina 88,550 (1924), and India 102,563 (1927). The USA had over 22 million in 1927.[30]

In light of these figures, it may come as a surprise that automotive mass production was not initially earmarked in the Five-Year Plan. The draft of the plan announced by Gosplan in June 1927 mentioned automobile construction only in passing. Over the next two years, however, American mass production technology clinched a central role in the Soviet industrialization drive, as plans pushed inexorably from the moderate templates of the planning agencies toward radical reconstruction and large-scale imports of technology. The struggles over economic development that roiled the 1920s—pitting Politburo rightists against leftists, shop floor youth against the economic bureaucracies, and regional interests into fierce rivalries over funds—found full reflection in the emergence of automotive mass production targets.[31]

The initial absence of automotive targets reveals the starkly diverging conceptions of development that separated the party maximalists from the moderates of the planning agencies. Gosplan's staffers were academics who had been educated in the lecture halls of prewar St. Petersburg; they understood economic planning to involve a careful massaging of markets into new equilibrium. To them, development implied designing state incentives to steer market activity. They projected that the Soviet economy would take a gradual departure from Tsarist legacies: in the near future, agricultural comparative advantage and a buildup in coal, steel, and railroads would form the basis of Soviet economic development. Hence Gosplan accorded little significance to the automobile industry: the control figures for 1927–1928 specified a target of 700 trucks.[32]

Such gradualism provoked Valerian (alias Nikolai) Osinskii (1887–1938), whose views reflected those of the party left. Osinskii was an old Bolshevik who had helped convince Lenin to abrogate Tsarist sovereign debts in 1918; in the early Twenties, he had warned about the implications for Russia of agricultural price deflation on world markets. Later he took on various roles in foreign economic diplomacy. In 1927, he was a delegate to the World Economic Conference in Geneva; in the 1930s, he repeatedly advertised the methods of Soviet economic planning to the West. Osinskii's affiliation with the party left in the Twenties debarred him from Stalin's inner circle and eventually cost him his life. But his efforts to push a large-scale technology transfer from the United States helped defeat gradualist alternatives and decentralized approaches to development within the economic bureaucracy.[33]

In the summer of 1927, Osinskii clashed in the pages of *Pravda* with Gosplan and *Vesenkha* officials over the role of automotive mass production in the Five-Year Plan.[34] Osinskii demanded that a new, large-scale plant with a capacity of 100,000 vehicles per year be included in the plan. His arguments drew from an alarmed diagnosis of comparative underdevelopment. In the United States, "the world's technologically most advanced country," the automobile was the key technical and economic innovation of the 1920s, Osinskii argued. Indeed, the automobile industry and its suppliers already contributed more value-added than any other American sector. In comparison, the Soviet automobile sector was puny. Wasn't the Five-Year Plan supposed to catapult the Soviet economy into the industrial future? How, then, could Gosplan think to do so without the automobile? Osinskii belabored cultural reasons, too. Just as it had done in America, the car would bind the countryside to the Soviet cities, connect peasants to industrial development, and hence help vanquish what he called, quoting Marx's famous dictum, the "idiocy of rural life." A homegrown

Soviet mass production of automobiles, finally, was a matter of military significance. "If in a future war we use the Russian cart against the American or European automobile," the result would be utter defeat, "the inevitable consequence of technological weakness."[35]

Gosplan chairman Stanislav Strumilin replied by stressing not future goals but present realities. He countered that no market existed in the Soviet Union that could absorb 100,000 vehicles a year. No significant demand for passenger cars was to be expected from urban workers in the near future. Agriculture might make use of trucks, but this would require furnishing significant credit, amounting to "supplying the peasants with automobiles at the state's expense." Instead, peasants should work their horses harder! Hoping to "compete with Ford" was an illusion. Strumilin recommended proceeding "gradually" and treating automobiles like tractors, of which the Soviet Union was importing large quantities and whose domestic production was only slowly beginning to increase. Full-scale motorization was premature in the Soviet Union, Gosplan submitted, as the country was too "technologically backward" compared to the rest of the world.[36]

To Osinskii, that was precisely the point. Strumilin was mistaken to take for granted the economic limitations of the present. The country needed to abolish its backwardness, which meant it needed to industrialize, which in turn required mass production and cars. He charged Strumilin of "tailism" (khvostizm)—the failure of revolutionary spirit to press forward regardless of circumstances. Certainly, peasants would not hold trucks in private ownership; trucks would reveal their full utility only as agriculture became increasingly collectivized. Regarding financing, consumer credit organizations of the kind that supported the market in America could be considered. In any case, the point of a large-scale factory was lowering production costs to American levels. Only high volumes would justify mass production techniques, whose economies would make themselves felt with especial force in the Soviet Union, where prices did not need to reflect profits, as in the USA. Finally, Osinskii returned to the military implications: it would hardly be possible to wage a future war with imported vehicles. Creating a homegrown motor industry could not wait: "defense considerations require this categorically." Within five years, the gap between the Soviet Union and the West would become unbridgeable.[37]

Osinskii, however, not only clashed with the cautious planners, but also had to contend with competing initiatives that emerged from the unruly administrative landscape of NEP. While the debate over Soviet automobilization raged in Pravda, at least three Soviet organs independently sought out automotive partners in the West.[38] In 1927, Glavmetall—the roof agency for the metal-building sector—negotiated with French and German car manufacturers about the possibility of a direct investment for a factory with a capacity of 10,000 vehicles annually. What the delegation had in mind was a factory that would assemble knocked-down imported cars, just as the branches of Ford and GM did in other countries. The Europeans were interested, but the venture foundered upon the "miserable import contingent" allotted to automobiles by the People's Commissariat of Foreign Trade.[39] In the summer of 1928, after Osinksii had publicly ridiculed as "complete nonsense" the idea of using European instead of American partners in building up the Soviet auto industry, a delegation from the Moscow Automobile Trust (in charge of AMO) traveled to Detroit. The delegation talked to Chrysler, General Motors, and other firms, but Charles Sorensen at the Ford Motor Company was most receptive. In Osinskii's unfavorable rendering of the encounter, Sorensen "burst out laughing" when the delegation suggested a factory with a capacity of 12,500 vehicles. Sorensen countered by offering a joint venture involving an assembly plant with an annual capacity of up to 150,000. Taken aback, the Moscow delegation stalled and instead agreed with an obscure Detroit truck producer, Autocar, on a moderate plan to retool AMO. (In his memoirs, Sorensen remembered finding the Moscow group "very difficult to deal with." His impression that they "lacked authority to go ahead" appears to have been accurate.)[40]

The third initiative was the one backed by Osinskii, and it involved making a brand-new mass production factory into a matter of Soviet-wide importance. In that matter, *Vesenkha* sent its vice chairman, Valerii Mezhlauk, to the United States. By spring 1929, rivaling negotiations were taking place in Detroit, with the Moscow Auto Trust vying for a separate agreement that would concentrate the automobile industry in the capital.[41] In the context of the Politburo's final approval of the "optimal" (maximalist) version of the Five-Year Plan in April of 1929, however, Osinskii got his way. A factory with an annual capacity of 100,000 was earmarked in the plan. Simultaneously, *Vesenkha* rejected a joint venture with Ford in favor of building the factory under Soviet auspices with American technical assistance. Sorensen agreed. In Dearborn in late May, Henry Ford and Mezhlauk put their signatures to a contract that granted *Vesenkha* Ford technical assistance in launching a large-scale car factory based on the Rouge.

The agreement marked a victory for Osinskii and the modernist faction among Soviet industrializers. With the signing of this high-profile agreement, Osinskii overcame Gosplan's hesitancy and sidelined the Moscow Auto Trust. Though rivalries continued throughout 1929, Moscow's agreement with Autocar was soon rescinded. In late 1929, as part of a larger restructuring of the economic administration, the Moscow Auto Trust was folded into a new roof organization, known as *Vato* (short for All-Union Automobile and Tractor

FIGURE 3.1. Ford executives posing with Soviet delegates after signing the technical assistance agreement between the Ford Motor Company and *Vesenkha*, May 31, 1929. Left of center, Charles Sorensen is seen linking arms with Valerii Mezhlauk. To Mezhlauk's left is Saul Bron, president of Amtorg. To Bron's left is Henry Ford. Photo: The Henry Ford.

Association). *Vato*, whose first chairman was Osinskii, oversaw the creation of several industrial "giants," such as the new tractor plants in Stalingrad, Cheliabinsk, and Khar'kov. Also under *Vato*'s jurisdiction were a new car factory in Yaroslavl, a ball-bearing factory (*Gospodshipnikstroi*), and a small automotive research institute (NAMI). The project that consistently garnered the greatest attention and the largest outlays, however, was the "Auto Giant" in Nizhnii Novgorod, an adaptation of Rouge technology.[42]

The Ford Agreement: Contexts

The perspective of development-oriented technology transfer allows us to place the 1929 Ford agreement in several larger contexts. First, the agreement formed part of a major shift in the overall Soviet strategy of engaging Western firms. As the Five-Year Plan unfolded, the so-called concessions to Western firms that had characterized NEP made way for comprehensive technical assistance agreements. With this switch, the Soviet state repudiated a strategy of hosting foreign direct investment in favor of pure technology transfers.

NEP concessions had bound foreign firms into agreements with considerable strings attached. Though details varied, most concessions granted foreign firms extraction rights (in sectors such as oil, asbestos, manganese, and gold) in return for royalties, minimum investment requirements, production targets, and export quotas. Concessions had clear advantages for the Soviet side: they brought in hard currency and helped develop critical export sectors—a process Trotsky called "the financing of our economy by the resources of world capitalist savings."[43] In practice, however, concessions were rife with conflicts between the investors, who chafed under the strict terms, and the Soviet side, which found that against expectations concessions had few sustained technological spillovers.[44]

Whole-scale industrialization required methods of appropriating Western technology that concessions could not furnish. In fact, as the compromises of NEP came under attack, it was the radicals and maximalists who most vocally championed direct imports of American technology. As Sergo Ordzhonikidze, who would head the mighty People's Commissariat of Heavy Industry in the Thirties, put it in 1928:

> If indeed we hope to catch up with and surpass American industry, we must absorb those technical achievements which exist in America. . . . How can this be done? We must invite foreign technical personnel, conclude technical aid agreements with them, and even more so, and first of all, send hundreds and thousands of our young engineers there, to learn how and what to do.[45]

Ordzhonikidze thus summed up the approach that came to dominate the Five-Year Plan: wholesale technology imports and personnel exchanges with Western firms. Concessions were officially terminated in 1930. That the shift toward technical assistance agreements was a fundamental part of the radicalization of development during the First Five-Year Plan can be gauged by their cost. Concessions *brought in hard currency*; the technical assistance agreements exemplified by the Ford deal, in contrast, *cost hard currency*, and in substantial amounts. For example, the lease of the Lena gold fields to a British mining consortium, perhaps the most significant of NEP concessions, brought in $17.5 million in investment between 1925 and 1929. The Ford contract, by comparison, was slated for expenditures of $30 million. The technical assistance agreements illustrate the sacrifices that the Soviet Union, a cash-strapped primary goods exporter, was willing to impose on its population in the pursuit of radical industrial transformation.[46]

It is telling in this respect that Ford's 1928 proposals to the Moscow Auto Trust, which projected a joint venture with significant capital investment on Ford's part, was rejected in favor of technical assistance in 1929. As Osinskii explained, the decision gave the Soviet side greater control over the process of technology transfer. The agreement with Ford combined the advantages of American assistance with complete "freedom of action." On the one hand, it allowed the Soviet Union "to take the matter of automobile construction into our own hands," while, on the other hand, it secured "continuous contact with American technology on the highest levels of development."[47] Osinskii also clarified why the Soviets chose the Ford Motor Company over its competitors. Unlike Ford, "Morgan's automotive trust" (referring to General Motors) was "only interested in selling us parts but not in developing automotive mass production in our country."[48]

Second, the Ford project occupied a central place in the larger landscape of Soviet industrialization. Measured by the scale of investment, foreign exchange outlays, and the significance attached to it by the political leadership, the Auto Giant ranked alongside the other megaprojects of the Five-Year Plan, such as the Dnepr dam, the steel and coal combines in Kuznetsk and Magnitogorsk, and the Stalingrad and Cheliabinsk tractor factories.[49] According to numbers compiled by the People's Commissariat of Foreign Trade in the mid-1930s, the expenditure on imports of equipment for the Auto Giant totaled 42.3 million rubles. That compared to 44 million for Magnitogorsk, 35 million for the Stalingrad factory, and 31 million for *Dneprstroi*.[50]

Finally, understanding the paradigmatic significance of the Ford contract requires some attention to the fine print. The agreement consisted of four substantial parts. First, Ford granted *Vesenkha* the right to manufacture and sell the Ford Model A passenger car and the Model AA truck in the Soviet Union. Second, Ford agreed to furnish *Vesenkha* with all proprietary technology—blueprints, patents, specifications—associated with the design and production of the Ford vehicles. Third, Ford agreed to offer consultation and technical assistance in the drafting, construction, and tooling of a mass production factory with an annual capacity of 100,000 vehicles. Finally, Ford agreed to open the Rouge to Soviet engineers and send Ford specialists to Russia. In return, the treaty obligated *Vesenkha* to import 72,000 knocked-down Model As over a period of four years at "the lowest net export prices." For consulting and proprietary knowledge *Vesenkha* paid at cost: the Soviet organs were responsible for expenses but exempted from royalties. The contract was slated for a period of nine years, during which, it was agreed, remarkably, that the Ford Motor Company would keep the Soviet side apprised of any and all technical innovations.[51]

On the one hand, these provisions reflected a standard template: all techni-cal assistance agreements of the First Five-Year Plan featured a combination of blueprints, patents, consulting, and personnel exchange. Most such agree-ments stretched over several years and included clauses that promised to keep the Soviet side up to date on technological developments during that period. By agreeing to such clauses, the Ford Motor Company followed many other Western firms in expecting that technical assistance would strengthen future trade relations.[52]

Other elements, however, were specific to this deal, and they laid the groundwork for a cooperation that would prove exceedingly favorable for the Soviet side. To be sure, Ford was cagey about credit and insisted that payment for machinery and automobiles was due in cash at the point of receipt. This disadvantage, however, was more than compensated by the fact that, unlike other Western firms, Ford did not charge royalties. The contract tied technol-ogy transfer to an export guarantee of Ford cars; this was the "price" that the Ford Motor Company charged for granting the Soviet side continuous access to its proprietary technology. Ultimately, the Soviet Union would honor only half of the agreed-upon imports. The nascent Soviet automobile industry, then, took ample advantage of the Ford Motor Company's open-source stance toward technological diffusion.[53]

Over the next six years, the Ford connection largely delivered what Osinskii had hoped for—"continuous contact with American technology on the high-est levels of development." In Charles Sorensen, in particular, the Soviets found a consistent champion of their goals, who saw to it that the members of successive Soviet delegations walked through open doors at the Rouge. Natu-rally, they had access to production, tooling, design, construction, and power generation; but they also got to observe the logistics and clerking departments—traffic, disbursement, purchasing, accounting, and auditing. Each department designated a contact liaison to the Soviet engineers.[54] Be-yond the terms of the contract, Ford even agreed to set aside Rouge toolmak-ers for customizing jigs, dies, and special machinery for *Avtostroi*, the Soviet agency responsible for the future Gaz.[55] "These Russians are great people," Sorensen wrote to the manager of Ford's English branch, exhorting him to grant Soviet engineers access to European subsidiaries. "Help them as much as you can."[56] The Ford Motor Company made use of its favorable terms to purchase machinery on *Avtostroi*'s behalf; indeed, Sorensen ensured that Ford's suppliers accepted Soviet visitors to their firms.[57] "I would say," So-rensen summarized in retrospect, "that they had full access to everything we were doing."[58]

The Soviets agreed. Dybets felt that Ford's staffers were instructed "to open up to us everything they have and teach us everything they know."[59] The

Soviets certainly appreciated the openness. In 1930, at the height of the technical assistance boom, *Vato* judged the Ford technical contract the "only one"
that was fully satisfactory; in contrast to others, it represented "the most solid
connection with American industrial technology."[60] In 1932, leading engineers
returning from Detroit gave a decidedly favorable evaluation of the Ford connection, calling it "a model" of successful technical cooperation. Ford had
opened his own factories and those of his suppliers to inspection and made
available the company's entire technical archive.[61] In 1934, Dybets's successor,
an engineer named Lomanov, reported to Moscow that Ford's factories remained "the most accessible for us" and continued to provide a "unique central
base" for acquiring know-how and blueprints. The unrestricted access granted
by Ford was "impossible to find in the factories of other companies," who instead hurried the Soviet commissions through their plants and provided little
technical support.[62] In the "technical dragnet" that the Soviet Union threw over
Western technology during the years of industrialization, the Ford connection
was a fat catch.[63]

The Dybets Commission in Detroit

Copying, borrowing, begging, and stealing foreign technology—the signature
activity of late developers—is not a simple matter of "ripping off." It is, in fact,
a proposition of considerable complexity. Just like innovation itself, technology transfer is a drawn-out process of adaptation and learning, fraught with
trial and error, dead ends, and misconceived fixes. It is both inherently inefficient and irreducibly creative. This is due to the complexity of technology itself. Much of technology is "tacit": it resides not only in the gadgets and machines but in knowing how to design, set up, use, connect, and improve them.
Transferring technology, then, involves three overlapping tasks, among which
purchasing machinery is only the first and most straightforward. More delicate
is the task of codifying the tacit elements. This requires drawing up observa-
tional reports, composing sketches and blueprints, drafting instructions, and
assembling endless lists of specifications and data. The third element is
people—consulting and hiring engineers and workers whose experience and
skill form indispensable repositories of technology.[64]

The nitty-gritty of technology transfer is where catch-up development hap-
pens in practice. The well-documented efforts of the Soviet engineers at the
Ford Motor Company offer a unique glimpse of how this process played out
in the context of wide technological disparities and a pressing timeline. A
daunting task confronted Stepan Dybets and his engineers when they moved
into the Rouge in the summer of 1929. Their assignment, as outlined by
Vesenkha, was "to study all technological processes, production organization,

and administration in Ford's factories." Dybets was instructed to deliver a comprehensive "design draft" for the new factory, which should answer these questions: What would be layout of the new plant, including auxiliary departments and workshops? How quickly could the Auto Giant be built? How many workers and engineers would be needed for tooling and operation? What machines and tools were required, and what was the timeline for buying and setting up the equipment? Finally, what was the volume of foreign exchange outlays, and how could the price tag be minimized? Moscow gave Dybets full discretion and full responsibility and asked him to kindly furnish all answers within four months.[65]

Dybets's commission adopted an Americanized name for *Avtostroi*, its sister agency in Nizhnii, and called itself "Autostroy." It used a Dearborn address, "c/o Ford Motor Co." (see figure 3.2).[66] Autostroy set up shop on the third floor of the Ford Motor Company's engineering laboratory. From there, Dybets and three assistants directed a group of Soviet skilled workers and engineers who procured "badges and tool checks" and spread out to the different departments of the Rouge. They took in everything from foundry to machine shop to tools and assembly; they looked over the shoulders of Ford's purchasing staffers and technical draftsmen.[67] Dybets told his staff to work "14–16 hours a day."[68]

On many issues, Dybets's group had to improvise. Mandated to economize on foreign exchange, Dybets and his team had to substitute Ford's first-rate machine tools for "less complex and expensive" ones. The matter was complicated by the fact that Ford was changing key specifications of the Model A at the beginning of 1930, and that Ford's calculations for capital depletion did not necessarily apply to Soviet conditions. Further difficulties arose from the fact that Ford received 25 to 30 percent of its parts from outside suppliers, all of which had to be registered and contacted. Meanwhile, *Vesenkha* changed its mind repeatedly about the target size of the new plant—numbers were revised from an annual capacity of 100,000 vehicles to 300,000 and even 500,000 a few weeks later, before finally being settled at 132,000. These constant changes "plagued not only Ford's employees but also our commission," and that was "reflected in our rapport with Ford."[69] Moscow's administrative turf wars contributed to the confusion. For the brick-and-mortar work necessary to construct the new plant in Russia, Dybets wanted to hire the Detroit architect Albert Kahn, as Ford's people recommended; *Vesenkha*, however, contracted with another company, the Cleveland construction firm Austin. Dybets doubted Austin's competency, writing to Moscow that Austin was "not the best construction firm in the USA," and "did not have the experience nor personnel appropriately qualified to complete this work"—an impression "confirmed by Ford and Chevrolet." Despite these objections, Dybets was told to go ahead and work with Austin. The relationship remained tense as construction proceeded at Nizhnii over the next two years.[70]

Despite all obstacles, Dybets was able to relay to Moscow the design draft on January 1, 1930. "After the commission had made itself familiar with the production in Ford's plants, and after consulting with engineers and workers of Ford's company," Dybets wrote home, "we determined the structure of the auto factory to consist of the following departments: steel foundry, press works, mechanical and assembly shops, tool and die shop, body shop, laboratory, heat treatment and a school." Dybets projected the force of construction workers at 12,650 (a number that soon proved too small). He included a detailed list of men to be hired from Ford.

With the layout plans finalized, the actual task of technology transfer began. The first step concerned the intangibles. Over the course of 1930, Dybets and his engineers took on the laborious task of relaying to Nizhnii the specifications of thousands of machine tools, descriptions of myriad production operations, and countless Rouge blueprints. Dybets's engineers created a complete inventory of all machinery in Ford's shops. Where Ford could not provide blueprints, Autostroy's technicians composed their own. Extensive illustrated reports of work processes and production setups formed the heart of the technology transfer. A typical example was the eighty-page typewritten report by engineer A. E. Sankov on the tool and die shop at the Rouge, replete with technical details, tables of specifications, and hand-drawn sketches. Another report meticulously documented the forty-nine consecutive operations necessary to produce a Model A cylinder block. Nizhnii received equally detailed reports on cold steel pressing, paint work, forging and foundry work, and so on.[71] Dybets summarized the work of the commission in these terms:

> We based the entire technical process on the methods of Ford's plants. Where some production method was not in use at Ford, we used the technical methods of his suppliers. We adopted production norms and selected machinery after reviewing the practice at Ford's plants in Dearborn and in Windsor [Canada]. We introduced a number of changes in the process, mainly in connection with the fact that the production program of *Avtostroi* consisted of 132 thousand vehicles against the 3–5 million vehicles put out by Ford's factory in Dearborn. Under these conditions our planners confronted an extremely difficult task—to preserve the principles of flow production and Ford's fundamental methods while adapting individual operations.[72]

Successive groups of Autostroy engineers made use of the clause of the 1929 agreement that allowed them to keep abreast of technological changes at the Rouge. In 1933, Dybets's successor, Lomanov, reported that Ford had "moved

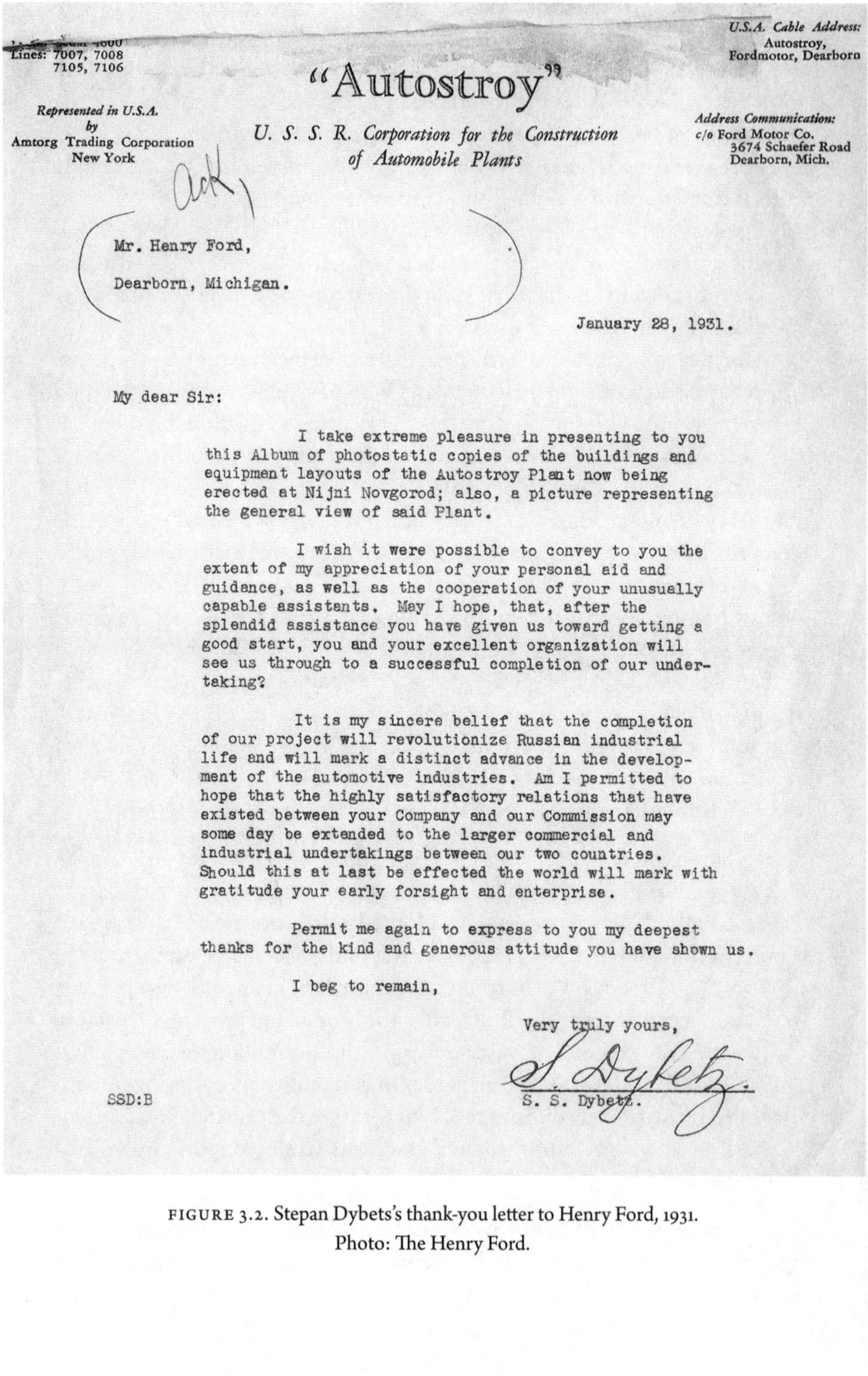

[illegible] 4600
Lines: 7007, 7008
7105, 7106

"Autostroy"

U. S. S. R. Corporation for the Construction of Automobile Plants

Represented in U.S.A. by
Amtorg Trading Corporation
New York

U.S.A. Cable Address:
Autostroy,
Fordmotor, Dearborn

Address Communication:
c/o Ford Motor Co.
3674 Schaefer Road
Dearborn, Mich.

ack,

Mr. Henry Ford,

Dearborn, Michigan.

January 28, 1931.

My dear Sir:

I take extreme pleasure in presenting to you this Album of photostatic copies of the buildings and equipment layouts of the Autostroy Plant now being erected at Nijni Novgorod; also, a picture representing the general view of said Plant.

I wish it were possible to convey to you the extent of my appreciation of your personal aid and guidance, as well as the cooperation of your unusually capable assistants. May I hope, that, after the splendid assistance you have given us toward getting a good start, you and your excellent organization will see us through to a successful completion of our undertaking?

It is my sincere belief that the completion of our project will revolutionize Russian industrial life and will mark a distinct advance in the development of the automotive industries. Am I permitted to hope that the highly satisfactory relations that have existed between your Company and our Commission may some day be extended to the larger commercial and industrial undertakings between our two countries. Should this at last be effected the world will mark with gratitude your early forsight and enterprise.

Permit me again to express to you my deepest thanks for the kind and generous attitude you have shown us.

I beg to remain,

Very truly yours,

S. Dybetz.

S. S. Dybetz.

SSD:B

FIGURE 3.2. Stepan Dybets's thank-you letter to Henry Ford, 1931. Photo: The Henry Ford.

FIGURE 3.3. Architectural model of Gaz, 1931. Photo: The Henry Ford.

forward significantly in comparison with the work methods fixed by us three years ago." This prompted a revised survey of Rouge operations—250 pages plus blueprints, layouts, and operation descriptions—updating Nizhnii on the recent technological innovations. The report covered new cost schedules, model changes, transformations in the shop layouts, and exciting new machining developments.[73]

The second step in the transfer of technology concerned the hardware. Having finalized the inventory of the new plant, *Avtostroi* began to splurge on machine tools. Outlays were enormous: by May 1931, *Vesenkha* had granted *Avtostroi* 40 million convertible rubles (roughly $20 million) for equipping the Nizhnii factory with 4,650 units of machinery from abroad. Of this sum, two-thirds went toward American orders and the remainder toward orders from Europe. In Europe, the Soviets acquired standard machine tools, while orders for specialized tools went exclusively to the US.[74] The significance of American machinery was decisive since Soviet factories could not provide machinery of similar quality. Only one-third of total outlays was slated for machinery orders within the Soviet Union.[75]

The bulk of orders was placed in 1931. The Ford Motor Company provided around $4 million of machinery, with the remainder of orders going to a large number of smaller machine suppliers of the American automobile industry.[76] A good number of these machines were routed through the Ford tool shop, which submitted them to performance tests before relaying them to the Soviet side.[77] In all of this, Autostroy proved a pesky and exacting customer, taking advantage of the fact that Soviet orders brought considerable relief to American machine builders buffeted by the Depression. As the Soviet side instructed suppliers, drafts of special tools had first to be approved by Autostroy, "and you will not begin to manufacture these items until finally approved drawings are returned to you." Autostroy asked that each machine be subject to a performance test, and that "one correctly machined sample from the performance test must be included with the shipment of the machine." Autostroy demanded that the tests be carried out in the presence of one of their inspectors, who had a reputation for being finnicky. As a Rouge toolmaker complained, the Soviet inspectors insisted on an absurd degree of machining precision that exceeded even Ford's standard tolerances. Over the quality of workmanship and machinery design, in fact, Autostroy dared to pick a fight, in which Ford ultimately relented by lowering the total sum of charges.[78]

Exchanging Personnel

But not only machines traveled across the Atlantic. The third step in the transfer of technology was a two-way exchange of people: Midwestern workers and engineers who traveled to Russia, and Soviet trainees who traveled to Detroit. While the machines took the route from New York City to the Black Sea ports, technicians and engineers more commonly boarded the ships crossing to German and Scandinavian ports, and from there the trains that connected to Moscow. During the early Thirties, the traffic was considerable (see tables 3.1 and 3.2).

The May 1929 agreement stipulated that Ford would provide "experienced and competent technical personnel" to Nizhnii. In practice, however, such official consultancy remained limited. Ford sent the technician Frank Bennett to Russia in December 1929. Over the next year, while the Auto Giant was under construction, Bennett helped Soviet workers set up two practice assembly lines for knocked-down Model As—one in Moscow and one in a shop in downtown Nizhnii.[79] As the Giant heaved into production, *Avtostroi* requested seventeen "first-class all-around men" for various positions in the machine and tool shops. The Ford Motor Company compiled a list of qualified volunteers, who spent six months in Nizhnii in 1932. They remained on the payroll of the Ford Motor Company, which billed the wages to the Soviets.[80]

In Nizhnii, this group joined a larger contingent of foreign workers who had signed up with Soviet recruitment agencies on their own accord, fleeing Depression-era America. Among them, for example, was Harry M. Reynolds, who lost his job at Ford in early 1932 after more than twenty years with the company. According to the form "Application for Autostroy—at Dearborn,

TABLE 3.1. Foreign specialists requested by *Vato*, 1931

Enterprise	Engineers (paid in dollars)	Foremen (paid in dollars)	Skilled workers (paid in rubles)	Total
Avtostroi, Nizhnii	30	35	468	533
Kar'khov Tractor	20	60	300	380
Stalingrad Tractor	10	20	110	140
Gospodshipnikstroi (ball-bearing plant, Moscow)	28	18	25	71
AMO Moscow	17	37	10	64
Cheliabinsk Tractor	6	1		7
NAMI	4			4
Other	18			18
TOTAL	133	171	913	1,217

Source: RGAE archives, f.7620, o.1, d.760, l.49.
Note: These numbers reflect requests by *Vato* to *Vesenkha*, not actual invitations extended.

TABLE 3.2. Foreign specialists in Soviet heavy industry, 1929–1935

As of January 1	Engineers and technicians	Workers	Total
1929	400		400
1930	600	512	1,112
1931	1,631	1,267	2,898
1932	2,050	4,008	6,058
1933	2,429	4,131	6,560
1934	2,031	3,118	5,149
1935	1,635	3,175	4,810

Source: Khromov, *Industrializatsiia*, 2: 263–77.

Michigan," Reynolds was married with two kids, and requested 600 rubles plus $50 per month.[81] A census drawn up by factory authorities in Nizhnii in late 1932 listed 181 foreign engineers and skilled workers in the new plant. Around half were "emigrants of the old Russia" who had lived and worked in the United States. Another contingent was made up of Germans, some of them arriving from America. The rest were "ethnic Americans," Austrians, and Hungarians. The highly skilled foreigners in Nizhnii were by no means just Communist fellow travelers. Rather, working for the Soviets was well-paid: most of the foreigners worked on a one-year contract and earned around 400 rubles plus $200 per month. The highest earner among the Americans was the engineer Herbert Ludwig, a specialist in body work, who made 1,200 rubles plus

$500 per month. (In comparison, the average wage of a Russian worker was 178 rubles.)[82]

A few among the American workers moving between the Midwest and Russia attained publicity. The brothers Victor and Walter Reuther, future union leaders, spent two years as toolmakers at Gaz in the mid-Thirties. Later disclaimers notwithstanding, they retained cherished memories of the experience.[83] The Reuther brothers left the Soviet Union before the political purges of the late Thirties, but many of their fellow migrants were not so lucky. Robert Robinson, the African American toolmaker who had left Ford for Russia amid some publicity, was arrested in 1937 and did not return to the United States before 1976.[84] The Italian-American Communist Joseph Sgovio, and Victor Herman, the Jewish Ukrainian-American Detroiter who set a world skydiving record above Moscow in 1933, were Gaz workers who survived the horrors of the Gulag.[85]

From the perspective of technology transfer, how effective was the work of foreign engineers and workers? The Soviet authorities certainly attached great significance to them. *Vato* instructed its departments to match foreign specialists with "young Soviet engineers, who, if possible, know foreign languages." Together these teams should "train our worker youth in practical questions."[86] At Nizhnii, a group of Russian workers would be assigned to work with a foreign foreman or specialist, a practice called *patronage*. Official reports claimed that patronage was successful. For example, line foreman Kosobutskii, a returnee from America, had thirty-three Russian workers operating fifty machine tools under his supervision. Kosobutskii's brigade reportedly overfulfilled the control figures by 197 percent in February 1932 and by 154 percent in March. Foreman Walter, skilled with milling machines but not proficient in Russian, was named a shock worker for the success of his brigade. Foreman Grondon, a former Ford worker and union organizer, instructed twenty-six Russian workers at the heat press.[87] Frank Bennett, the Ford production manager who helped set up the practice assembly shop in Nizhnii, witnessed a gradual process of learning by doing. When he arrived, he observed that the problem for the workers was "handling tools. The people did not know how to use them." However, "they eventually grew into it so that we were turning trucks and cars off the same line"—a scheduling challenge that the workforce was apparently able to meet. After a period of trial operations, the assembly shop found a rhythm. "They were pretty well moving when I left," Bennett recalled. "They could get along by themselves."[88]

Just as often, however, the authorities' expectations were frustrated. Both the recollections of Western engineers and the official documentation suggest as much. The foreign specialists struggled to break through their cultural isolation. Many rank-and-file workers regarded them with the same suspicions they harbored toward the "bourgeois" specialists.[89] An American engineer recalled being told by workers, "We ourselves made the revolution, and we ourselves will put industry in shape."[90] Vice versa, the Americans often were appalled by what they regarded as a lack of education and discipline among the workforce. As one of the Ford employees present in Nizhnii in 1932 wrote, "Teaching the men here is very difficult as they are very green (fresh off the farm)." He added, "You get very little cooperation from the foremen."[91] Another described the workforce as "ignorant peasants who have never seen a tool beyond a hammer and a saw and who take no interest in their work anyway."[92] In this context, *Vato* had to concede, "A systematic work to adopt and assimilate the knowledge and experience of the foreigners is not being conducted." It often remained unclear which factory department was responsible for the foreign specialists, so it was up to the foreigners' own initiative to work for the often considerable salaries they earned. Precious foreign exchange was thus wasted.[93] Such problems, which continually irked the higher organs, are evident from this decree of January 1931, signed by Osinskii:

> The board of *Vato* makes it the responsibility of all workers in the *Vato* system to exercise an especially attentive attitude towards the utilization of foreign technical assistance and the foreign specialists. The Soviet state expends great means on foreign technical assistance in order to accelerate the transfer of the experience of leading technology into socialist industry. All kinds of "theories" and talk that "Americans are good in America," or "we can manage by ourselves" and so on, is economically and politically harmful. All actions that interfere with us making use of foreign technology must be decisively stopped.[94]

From the perspective of technology transfer, then, the impact of foreign engineers and workers on Soviet industrialization may well have been limited. In contrast, the Soviet authorities found that sending delegations to work and study in Western firms—a practice known as *komandirovka*—proved highly useful (for numbers, see table 3.3). As the People's Commissariat of Heavy Industry (NKTP) concluded, the *komandirovka* was the "most effective" way to take advantage of the technical expertise of Western firms. Learning and working on the shop floors and in the research laboratories of Western firms allowed Soviet engineers to absorb technological lessons "more quickly and comprehensively" than they could from the Western specialists in Soviet factories. What was more, being present in Western firms gave Soviet engineers exposure to methods "which foreign firms purposely conceal from us."[95]

It is, then, no surprise that consecutive Soviet delegations made full use of the Ford Motor Company's open door. The presence of Soviet students, workers, and engineers at the Rouge was a common sight in the Thirties. By 1933,

TABLE 3.3. *Vesenkha*/NKTP personnel dispatched abroad, 1930–1933

	To Europe	To USA	Engineers	Workers	Planning personnel	Total
1930	752	638	923	344	123	1,390
1931	327	158	235	195	55	485
1932	291	21	215	74	23	312
1933 (Jan–Nov)	282	103	272	93	20	385

Source: Khromov, *Industrializatsiia*, 2: 262.

280 Soviet engineers and workers had completed *komandirovki* at the Ford Motor Company.[96] Asked by *Vato* to evaluate their Rouge sojourns, Soviet students uniformly lauded their experience. They reported that Ford's technicians were friendly and forthcoming, cooperation was smooth, and no secrets were being withheld. Management was "obliging when we requested an explanation," and fellow workers provided "the highest form of collaboration" and "gave all of their experience."[97]

Some *komandirovki* consisted of rank-and-file workers. For example, in May 1931 Nizhnii sent fifteen workers to the Ford Motor Company "to study the construction of automobiles, according to the treaty on technical assistance." Their sojourn was set for six months. All of them were considered politically reliable, most of them were listed as "metal-workers." They differed mostly in age. Ivan Rykov, electrician, was born in 1888; Antonii Privalov, metalworker, was born in 1901; German Piskarev, metalworker, was born in 1910.[98]

The first Soviet automobile designers—a cohort famed after World War II for their cars and tanks—also went through the Ford "school." Andrei Lipgart, for example, was part of Dybets's group of engineers in 1930. Lipgart designed the first Soviet passenger car in 1935 (the M-1) and remained chief design engineer at Gaz until 1951. Several heavy trucks and tank improvements are credited to Lipgart, as well as the famous postwar Gaz *Pobeda*.[99] One of Lipgart's closest collaborators was A. M. Kriger. Born in 1910 and educated during the cultural revolution, Kriger was an exemplary "promotee"—a beneficiary of Stalin's social revolution. He graduated in 1932 and began at the newly finished Gaz as an automotive designer. In December of 1933, Gaz glowingly recommended Kriger for a six-month sojourn in Detroit. Kriger had "shown himself to be a knowledgeable and energetic worker with initiative" who had "delivered in comparatively short time a number of constructions" that had improved Gaz's models. In 1935, in preparation for the M-1, Kriger was again sent to the United States. By 1942, he was deputy chief of construction and design at Gaz. In this capacity, he supervised the development of the Gaz-51 truck, which became a Soviet export best seller well into the 1970s. For the Gaz-51,

Kriger received the Stalin prize in 1947. Kriger later was head of construction and design at the auto factory in Moscow—the former AMO—for nearly thirty years, 1954–1982. He died in 1984.[100]

Most important from the perspective of mass production, however, was the fact that leading Gaz shop engineers spent time in Detroit. These engineers formed the factory's skilled core in the late Thirties and during World War II. Unlike Dybets and Osinskii, who had orchestrated the technology transfers of the First Five-Year Plan, members of this group were spared by the purges. Engineers like Paryshev, *nachalnik* (superintendent) of the Gaz body shop, or Troitskii, *nachalnik* on the final assembly line, had worked at the Rouge and retained technical leadership positions at Gaz throughout World War II.[101]

Technology Transfers and Foreign Exchange

The global Great Depression affected the Soviet Union's foreign trade just as it did all primary goods exporters: it induced a catastrophic fall in the terms of trade.[102] With grain prices on the world market in free fall, Soviet exports brought in less and less hard currency to pay for imports.[103] The global economic crisis therefore sliced the First Five-Year Plan in two halves: a remarkable boom in Soviet foreign trade was followed by an equally sharp bust. The "optimal" version of the First Five-Year Plan, adopted in April 1929, had confidently projected a continual expansion of Soviet exports—and hence a growing capacity to import—well into the next decade. And, indeed, between 1928 and 1931, Soviet imports and exports expanded rapidly, defying the contraction in global trade. In 1932, however, both imports and exports declined sharply, and by 1934, they had returned to levels that obtained prior to the First Five-Year Plan.[104] The turnaround was largely a result of a gaping hole that opened up in the Soviet balance of payments in 1931. That year several developments conspired with the declining terms of trade to force a radical curtailing of Soviet imports. A poor harvest made grain procurement increasingly difficult and violent. Soviet exports met greater resistance as developed countries mounted trade barriers and campaigned against Soviet export dumping. In the summer of 1931, as financial crisis ripped through the West, interest rates on commercial loans rose steeply.[105]

As a major component on the debit side of the balance of payments, technical assistance mirrored the boom and bust in foreign trade.[106] From 1921 to 1933, the Soviet Union authorized 170 technical assistance agreements; of those, 117 alone were concluded between 1929 and 1931. By the end of 1933, however, only 40 such contracts remained active; by 1938, 8 remained.[107] Similarly, the bulk of Western machinery orders was dispatched in 1929–1932; by 1933, the number of orders had fallen below pre-Plan levels.[108] The 1931 foreign exchange crisis forced the Soviets to sharply curtail imports of machinery and to revise or phase out the connections to Western firms. In late 1933, the economic organs decreed "maximal substitution" of imported equipment with Soviet machinery; in the automobile and tractor factories—Stalingrad, Cheliabinsk, and Gaz—the importing of machines was henceforth restricted to "singular cases."[109] By the dawn of the Second Five-Year Plan (1933–1937), wholesale imports of technology gave way to targeted acquisitions of high-quality machinery and industrial espionage. Foreign exchange outlays now went increasingly toward defense-related technological inputs, in particular in the aviation industry. Meanwhile, the Soviet Union began exporting its own technical assistance in order to raise hard currency. For example, the Soviets sponsored a venture called *Turkstroi* that helped get a textile combine off the ground in Turkey in 1933.[110] Supervising the construction of grain elevators in Iran was slated to bring in 4 million gold rubles in 1935.[111]

As we have seen, foreign hard currency delineated the most visible constraint on Soviet industrialization; little surprise that Stalin equated foreign exchange reserves with "the interests of the state."[112] In the summer of 1931, the dual problem of insufficient grain procurements and a dwindling reserve of foreign exchange was the single most vexing issue on the Politburo's agenda and the cause of sharp conflicts among the Soviet leadership.[113] The problem became so severe that Stalin decided to abruptly terminate imports from the USA. "In view of the hard-currency problems and the unacceptable credit terms in America," he instructed the Politburo, "I am opposed to placing any new orders whatsoever in America." Stalin also asked that existing contracts be wound down and orders, wherever possible, transferred to Europe.[114]

The turnaround regarding imports from the USA not only caused Sergo Ordzhonikidze to throw a tantrum in front of the Politburo.[115] It also embarrassed his subordinates in the *Vesenkha* system, especially those among the maximalist faction who had consistently advocated the adoption of American technology. Nevertheless, Stalin's decision was immediately transmitted down the hierarchy. "In connection with the decision to transfer orders for machinery placed in the USA to Europe," Dybets wrote to the board of *Vato* in September of 1931, "it is necessary to quickly command abroad three *Avtostroi* engineers." The group was charged with "replacing American equipment with European . . . under partial reworking of the technical specifications." The changes considerably delayed equipment deliveries to the construction site in Nizhnii.[116]

Though the Ford connection remained a priority for the Soviet side, it did not escape the readjustment of relationships with Western firms. In November 1934, Autostroy tersely informed the Ford Motor Company that it considered the 1929 agreement canceled. Ford's staffers concluded that the reason was Autostroy's evident underfulfillment of the terms: only slightly more than half of the 72,000 knocked-down Model As stipulated in the agreement had been purchased by the Soviet side; of an anticipated volume of $33.6 million, $17 million had been paid.[117] Remarkably, Ford's staffers shrugged off this shortfall and offered a successor agreement, which was signed in March 1935.[118] The company would continue to host Soviet engineers; in return, the Soviet side agreed to refrain from exporting homemade Fords and committed to purchasing parts and replacements exclusively in Dearborn. Relations cooled somewhat: Sorensen asked the Soviet engineers "to move out of the Rouge office," and as a purchaser of parts and machinery, Autostroy would henceforth be "treated as any outside customer."[119]

At the same time, however, the Ford Motor Company remained hospitable to Soviet junkets. In late 1935, as Gaz prepared to develop the first home-designed passenger car, director Sergei D'iakonov traveled to Detroit and convinced Sorensen to release Model B blueprints.[120] Sorensen also shared photographs of Ford's landmark V8 engine.[121] In 1936, Sorensen saw to it that the Ford Purchasing Department would be "phoning Ford suppliers and arranging for Autostroy representatives to go through their plants."[122] Later that year, when other American steel plants turned away a Soviet delegation, the Ford Motor Company agreed to have the group spend two weeks at the Rouge steel mill.[123] As late as 1937, Sorensen welcomed a group of thirty-five Soviet engineers at the Rouge and arranged for them to visit some of Ford's machine tool suppliers.[124]

The Ford Motor Company also welcomed high-profile visitors from the Soviet apparat. In March 1936, Sorensen's office agreed to show "Mme Molotov" through the Rouge, who was in the United States at the head of a commercial delegation.[125] Later that year the People's Commissar of Foreign Trade, Anastas Mikoyan, stopped by. Mikoyan lunched at the Dearborn Laboratory with Henry and Edsel Ford. Mikoyan freely acknowledged how much Soviet technology owed to American firms.[126] Sorensen recalled that contacts with the Soviet Union continued "right up until World War II started in 1941." He was sorry, however, to lose touch with Valerii Mezhlauk, with whom he had negotiated the 1929 contract. "I never heard from Mezhlauk again. I am at a loss to understand why."[127] Like Dybets, D'iakonov, and Osinskii, Mezhlauk fell victim to Stalin's purges. He was executed on July 29, 1938, in Moscow.[128]

The Auto Giant at Work

Sergei Sergeevich D'iakonov was appointed general manager of the new factory in Nizhnii Novgorod in July 1932. Born near Moscow, D'iakonov had been a party member since 1918 and held an engineering diploma from the Leningrad Polytechnical Institute. At age thirty-three, D'iakonov was a few years too

TABLE 3.4. Gaz share of Soviet automobile production, 1932–1940

Year	Total Soviet production	Gaz production	Percentage of total
1932	24,000	7,500	31.25
1933	49,000	26,600	54.29
1934	72,000	49,300	68.47
1935	97,000	63,600	65.57
1936	136,000	86,300	63.46
1937	200,000	135,700	67.85
1938	211,000	145,600	69.00
1939	202,000	N/A	N/A
1940	146,000	87,100	59.66

Source: TsANO archives, f. 2435, o.2, d.8.

old to be one of Stalin's promotees; rather, he was of the youngest generation to be swept up in the purges of 1937–1938. But that lay in the future. At the time of his arrival in Nizhnii, D'iakonov was at the apex of his career; before that, he had served in engineering positions in Moscow and had been Osinskii's deputy chairman on the board of *Vato*. D'iakonov replaced Stepan Dybets, whose stint at the helm of the Nizhnii factory had lasted only six months (January to June, 1932). Dybets moved to Moscow and occupied various posts in Ordzhonikidze's People's Commissariat of Heavy Industry before assuming the chairmanship of *Gutap* (the Head Administration of the Auto-Tractor Industry, *Vato*'s successor organization) in 1934. Within the hierarchy of the Soviet command economy, Dybets was now D'iakonov's boss, while the former head of the standing commission at Ford in turn reported directly to Ordzhonikidze.

Under D'iakonov's leadership, the Auto Giant grew into the linchpin of the Soviet motor vehicle industry. In 1933, the new factory complex took on the name Gaz (*Gor'kovskii Avtomobil'nyi Zavod*) after Nizhnii Novgorod was named for Maxim Gorky, the city's famous scion. Accounting for roughly two-thirds of total Soviet vehicle output after 1934, Gaz was at the center of the remarkable boom of the new Soviet automobile industry (see table 3.4). During the Second Five-Year Plan, Gaz made steady progress. The factory complex underwent two major phases of expansion, in 1935 and 1938. In 1935, D'iakonov announced the factory's "liberation from import dependence, in particular, from Ford's technical assistance."[129] In 1936, Gaz discontinued the Ford Model A and presented the first Soviet-designed small car, the Molotov-1.[130]

But severe problems continued to plague the Soviet River Rouge. These problems were not restricted to Gaz. Reflecting the difficulties of Soviet industry at large, Gaz struggled with a largely unskilled workforce, a chronic labor shortage and high turnover, severe problems of managerial coordination, and pervasive bottlenecks in the supply of parts and raw materials. In a factory built on flow production principles and equipped with assembly lines, these problems often proved debilitating. Complicating matters, the Soviet labor regime of the 1930s battened on mobilization strategies that militated against Fordism. Norm setting, piece rates, and Stakhanovism emphasized individual work performance and were difficult to reconcile with the principles of flow production. In an ironic turn of events, Fordism took root only very partially at Gaz during the Second Five-Year Plan. Only in World War II, faced with an acute shortage of skilled labor and operating under an increasingly repressive labor regime, did Gaz rediscover Fordism as a powerful tool of labor mobilization.

Amid ongoing delays in supply deliveries, an unabated housing shortage, and general disarray, the newly completed factory started up production in January 1932. The first Ford AA light truck made entirely of Soviet-produced parts rolled off the assembly line on January 29. By March, production was halted for several weeks for lack of supplies. (Ordzhonikidze blamed the breakdown on the presence of wreckers.) In the first six months of 1932, the giant factory turned out a meager 1,008 vehicles. Production picked up considerably during the last quarter of 1932, with an output of 3,721 AA light trucks. The first 34 Soviet-produced Model As were finished in December of 1932. But all in all, the Soviet River Rouge missed the planning targets for 1932 in spectacular fashion, producing only two-thirds of the requested number of trucks, and 5 percent of the requested number of Model As.

Apart from the fact that "many construction and assembly factors remained incomplete," the poor showing for that year was due to the many difficulties that the Soviet workers and engineers faced in operating their brand-new factory. As D'iakonov reported, in 1932 "familiarization with the technology" had "barely begun." The low skill level among workers was particularly vexing to management, since incorrect operation could damage Gaz's state-of-the-art Western machine tools. D'iakonov's 1932 workforce survey concluded with these "distressing results": 54 percent of workers hired at the factory were peasants; 63 percent were younger than twenty-five; labor turnover for the entire year was 133 percent. This meant that in order to arrive at a workforce of 22,475 by the end of 1932, factory management had hired close to 30,000 people. The reasons why workers failed to stay put, however, lay not only in the drudgery of the assembly shop. Rather, dismal living conditions at the factory, where housing and even food supply was insufficient, was a major reason for the instability. Labor turnover varied markedly among the skills ranks: almost half of the unskilled workers who arrived at the factory left within the year, while only one out of twenty highly skilled workers quit.[131]

FIGURE 3.4. Cab mounting on the assembly line at Gaz, 1933. Photo: ITAR-TASS/Alamy.

The problems continued into 1933. The annual survey for that year found that four out of five Gaz workers were younger than thirty years old. More than half had a peasant background, and almost one in five was illiterate or possessed only rudimentary reading skills.[132] As in other Soviet metalworking factories, typical Gaz workers were young women and men who had only recently left the villages where their families had lived for generations. They had no skills or education to speak of.

These predominant characteristics—young, unskilled, and from peasant families—distinguished the workforce at Gaz from that in factories that had existed before the First Five-Year Plan. In the older industries, workers experienced the decline in living standards and the erosion of labor autonomy during the First Plan as a catastrophic disruption of their working-class traditions. The workers of the textile industry, for example, organized a number of strikes in 1932 that caused considerable exasperation among the party leadership.[133] The workforce at Gaz, however, was entirely different in composition and outlook. The young peasant workers flooding into the Gaz shops in 1932 had no working-class tradition to defend. Uprooted by collectivization, many of them led peripatetic existences, drifting back and forth between the countryside and the shop floor, often abandoning one factory position for another in the hope of better conditions. The fundamental problem facing Soviet managers of labor in the 1930s was the mobilization of this unskilled workforce.

The declared goal, repeated like a mantra in the quarterly and annual reports, was twofold: to raise labor productivity and to lower production costs. Obviously, these goals were interrelated: higher labor productivity would tend to lower unit costs. In turn, however, lower unit costs did not solely stem from higher labor productivity, but depended on a whole host of factors, such as the cost of raw materials, supplies, and the depreciation of machinery and fixed capital. But management at Gaz had little control over supply costs, and decisions over capital stock were in the hands of the Commissariat of Heavy Industry. So D'iakonov and his staff had little choice but to focus on labor.

To counter turnover, raise skill levels among workers, and improve labor efficiency, management at Gaz followed three strategies. First, workers were encouraged to attend three-month technical training programs (so-called technical minimums) at factory schools. This education measure affected roughly one-third of the workforce during the Second Five-Year Plan. In 1935, for example, 10,500 Gaz workers completed the technical minimum, out of a workforce of 30,000.[134] Second, Gaz gradually adopted incentive payments (progressive piece rates and bonuses for overfulfilling work norms) in almost all factory departments—even in the assembly shops that did not easily lend themselves to these methods. Finally, Gaz, like every branch of Soviet industry, was swept up in the Stakhanovite movement.

Stakhanovism was born in a Donbass coal mine when Aleksei Stakhanov set a record for tons of coal mined in a single shift. Stakhanovism's most prominent emulator in the metalworking industries, however, was a machinist at Gaz. On September 10, 1935, Aleksandr Busygin, a graduate of the technical minimum, turned out 966 crankshafts in a shift that, according to the "American" norm, should yield 675. By the end of 1935, 2,000 workers at Gaz had reportedly overfulfilled their norms by more than 140 percent.[135]

On the one hand, Stakhanovism was a continuation of the populist strand of the Soviet rationalization movement. It pitted grassroots worker initiative

FIGURE 3.5. The Ford Model A–based lineup of Gaz vehicles on factory premises, 1935.
Photo: The Henry Ford.

FIGURE 3.6. Gaz spring shop and forge, 1935. Photo: The Henry Ford.

against technical experts and factory middle management. According to the
party committee of the Gorky region, the successes of the Busyginites at Gaz
"sharply disclosed the ills and shortcomings of the leadership apparatus of the
factory management," who failed to adjust work norms and supply schedules
to the demands of the record setters.[136] On the other hand, Stakhanovism was
quickly co-opted by the party leadership, who after some hesitation used the
movement to push through a comprehensive revision of industrial work
norms across the entirety of Soviet industry.[137] The automobile industry was

no exception. In February and March 1936, a branch conference of the auto-tractor industry convened Stakhanovites, factory management, *Gutap* leadership, and union and party members in Khar'kov, Ukraine, to assess the impact of Stakhanovism on productivity.

The conference revealed that Stakhanovism caused considerable disruption in factories based on flow production. While officiously lauding the "significance of Stakhanovism" for the auto-tractor industry, the conference report noted that "the development of the Stakhanovite movement led to a great splintering of norms." As a result, each factory now operated with "more than fifty thousand norms." Confusion surrounding the norms led to "frictions between workers and the norm-setting staff and the shop administrations, and led to superfluous revisions of norms and waste of work time." True, the report submitted, "everywhere the army of Stakhanovites reache[d] new heights of socialist technique." Nevertheless, one could not "ignore the fact that a significant number of workers did not fulfill the norms." The main reasons lay in "the significant number of inner-factory defects," such as "the low skill level of newly hired workers and the poor participation of the engineering and technical staff in helping the workers master the new norms."[138] Regardless of the excitement surrounding Stakhanovism, the movement could do little to remedy the underlying structural problems limiting productivity growth: supply bottlenecks that inhibited effective coordination, made a mockery of work schedules, and caused seize-ups throughout the entire production process. The output records achieved by Busygin and his followers could sharply raise productivity at certain points, but they could not solve the problem of bottlenecks, and often indeed exacerbated them.

Machinery, the conference recognized, stood idle for reasons outside of the control of the workers operating them, such as "missing materials and parts at the workplace, interruptions in feeding the instruments, and power-outs." Gaz was singled out as a negative example in the *Gutap* system: there the situation was so bad in the summer of 1936 that the motor assembly line stood still for entire shifts. On thirteen days in June of 1936, the main assembly line at Gaz was idle for an average of more than two hours in a workday of two seven-hour shifts (see table 3.5).

In the wake of the Khar'kov conference, more than 32,000 of Gaz's norms were revised upward, increasing on average by 28.7 percent. Piece rates and other "stimulating" wage systems, which had dominated close to 60 percent of operations at Gaz in early 1936, were introduced more broadly after the conference, which decided that they should eventually cover 90 percent of workers.[139]

The conference concluded that the responsibility for the problems in *Gutap*'s factories lay with the engineering-technical staff and the factory

TABLE 3.5. Assembly line downtimes in hours per day at Gaz, June 1936

June ...	1	2	3	4	5	7	8	9	10	11	13	Average
Main assembly line	1.6	7.6	1.6	2.6	0.25	1.75	1.4	2.85	0.5	1.75	.5	2.04
Body assembly line	4.1	3.4	4.1	2.85	3.4	4.35	5.2	3.75	5.35	4.15	6.25	4.26
Motor assembly line	7.0	3.5	3.9	5.3	5.7	7.5	6.8	7.1	5.6	5.9	5.8	5.83

Source: RGAE archives, f. 7622, o.1, d.58, ll. 18/19.

administration. It was their task to help Stakhanovism penetrate shop floors even more pervasively. What the report did not spell out was that the injunction to abet record chasing in the production process confronted factory management with a "cruel dilemma":[140] either support Stakhanovism and accept the attendant disruption of production flow, or discourage Stakhnovism and antagonize party activists and the leadership in the higher rungs of administration.

It was a dilemma D'iakonov could not solve. For three days at the end of March 1937, Gaz party activists convened with middle management, shop superintendents, foremen, and Stakhanovites to air grievances and lay blame. The protocol of this conference provides a jarring insight into the production realities at Gaz in the last year of the Second Five-Year Plan.[141] The proud Soviet River Rouge operated on a basis far removed from the ideas of Fordist flow production. "In our auto factory technological thinking is poor," complained Gaz's chief mechanic. "Many decisions are made on the go, unplanned and without sufficient preparation, causing very many blunders and errors and crippling rationalization." Engineer Belogub was responsible for intrafactory transport, one of the key components of flow production. Belogub complained that the conveyor connecting the foundry with the mechanical shop had to be rebuilt after the expansion of the foundry because the planners had not considered the problem. "In January 1936," Belogub continued, "we planned the so-called Busygin conveyor. But the conveyor is idle until this day." What was worse, Belogub reported that there were auxiliary shops on the factory premises where the level of mechanization was so low that they practically worked with "handicraft methods."

Particularly damning were the reports from the vaunted assembly lines. The foreman on the main conveyor complained about "the poor work of the supply shops, which send unsuitable and defective parts to the assembly line." As a consequence, entirely defeating the purpose of flow production, "a whole range of parts in the already assembled cars [had] to be retrofitted." In March alone, of 1,300 finished cars roughly one-third had to have their motors replaced after final assembly, "very negatively" affecting quality. The factory leadership, charged the foreman, "sits out these deficiencies, and nobody presently cares about the daily struggle to fulfill the schedule."

The superintendent of the all-important Ford AA assembly shop, Pirogov, concurred. "Only some 10 to 15 parts" were defective, but this was "entirely sufficient to upset work at the assembly line. Hence: many stoppages and high labor turnover." Since work on the line was subject to piece rates, downtimes significantly lowered wages. Pirogov reported that during the month of February unskilled and semiskilled workers "earned 120–130 rubles"—this compared to an average wage of close to 300 rubles. As a consequence, workers could not be persuaded to stay on the line. "Discharge applications began to arrive in bundles." Pirogov concluded: "On the assembly line there is little culture. People come and go. The dirt prevents us from putting out a quality car."

Aleshin, a Stakhanovite from the assembly line of the Molotov-1, vented that "a year already they are assembling the M-1, and still they haven't learnt how to work properly: they torment us with downtimes. In three months the conveyor has stood idle for 375 hours. The workers work piece-rates, they earn little, and run. The workshop supplies useless parts. On the conveyor they have to saw them off."

In the conference minutes, D'iakonov came across as a weak and negligent director. The party activists blamed D'iakonov, his technical staff, and the shop superintendents for carelessness, disinterest, and lack of initiative. But in reality, D'iakonov and his staff possessed neither the necessary authority among the workers nor the power to influence crucial supply and scheduling decisions. Lack of coordination and technical inefficiency was systemic, not owed to personal or political shortcomings. In this respect, Gaz remained representative of the structural difficulties of Soviet industry in the 1930s. These difficulties militated against the logic of flow production and made the heady celebrations of Fordism of only ten years earlier largely academic.

Without comment, D'iakonov passed the report of the March 1937 conference to his superior Dybets in Moscow. Dybets left marginalia in red pencil—heavy underlining, exclamation marks—on every page of the report. While it is unlikely that Dybets was surprised by the findings of the conference, it is safe to assume they caused him considerable alarm. The conference took place only two weeks after Sergo Ordzhonikidze, Dybets's political sponsor, committed suicide—an event that adumbrated the perilous atmosphere of the Great Terror. Dybets was arrested in October 1937. On November 26, the

Russian-American former Wobbly, who as head of *Vesenkha's* standing commission in Detroit had personally supervised the transfer of Ford automotive and production technology to central Russia, was executed. Sergei D'iakonov outlasted his boss by several months. But on April 22, 1938, D'iakonov, his 1934 Lenin award "for the organization and mastery of assembly line mass production" notwithstanding, was fired as Gaz director. He was arrested in July and executed on September 7.[142]

Arrests and executions, of course, did not solve the underlying problems of automobile production at the Soviet River Rouge. In 1938, Gaz, for the first time since 1933, did not meet the plan. Gaz's new director, Ivan Loskutov, delivered a voluminous and frank explanation for this failure to Moscow. Loskutov noted "the sharp disproportion in productivity between the supply and manufacturing shops." In all of 1938, Loskutov elaborated, the main assembly line had lain idle for an average of two hours and twenty minutes every day, mostly "for lack of metal and supply parts." Loskutov got to the heart of the matter: "Since the fundamental character of the factory is flow-mass production, stoppages in the main operations stall the work of all flow lines." Uneven deliveries coming from the supply shops "caused the interruptions in the assembly shops." Labor turnover had hardly improved. Gaz lost 17,581 workers in 1938 while hiring 20,247. Loskutov noted that it took a newly hired worker roughly two months to get within 80 percent of the work norms, which necessarily slowed down everyone else on the production lines.[143]

Equally worrying was the fact that, for all its vaunted flow principles, Gaz continued to rely on an army of auxiliary workers who carried parts and supplies from shop to shop. Loskutov noted that "storage spaces, as usual, remain strewn about the factory compounds" and "loading and unloading operations are not mechanized." In consequence, the number of workers in auxiliary crews (loaders, carriers, and so on) rose from 18,431 to 20,878 over the course of 1938—a staggering 40 percent of the overall labor force. "The increase in the number of auxiliary workers, the large amount of defective output, downtimes, labor turnover, poor labor discipline, the slow implementation of measures to liquidate the remains of wrecking"—this list of shortcomings hampered any attempt to increase productivity and meet the plan.[144]

Undeterred by these recalcitrant operational problems, Moscow drew up a new expansion plan for the auto industry. In March of 1939, the 18th Party Congress officially adopted the Third Five-Year Plan, notionally encompassing the years from 1938 to 1942. In the parlance of 1939, the Third Plan would complete "socialist construction" and bridge the way for the introduction of Communism. In contrast to the Second Plan, which had emphasized operations, the Third Plan again projected huge programs to expand the Soviet industrial base. For the auto industry, this once again meant using River Rouge as a model. Just as the Rouge supplied numerous Ford assembly plants across the US, Gaz was to send knocked-down AAs to locations in the Caucasus region, Central Asia, and Siberia. According to the scheme, Gaz was to deliver 190,000 sets of parts yearly to future assembly shops in Rostov-na-Donu, Tiblisi, Ufa, Omsk, Irkutsk, and Tashkent. Moscow allotted 1 billion rubles (roughly 2 percent of the 1939 budget) to the scheme, on a completion schedule that coincided with the end of the Third Plan in December 1942.[145] By late 1940, Gosplan put the factual capacity of Gaz at 180,000 vehicles. The Omsk assembly branch was under construction, and Rostov had begun operations. Tashkent and Irkutsk were still in the planning phase.[146]

The German attack on the Soviet Union in June 1941 made these plans obsolete. But as the German advance forced the Soviets to relocate entire production facilities to the east, Gaz, which lay safely beyond the reach of the front, returned to the attention of production planners. In consequence, the city of Gorky benefited from the preferential supply of resources and raw materials. At Gaz, war production triggered a surprising comeback of Fordism. Faced with the peculiar conditions of war production, a severe shortage of skilled labor, and a clear preference of quantity over quality, the Gaz engineers returned to mechanized flow. As men left for the front, women in increasing numbers took their places on the Gaz shop floor; already by the end of 1941, the share of women in the overall workforce was projected to increase to almost two-thirds.[147] The women moving into the factory were unskilled and had little production experience. As we discuss in chapter 5, to mobilize the newcomers' labor, Gaz management doubled down again on flow production principles.

Conclusion

This chapter has described the rise of Gaz and the making of Soviet automotive mass production as part of a specific strategy of industrial upgrading employed by the Soviet Union during the First Five-Year Plan. In 1929, the Soviet leadership terminated direct investments of Western firms in Russia and instead embarked on an aggressive strategy of wholesale technology imports from the West. This shift coincided with the victory of Stalin and the maximalist faction in the political struggles over industrialization. Technology imports from the West expanded massively between 1929 and 1931; this surge luridly testifies to the radicalization of Soviet economic policy, since paying for these imports required the merciless mobilization of economic resources in order to raise foreign exchange. The foreign exchange crisis of 1931 quashed the most expansive dreams of technical assistance; yet targeted Western connections, including the well-oiled connection to the Ford Motor Company, persisted through the mid-1930s.

The contract with the Ford Motor Company had a preeminent place among the many technical assistance agreements with Western firms concluded during the First Five-Year Plan. The Ford agreement not only harbored rich symbolic significance. Thanks to the company's open-source stance—a policy that derived from the company's producer-populist roots—Sorensen and his staffers gave the Soviet engineers almost unlimited access to Rouge technology. They actively supported the Soviet side in extensive copying and observation, the acquisition of machinery, and the exchange of personnel. The copious documentation that Dybets relayed to central Russia from Detroit laid the foundation of Gaz. Voluminous Soviet imports of machinery soaked up immense outlays of foreign exchange. Western specialists, hired by the Soviet authorities with high hopes, appear to have had limited impact. By the mid-1930s, most of the Westerners had left the Soviet Union; others fell victim to the purges of 1937–1938, just as did the senior figures who had coordinated the transfers, such as Nikolai Osinskii, Stepan Dybets, and Sergei D'iakonov. A cohort of Soviet engineers and skilled workers who had enjoyed work experience at the Rouge in the early Thirties most enduringly linked Detroit and Gorky. These men returned from America into midlevel engineering roles; escaping the purges, they moved into senior positions after 1938 and then oversaw Gaz's flow production during the war.

Indigenizing flow production at Gaz was hardly a smooth process. As production realities during the 1930s made clear, two major problems confronted Fordism at Gaz. One was the ongoing difficulty of the command economy to allocate resources. Laments of Gaz management and technical staff about tardy, incomplete, or defective deliveries of steel, machine tools, and raw materials dominated the accounting and plan fulfillment reports. The second problem was less obvious and more difficult for management to articulate, because doing so would have amounted to questioning the tenets of Soviet labor policies in the 1930s. These policies were geared toward worker performance, not technological efficiency. Stakhanovism and progressive piece rates encouraged uncoordinated performance records but did little to assuage the fundamental problem of production coordination in a giant factory built on flow principles. It was no surprise that Busygin, Gaz's poster-boy Stakhanovite, achieved his crankshaft record in the supply shop and not on the assembly line. The emphasis on worker performance left engineers and management on the defensive. In the 1920s, the most radical Soviet rationalizers claimed that Taylorism, with its obsession over individual performance, was superseded by Fordism, with its emphasis on mechanization and flow. The 1930s, then, saw an ironic turn of events. At Gaz during the Second Five-Year Plan, Taylorism trumped Fordism, a development that stood in tension to the purpose of the vast technological transfer from Detroit during the First Plan.

TABLE 3.6. Gaz production figures, 1932–1938

Year	Output of vehicles	Number of employees (average figures)	Labor Productivity (vehicles/ employees)	Unit production cost of one Gaz AA, in rubles
1932	7,559	22,475	0.34	9,714
1933	26,661	26,695	1.00	4,926
1934	49,300	29,936	1.65	3,935
1935	63,642	30,239	2.10	3,536
1936	86,267	40,365	2.14	3,894
1937	135,718	46,312	2.93	3,928
1938	145,601 (AA and M-1 only)	48,138 (1st quarter)	3.02	3,907 (1st quarter)

Source: TsANO archives, f. 2435, o.1, d. 169; d.171, ll.3–7; o.2, dd. 6/8.

Even so, efforts to increase efficiency in the 1930s were not entirely in vain. Despite supply bottlenecks, incongruous labor policies, and the self-lacerating removal of technical personnel during the purges, Gaz did increase output and even, by a rough measure, labor productivity. In 1937, Gaz produced over 135,000 vehicles, or on average 3 cars per worker employed. That was certainly below the 8.7 cars per worker that the Ford Motor Company registered in 1933. But it was a big improvement over the 0.34 cars per worker that Gaz put out in 1932 (see table 3.6). The legacy of the Rouge connection was revived after 1938, as central authorities, spooked by the dislocation of the purges, began to back administrative and technical staff in industry and doubled down on labor discipline, which was increasingly enforced with draconian measures. Piece rates were phased out.[148] At Gaz, this allowed middle management and engineering staff to reassert the organizational discipline of flow production, a process that coincided with the beginning of the Third Five-Year Plan and that continued during the war.

The return to flow production during the war also marked the resurgence of the technical-modernist discourse of the engineers. One Gaz engineer described the tank assembly shop of 1943 in these terms:

The entire mechanical shop is divided into sections on the basis of parts produced. . . . Every section puts out a finished part, which goes to the main assembly line. Each section, in turn, consists of individual assembly lines, laid out on the basis of processing parts and the sequence of assembly; it is where the individual parts flow, where they are processed, and whence they move to the main conveyor. . . . The assembly lines are laid out according to the sequence of processing parts. . . . The entire design of the assembly lines, the shop, and the building is based on the principle of the shortest passage of parts and optimal conditions of transportation. Hence, all assembly lines transverse the building from the south, feeding the assembled parts northwards, where the factory's main conveyor is located.[149]

Similarly, Giovanni Agnelli, Fiat's chief executive, described flow production at the brand-new Mirafiori in a mixture of engineering jargon and organizational dream:

Organic sequence of production phases on a single floor; organization of the factory into sectors devoted to the production of individual groups and completed parts; lateral positioning of the production sectors next to the assembly lines according to the sequence of parts into assembly; positioning of the production lines in every sector according to the sequence of parts in sector production; systematic positioning of every element of production in a line of machine tools, corresponding to the sequence that occurs in executing the individual phases of production; result of the rational layout: elimination of material transports in the course of production.[150]

Agnelli, of course, could have been talking about the layout that Gaz's chief engineers brought from Detroit, made the basis of factory construction, and rediscovered under the conditions of war. And in a sense, Agnelli *was* talking about Gaz. Based on the operation of Ford's River Rouge, flow principles had become the universal grammar of mass production in the 1930s.

4

Nazi *Fordismus*

According to present German ideas, an enterprise in Germany is only justified
to exist insofar as it submits to the general political and economical
requirements of the State.

—ERICH DIESTEL, MANAGING DIRECTOR OF FORD COLOGNE, 1938

We have been told by Mr. Schacht that if we would continue to play the game
with Germany for another five years, we would be glad we came here.

—R. K. EVANS, MANAGING DIRECTOR OF OPEL, 1934

ON THE NIGHT of October 21, 1937, William Werner returned to the Detroit
Book Cadillac after a long day at the Buick factories in Flint. A telegram was
waiting at the reception: Werner's superiors had cabled from Saxony. It had
transpired, the telegram informed Werner, that Ferdinand Porsche, the protégé designer of Hitler's "people's car," and Otto Dyckhoff, Porsche's lead engineer, had successfully recruited a dozen German-Americans from the Ford
Motor Company to staff the planning bureau of the projected Volkswagen
plant. Werner might want to look out for similar opportunities for his own
firm, Auto-Union. Werner picked up pen and stationery and replied. All had
gone well so far, he was happy to report: the reception at the American firms
had been extremely cordial. He and his group were looking forward to their
sojourn at River Rouge in three days' time. Regarding Porsche's headhunting
campaign, yes, he had been made aware of such efforts. Werner said he would
look into the matter with care but doubted that much could be achieved. He
felt that only experts with considerable skills in designing and constructing
machine tools were worth hiring. Such engineers, however, were "very expensive and mostly Americans."[1]

Werner was right, but that difficulty had not deterred the Volkswagen
people, who took advantage of the fact that many of the highly skilled

toolmakers in the employ of American factories were of German origin. By the time of Werner's stay in Detroit, Volkswagen had indeed already culled several experienced German-American engineers from the skilled core running the Rouge. Among those recruited was Hans Mayr, superintendent of the Rouge press shop, a German-born toolmaker who had worked for Ford since 1923. Mayr was joined by a colleague, the Ford press designer Karl Luik. Porsche and Dyckhoff hired Luik "on the basis of his prior activity in the United States" and expected him to set up the Volkswagen press shop. Along with Luik and Mayr came Hans Riedel, one of the superintendents at the Rouge body shop, and Joseph Werner, who had designed tools for the vaunted Ford V8 engine block. Joseph Werner (no relation to William) had first moved to the United States in 1927 "after reading two books by Henry Ford," as he recalled. His recruitment came unexpectedly: "My wife received a phone call one day in spring 1937, asking me to see a Dr. Porsche in the Book-Cadillac Hotel." At the meeting, Porsche and Dyckhoff showed him a photograph of the Volkswagen prototype and told him, "We want you to introduce American mass production methods into the manufacture." Mayr, Luik, Riedel, and Werner, Ford veterans and American citizens all, left the United States in 1937 and set up shop in the Volkswagen planning bureau in Stuttgart.[2]

The transatlantic migration of engineers from Detroit to Nazi Germany mirrored the movements of personnel and machines into Soviet Russia only a few years earlier. Both regimes regarded automotive mass production as a strategic sector of twentieth-century national economies—indeed, as one of the core areas of comparative underdevelopment vis-à-vis the United States. To both regimes, automotive mass production was a technology that had to be mastered if they were to prevail in an American-dominated world order. Both regimes accordingly sought to upgrade this sector, not only for economic bragging rights and civilian propaganda, but also, crucially, in order to boost national technological capabilities and to support state-orchestrated projects of rearmament. Both regimes sent engineers to the Midwest and took advantage of the fact that Detroit was a city of migrants: they hired workers and engineers who not only had acquired sought-after production skills in the Motor City but also spoke a common language in which to transmit them. For both Soviets and Nazis, industrial upgrading was an irreducibly transnational affair that required engaging with American corporations in attempts to acquire their proprietary technologies.

But given two profoundly different industrial structures and economic systems, such engagement took quite different forms in each case. Stalin and the Bolshevik leadership sought to transfigure an impoverished agrarian economy whose development deficit was at once deep and encompassing. As we saw in chapter 3, they sought to heal this deficit by copying the Western technological arsenal in its entirety. Accordingly, the Soviet importation of Fordism was only one part—albeit a central one—of a much larger, comprehensive campaign of technology transfer.

Germany's development deficit vis-à-vis the United States was of a different character. Unlike the Soviet Union, Germany boasted a highly developed industrial base in its own right, centered around classic producer goods, such as coal, steel, machine tools, and instruments. In the electrical and chemical sectors, German corporations operated on the forefront of global innovation, and indeed had a thing or two to teach their American competitors.[3] And yet, when it came to automotive mass production, Germany was a developing nation. Germany's engine makers, such as Daimler-Benz or BMW, could not match America's. The single high-volume factory in Germany, that of Opel, was gobbled up by General Motors in 1929. Though Germany's machine tool builders were a proud and venerable branch with considerable export clout, they were unequipped to supply mass production factories. Germany's development deficit was therefore circumscribed but sharp. Acquiring automotive mass production was of neuralgic significance: it not only harbored the potential of a growth-generating consumer and export sector, but it was also—more immediately urgent to the Nazi regime—of primary military-strategic significance. Accordingly, the Nazi regime did not purchase bulk machinery and entire technological systems wholesale, Soviet-style. Instead, it resorted to targeted industrial reconnaissance and the recruitment of American specialists—that is, to Detroit missions such as those of Porsche, Dyckhoff, and William Werner.

When it came to building a capable domestic automotive industry, however, there was another decisive difference between the two regimes: both Ford and General Motors had sizable investments in Nazi Germany. In stark contrast, as we saw, Osinskii and the Supreme Economic Council had rejected an offer by the Ford Motor Company to build a plant on Russian soil, and opted for a standing commission in Detroit instead. The Soviet procedure had the advantage of keeping the Americans at arm's length and of retaining greater control over how technology would be appropriated. At the same time, it required enormous amounts of hard currency, which the Soviet leadership raised through a merciless campaign of primitive accumulation at home. The Nazi regime, in contrast, ensnared the American multinationals operating in Germany in a web of political pressure and economic incentives, and in doing so found ways, remarkably, to appropriate the Americans' technology without spending significant amounts of US dollars.

American Multinationals in the Nazi Political Economy

To understand how the Nazi regime acquired mass production technology while saving hard currency, we have to come to terms with the political economy of Nazi Germany—both its domestic structure and its place in the international arena of the Thirties. The paramount limitation governing Nazi foreign economic policy was one that the Soviet leadership—or, for that matter, the governments of all import-dependent nations in the Thirties—would have recognized: a chronic and severe shortage of foreign exchange. This predicament was a legacy of the Depression. By the end of the 1920s, as a result of reparations and plentiful American loans, Germany had garnered the dubious distinction of carrying the single greatest nominal external debt burden in the world. In the brief boom between 1924 and 1929, exports and revolving loans had assured debt service. The Depression, however, severed Germany from its export markets, and the global financial crisis of 1931 brought down the edifice of international credit. In response, the last Weimar governments imposed stringent controls over capital outflows and erected import barriers to economize on foreign exchange. They also began subsidizing exports to plaster the widening gap in the balance of payments.[4]

When they came to power in 1933, the National Socialists inherited this makeshift system of trade management and capital controls; they did not create it. What they added was turning this system from an emergency measure into a tool of strategic economic policy. Nazi authorities strengthened the state's grip over foreign exchange, cut down on imports, and fortified export promotion. They elbowed industry into developing import substitutes, such as artificial fiber, synthetic rubber, and gasoline from coal hydrogenation. Central control over foreign exchange (and hence imports) allowed the Nazi authorities to systematically privilege strategic sectors (metalworking, aviation, steel) with hard currency while starving consumer industries (such as textiles). The desired result was a shift in resources from consumption to rearmament. Hjalmar Schacht, Reichsbank president and economics minister, laid the fundamental building blocks of this system in 1934 with his "New Plan." The plan's essential features remained in place until the Nazi economy collapsed in 1944.[5]

The second salient context for how Nazism appropriated American technologies of mass production was the domestic "steered market economy"—the system by which the regime sought to make use of private industry for national purposes. How this system worked in practice has gained clarity over the last fifteen years, as abstract debates over whether the Nazi economy was "socialist" or "capitalist" have made way for scholarship that has begun to reconstruct in detail the negotiations between Nazi state organs and German businesses.[6] What emerges from this scholarship is the view of a Nazi state that harnessed property rights, markets, and the law to its goals. The system involved an implicit two-way bargain. On the one hand, the state would respect the property rights of businesspeople (as long as they were not Jewish) and granted them freedom to select contract partners, make investment decisions, and choose production strategies. On the other hand, the state expected industry to support the regime's overarching politico-economic demands (such as the development of import-substituting products, military-industrial buildup, and rearmament). The regime portrayed these demands as coterminous with the collective interest of the *Volksgemeinschaft*. It expected German firms to meet these demands by employing their own initiative, using their own resources and expertise, and deploying their own innovative strategies and know-how. If firms delivered desired results or, better yet, came up with ideas and improvements of their own, then rewards, promotions, participation in shaping the larger political economy, and profits beckoned. Refusal to comply, or failure to deliver results, incurred the threat of reprisals.

This expectation of active performance in service of the regime, including the always implicit threat of punitive action, echoed the notion of *Dienst* that right-wing postliberals had developed in Weimar times. It remained a strong ideological tenet throughout the Nazi period. As Hitler put it in 1936, "the Ministry of Economics has merely to set the national economic tasks, and private business has to execute them." In light of the slow development of synthetic fuel and rubber, however, Hitler also stated: "Either we possess a private industry [willing to] wrack its brain over production methods" or "we no longer need a private industry."[7] Such views could be flanked from the side of business. As the president of the Munich section of the Chamber of Commerce, Albert Pietzsch, argued in a memorandum on "economic steering," the National Socialist state should restrict itself to issuing demands and controlling results. It should leave execution to individual firms, who would coordinate among themselves in adequate "bodies of self-administration." These arrangements would mobilize the "creative initiative" of private businesses and enlist them into "responsible cooperation" in meeting the regime's goals.[8] (As we discuss in chapter 5, such notions resurfaced when Albert Speer gave the tightening of state steering in 1942 the ambiguous moniker "industrial self-responsibility.")

Principled noncooperation on the part of industrialists, however, turned out to be rare; at least in the regime's prewar years, the stance of the great majority of businesspeople fell somewhere between grudging accommodation and active support. Only in a few high-profile projects did private industry fail the regime: in aviation, iron and steel, and, as we shall see, in the case of the

Volkswagen—and only then did the Nazi state step in and run the industrial plant itself.[9]

The Nazi state treated multinational corporations very similarly to domestic firms. It subjected them to foreign exchange management and economic steering. That is, within the framework of capital controls, the regime gave foreign corporations considerable autonomy; at the same time, however, the regime expected them to show cooperation and even initiative. Nazi authorities were well aware that the likes of Ford, General Motors, Standard Oil, and IBM, which held substantial fixed investments in Germany, constituted crucial sources of capital and technology. Because of this, the regime not only tolerated but in fact encouraged the presence of multinationals in Germany—as long as they supported the military-industrial buildup. Hitler repeatedly reassured American business representatives that "he would tolerate no discrimination of foreign capital"—but added the caveat that it had to be "invested for legitimate economic purposes."[10] An internal party circular clarified what this meant with somewhat greater precision and frankness: foreign capital was welcome "as long as [it] subordinates its activities in Germany to the demands of state policy."[11]

In practice, the regime both cajoled and harassed multinationals into putting their capital and proprietary technology in the service of Germany's military-industrial buildup. Capital controls were key. By preventing multinationals from repatriating profits, the Nazi authorities compelled them to channel their proceeds into plant expansion, technological upgrading, and joint ventures with domestic firms. This strategy was successful: between 1929 and 1940, the book value of American foreign direct investment in Germany rose by almost 50 percent, almost exclusively as a result of reinvestment.[12] Standard Oil's German subsidiary, for example, contributed substantial outlays to a key refinery for synthetic jet fuel.[13] IBM transferred the manufacture of its proprietary punch card tabulators to the German branch.[14] General Motors–owned Opel built a brand-new, state-of-the-art, flow production factory for trucks.[15] Ford put its machines, expertise, and personnel toward a military-sponsored truck development job.[16] The regime further expected American multinationals to "Germanize" their products—that is, to source local raw materials and make use of domestic suppliers. Often, this required instructing German firms in American best practices: for example, GM-owned Opel began pushing German machine tool manufacturers to build to American specifications.

More broadly, the regime inserted multinationals into the framework of foreign exchange management and export promotion. By withholding dollar allocations, the authorities steered the branches of Ford and GM into barter agreements with their parent companies, who supplied machinery and scarce raw materials (such as rubber and iron ore) against goods deliveries from

Germany. Export premia, finally, persuaded Ford and GM to use their international distribution networks to support the German balance of payments.[17] All of this took place in an environment in which foreign-owned corporations faced grassroots hostility from the steered press, from lower-level party organizations, and from the German-dominated trade associations. This groundswell of nationalist hostility served to push multinationals closer to the authorities, who periodically promised to rein in the troops in return for compliance with the regime's programs.

Why did multinationals cooperate at all with Hitler's odious regime? This question has exercised historians, and they have offered varying answers: American executives were naively deluded about Nazi aims;[18] they were cynical profiteers tacitly complicit in the regime's crimes;[19] they were level-headed pragmatists only interested in safeguarding their investments.[20] Evidence, to be sure, may be adduced for each of these claims. Fundamentally, however, American corporations complied for two reasons. On the one hand, the Nazi rearmament boom presented them with a solid growth market in an otherwise brittle post-Depression international environment.[21] On the other hand, American corporations encountered in Germany an activist state whose methods were far from exceptional in the landscape of the global Thirties. In an atmosphere of nationalism and military buildup, the Nazi regime was not alone in dragging multinational corporations into the contentious politics of industrial upgrading. It might even be said that the Nazi authorities were not immeasurably more demanding than other governments.

Ford and General Motors encountered nationalist headwinds and state-orchestrated industrial policy everywhere they turned since the late 1920s. The struggle was particularly pronounced in nations that harbored a domestic automobile sector terrified of the overweening American competition. In Italy, Mussolini's regime sought to protect and build up a national champion, Fiat, and hence prevented Ford from gaining a foothold there.[22] At the same time, Fiat's engineers made vigorous use of the open door at the Rouge and intensified their technological reconnaissance in the run-up to the expansion of Mirafiori. In France, where Ford had established an assembly branch in 1929, the company faced familiar government pressure to nationalize its ownership, use local suppliers, and bring manufacturing capabilities to the domestic market. The Ford branch duly merged with a French company, Mathis. In order to gain access to "French-only" government subsidies, and in order to be eligible for military contracts, Ford eventually built a new factory, partially with fresh funds from Dearborn. The location—Poissy, close to the French capital—was chosen because it was compatible with French mobilization plans. When Poissy opened in 1939, it produced not cars but military trucks and aircraft engines. Ford's experience in France closely mirrored that of General Motors in Germany. Here the authorities not only goaded the Americans into building a new truck factory but also made them agree to a location—Brandenburg, just outside of the German capital—that satisfied strategic requirements. Meanwhile, General Motors chose not to get involved in France, even when offered a merger with one of the domestic Big Three, Citroen. It seemed unwise to put fresh capital into the volatile French market.[23]

In Japan, authorities began exerting pressure on both Ford and GM after the invasion of Manchuria in 1931, when they became increasingly concerned about the military need for a domestic motor vehicle industry. Both corporations had established successful assembly plants in the 1920s, where imported kits of knocked-down vehicles were put together. Now the Americans were told to replace these imports and begin sourcing parts on the domestic market—a development that benefited Nissan and Toyota, who jumped at the opportunity to act as suppliers. Increasingly under pressure from the authorities to expand Japanese ownership stakes, both Ford and GM sought mergers with Japanese companies. A series of joint venture initiatives that involved Ford, GM, Nissan, and Toyota in various combinations dotted the years from 1934 to 1939: the Americans desperately sought to bolster their national credentials, while the Japanese companies hoped to secure continuous technological inputs by aligning with the Americans. Each proposal, however, was ultimately vetoed by the increasingly powerful military, who eventually forced the Americans to close up shop.[24] Given such headwinds, it was no surprise that General Motors considered Japan a more difficult business environment than Nazi Germany.[25] Indeed, it appears that Japanese military authorities, who consistently adopted a hard stance against foreign corporations, understood the value of technological engagement with them less clearly than did their German counterparts.

What comes into view in these comparisons is the political economy of transnational development competition, in which states tangled with multinational corporations over the terms of engagement. In bringing state power to bear on foreign multinationals, and in using capital controls and the threat of nationalist reprisals as primary tools in this endeavor, the Nazi regime was not unique. By forcing multinationals to nurture domestic suppliers, by cajoling them into joint ventures with domestic firms, by encouraging new fixed investments, and by pushing for technological transfers, the Nazi regime mirrored other activist states during the Thirties.

Indeed, the Nazi "steered economy" developed an arsenal of mechanisms that was hardly sui generis, but rather resembled a common set of methods hit upon by other twentieth-century authoritarian states in pursuit of economic upgrading. Consider the core features that social scientists have identified with twentieth-century "developmental states": a state negotiating with businesses

on the basis of "market-conforming methods of state intervention"; social coalitions between business elites and state actors; a tight control over labor
along with wage retrenchment; a purposive industrial policy aimed at factory-
level rationalization as well as at changing the overall industrial structure of
the country; a focus on transferring technology from abroad and diffusing it
at home; foreign exchange management as a primary tool of economic policy;
the trial-and-error, improvisatory character of the steering process; and an
environment of ideological mobilization and targeted repression.[26] Pondering
this catalog, it is hard not to see the Nazi rearmament economy in action.

This, then, was the politico-economic context in which the Nazi appropriation of Midwestern Fordism took place. Such appropriation followed three
main channels. The first was the regime's strategic use of Ford and General
Motors as multinationals with investments in Germany. This channel involved
binding the Americans' local branches into Germany's political economy,
coaxing them into releasing proprietary technology, and transferring their
production protocols. It also involved a remarkable degree of personal diplomacy between American executives, German state officials, and Nazi party
brass. The second channel was the state-sponsored development of a German
River Rouge replica—the Volkswagen plant. This involved the type of
technology-transfer-by-personal-migration exemplified by Porsche's recruitment of German-American engineers. This chapter explores these two channels in detail. The third channel, finally, was the type of targeted industrial
reconnaissance exemplified by William Werner's Detroit mission in the fall of
1937. We explore its impacts in chapter 5, where we follow Werner's ascendance
from automotive executive into the highest echelons of the German war
economy.

The American Challenge and the "People's Car"

The political urgency that automotive mass production assumed in the Nazi
economy, and the fractious conflicts around it, must be seen against the backdrop of the difficulties experienced by the German auto industry during the
Twenties. These difficulties were neatly laid out in an engineering report presented to the Reich Association of the German Automobile Industry in 1925.
Under the title "The Existential Struggle of the German Automobile Industry,"
the report presented some stark facts. In the production of cars, Germany was
trailing the world's foremost economic powers—France, Britain, the United
States; when it came to the ratio of inhabitants to cars in use, Germany (360:1)
was even lagging behind Argentina (101:1). The most dangerous competitor,
of course, was the United States: it took American carmakers six days to match
the number of vehicles Germany put out in a year. If Germany were to acquire

broad motorization, there were only two options: "either we buy American cars, or we build our own." The first option had merit: American cars were sturdy, affordable, and of high quality. Choosing this route, however, would imply "the death of the German automobile industry" along with all its supply firms, affecting up to 160,000 workers—and lest the point be lost, the report added that this would be "a death from which no resurrection is possible." The second option, however, also involved a daunting proposition. Building up a competitive car industry would require a comprehensive technological over-haul: introducing flow production, upgrading machinery, and bringing foundry work up to American standards. It would also require sacrifices: "all so-called small workshops must disappear" and all undercapitalized carmakers "must either merge or also die." Wages would have to remain low. The state would have to support the industry through tax policy and robust tariffs.[27]

The obstacles to introducing the deep runs characteristic of Detroit were indeed high. Weimar's carmakers, small and medium-sized firms with shaky capital, produced too many types too expensively with outdated methods. After the stabilization of 1924, they confronted not only dim export prospects but narrow domestic demand. The inflation had hollowed out middling in-comes and left many Germans poor and a few very rich: this assured an auto-mobile market in which some carmakers, like Daimler and Benz, built limited numbers of luxury limousines while others, like BMW, made most of their money selling motorcycles, which remained the most widespread mode of motorized transportation. Only the well-off could afford to maintain a private automobile, since paying for fuel, tires, oil, taxes, and insurance exceeded the means of middling households. Most automobiles, therefore, were used as capital goods by small businesses, firms, doctors, or roving salesmen. This was the customer base of Opel, whose twelve-horsepower Frog exhausted the de-mand of the slim Weimar professional class, thus allowing it to build a respect-able 120,000 units between 1924 and 1931.[28]

The remedies suggested in the 1925 report—firm combination and mass production, tariffs and state support—were more easily listed than imple-mented. There were only two automotive mergers of consequence in the Wei-mar period: a bank-orchestrated combination of the high-end players Daimler and Benz in 1926, and a bailout of four Depression-battered carmakers by the state of Saxony in 1932 that resulted in the formation of Auto-Union (William Werner's home firm). Other merger plans foundered on the resistance of fiercely independent proprietors. Most importantly, the refusal of the domi-nant Opel brothers defeated any national consolidation scheme—until the Opels stunned the public by selling out to General Motors in 1929.

Many carmakers succumbed to the lure of Fordism and set out to introduce modern manufacturing methods on their own, often borrowing American capital to do so. They introduced some assembly lines, often nonmechanized, and thus created what an industry observer in 1931 called "a hint of flow production." The most immediate result was overcapacity: productivity tripled between 1925 and 1929 but plant was heavily underutilized. When the Depression hit, many car builders scrapped their flow systems and retreated back into higher price classes.[29] Labor and the press spoke of "rationalization led astray."[30] Neither was state support unambiguous. For a period of three years, the industry got its tariff—prohibitive rates protected carmakers between 1925 and 1928. However, once tariffs reverted to standard levels (between 30 and 75 percent, depending on price class), imports surged back into Germany: in 1929, four out of ten new registrations were foreign makes. Automobile firms asked the state to lower vehicle taxes and slash import duties on gasoline to lighten maintenance costs. Concerned with fiscal priorities, the government shrugged. Carmakers pleaded "imprudent and unfair" treatment and accused the state of "automobile hostility."[31]

The woes of Weimar carmakers, however, were only one national variation on a common European theme.[32] Everywhere auto firms clamored for protection against the American competition; everywhere they sought to either gang up against Ford or GM, or do as Opel did and break ranks by merging with the Americans. France's tariffs on automobiles hovered around 45 percent; Britain's McKenna duties stood at 33 percent; Italy's rates rose from 60 percent to prohibitive as the decade progressed.[33] Numerous merger initiatives dotted the Twenties and Thirties. An early such initiative was the 1918 attempt of nine French carmakers to band together and copy Ford; in 1926, French firms considered a "general entente". These initiatives came to naught: proprietors found it impossible to agree on terms. American buy-ins also remained rare: In 1929, a joint venture between Ford and Fiat fell flat. British carmaker Austin asked first Ford, then GM for a merger; Citroen approached both American firms in 1934. Each time the Americans declined. GM's investors remained skeptical of the European makes, while Henry Ford and his executives were notoriously loath to compromise on production and design. GM's acquisition of Opel was the conspicuous exception proving the rule.

Often such defensive merger schemes revolved around the concept of a "people's car"—a European answer to the Model T. Here, too, the choice was either to beat the Americans or join them. A 1931 pamphlet by the title *Das Volksauto* exemplified the thinking. If Germany wanted to "ruthlessly drive out the Americans," its leading automobile firms would have to set aside their differences and join forces to produce an affordable, reliable family vehicle with reasonable power and innovative design. This people's model would depart from the weakling minivehicles—glorified runabouts with roofs—put out by Weimar Germany's small firms. But neither would it be the "monstrous crossbreed between railroad car and horse-drawn coach" that the established carmakers offered the upper classes. Collectively built, the people's car could surpass even the Americans and challenge them in export markets across Europe and the world. If German carmakers failed to cooperate, however, there was only one alternative: accept defeat and invite Ford to build a people's car for Germany. In this case, at least Opel might be wrested back into German hands and General Motors forced to retreat across the Atlantic.[34]

The sense of embattlement vis-à-vis the Americans explains why German carmakers reacted with excitement when the National Socialists took power in January 1933. With Hitler, whose automotive enthusiasm was well known, the industry hoped to get an administration more responsive to their appeals than its predecessors. Shortly after Hitler's appointment, the Automotive Association asked the new chancellor to deliver the keynote address at the International Automobile Exhibition in Berlin—a request Hitler "gladly" accepted. Addressing the assembled car industrialists at the opening ceremony on February 11, Hitler told them what they wanted to hear. Previous administrations had "done heavy damage to German car manufacturing," Hitler said. In contrast, the new administration would actively promote what was "possibly the most important industry today." He announced a "program for motorization" that included long-anticipated tax cuts, investments in road infrastructure, and subsidies to motorsports. That May a good mood prevailed at a meeting between the leading German carmakers and Hitler. The new chancellor confirmed that he considered the motor industry the "most immense and most successful industry of the future." Much to the satisfaction of the auto industrialists, he accorded the motor industry a key role in the overall task of economic reconstruction.[35]

Indeed, the motor vehicle industry experienced a strong recovery after 1933 that outpaced industrial growth at large. Fundamentally, the auto industry rode a cyclical rebound that had already reared its head in the summer of 1932. But carmakers also benefited from the regime's now favorable policies. A host of measures—tax incentives, allowing roadside parking, simplifying drivers' licensing, lowering insurance and registration fees, and so on—eased maintenance costs. *Autobahn* construction had high propaganda visibility; at least as significant, however, was the improvement of thousands of kilometers of regular roads. The regime's foreign exchange controls effectively ended import competition.[36] It helped that the motor vehicle enjoyed something of a cultural renaissance under National Socialism. Cars were highly compatible with Nazi ideology and assumed a central place in the regime's propaganda. The "National Socialist Motor Corps" introduced thousands of young men not only to motorized vehicles but also to swastikas and paramilitary spectacles.[37] Benefiting from robust government subsidies, the Silver Arrows of

Mercedes-Benz and Auto-Union began dominating the international race circuit.[38] The International Automobile Exhibitions, held every winter in Berlin,
lost their sober trade fair feel and became carefully orchestrated pageants reminiscent of the Nuremberg party rallies, attracting tens of thousands of specta-
tors. Each year the event culminated in a speech in which Hitler extolled German motorization.[39]

If German carmakers and the new regime started out on a good note, however, soon the auto industry came to feel the double edge of Nazi economic
steering. The regime had demonstrated its support of the carmakers; now it
began to put demands on them. Addressing the Berlin Auto Exhibition in
March 1934, Hitler reminded his audience that the distance between Germany
and America remained vast. Germany had a half-million cars; closing the gap
would require twelve million. Hitler squarely presented the assembled auto
industrialists with a "task": if Germany were to achieve mass motorization,
Hitler demanded, "then business must create and construct for the German
people an adequate motor car." For years, Hitler had been accusing German
carmakers of producing models that were too expensive. Now he returned to
the theme: the main obstacle to a popular car was "adjusting the price to the
financial means" of "millions." In doing so, carmakers might follow the radio
industry, which over the previous year had formed a consortium to develop a
cheap, basic radio model—the *Volksempfänger*—that had quickly found more
than half a million customers. Even though Hitler did not invoke the term in
his speech, everyone understood the reference: the dictator had just revived
the long-lingering idea of a Volkswagen.[40]

Hitler's speech at the 1934 Berlin Auto Show marked the opening volley for
one of the Nazi regime's more madcap episodes: the flopped attempt to mass-
produce a German "people's car." Indeed, the history of the Nazi Volkswagen
is to a large degree a story of what did not happen. To briefly review the project's many egregious failures: Under National Socialism, the Volkswagen remained no more than an endlessly stoked expectation. German carmakers did
not like the idea of a people's car and failed to produce one. In 1937, the sprawling German Labor Front co-opted the project, but it, too, failed to deliver a
single Volkswagen to German customers during the Third Reich. Over 300,000
would-be purchasers faithfully submitted their savings toward a car to the
Labor Front, only to see their claims evaporate during the war. (In 1948, they
filed a class action suit.) Construction on the Volkswagen megaplant was
begun in 1938; unfinished, it was turned over to war production in 1939. Farci-
cally, the first articles mass-produced in its enormous halls were not innovative
motor vehicles but disposable jet fuel tanks made from plywood.[41] And
throughout the war, largely as a result of raw material and labor shortages, the
plant operated well below capacity. With good reason, therefore, historians

have lampooned the Nazi Volkswagen as a vast misallocation of resources, as propagandistic hubris meeting harsh economic realities, as a manifestation of the dictator's quixotic megalomania, and as the symbol for the "failure of a National Socialist consumer society."[42]

Taking a step back and considering the international background, however, reveals some fresh plot twists in the seemingly familiar Volkswagen story. Three issues stand out. First is the comparative context in which Hitler revived the project: the development deficit vis-à-vis the United States. Hitler's demand that German carmakers develop a people's car reflected his longstanding conceit that competing with America required combining *Lebensraum* with Fordism. Second was the context of the European Thirties, in which the Nazi Volkswagen paralleled other nations' efforts to upgrade their car industries by making domestic firms cooperate—a goal that, as we saw, proved elusive not only in Germany. In keeping with this context was also the notion that developing a people's car might proceed as a joint venture *with* the Americans rather than against them. Before the Volkswagen became inextricably connected with Porsche's famous "Beetle" design and fused with the command-consumption politics of the Labor Front, there was a real possibility that the German people's car would be the spawn of a cooperation with an American multinational. It is important not to be fooled by hindsight here: Porsche only earned the dictator's full backing in the summer of 1936. Before that, as the evidence presented in the rest of this chapter shows, the regime repeatedly encouraged both Ford and General Motors to design and mass-produce a German people's car.

Third and finally, the Volkswagen tussle showcases the making of a crucial element of the Nazi "steered market economy": how the regime learned to deal with foreign corporations that held fixed investments in Germany. It was the specter of the Volkswagen that first brought GM and Ford in close touch with the regime. Though neither corporation proved willing to put fresh dollars behind the project, both nevertheless learned to negotiate the political economy of the Third Reich in the process. The regime, in turn, figured out how a mix of political pressure and economic constraints could mobilize the Americans' resources in the service of Nazi political goals and squeeze mass production expertise from them. The process did not follow any blueprint; rather, the Nazi state muddled and improvised, with the military, party, and ministries not always proceeding in unison. This polycratic environment made personal diplomacy and informal connections critical, which involved not only American executives and regime representatives but also unlikely figures like the deposed kaiser's grandson, Prince Louis Ferdinand of Hohenzollern, who came to broker between Dearborn and Berlin. What held together the regime's various activities, however, was a basic imperative: to bolster a German re-armament economy that was chronically bereft of hard currency. The next section follows, play-by-play, how in the wake of Hitler's Berlin speech Nazi transnational industrial policy took shape.

Jockeying for the Volkswagen

"Who will build the people's car?" asked the magazine *Motor und Sport* after Hitler's appearance at the 1934 Auto Show.[43] Over the next three years, this question prompted an intense round of jockeying for the Volkswagen. Four camps were party to the contest. The first was the Automotive Association, dominated by the three big players Daimler-Benz, BMW, and Auto-Union. The leaders of these firms belonged to a generation of industrialists whose conservative outlook had been shaped during the Weimar period. Appreciative of state support but wary of state intervention, they continued to doubt that car ownership could be expanded beyond higher incomes. As BMW founder and director Franz-Josef Popp repeatedly insisted, for the foreseeable future the bus would remain the true people's car. The key obstacle, the association maintained, was not the price of a car but the cost of maintaining and driving one, and it was up to state policy to remedy this problem. Unnerved by the prospect of a state-subsidized competitor, the Auto Association would have liked to have seen the idea of a Volkswagen stillborn. To placate the regime, however, the association saw itself compelled to turn to a second contestant, the engineering firm of Ferdinand Porsche. They asked Porsche to design a Volkswagen prototype. Behind closed doors, however, the members of the association made no secret that they hoped Porsche would fail.[44]

Porsche was an automotive engineer of Czech-German origin who had made his career as technical director of Daimler-Benz in the 1920s. Something of a gadfly, he fell out with his superiors and quit the company in order to found his own design bureau in 1930, where he pursued a project dear to him: "a car for the broad masses." In Depression-era Germany, however, his prototypes attracted little interest, and in spring 1932 Porsche toured the Soviet Union and even considered relocating there.[45] Porsche's breakthrough came with the development of a race car for Auto-Union; this matter occasioned a first meeting between Porsche and Hitler in early 1933. The new chancellor took a liking to the designer and began treating him as a protégé. Porsche in turn began to make extensive use of the personal access he enjoyed to the dictator. He nurtured greater ambitions than designing a car for the association; as they correctly suspected, Porsche sought "to become technical director of a special plant, yet to be built, for producing the Volkswagen."[46]

The third contestant was Opel, Germany's largest carmaker and a 100 percent subsidiary of General Motors. Opel was GM's flagship foreign investment and the anchor of its overseas empire. The branch answered to GM's Overseas Office in New York, whose head was James D. Mooney, a cosmopolitan who regarded corporate elites as architects of international peace and order. This worldview infused GM's activities in Germany. Opel's leading executives were Americans who frequently traveled to New York and back; engineers often arrived from Detroit. Communications were bilingual. Most Germans accordingly regarded Opel as an American company, which provoked recurring expressions of nationalist hostility. The Automotive Association counted Opel among its members but regarded the firm with suspicion because of its American ownership and strong competitive position. Alone among German factories, Opel's Rüsselsheim plant, replenished by capital from New York and machinery from Michigan, had the capacity to support mass production runs. Hence Opel's executives saw their firm as the natural home of a future Volkswagen.[47]

The fourth contestant was Ford's German subsidiary, Ford AG, located in Cologne on the banks of the Rhine. In the scuffle surrounding the Volkswagen, Ford AG was in the weakest position. Having opened in 1931 at the nadir of the Depression, the branch had yet to turn a profit or produce to capacity. Notwithstanding the Weimar infatuation with all things Ford, the Cologne subsidiary suffered on account of its American brand. As an executive complained in 1932, the German public treated Ford AG with "malicious agitation"; its fellow carmakers saw it as "an American enterprise with whom true Germans ought not to do business."[48] Cologne also suffered from an awkward management setup. All decisions of import had to be cleared in Dearborn, Michigan, where Edsel Ford and Charles Sorensen kept Henry apprised. But unlike GM at Opel, Ford AG had no American executives on the ground in Cologne. Responsible for communications with Dearborn was Heinrich Albert, whose qualifications had nothing to do with automobiles; rather, he was a trained lawyer, former diplomat, and minister emeritus of an early Weimar administration. Besides his duties for Ford, Albert also acted in an advisory capacity for other American corporations with investments in Germany, such as IBM, Gillette, and Woolworth.[49]

The four contestants had to reckon with a regime, finally, that had no scruples in playing them against each other. The main figure they had to deal with was Wilhelm Keppler, the "chargé of the Führer for economic affairs." During the regime's early years, there were few matters of economic policy that lacked Keppler's involvement. As board chairman of the state-orchestrated coal hydrogenation trust *Brabag*, he was active in import substitution. He was involved in the expropriation of the airplane maker *Junkers*; the landmark 1934

FIGURE 4.1. James D. Mooney (center), as head of GM overseas operations responsible for Opel, aboard the *Europa*, 1931. Photo: Getty.

Law of the Order of National Labor bore his imprint. As "special commissioner for raw material questions," Keppler negotiated with industrialists regarding artificial fibers, synthetic petroleum and rubber, iron ore, chemicals, and industrial fats.[50] Keppler was universally described as lacking charisma and smarts; GM's James Mooney, who came to deal with him extensively, found him "pleasant" but "not a very strong character or personality."[51] The American officer who interrogated Keppler after the war flatly called him "a man of limited intelligence."[52] Keppler, however, inhabited a central node in the network politics of the early regime. As one businessman described Keppler's value, "most importantly, he has Hitler's ear."[53]

Over the spring of 1934, the Automotive Association, Opel, and Ford began sounding out the significance of Hitler's Volkswagen injunction. The association aired the industry's "strong caveats" in a memo issued in April, which reiterated that high raw material prices, a narrow market, and onerous maintenance costs—and not a high vehicle price—stood in the way of mass motorization. At a meeting between association members and ministerial authorities, a chancellery secretary responded that the German auto industry "was constructing cars that were much too expensive and did not reflect the income of the broad populace." A price target of 1,000 marks was floated, an unheard-of level that struck the industrialists as preposterous. The association balked at prescriptions but promised to investigate the matter further.[54]

Next in line were Opel's managers. The Automotive Association's executives had failed to secure a personal meeting with Hitler, but when James Mooney asked for an audience, the chancellor made himself available.[55] In the run-up to the meeting, Hitler signaled his "energetic" reassurance that foreign capital would face no discrimination in the automobile industry; this explicitly included "the capital of General Motors."[56] Accordingly, a congenial mood prevailed at the May 2 meeting. Mooney arrived with a Volkswagen proposal in hand: he offered to lower the price of Opel's popular P-4 model to 1,400 marks in return for demand guarantees, a ceiling on raw material costs, and a cap on dealers' commissions. According to Opel's account, Hitler talked at length and even "characterized the 1.2 l Opel as his conception of the true 'Volkswagen,' the car for the German masses, the goal which he had expressed at automobile shows and elsewhere." Though the meeting yielded nothing concrete, Mooney and his colleagues came away with the impression that Opel's small car might soon be accorded the official designation of Volkswagen.[57] Upon returning to the United States, Mooney thanked Hitler for the meeting in a remarkably effusive letter that commended the dictator for his "strong and farsighted leadership" and for leading Germany to "peace, cleanness, and hard work."[58]

FIGURE 4.2. Wilhelm Keppler, powerful broker in the Nazi regime's
economic politics during the early years, 1936.
Photo: Sueddeutsche Zeitung/Alamy.

In the meantime, Ford's branch in Cologne began its own diplomacy. As
Heinrich Albert reported to Dearborn, the German minister of economics had
reassured him that "no difficulties shall be placed in the way" of firms "working
entirely or partly with foreign capital," provided that these firms made use of
German workers and suppliers. Albert also learned that the regime attached
considerable importance to the Volkswagen issue. Since the idea was "propagated by the Chancellor himself," and in light of Ford AG's ongoing difficulties,
Albert recommended "a strong intellectual and practical cooperation in this

matter by Ford proposing a suitable model." This might ingratiate the Cologne branch with the regime and help assuage nationalist hostility.[59]

Unbeknownst to Albert or Mooney, meanwhile, the War Ministry got involved. The military was interested in removing sensitive industries from the French border, and the factories of Opel and Ford seemed natural targets. The military thought that Ford AG, in particular, might be easily goaded into relocating if given proper incentives: presumably, Ford AG was "vitally interested in having the support of the German government," since Ford sales were confronting "considerable mental resistances" on account of the American ownership. In consultation with officials from the city of Hamburg, the military decided to "suggest to Henry Ford to erect a new factory" in that city. Hamburg authorities promised to support the project through a generous property lease, tax incentives, and guaranteed government orders. Because Ford AG's liaison, Heinrich Albert, had served a Weimar administration, however, Hamburg and the military mistrusted him and sought to avoid dealing with him. They decided to appeal to Dearborn over his head.[60]

In doing so, the Hamburg authorities contacted the kaiser's grandson, Prince Louis Ferdinand von Preussen. Why this choice? On the one hand, Louis Ferdinand enjoyed privileged admission to Berlin political circles on account of his pedigree. On the other, Louis was known to possess personal access to Henry Ford: in 1929, he had embarked, at age twenty-one, on a *Bildungsreise* to the Americas and ended up spending three years working for Ford. He had read *My Life and Work*, met Samuel Crowther, and entertained the hope that Ford might involve him in the German branch. Back in Germany in December 1932, Louis was swept up in the political turmoil that culminated in Hitler's appointment to chancellor. In the elections of March 1933, he voted for the National Socialists, whom he considered a "youth movement" that was preferable to the "old-fashioned and merely traditionalistic" conservatives that had launched Hitler to power. That spring Louis met with Hitler at the chancellery, where they talked at length about automobiles, motorization, and Henry Ford.[61] Despite Ford's nimbus among leading Nazis, however, Louis reported to Dearborn that the Ford Motor Company could not expect "any special favors" from the German authorities, who were impatient with the weakness of Ford's Cologne branch. Louis counseled an aggressive approach:

In my opinion Mr Ford has only t[w]o ways to choose with his German plant: To close down or to go ahead in a real Ford way, that means in a big way. . . . It is absolutely beneath the dignity of the Ford Motor Company to be satisfied with 5 percent of the German business, whereas Opel-General Motors sell almost 50% of all cars made in Germany. It will be necessary to change the name of the car into a German name and also change the

location of the plant, and build a real production plant, where we can produce everything, and not have to rely on other firms.[62]

Louis was therefore energized when Hamburg's representatives asked him
to talk to Henry Ford about a new German investment. After Hitler gave the
green light to the mission, Louis and a Hamburg official set out for Dearborn.[63] They conferred with Henry Ford, Edsel Ford, and Charles Sorensen
and made their case that Ford AG should build a brand-new factory on the
banks of the Elbe River. Sorensen, however, gave the mission a reply he described as "non-committal." He found Hamburg's proposals "very indefinite"
and explained that the Cologne plant, which he considered "ideal," had to be
fully utilized before new investments could be entertained.[64]

But the Germans were undeterred. In order to stress that the Hamburg
proposal had Hitler's backing, Keppler personally dispatched a letter to Louis
Ferdinand. In Dearborn, the prince sat down with Henry and Edsel Ford and
read Keppler's missive to them aloud. Here is what the Fords heard: "The
Führer decidedly favors the foundation of new motor car factories in order to
create the Volksauto." Hitler expressly did "not wish any discrimination whatsoever of foreign capital among the German industries." Since Germany was
"utterly backward" as far as automobiles were concerned, the country was "trying to multiply the present amount of motor cars for the coming years." Any
expansion plans in Germany on the part of Ford were therefore welcome. The
only caveat: any new factory would have to be located in central Germany,
removed from the Western border.[65]

Dearborn, however, remained unimpressed. As Sorensen put it, "nobody
here could see any reason why we should move out of Cologne."[66] Louis Ferdinand, in contrast, relayed to Germany his impression that Ford had expressed a "principle [sic] willingness to construct a Volkswagen in Germany."
Louis also asked Keppler to receive two Ford emissaries. Keppler agreed to do
so but cautioned that "Ford would have to decide quickly or else others would
get the business."[67]

Indeed, Keppler simultaneously upped the ante against GM. He told R. K.
Evans, the senior American at Opel, that he considered "only the Opel company . . . capable" of shouldering the Volkswagen. Should Opel hesitate,
however, "somebody else would be instructed to undertake the project."
Evans concluded that Opel's prosperity depended on placating the regime
and recommended that GM take up the Volkswagen project. As Evans relayed his impressions to New York: "If industry is generally willing to cooperate . . . there will be full recognition of capital rights, opportunity for a reasonable return on investment, and no undue interference in the conduct of
business."[68]

In December 1934, Keppler received A. M. Wibel and Herman Moekle, two accountants that Ford had sent from Dearborn. Both Heinrich Albert and Louis Ferdinand attended the meeting. According to Albert's protocol, Keppler took the position that "the construction of a popular car should be developed organically by the initiative and creative power of a single and individual motorcar undertaking." For this reason, Keppler was "eager to get the cooperation of Mr. Ford whose genius for mass production he knows." In light of Keppler's assurances to Opel, this amounted to a remarkable bluff. Wibel and Moekle, however, reiterated why Ford remained hesitant: bringing Cologne to full capacity would have to precede any expansion. The meeting adjourned without concrete results.[69] A few weeks later, a disappointed Louis still hoped that Henry himself might come to Germany to continue the talks.[70]

GM's headquarters, meanwhile, concluded that cooperating with the regime would be advantageous. A few days after the inconclusive meeting with Ford's emissaries, Mooney offered Keppler a "compromise."[71] Opel would indeed agree to build a new factory in central Germany. This new plant would not make Volkswagens, however, but rather host the firm's growing truck program. Over the fall, Opel's executives had been scouting locations for a new plant, including Hamburg. In coordination with the military authorities, however, Opel finally settled on Brandenburg, outside of Berlin. Apprised of this proposal, Keppler responded with "great joy." As he wrote to Opel, "the solution that has been suggested in America" had found "applause in certain quarters." Keppler hoped that "your American friends" would deploy their technical expertise to build a factory both prolific and flexible, which would be ideal from a military-strategic perspective. He also recommended "soon expanding the Rüsselsheim works for the production of the Volkswagen."[72] In January, Opel presented layouts and equipment schedules to military officials in Berlin.[73] After Hitler gave his approval, things moved fast: on March 22, 1935, GM's finance committee in New York approved the new investment, which amounted to 11 million marks.[74] On March 31, the press announced the new factory. Ground was broken on April 12; the first Opel Blitz truck rolled off the line in early November.

As Opel's investment hit stride in Brandenburg, Keppler brought new pressure on Ford. The first issue was standards. In 1935, the military pushed a unified system of technical norms on the automobile industry, which every German carmaker, including Opel, quickly adopted. Since Ford AG produced cars of American design, however, assimilating German standards (which included the metric system) posed a considerable challenge. The second issue arose when Keppler again asked Louis Ferdinand to approach Dearborn on his behalf. This time, Keppler asked that Ford buy into an ailing German carmaker, Stoewer, whose workshops were located in Stettin on the Baltic Sea. In a reprise of the Hamburg affair, Keppler sought to goad Ford away from the Western border and bind the firm into the German automobile industry.

The matter came to a head when Keppler received Heinrich Albert and Louis Ferdinand in January 1936. Keppler began by comparing Ford unfavorably to Opel. Opel "had always been on good terms with the Government and Party organizations," Keppler said, while Ford "was always coming to complain, never to offer anything." Only recently had Opel begun operating its brand-new truck factory in Brandenburg, a strategically desirable location. Ford AG was aware that the government did not approve of its plant location on the Rhine; why was Ford so unresponsive? Keppler then said something sharply revealing about how the Nazi regime "steered" foreign firms into compliance. Perhaps, Keppler said, Ford AG might eventually obtain an official letter of recognition as a fully "German" firm. However,

> not paper and recognition but disposition and atmosphere [were] decisive. This atmosphere could only be created by Ford doing something which Government and Party wanted. Then the competent departments would have a means of rendering Ford popular. It was the way of things in Germany that the totality of the State seized hold of the entire life [sic]. Without good relations with the Government Authorities and Party departments the opposition to a foreign undertaking could not be removed and the naturalization of the latter as a German undertaking not be achieved.

Lest the point be lost, Keppler said that there would be no budging on the issue of standards, and that he would "urgently recommend" that the Ford Motor Company consider an affiliation with the Stoewer works.[75]

Making the Americans Play Ball

We may pause our play-by-play here: By 1936, the patterns of the regime's relationship with the American multinationals had been set. Together with the military authorities, Keppler had roped the Americans into a type of informal project competition. A mixture of personal diplomacy, selective information, and calibrated political pressure succeeded in making the Americans, willy-nilly, "work towards" the regime's goals.[76] If these bullying tactics bore a distinctly Nazi stamp, the demands that the regime put on the American corporations were, from the perspective of transnational industrial policy, generic: Keppler pressed the Americans for new fixed investments (Volkswagen), joint ventures with domestic industry (Stoewer), and technical assimilation (standards). These methods had also already yielded one significant result: to avoid shouldering the manufacture of the Volkswagen without alienating the regime, General Motors had built a truck factory in Germany in coordination with the military authorities—a significant new fixed investment that combined cutting-edge mass production facilities with military adaptability.

Moreover, Keppler was right: on the whole, General Motors proved more responsive than Ford to the regime's demands and forged a closer relationship with its highest officials. Opel's American executives began building on the connections established during the Volkswagen tussle. With the truck factory, Opel opened a direct line to the army procurement office and its influential military head, General Georg Thomas. Thomas had been "very pleased" when New York authorized the Brandenburg investments in early 1935; over the next few years, the plant sold a considerable share of its Opel Blitz trucks to the army and later agreed to produce a special four-wheel design at the army's behest.[77] By 1938, Mooney's second in command, Graeme Howard, characterized Thomas's attitude as "a helpful, cooperative, and understanding friendship for General Motors and Adam Opel A.G."[78] Cyrus Osborn, the senior American executive at Opel after 1937, counted Thomas's department and the Ministry of Economics among those who "recognize[d] the advantage to Germany of Opel's association with GM."[79]

By 1938, Opel's contacts included Erhard Milch and Ernst Udet, the leading officers at the Aviation Ministry, which was in charge of the Luftwaffe's sprawling bomber development complex. Meetings with Milch and Udet were sociable: "We had a very nice luncheon, did a little serious drinking, and reviewed many business matters," as Howard described the proceedings. In September 1938, minister of aviation Hermann Göring hosted William Knudsen, who had succeeded Alfred Sloan as GM's president, outside of Berlin. According to Opel's report, Göring thanked Knudsen for the "valuable assistance which the General Motors Corporation, in particular Opel," had rendered in connection with "the creation of foreign exchange" through automobile exports and "in the fitting out of Germany's new Army and Air Force." Göring expressed his satisfaction that Opel was introducing American industrial methods into Germany. He hoped that Opel might consider manufacturing aircraft engines in a new factory "equipped with American machines." Knudsen's replies were noncommittal, though Opel later did begin producing a special type of aircraft engine gear for the Aviation Ministry's bomber program.[80]

Along with their German colleagues at Opel, then, GM's American executives actively cultivated high-level connections in Berlin.[81] However, these efforts must be seen in the context of the pervasive hostility that confronted Opel on the part of aggressive local party organizations and a nationalist-minded public that railed against the firm's American ownership. In particular, Howard's and Osborn's conferences with the Aviation Ministry transpired amid an aggressive challenge to GM's hold over Opel. In 1938, the party boss (*Gauleiter*) of Hesse, where Opel's Rüsselsheim plant was located, sought to interfere in Opel's management and demanded that a National Socialist of his choosing be installed as "plant leader" (*Betriebsführer*). In doing so, the *Gauleiter* had the support of several German executives at Opel. GM, however, responded forcefully to these challenges. Mooney and Howard cut loose the Nazi-leaning Opel director Rudolf Fleischer and installed in his stead the American Cyrus Osborn, whose allegiance to General Motors was without question and who, with "shaky" German, reinforced the American presence at Opel.[82] The Americans were able to reassert their authority largely because they could count on the backing of ministerial and military higher-ups in Berlin, who vowed to set the *Gauleiter* straight. Broad-based nationalist hostility, then, gave a sharp edge to the regime's politics toward multinationals: it drove the Americans to seek protection from the Berlin authorities, which in turn allowed the regime to reinforce its demands. As Osborn explained the rationale, "in the interest of the protection of our entire investment in Germany," it was necessary "to co-operate with high and important government departments in the furtherance of certain of their projects."[83]

Like Opel, Ford AG encountered nationalist hostility among the public. It faced the antagonism of the Automotive Association, described by Heinrich Albert as "a formidable opponent" who was happy to seize on every opportunity to denounce Ford AG and its products as insufficiently German.[84] This stigma was effective: until 1937, government officials, military agencies, party members, and affiliates of professional associations refrained from purchasing Ford cars. Albert estimated that this silent boycott reduced Ford's customer base by at least one-third, but that was not the only problem: "What makes government orders so important," Albert wrote to Dearborn, "is the fact that they would imply the official recognition of our works."[85] For much of the first four years of the regime, Albert was engaged in what he called "fighting for equal rights"—for an official recognition on the part of the government that Ford AG was a "German" firm.[86]

Adding to Albert's worries, many of the regime's supporters struggled to reconcile Ford AG's apparent reluctance to support the regime with the nimbus that Henry Ford enjoyed among Nazis. This peculiar good-czar phenomenon led to repeated attempts, similar to Louis Ferdinand's sortie in the Volkswagen matter, to appeal to Dearborn over Cologne's head. Among dealers and middling party men in particular, Henry Ford was popular while Cologne had a poor reputation. In 1935, a Dearborn sales agent visiting dealers in Germany reported widespread discontent with Albert's management and threats against him. Hamburg circles still had not accepted Dearborn's rebuke in the Volkswagen matter. They urged that "some kind of contact should be established direct with the higher Ford officials in Detroit" and that headquarters replace Albert with "an American, working directly under and reporting to

Detroit"—essentially replicating the setup of Opel.[87] As late as 1939, one dealer calling himself "a supporter of Ford ideas" addressed Henry and Edsel Ford directly to express his concern that "the methods used at Cologne are widely at variance with your first principles." He urged a fuller and closer co-operation with the aims of the Nazi economy.[88]

Like GM's executives, Albert reacted to this pressure by moving closer to the regime. After Keppler had warned Ford AG to show initiative, Albert increasingly began adopting the regime's arguments in his correspondence with Dearborn. Albert had responded with annoyance to the entreaties of the Hamburg authorities; now he urged Edsel Ford and Charles Sorensen to placate Keppler and buy out the Stettin Stoewer works. The reason for doing so, Albert argued, was primarily "psychologic"—"to win the good-will of Party and State by doing them an economic service."[89] He also recommended accepting the military's standardization demands and intensifying exports "on account of [their] national importance."[90] Dearborn's responses were mixed. On the one hand, Edsel Ford and Sorensen began supporting Cologne's exports through Dearborn's distribution networks. They also accepted the constraints of Nazi foreign exchange management and began supplying Ford AG with raw materials through barter agreements. On the other hand, in the Stowever matter, Sorensen upbraided Albert for being "too impressed with the necessity of co-operating with the Government Authorities" and told him to drop the deal, thus passing up the regime's second request to expand investment in Germany.[91] A few weeks later, Albert suggested that Henry and Edsel direct a personal letter to minister of economics Hjalmar Schacht to support Ford AG. The Fords rejected the idea as "too committal."[92]

Why was the Ford organization apparently less eager than General Motors to engage with the regime? There were obvious reasons. For one, while Ford AG's numbers crept into the black in 1935, the plant still ran at only 40 percent capacity.[93] Under these circumstances, a large-scale expansion program of the type suggested by Keppler seemed far-fetched. Because Opel was the major contributor (and beneficiary) of the Nazi motorization boom, in contrast, the firm accumulated profits quickly. Unable to remit these profits across the Atlantic, GM's management had good reason to reinvest them instead.[94] Moreover, the Ford Motor Company expected its overseas branches to produce American-designed cars, which made it difficult to adapt to national technical standards. Standards delivered a concrete way of answering the question, Which industrial sphere of influence mattered more for Ford AG: that of the global Ford branch network or that of the German rearmament economy? When Albert asked, apropos the standardization issue, whether Dearborn would be "willing on principle" to have Cologne build a model specifically designed for the German market, Sorensen responded with an emphatic "no."[95] Opel, of course, had no such problems.[96]

But there were also ideological differences. Both firms' executives, to be sure, nurtured the conceit that they conducted their affairs with the Nazi regime on strictly business terms and without regard for politics. However, they derived rather different implications from this premise. Sorensen early on compared the Nazi regime's meddling to that of the New Deal, which Henry Ford famously detested. "You have in Germany what I call an N.R.A.," Sorensen wrote to Prince Louis Ferdinand. "Prices will be determined by them, and they are even talking about design. I am not sure that Mr. Ford would accept this kind of a plan anywhere in the world."[97] The Ford Motor Company did not like to be told what and how to produce. Hence the regime's demands in matters of plant expansion, the Volkswagen, and standardization struck Edsel Ford and Sorensen as an imposition. At the same time, they were happy to let Albert deal with the regime for them.

GM's executives also saw the regime's demands as intrusive, but they fundamentally accepted the need to come to terms with them. Mooney wondered about "the best manner in which we can accept the considerable domination of our operations . . . on the part of the government."[98] Sloan expressed the view that local political circumstances should not concern General Motors even if management "might not wholly agree with many things that are done." As he stated the principle in 1939, a multinational "should conduct its operations in strictly business terms, without regard to the political beliefs of its management, or the political beliefs of the countries in which it is operating."[99] GM's executives took this principle to mean that playing ball with the regime was the correct course of action as long as it strengthened Opel's position and secured its earnings.

Ford, GM, and Nazi Industrial Upgrading

How did the mix of pressure and incentives that the regime applied to Ford and GM affect the buildup of mass production capacity in Nazi Germany? Broadly speaking, both firms recovered from the Depression riding the Nazi motorization boom and, by the mid-Thirties, grew into pillars of the rearmament economy. As Albert became increasingly willing to accommodate the authorities, Ford AG's position improved, and the firm grew from a marginal and money-losing branch to a well-equipped provider of cars and trucks. In 1935, Ford AG began cooperating in the regime's export promotion schemes and foreign exchange management: Cologne shipped automotive parts to Dearborn and received dollars in return. The German authorities then required Ford AG to exchange these dollars into marks, albeit at a favorable rate that included a 25 percent export bonus. In 1936, Dearborn began shipping tires and iron ore to Ford AG in return for parts, thereby supplying Cologne with indispensable imports without requiring transactions in hard currency. Again, the German authorities compelled Ford AG to sell a share of these sensitive imports to other German producers, albeit at favorable prices. The success of these agreements explains why in 1937 ministerial and army departments finally granted Ford AG the much-coveted official designation "German firm." In 1938, the first major government order followed, with the army requesting over 3,150 V8 trucks, and by the fall Ford AG reported that "business with the authorities developed extraordinarily." Vigorous export business and government orders meant that Ford AG was now producing behind demand. By the outbreak of war, Ford was responsible for almost one-fifth of German truck production.[100]

In 1938, Dearborn also agreed to a joint venture. The project involved the Berlin firm Ambi-Budd, a supplier of automobile bodies. Under the terms of this cooperation, the military provided designs for the truck as well as specifications for machinery, Ambi-Budd provided the facilities and technical supervision, and Ford AG sent engineering staff, built machinery, and set up assembly. The plant operated from late 1938 to 1941 and put out more than 1,800 troop transporters and personnel carriers. Though this operation was on a much smaller scale than Opel's Brandenburg facility, it followed a similar logic: the military procurement agencies contracted directly with the American-owned firm for the production of trucks in a strategically desirable geographical location.[101]

Ford AG's significance in the rearmament economy, however, was dwarfed by that of Opel. Simply put, Opel was a much larger concern: over the course of the Thirties, the firm rapidly expanded to become the largest car manufacturer in Western Europe, and its Rüsselsheim and Brandenburg plants came to form the two cornerstones of Nazi Germany's automotive mass production. Funded by profits that could not be repatriated to the United States, Opel's gross investment in real estate, plant, and equipment tripled from 46.6 million marks to 143.4 million between 1929 and 1939. At both branches, capital replenishment concentrated on factory machinery, for which net investment stood at close to 100 million marks by decade's end.[102] Other expansion projects included a new forge, a press shop for car bodies, and a tool shop that allowed Opel to build 70 percent of its machinery in-house. Brandenburg boasted a state-of-the art power plant "recognized as one of the most modern and efficient in Europe." As Osborn concluded in a summary report he relayed to New York in 1940, several years of modernization and expansion had made Opel "the most highly developed and most efficient motor car producer in Europe."[103]

FIGURE 4.3. The final assembly line at Opel's Brandenburg truck factory, 1936.
Photo: Sueddeutsche Zeitung/Alamy.

The Brandenburg plant was a major prize for Nazi rearmament: it became the army's main source of trucks. When Brandenburg opened, it garnered "the admiration of all experts": its architecture and equipment exemplified modern mass production. The shop floor was spacious and light-filled and featured powerful machines, precise coordination, and partial automation. Fully laid out according to flow principles, the brand-new plant accomplished the entire fabrication from raw materials to finished truck under one roof. It boasted twenty-seven conveyors linking 1,200 modern machines, among them highly specialized tools built according to American specifications.[104] A little more than a year after the plant started up, a major expansion to the tune of 4.58 million marks was agreed upon with the army, in order to incorporate the production of a new four-wheel-drive truck.[105] Already in 1936, the first year of full operations, Brandenburg produced 15,000 trucks. By 1940, that number had reached 19,600 units. In this period, Brandenburg accounted for over one-third of German truck output, of which a considerable number went toward exports.[106]

These facts explain why, by the outbreak of war, GM's executives and the Nazi authorities both regarded their relationship as successful.[107] For GM, the Opel subsidiary had developed into a significant asset under the conditions of Nazi economic steering and exchange management. Benefiting from the regime's aggressive export promotion, Opel had become GM's most prolific hub in overseas markets, delivering knocked-down kits to all major GM-owned assembly plants within Europe and beyond. As Osborn explained in 1940, GM's "position in the world markets is appreciably stronger because of Opel." It helped that Opel cars captured markets that were unavailable to GM's more expensive American brands: Opel trailed only Chevrolet among GM's exports. Opel passenger cars and trucks sold from assembly plants outside of Germany garnered approximately $20 million—income that GM derived from Opel despite the inability to directly repatriate profits.[108]

For the Nazi regime, it mattered that Opel's share of German car exports hovered between 40 and 65 percent every year after 1933. The firm's outstanding role in international markets made it an important source of foreign exchange. Equally important, Opel's two factories featured modern mass production technology that the regime was only too happy to exploit after the outbreak of war. To be sure, Rüsselsheim was idle for several months after the German invasion of Poland, as civilian vehicle production was severely curtailed. Soon, however, the plant became a successful supplier to the sprawling system of German aircraft production. In January 1942, the now Germanized management boasted that, exceptionally, Opel was building aircraft components and airframes "on the moving line." The military authorities ordered Germany's leading aircraft engineers to "observe how production is done" at

Opel.[109] Unlike Rüsselsheim, Brandenburg faced no downtime after 1939. Throughout the war, the plant put out the flag vehicle of the Wehrmacht's motor fleet, the three-ton Blitz truck.

Enlisting the American multinationals allowed the Nazi rearmament economy to acquire American machinery without taxing hard currency accounts. In this way, the Americans effectively dollar-subsidized technological transfers into Germany. For Ford, the first significant transfer of this type took place in 1935, when Dearborn sent V8 cars, parts, and machinery worth some 3 million marks to Cologne in exchange not for dollars but for newly issued shares of Ford AG. It was understood that this constituted a long-term credit that lacked a fixed repayment date.[110] As Albert explained to officials at the Ministry of Economics in terms they will have appreciated, these V8-related imports "supply the German political economy with values which are not reciprocated. . . . They signify a rational addition to German production."[111] In 1938, Ford Cologne ordered more than $56,000 in American machine tools through Dearborn. The orders were paid for not with dollars but with parts and sundries shipped from Cologne to Dearborn. Though deliveries were temporarily held up by the outbreak of war, machine imports for 1939 exceeded $100,000 against barter and appear to have continued into 1940.[112]

Similar technology transfers, extorted by exchange controls, took place between GM and Opel. Capital controls ensured that Brandenburg had to teach German suppliers how to manufacture a range of truck components. The plant also required specific American machines, for which the exchange offices refused to allocate dollars; so Opel's engineers coaxed the blueprints from the American supplier and built the machines themselves.[113] The senior American engineer on the ground at Opel tested German-built machines and found that they could not "stand the gaff" as the American machines did. He suggested an elaborate scheme for upgrading: German machines should be shipped to America and tested there; "then, according to the results, we should get the German manufacturers to make better tools."[114]

German machine tool builders, however, did not necessarily jump at such proposals, as Otto Dyckhoff, Opel's chief production engineer, found out the hard way. In 1937, Dyckhoff sought permission from the Economics Ministry to import a Gleason machine for Brandenburg. The ministry told Dyckhoff to use machines from Klingelberg, a German manufacturer, instead. Dyckhoff replied that they had tried out Klingelberg's machines but found them irredeemably inferior. The ministry responded that no import dollars could be allocated; instead, Opel should help Klingelberg develop a better machine. When Klingelberg's engineers learned of this, however, they indignantly denied that their machines were subpar; also, they submitted, not every

American machining "fad" was worthy of imitation. To this, Dyckhoff reacted sharply. "Your current construction," he wrote to Klingelberg, with carbon copy to the ministry, "is not a high-performance machine for mass production." It was necessary to keep abreast with American technology, he continued, "for reasons of national economy, since, as you will be aware, the defense capabilities and food supply of the German people depends on industrial exports, not least automobile exports." Without high-performance machinery, it was impossible to "solve the problem of the Volkswagen or that of automobile exports." Chastened, Klingelberg agreed to develop a special-purpose machine to American specifications, so that the German auto industry could "compete on world markets even without using American machines."[115] In this way, indirectly but forcefully, the combined pressure of exchange control, economic steering, and political bullying contributed to technological learning. The episode throws some light on how German manufacturers in the Thirties were pushed to make better tools—or at least the kind of American-style tools that firms seeking to exploit economies of scale asked them to build.[116]

Finally, the "tacit" nature of technological knowledge required exchanging personnel across the Atlantic. Opel's managers emphasized that "the best German men in our organization are those who had some foreign experience" and sought to regularize training programs and personnel exchanges with Detroit.[117] Not by coincidence, the top three engineers at Opel had considerable exposure to American factory realities. The first was Gerd Stieler von Heydekampf, a Berlin-born machine tool engineer who, like so many of his generation, spent much of the 1920s in American factories. In the wake of the Depression, Heydekampf returned to Germany, joined Opel, and quickly ascended to the board of managers. As head of purchasing, Heydekampf began to deal extensively with the Ministry of Economics and the military authorities. In 1938, at only thirty-three years of age, Heydekampf was put in charge of the Brandenburg plant.[118] Heinrich Nordhoff had studied with Heydekampf at Berlin's Technical University in the 1920s. Instead of moving to America, Nordhoff did "the next best thing" (in his own words) and joined Opel, which sent him on several trips to Detroit. Nordhoff joined Opel's board of managers in 1936 and began to play an influential role in the firm's diplomacy with the regime. By 1940, Osborn credited the "healthy atmosphere" in the firm's relations with the government to Nordhoff's skillful diplomacy. Nordhoff succeeded Heydekampf at the helm of Brandenburg in 1942.[119] The third high-profile engineer was Otto Dyckhoff, who, as we just recounted, tangled with German manufacturers about the quality of their machine tools. As Opel's chief production engineer, Dyckhoff was responsible for equipping Brandenburg with machinery in 1935.[120]

The careers of these men illustrate how American mass production know-how percolated through German industry. Opel's leading engineers marched straight from orchestrating Nazi motorization to running war production, and many continued into the West German economic miracle. Dyckhoff left Opel in 1937 to work for Porsche's Volkswagen plant (more about this presently). In 1941, he was put in charge of a BMW "flow plant" for aircraft engines.[121] Heydekampf left Brandenburg in 1942 for a management position at Henschel, one of the pillar firms of the Nazi war production machine. In 1943, he relieved Ferdinand Porsche at the helm of Nazi Germany's tank program. After the war, Heydekampf emerged as one of the leading players in the burgeoning West German automobile industry.[122] Nordhoff, finally, was in charge of Brandenburg until the Red Army dismantled the plant in 1945. In 1948, the British occupation forces invited him to take the helm of the reconstituted Volkswagen works, where Nordhoff remained until his death in 1968, making his name synonymous with West Germany's *Wirtschaftswunder*.[123]

Porsche's Americans

Meanwhile, what *of* the Volkswagen? In July 1936, Ferdinand Porsche presented the latest prototype of his "Beetle" design at Hitler's holiday retreat in upper Bavaria, and the dictator decided he had finally seen "his" Volkswagen. Hitler had declined to commit to a model for more than two years, but sent encouraging signals in Porsche's direction even as Opel's managers remained hopeful to win the Volkswagen designation for their popular P-4. At the same time, Hitler was fed up with the Automotive Association, who feared the Volkswagen and had become openly hostile to Porsche. Much to Porsche's delight, the dictator proposed that the new Beetle prototype should find its mass production home in a special plant built as a private-public undertaking independent of the German carmakers. At this juncture, the idea to involve the American multinationals was unceremoniously shelved: the Volkswagen, Hitler said, was now "a purely national matter" from which "firms oriented towards America" would be excluded.[124] The Americans were kept in the dark about this reversal. In September 1936, Mooney sought a meeting with the dictator, hoping to propose a further price reduction to the P-4 in order to finally win the Volkswagen designation for Opel. Hitler declined and sent Keppler instead, who, when prodded about the Volkswagen, grew "rather vague."[125] A year later, GM's executives still wondered if some kind of financial participation in Porsche's project might be advisable.[126]

Opel's input proved unnecessary: the question of how to fund the future Volkswagen plant received a quintessentially Nazi resolution when the

German Labor Front decided to take up the project. With the Volkswagen, the Nazi labor organization found a way to put to work the considerable assets it had confiscated from Weimar's crushed labor unions: these funds, together with the layaway savings of hundreds of thousands of hopeful future Volkswagen drivers, constituted the plant's main source of financing. The Volkswagen also fit into the front's ideological program: like no other Nazi organization, the Labor Front propagated the idea of a racially inflected "people's community" of German-Aryan workers and toilers. A people's car factory that was publicly sponsored, operated on a nonprofit basis, and ran with modern mass production equipment, corresponded well with this ideology.[127]

Porsche had not initially conceived of a separate factory. Though he had flirted with "people's car" ideas since the 1920s, Porsche initially approached the project as an automobile designer—that is, he began with the example of the Model T. As Porsche argued when he first presented his ideas to the Automotive Association, any German people's car would have to begin with an audacious new construction, one that would meet rising expectations for strength, durability, and comfort. Like the Model T, such a design would require careful preparation so that it could be produced "principally unchanged for more than ten years." To organize production and distribution of his people's car, Porsche proposed merging several existing German carmakers under one administrative roof.[128] Porsche's initial ideas therefore very much echoed the Volkswagen hopes of Weimar times, in which national mergers would beat back the American competition both at home and on export markets.[129]

With Hitler calling for a separate factory for Porsche's design, however, a whole new prospect opened up: now it would be possible not only to replicate the Model T but to copy the mighty River Rouge. Thus a new chapter in the Nazi appropriation of mass production began, which resembled Soviet efforts: Porsche hastily assembled a small team of engineers and planners to study the Rouge's layout and operations, acquire machinery, and hire specialists from Ford. This Volkswagen committee consisted of the designer himself, as well as Bodo Lafferentz, who represented the Labor Front, and Jakob Werlin, an executive from Daimler-Benz who had first introduced Porsche to Hitler. Finally, Porsche managed to recruit Otto Dyckhoff, Opel's technical director—a fact that GM's executives acknowledged as a loss.[130]

In June 1937, the team set out for Detroit. Though the details of the group's activity at the Rouge are lost, it is clear that they were welcomed in Dearborn and got a chance to speak to Henry Ford. A German Ford dealer close to Werlin introduced the group.[131] Werlin recalled an "animated" conversation with Ford, who opened the Rouge to inspection, just as he had for the Soviet delegations several years before. (Asked why the company was so hospitable to foreign engineers, Ford reportedly replied, "We have no secrets. If better cars are built in the future, I will build them.")[132] During the group's stay, one of Porsche's Silver Arrows won a prestigious international race on Long Island; Ford cabled to congratulate. The designer thanked him and reported that he had spent three weeks "all over" the Rouge, which he called "the most wonderful factory I have ever seen."[133]

Over the next weeks, Dyckhoff and Porsche hired from the Ford Motor Company the technical leadership of the future plant. Tapping into the large German-American cohort among the highly skilled core at the Rouge, Volkswagen recruited the toolmakers Henry Esfeld, Karl Luik, and Joseph Werner; Hans Riedel, a superintendent at the Rouge body shop; Hans Mayr, the superintendent of the press shop; and the specialists Rudolf Stephan, Reinhold Ficht, and Willy Rechenbach. All of them occupied leading technical positions at the Rouge and boasted at least ten years of Ford experience: like many aspiring German machinists and engineers, they had moved to the United States in the 1920s to join the world's leading automobile firm. The veteran in this distinguished group was Mayr, who had first left Germany before World War I and earned his chops at Highland Park. After a stint back in Germany, he returned to the Ford Motor Company in 1923 and worked his way to the helm of the Rouge press shop.[134]

Porsche's Americans sold their houses and cars and moved their families to Stuttgart, where they joined the Volkswagen planning bureau. Joseph Werner and Hans Mayr began reworking Porsche's Volkswagen model for mass flow production. The key, as Werner recalled, was in the "little things": for example, Werner pointed out "that you simply couldn't grind one thousand gears a day"; instead, he introduced the more time-efficient "American method" of shaving the gears. Dyckhoff, Mayr, Werner, and Esfeld drew up production plans and determined the makeup of the machine park.[135] Fritz Kuntze, another Ford veteran, also joined the group. Kuntze had been in charge of the Rouge power plant for several years before returning to Germany in the spring of 1937 and signing with Dyckhoff. Kuntze was largely responsible for sketching the basic layout of the future plant, based on his knowledge of the Rouge. His layout adopted the high degree of backward integration boasted by the Rouge and included press shops, a body shop, and a machine shop, a forge and a foundry to supply the raw parts, as well as a steel works and a power plant. Myriad conveyors would emulate Rouge-style flow. Capacity was slated to reach 1.5 million vehicles (though in reality this figure was not obtained before the 1960s). Volkswagen then hired the architectural firm Mewes, which had built Ford's factory in Cologne. Mewes worked the elements sketched out by Kuntze into the characteristic fusion of functionalism and fascist monumentality that still gives the Volkswagen headquarters its unsettling vista today.[136]

Kuntze kept a daily log, which offers an interesting glimpse at the lives of the newly recruited returnees. Shortly after arriving from Detroit, Kuntze completed a two-week training sponsored by the Labor Front, where "capitalists as well as native and foreign managers" received ideological instruction. It is unclear how many of his fellow German-Americans had to do the same. Kuntze, in any case, seemed to enjoy the mobilizational aspects of Nazism, often recording political events in his log (February 20, 1938: "Sunday. Magnificent weather. The Führer's great speech." March 14, 1938: "Austria is ours."). Like Porsche himself, Kuntze kept a portrait of Hermann Göring in his office. Kuntze's log also gives the impression that the German-Americans formed a tight-knit group that socialized after hours and visited each others' families on weekends. Into the war, they maintained a sense of esprit de corps (May 8, 1942: "Gathering Mayr, Riedel and all Americans: stick together against the white collars!"). However, the stresses of war production also produced fierce altercations (July 9, 1942: "Severe clash with Mayr over work shop tasks: yelled at us terribly.").[137]

The original group of nine did not remain the only German-Americans at Volkswagen. In November 1938, Dyckhoff returned to Detroit; this time he targeted foremen, toolmakers, and other skilled German-Americans working at the Rouge. Among those recruited were William Ruf, "foreman of the motor block department"; John Rumpf, "foreman of the axle department"; William Fritzke, "foreman of the tool shop"; Theodor Koch, "foreman of the crankshaft department"; and Oscar Messerschmidt, "foreman of the piston and cylinder department." Messerschmidt, who was an American citizen, sailed with his wife and five children from New York on January 4, 1939, expenses paid by Volkswagen. On the same boat were thirty-nine-year-old John Neuse and his wife, American citizens "born in Germany and naturalized in Detroit." Overall, more than two dozen former Ford workers made the passage to Germany in the first months of 1939. In Germany, this new group of skilled labor migrants took up supervisory positions at a pilot plant of Volkswagen's, where selected German youth completed preparatory machinist apprenticeships.[138]

Along with these Rouge recruitments for Volkswagen, the Labor Front sought to win skilled workers for German industry at large. In the winter of 1938–1939, the Front's agents took out ads in German-language newspapers across the Midwest, and eventually persuaded more than seven hundred skilled workers in Milwaukee, Chicago, Cleveland, and Detroit to resign their American jobs and relocate to Germany. With the campaign, the Labor Front sought to alleviate the severe shortage of skilled labor that haunted German industries. But the returnees also brought hard currency with them—$202,012, according to the FBI's subsequent calculations—a modest but much-needed contribution to Volkswagen's purchases of American machine tools. Those recruited in this campaign found employment across German industry; a few wound up at Volkswagen. [139]

When this final group of returnees arrived, construction at the main factory complex was nearing completion, but equipment and machinery had not been fully set up. The reason for these delays was that Volkswagen was a project of the Labor Front, which stood outside of the main circuits of the Nazi rearmament complex. The authorities did not include the plant in their military planning and did not prioritize it in their allocations of labor, steel, and machinery. Thus the outbreak of war in September 1939 saw the factory unprepared. Before the plant could produce a single Volkswagen, the military authorities suspended passenger car production across the motor vehicle industry. For several months, the works was cut off from raw materials deliveries; scheduled arrivals of American machinery were indefinitely postponed. Retooling for armaments purposes was awkward and slow. By early 1940, the great production halls stood "unused and empty," as Porsche had to admit.[140] Under these circumstances, several of the Ford veterans packed up and returned to the United States before the German authorities could seize their American passports.[141]

The majority of Porsche's initial group of recruits, however, remained and led Volkswagen into war production. Orders from the aviation sector—aircraft parts, and those plywood fuel tanks—provided some early relief. Next, the factory began repairing damaged Ju-88 bombers, and this remained one of the plant's main activities during the war. In the summer of 1940, the factory began to put out military versions of Porsche's Beetle design: jeeps, amphibians, and communications vehicles. These amounted to more than 66,000 units over the course of the war.[142] Throughout the war, Volkswagen's technical leadership and production engineering was in the hands of Porsche's German-Americans. Fritz Kuntze, formerly in charge of the Rouge's energy supply, ascended to the head of the power plant and supply departments more generally. Hans Mayr held the position of technical director. Karl Luik headed the press shop, and Joseph Werner oversaw final vehicle assembly. In these roles, the Americans put their expertise at the disposal of the Nazi war production machine and became complicit in its crimes. Hans Mayr and Porsche sought to exploit the industrial capacities of occupied France for Volkswagen (albeit with mixed success). Ford veterans Hans Riedel and Rudolph Stephan organized the underground relocation of Volkswagen operations in 1944: in repurposed mine shafts, forced laborers toiled under inhuman conditions on improvised assembly lines. By 1944, more than half of the main factory's 8,771 workers were POWs and so-called foreigners working under coercion.[143]

After the war, the US Strategic Bombing Survey concluded that, despite being "the largest factory of its type in Germany" and boasting "the largest press shop in Europe," at no time had the gigantic works operated above 50 percent of capacity.[144] The production engineer who handed the plant over to American forces in 1945 concurred: during the war, flow production had remained "highly unfinished, and the stipulated production quotas were never reached for want of material and because the machinery was incomplete." He noted, however, that "in technical regard, it was tried as much as possible to work with modern production methods" and discerned "a certain advantage over other German firms" because "our technical leadership had practical experience in the American vehicle industry."[145]

In 1945, US military intelligence identified thirteen former Americans at the plant, among them five of Porsche's recruits from 1937, all of them in leading positions.[146] Several of them were arrested and eventually disbarred from further employment at Volkswagen. Hans Mayr, the most high-profile of the German-Americans, was forced out. Hans Riedel returned to the United States. At least three American veterans, however, continued their career at Volkswagen. Fritz Kuntze was allowed to return but had to accept a demotion from heading power plant operations to managing the plant's vehicle fleet. More impressive were the postwar careers of two other Americans. Joseph Werner, Porsche's recruit number one, returned to the helm of Volkswagen's production engineering department and visited the United States as part of a technical reconnaissance mission in 1951. He subsequently helped launch Volkswagen's first fully automated branch in Hanover, which opened in 1957. Werner's closest associate in this endeavor was Otto Höhne, whom the Labor Front had culled from his Chicago assembly line job in 1939. Höhne worked his way up through the ranks during the war. In 1959, Höhne became Volkswagen's director of production; in 1960, he joined Volkswagen's management board. Upon his retirement in 1972, Volkswagen's accolades stressed his American credentials: "The knowledge of modern work methods in car manufacturing, which Otto Höhne brought with him from America . . . put him in a position to bring Volkswagen up to the technological standard it currently enjoys."[147]

Conclusion

In 1938, German consular staff in the United States decorated two prominent American businessmen with an award that the Nazi regime bestowed on foreigners who, according to the official designation, "had been of service to the Reich." One of the recipients was GM's overseas chief executive James Mooney, who accepted the Order of Merit of the Cross of the German Eagle, First Class, from the German consul in New York on August 17. The other awardee was Henry Ford. In a brief ceremony at the Dearborn Laboratory, two German diplomats pinned the Grand Cross of the German Eagle, the award's highest rung, to Ford's chest. The occasion was Ford's seventy-fifth birthday on July 30. A year earlier, Thomas Watson, IBM's chief executive, had received a similar decoration from Hjalmar Schacht at the occasion of the International Chamber of Commerce's Berlin conference.

There were two contexts for these remarkable gestures of recognition. Mooney's and Ford's awards occurred, first, as part of an effort of Nazi diplomats to strengthen pro-German voices on the American right at a time when diplomatic relations were deteriorating. Over the course of 1938, German consular staff gave more than a dozen eagle crosses to Americans. Apart from one celebrity, Charles Lindbergh, the other awardees were lesser-known figures, such as the Stanford historian Ralph Haswell Lutz and Oberlin professor Karl Geiser, the translator of Sombart's works for Princeton University Press. Such bestowals ceased after the pogroms of November 1938 had turned American public opinion firmly against Nazi Germany.[148] An equally important reason for the decorations of Watson, Mooney, and Ford was the Nazi regime's transnational industrial politics. The awards reflected the close, if tense and quarrelsome, relationships that American multinationals developed with the Nazi regime over the course of the Thirties. Watson received his decoration for "bettering economic relations," as the *New York Times* reported; Mooney his "in recognition of his services in the development of the Adam Opel AG in Germany," as American military officials later concluded.[149]

Connections such as these have prompted historians to ask questions about complicity. Did American businesspeople sympathize with the Nazi agenda? Did their firms collude with the Nazi regime? Were there alternative courses of action they chose to forgo? Though these questions remain urgent, this chapter has adopted a different angle: we asked how the Nazi regime managed to rope the powerful American carmakers into serving the needs of motorization and rearmament in the first place.

It turns out there was a certain method to the madness. The regime subjected Ford and GM to the general line of economic steering. The framework mechanism was capital controls. By refusing to allocate foreign exchange, the authorities pushed GM and Ford to support the exports of their German branches and to provide them with crucial raw materials against barter or book debits. The branches also acquired American machine tools without taxing the Nazi hard currency coffers. Since Ford and GM were debarred from repatriating profits, they recycled earnings into plant, machinery, and other fixed investments. Thus GM's considerable frozen dividends effectively constituted a forced dollar loan for the comprehensive modernization of Germany's crown carmaker, Opel. Locked in behind capital controls, the Americans also had little choice but to nurture domestic suppliers, which involved sharing American technology and imparting American know-how. The regime reinforced these pressures by keeping the Americans in a peculiar pincer: grassroots nationalist sentiment pushed their executives to seek cover from the authorities in Berlin, who in turn pressed home their economic demands.

The effects were considerable. Led by Opel, the automobile industry developed into a leading sector of the German economy and became a cornerstone of the Nazi rearmament complex. Already by 1934, Germany had overtaken France in motor vehicle output and held a global third place behind Britain. Opel accounted for 44 percent of this surge. By 1936, Germany's automobile industry was also the globe's third largest exporter. That year Opel's share of German vehicle exports was 43.5 percent. By 1938, the automobile industry had outpaced machine tools and chemicals in German exports earnings, and half of that share belonged to Opel. Of the domestic market, Opel captured between 37 and 45 percent each year before the war.[150] General Motors established a model truck plant in Brandenburg and put the facilities at the army's disposal. Opel instructed German toolmakers how to build to American specifications. Production engineers and skilled workers familiar with American methods spread out through German industry, connecting the Nazi industrial boom to the technology frontier across the Atlantic.

The Nazi state thus decisively shaped how complex mass production migrated into Germany. In this, it mirrored the Soviet state. The conspicuous difference between the two was this: the Nazi regime expressly encouraged the activities of American corporations in Germany, as long as they supported the military-industrial buildup. The Soviet leadership, meanwhile, evicted American firms from Russian soil and embarked instead on a campaign of comprehensive technology import, and it accepted the economic and social dislocations this strategy entailed.

Looking out over the twentieth century, both the Soviet and the Nazi strategy are thrown into revealing comparative light. The Soviet strategy stands out in its extremity: banishing foreign firms and buying all technology abroad was a perilous gamble, a mad rush to quickly attain economic independence no matter the cost. The Nazi engagement of America's powerful carmakers, in contrast, has recognizable resemblances to the strategies by which other authoritarian late developers sought to foster domestic automobile sectors. Like Nazi Germany, the regimes of interwar Japan, postwar Brazil, South Korea, and late-twentieth-century China—to pick out obvious examples—began dealing with foreign corporations in a context of foreign exchange constraints, and all of them deployed capital controls as a policy tool. All of them both courted and pressured foreign corporations, asking them to commit to joint ventures, cultivate local suppliers, share technology, and support exports.[151] To be sure, the exact mechanisms varied, and the outcome in each case depended heavily on the shifting international environment and on the balance of power between states and multinational corporations. Nevertheless, seen from the perspective of strategic industrial upgrading, it is doubtful that Nazi Germany developed a "unique and distinctive economic system."[152] Instead, in seeking plausible historical comparisons for the economy of 1930s Germany, historians might look to the many other authoritarian, activist, and development-oriented states of the twentieth century.

5

War of the Factories

Oh, but there is nothing that will not have to be produced in masses!
—ADOLF HITLER, JULY 1944

IN EARLY NOVEMBER 1941, Hermann Göring summoned the elite of the German armaments complex—military brass, industrialists, bureaucrats—to the Aviation Ministry in Berlin. The topic to be discussed sounded innocuous—"rationalization in the armaments industry"—but the assembled men soon realized that they were in for a dressing-down. Göring used the occasion to roundly accuse them of failure. According to the protocol of the meeting, Göring opened by declaring that, "in terms of rationalization, German industry must become equal to America"—a goal that armaments producers had to date approached much too hesitantly. The USA, which was supplying Germany's opponents, was vastly superior in terms of mass production, and the time for factories to update their methods was now. "Germany too must finally arrive at flow production," Göring said, and "craft production must disappear entirely." Göring then proceeded to "sharply attack" the assembled industrialists. Henceforth, firms would be held responsible if they failed to meet production quotas. Time was of the essence: soon American war production would accelerate beyond reach. "Europe stands against America!" Göring exclaimed. "Assembly line production" was now "decisive."[1]

In the military context of November 1941, Göring did not have to explain the urgency of this program. As Göring said pointedly, the campaign against the Soviet Union "had brought surprises." It was beginning to sink in that, largely because the Red Army marshaled a better and more plentiful arsenal than expected, the core objective of Operation Barbarossa—to defeat the Soviet Union within a few months—had failed. A day before Göring's rebuke, the German Military High Command had concluded that the Moscow-bound Army Group Center had lost 40 percent of its fighting power since the beginning of the invasion in June. Tank divisions were decimated by two-thirds. Göring's home department, the Luftwaffe, was little better: German combat aircraft were being shot down almost as fast as the factories could replace them.[2] The situation was sufficiently grim to drive Göring's top official at the Aviation Ministry, Ernst Udet, to suicide. On December 4, the exhausted German attack ground to a halt in the outskirts of Moscow. Three days later, Japanese planes bombed Pearl Harbor. America's long-anticipated entry into the war was official, and Germany now faced a two-front war of uncertain duration.

In his outburst, Göring conveyed a basic truth about the war that was escalating in the winter of 1941: its outcome depended on the factories. Even more than the trench warfare of 1914–1918, with its wood-framed planes and clumsy tanks, World War II was a gigantic contest of military matériel. Whoever could outproduce the enemy in guns, tanks, fighters, bombers, ships, and ammunition—stuff made out of metal, much of it on assembly lines—would surely emerge victorious.[3] As Göring also knew, Germany was not entering this new phase of industrial competition from a favorable position. Despite the German occupation of Western Europe, and despite drastic measures since the Thirties, the Nazi economy remained short on all the basic ingredients necessary to equip a large-scale war: coal, steel, fuel, raw materials, and labor. With America's entry, the contest became extremely lopsided against Germany. In 1941, the United States produced more steel than all other belligerents combined, and, drawing on this supply, the United Kingdom was putting out almost twice as many military aircraft as Germany. That fall Göring and other Nazi leaders received from the statisticians reports that spelled out in alarming detail the desperate economic and military situation of the Third Reich.[4]

A different regime might have tallied up the prospects and sued for peace. But for the leadership of the Third Reich, this was inadmissible. It would have meant relinquishing the core goal that Hitler had first articulated in the Twenties and that his regime had been building up to in the Thirties: to make Germany a continental power that could match the United States. As Göring's exclamation—"Europe stands against America!"—made clear, the existential threat that had haunted the German right since Weimar days materialized with terrible concreteness in December 1941: now America's industrial might would directly confront Germany's in the theaters of total war. Instead of giving in, the Nazi leadership responded to the strategic debacle unfolding in the winter of 1941–1942 the only way it knew: by way of escalation. The same day Göring chastised the industrialists about rationalization, he laid out guidelines for putting Soviet POWs to work in German industry, opening the way for the massive deployment of forced labor into Nazi war production.[5] On December 3, Hitler decreed tighter state control of industry and an intensified focus on "rationalization." Given the shortages of raw materials and labor, the military should renounce demands for fancy weaponry in favor of durable, mass-producible designs. In the same decree, Hitler empowered "seasoned technicians" to review firms and impose more efficient production methods.[6]

The type of "seasoned technician" Hitler had in mind was exemplified by William Werner, the German-American engineer who led a group of Auto-Union specialists to Detroit in the fall of 1937. Since then, Werner had enjoyed a steep ascent within German industry that culminated in his appointment as leading rationalization consultant in Göring's Aviation Ministry. In May 1941, Göring had chosen Werner to lead the ministry's Industrial Council, a task force that was founded at Werner's suggestion and aimed at submitting Germany's sprawling aircraft industry more tightly to ministerial control. Much of what Göring offered in his November 1941 harangue had indeed been developed by Werner's Industrial Council. Nor did Werner's career within the Nazi armaments complex stop there. After Albert Speer took over the Ministry of Munitions in February 1942, Werner assumed a crucial liaison role between Göring's and Speer's rivaling bureaucracies and began acting as one of the system's chief enforcers.

William Werner's ascent to the commanding heights of Nazi Germany's wartime industrial complex, which we follow in this chapter, illustrates how the state-led pursuit of mass production that began in the 1930s intensified under the conditions of total war. With greater force than before, the Nazi regime sought to bind industry to the war economy; this in turn required tightening the screws of economic steering. The armaments bureaucracy, which combined the Munitions Ministry headed by Speer and the Aviation Ministry (headed by Göring but in fact run by his first official, Erhard Milch) began telling firms what to produce, how to produce, and whom to hire. As state steering narrowed firms' room for discretion, the collaborative relationships of the 1930s grew acrimonious. Often the firms that supplied arms to the military resisted the demands of the ministries. Firms did not like to share scarce resources, such as machine tools and labor, with each other. Firms were wary of licensing their own designs to their competitors; or, vice versa, they resented having to assemble engines, vehicles, tanks, or aircraft whose prototypes had been developed by other firms. Firms were slow to share engineering know-how across sectors, as the authorities requested; they resented interference in their production protocols.[7]

To put pressure on the firms, Speer and Milch availed themselves of men like William Werner: technically competent and politically committed engineers whom they endowed with the authority "to intervene into the firms and fully reconfigure their production setups."[8] Besides Werner, this new group of rationalization enforcers included figures we have already encountered: during the war, Otto Dyckhoff and Hans Mayer of Volkswagen and Heinrich Nordhoff and Gerd Stieler von Heydekampf of Opel brokered between the ministries and the firms, bridging the distance that separated the commanding heights of the armaments complex from the shop floors. Their activities merged state steering, shop floor rationalization, and labor coercion. These high-profile production engineers, whose American credentials lent them authority vis-à-vis both the ministries and the firms, connected the state apparatus to the sphere of economic execution in the factories.

Werner's career, then, sheds light on a crucial but little-explored realm of the Nazi war economy: the institutional interface that bridged the ministries and the shop floors. The existing scholarship has, on the one hand, amply explored the level of the firms, and documented in particular their pervasive exploitation of forced labor.[9] On the other hand, the literature has long focused on the very top of the administrative pyramid, and in particular has debated the role of Albert Speer. In an older, now debunked narrative, Speer was personally responsible for implementing reforms that unleashed a "production miracle"—the surprisingly steep increase of armaments output that the Nazi war economy registered during the last three years of the war. This narrative, however, has always suffered from too closely echoing Speer's own, hardly disinterested, rendering of the issue.[10] More recently, in contrast, economic historians have shown that the late-war production boom drew on dynamics for which Speer could hardly claim credit: they were the predictable effect, as the new consensus has it, of the continuous buildup of armaments capacity since the 1930s, and of systematically channeling more labor and resources into the arms sector during the war. In particular, historians have evoked the learning effects inherent in mass production to explain why the Nazi arms complex became more prolific.[11] On this basis, historians have described the late-war boom as "the result of an inevitable development" that would have happened "even without Speer." Because of the economies of learning, production increases constituted a "quasi-natural development" that owed little to the dedicated rationalization measures touted by Speer's ministry.[12]

This commendable demolition of the Speer myth, however, has left us with the somewhat implausible image of a wartime state steering apparatus that was entirely ineffectual and disconnected from what happened on the shop floors. Our discussion of the Ford Motor Company in chapter 1 bears recalling here: what economists call economies of learning hardly arises automatically but is in fact the result of myriad, hands-on shop floor improvements and constant trial and error. We also pointed to the crucial role of the skilled core in orchestrating these improvements. The shop floor skilled core, however, was the natural habitat of Werner and the newly empowered group of technocrats peopling the middle rungs of the ministerial steering system. This perspective pushes us beyond the fixation on Speer and toward the mesolevel of the Nazi arms complex, where ministerial dictates were executed. And here we encounter a Nazi state that sharply increased its ambition to coercively control the economy after the crisis of 1941–1942. Backed by Speer and Milch, Werner pronounced incessantly that it was necessary to match American mass production methods in total war, and he aggressively sought to enforce those methods, like flow production, in the face of polycratic frictions and economic shortages—with decidedly mixed results, to be sure, but hardly without consequences. Seen in this light, what changed in 1942 was not the catalog of rationalization measures but the determination of the state organs to impose them on a sea of private firms that increasingly had other ideas.

This perspective matters on two levels. First is the international comparison: the emergence of a more aggressively coercive wartime state was not a uniquely Nazi pattern. All belligerents found ways to strengthen the state's grip over the economy for total war. All warfaring states used government power to ramp up capital investment and shift resources from consumption to industry. All states intervened directly in the production sphere. The Japanese "control associations," which were staffed by industry representatives and enjoyed authority to impose best practices on their members, very much mirrored the production committee system adopted by the German arms complex after 1942.[13] In the United States, the military procurement agencies prescribed production protocols to firms and dictated prices to contractors. Firms had to accept this because the greater part of the industrial plant newly created for the war—such as Ford's Willow Run bomber factory—was financed and owned by the government, even if it was operated by the contractor (so-called GOCO plants). A similar arrangement prevailed in Britain.[14] When it came to mobilizing resources for war, the Soviet leadership enjoyed the advantage of having already built a command economy during the Thirties. Yet it, too, strengthened central authority over the allocation of resources and doubled down on updating production protocols.[15]

Second is the perspective of how the German industrial apparatus indigenized and elaborated on the technology transfers of the 1930s. During the war the German economy underwent what one economic historian evocatively called a "crash course" in mass production.[16] William Werner allows us to understand how this worked in practice; how war technocracy, backed by the state, facilitated this crash course; and how tacit technological knowledge—production protocols, organizational capabilities, technical experiences—diffused throughout the industrial system.

William Werner: Göring's American

William Werner leveraged his transatlantic biography into a stellar National Socialist career in the lead sectors of the mid-twentieth century: automobiles and aircraft. He was born in New York in 1893 to German parents. Upon relocating to Germany in 1907, he retained his American citizenship. This made him exempt from the World War I draft: Werner avoided the trenches, became a toolmaker, and worked for various machining firms across Germany. In 1926, as did so many aspiring German engineers during these years, Werner made the pilgrimage to the Midwest, where he worked and studied operations at Chrysler. Upon his return, the Saxon luxury carmaker Horch appointed him technical director, a position he was able to retain when Horch was folded into Auto-Union during the Depression. By the late Thirties, Werner had made Auto-Union into the second-ranking German carmaker after Opel.[17]

As an engineer, Werner was a rare dual talent. He was an avid automobile designer, and together with Porsche, he made the Auto-Union Silver Arrow the era's standout race car. During the Thirties, however, Werner focused his attention on the shop floor, and his contributions in this sphere formed the foundation of his wartime career. What recommended Werner was his consistent American orientation. As a production engineer at Auto-Union, he kept abreast of developments in the US, corresponded with American carmakers, and retained his membership in the American Society of Automotive Engineers.[18] Werner came to proselytize for two American methods with particular vigor. The first was flow production, for which he, as a trained toolmaker, emphasized the crucial role of sophisticated machines. The second was modern, automated foundry operations, inspired by what he had seen at River Rouge. By 1938, he was regarded as "one of the best production engineers in Germany."[19]

Werner flourished under the Nazi regime. It is unclear whether or not he joined the Nazi party.[20] But he certainly embraced the regime's goals as his own. During the Volkswagen melee, Werner was the lone voice in the Automotive Association urging his colleagues to stop bickering and follow the dictator's demands.[21] In 1938, Werner reminded Auto-Union staffers not to do business with Jewish-owned suppliers. As the Auto-Union plant leader (*Betriebsführer*), he exhorted his workers to compete "with joy" in the Nazi Labor Front's contest for the "model factory" award. Werner gifted an Auto-Union-themed "Adolf-Hitler-Book" to every worker in honor of the dictator's fiftieth birthday in April 1939. As late as New Year's 1944, Werner's office made a point of circulating to Auto-Union staffers a special print of a speech by Nazi propaganda minister Joseph Goebbels.[22]

Werner, then, was hardly an apolitical technocrat. Rather, his career sheds light on an often-overlooked milieu of the functional elites who flourished

FIGURE 5.1. William Werner (left) and Ferdinand Porsche conferring over an Auto-Union Silver Arrow, 1938. Photo: Getty.

under National Socialism: the engineers.[23] The worldviews of the engineers resonated with a Nazi ideology that extolled technological progress as an expression of German creative "genius." Engineers benefited from the regime's military-industrial buildup, which afforded them ample career opportunities and furnished them with radically expanded spheres of influence. Engineers like Werner were not the powerful industrialists, military commanders, and SS officers who stood trial in Nuremberg, nor the academics, lawyers, and desktop perpetrators that have become the focal point of a more recent historiography.[24] Though engineers like Werner, Otto Dyckhoff, or Gerd Stieler von Heydekampf were professionally indisposed toward elaborate pronouncements of ideology, they expressed their support of the regime through their actions: throughout the war, they kept the Nazi production machine running long after it was clear that the cause was lost. Like the Volkswagen builder turned tank designer, Ferdinand Porsche, or the rocket scientist and V2 developer, Wernher von Braun, William Werner remained unperturbed that he was putting his technical brilliance in the service of a criminal regime.[25]

In the hothouse of Nazi war production, American credentials bolstered careers. At some point in the late Thirties, Werner must have renounced his American citizenship, as did his fellow German-Americans at Volkswagen. But it is testimony to the strong hold that American technology had over the Nazi imagination that William Werner never Germanized his first name.

The beginnings of Werner's ascent into the command centers of Nazi war production can be dated to his return from Detroit in November 1937. On that trip, as described in the opening pages of chapter 1, Werner and his engineers visited thirteen different auto factories and toolmakers in southern Michigan, including Chevrolet, Pontiac, and the Rouge. This industrial reconnaissance mission yielded detailed descriptions of myriad machine tools and work processes, along with several hundred high-resolution photographs. The report distilled a simple conclusion from the material: American practices saved raw materials and labor. Flow production allowed employing inexperienced workers to great effect; sophisticated machines could be tended by unsophisticated workers.[26]

Back in Germany, Werner presented these findings to industrialists and engineers in a series of lectures, which he set in the context of rearmament. "What primarily interests all of German industry today," Werner said, "[is] higher output with fewer skilled workers." In his presentations, Werner treated his audiences to dozens of photo slides of machines from America that were designed to synchronize the work flow and bind workers to the production process. To illustrate the potential for material savings, Werner chose an example that would become a minor obsession of his consultant work during the war: the casting of parts such as engine blocks and crankshafts. In foundry work, Werner said, the outdated German methods resulted in wastage that was "unacceptable" under the shortage-prone conditions of rearmament. As a good modern counterexample, Werner presented images from the Rouge foundry, which cast entire crankshafts in one go with less than 1 percent of waste. Just like at the Rouge, German foundries and forges needed to be turned into "precision workshops," Werner said.

In his talks, Werner conceded that the principles he presented were not, strictly speaking, new. But he insisted that rearmament now required their "clear recognition and radical implementation" throughout German industry at large.[27] Evidently convinced that his American credentials made him the right person for the job, Werner therefore took it on himself to target deficiencies at the largest German aircraft producer, Junkers. In a memorandum addressed to Junkers, Werner rehearsed his lecture on the superiority of the forging and casting methods he had witnessed at the Rouge. In stark contrast to these best practices, Werner charged, Junkers foundries wasted a staggering 88 percent of raw steel allotments! It was necessary to install "modern forging machines" and update casting techniques. The war and its shortages made such measures "imperative," Werner argued, and the leading firms of the aircraft engine industry could hardly "afford to evade them." Surely, Junkers was aware that "American producers have been tackling the problem of mass-producing aircraft engines with immense energy." To underscore his point, Werner attached an article from *Automotive Industries* that described how Packard was retooling to make Rolls Royce engines.[28]

Werner's confrontation with the aircraft industry paralleled developments elsewhere. As Fordism migrated into aviation, pushy automotive engineers clashed with the established aircraft firms across belligerents, and everywhere they could count on the state to back them up. In the United States, for example, Charles Sorensen tussled with the aircraft designers of Consolidated, who argued that building bombers was fundamentally different than building cars, and that the mass production protocols of the auto industry did not apply to aircraft. Sorensen, however, mobilized the military's support, and Consolidated was told to license its designs to Ford. Though the process was hardly smooth, it famously showed results in Willow Run, the factory that turned out "Liberator" bombers in flow production. In Britain, Rolls Royce engineers were told to seek out personnel from Ford's English branch to adapt their craft-made engines to mass production with machine tools shipped from the United States.[29]

Similarly, Werner called upon the state to impose the protocols of automotive mass production onto the aircraft sector in Germany. No longer could it be "left to the individual firm" to improve production, Werner argued to officials at the Aviation Ministry. "Given the seriousness and immense

significance" of upgrading industrial methods, Werner considered it imperative "to involve the Aviation Ministry and its powers."[30] Other engineers, too,
criticized the aircraft industry as too sluggish and called for endowing the
Aviation Ministry with "dictatorial powers" over firms.[31]

The Aviation Ministry welcomed such arguments, since conflicts between
the ministry and the aircraft firms were sharp. Junkers, the leading aircraft
producer, presided over a decentralized landscape of smaller aircraft developers. The firm consisted of more than a dozen suppliers, subcontractors, and
license takers; its rationalization strategy was geared toward taking advantage
of the organizational "economies of scope"; its production realities did not
measure up to visions of flow production and conveyor belts.[32] Over the
course of 1940, however, it became clear that the Junkers system failed to meet
the demands of the air war over Britain. The Aviation Ministry looked with
increasing alarm across the Atlantic, anticipating—like Werner—an imminent
upsurge in American output of fighters and bombers, based on the deep capabilities of the American automobile industry. These worries triggered a drawn-
out rearrangement of the aircraft complex, as the Aviation Ministry moved
forcefully to reassert its dominance over the industry.[33]

In this process, William Werner was a key figure. For the ministry, he was
the ideal man: a seasoned flow production expert from the automobile industry who seemed to be both capable and willing to whip the struggling aircraft
industry into shape. How this could work emerged in early 1941, when the
chief official in the Aviation Ministry, Ernst Udet, hired Werner to inspect
aircraft engine production at BMW. In 1940, the Bavarian engine maker had
fallen woefully short of the output quotas for its 801 double radial engine, one
of the workhorses of German combat aircraft. BMW's director, Franz-Josef
Popp (whom we encountered in the previous chapter arguing that the bus was
the true "people's car"), refused to accept blame for this failure and pointed to
shortages of parts, machine tools, and skilled labor instead. More alarming to
the ministry, Popp made no secret that he disliked the 801 and preferred developing a new engine. Popp's reluctance shows how the goals of firms could
diverge from those of the arms bureaucracy. As Popp saw it, control over resources and technical development should remain within BMW. As Udet saw
it, a firm like BMW should subordinate itself to the overall strategy of aircraft
production and put its technical expertise at the Aviation Ministry's disposal.
Udet wanted the BMW 801 in large quantities as fast as possible and considered Popp's prevarications "downright criminal foolishness."[34]

Udet cited Popp to Berlin, informed him that he considered BMW's performance "catastrophic and unacceptable," and announced that he would send
a certain William Werner to inspect operations at BMW.[35] Werner traveled to
Munich and delivered his report to the Aviation Ministry in February 1941. It

addressed both organizational and technological problems. First, Werner criticized BMW's decentralized nature: the firm's five subsidiaries, cobbled together in a series of acquisitions, engaged in rivalries and failed to coordinate their efforts. Werner argued that BMW should emulate his home firm Auto-Union, which had a centralized protocol for the firm's eleven subunits and shared resources, workers, and machines across divisions. Second, Werner identified deficits in BMW's shop practice. The main shops in Munich and Spandau "could be used for making different types of engines," an arrangement that "did not correspond with the current level of aircraft engine production." Instead, Werner advised, BMW's divisions should specialize and turn themselves into "explicit high-volume shops." The machines in use at BMW were "beyond discussion"; given the shortage of skilled workers, high-capacity machine tools were needed that could "dispense with a worker's dexterity" and that were designed to move the engines along more evenly and more quickly.[36]

BMW's management acknowledged that Werner's critical review had inflicted "an embarrassment." It prompted the firm to scour the industry for engineers with American credentials. First, BMW tried to headhunt Gerd Stieler von Heydekampf, the director of Opel's Brandenburg truck plant. When Opel submitted that Heydekampf had no experience with aircraft, BMW's managers replied that their main hope was to hire "a mass production man." Opel refused to release Heydekampf.[37] But BMW did manage to land Otto Dyckhoff—the engineer who had defected from Opel to Volkswagen and orchestrated the recruitment of German-Americans in 1937–1938. By the spring of 1941, Dyckhoff had grown impatient with Volkswagen's subordinate role in the war economy; he left and assumed the directorship of one of BMW's engine branches.[38]

Evidently impressed with Werner's intervention at BMW, Göring took up his proposal to strengthen the Aviation Ministry. In May 1941, Göring created an executive organ that had the explicit purpose of pushing the methods of automotive mass production into the aircraft sector. This new organ was the Industrial Council at the Ministry of Aviation, whose leading figure was William Werner. As Werner put it, the council should be "endowed with all necessary authority" over the decentralized aircraft industry, so it could ensure that "the most rational production methods" would be widely implemented.[39] To the firms, the Aviation Ministry introduced Werner as their new rationalization liaison. Firms were encouraged to turn to Werner with any questions they might have about improving production methods; in turn, they were required to divulge all information that he might request.[40]

Having installed William Werner at the Industrial Council, Göring next endowed Erhard Milch, the ministry's ambitious state secretary, with far-reaching authority over industrial resources. Because of long-standing bureaucratic

FIGURE 5.2. William Werner (left) with Ernst Udet and Erhard Milch
in front of aero-engines at BMW, 1941. Photo: BMW Archive.

rivalries, Milch's powers remained limited in practice; but the move signaled
the expansive vision of state power over industry that Aviation Ministry officials were developing on the eve of the invasion of the Soviet Union. Göring's
decree gave Milch the right to requisition machines, buildings, and raw materials from across firms and to move around managerial personnel "without regard to private contracts." Milch justified these powers with the sharpening
threat of losing the aircraft production race against Britain and the United
States. "The current strength of the air force is in no way sufficient to achieve
victory," Milch said in a mid-June meeting with the military procurement
agencies. Therefore, he believed, the strength of the Luftwaffe needed to increase fourfold. To achieve that purpose, Milch claimed "the right to confiscate
every factory in Germany" for the aviation industry.[41]

Milch's expansive vision of state power aligned with Werner's ideas about
state-imposed rationalization. Beginning in the summer of 1941, Werner's
career followed that of Milch, for whom Werner became a protégé. Thus, in
late October, Milch presented Werner to the chief of the military procurement

office, Georg Thomas (the officer who negotiated the construction of the Brandenburg truck plant with GM officials, discussed in chapter 4). Thomas asked Werner to lay out his rationalization plan. Once again, Werner performed the part of American-style rationalization consultant with bravura. Compared to "American methods of mass production," Werner said, German industrial practices were "antediluvian." He recommended the following program: Modern forging and casting techniques had to be introduced. Specialization was necessary: each production program should involve no more than three factories. Firms had to share their know-how, and factories had to adopt the methods of the most efficient producer.[42] Less than three weeks later, Göring pressed home precisely these themes in his reprimand to the assembled armaments managers in Berlin.

In the winter of 1941–1942, with the Third Reich's strategic position in the balance, the pressure within the Nazi aviation complex was released in a momentous reshuffling. In December, Udet's suicide cleared the way for his rival, Erhard Milch, to assume the helm of the Aviation Ministry. By early 1942, the directors of the most powerful firms of the aircraft industry—Messerschmidt, Heinkel, and Junkers—had been demoted. At BMW, the ministry ousted Popp and replaced him with a troika of production engineers. "Show me that you can run this shop," Milch told them; otherwise, he would "put someone above your heads." BMW's new management vowed to follow the ministry's directive and focus on the 801 engine that Popp had resisted.[43] As Milch's protégé, William Werner saw his influence measurably increase. In early 1942, Werner took his place in the weekly executive meetings at Milch's office at the Aviation Ministry.

Enforcing Fordism in the Nazi War Machine

Werner's rise over the course of 1940–1941 illustrates how the Nazi war economy radicalized as it confronted military setbacks and alarming assessments of comparative industrial weakness. Wielding the state's coercive powers, the Aviation Ministry sought to impose tighter control over the aircraft firms. Werner's ascent, however, makes clear that this was by no means a development that neatly pitted "the state" against "business." Rather, the political goals of the regime found support among production engineers like Werner, whom the bureaucracy recruited from the firms themselves. Werner in turn was eager to put his expertise at the regime's disposal. In the Nazi armaments bureaucracy that emerged from the winter crisis of 1941–1942, Werner established himself as an enforcer of the regime's industrial demands.

The reorganization of the war economic administration culminated with the appointment of Albert Speer to the post of Minister of Arms and

Munitions in February 1942. Hitler charged Speer's ministry with subordinating the entire German economy to the needs of war production.[44] Previously, military procurement had relied on an armaments market in which the military departments placed their orders directly with the firms. As we saw in the previous chapter in the case of General Thomas and Opel's American executives, this market relied on closely cultivated relationships between the military and individual firms. Now, Speer's bureaucracy stepped between the firms and the military: orders would henceforth be channeled through the ministry. Backed by Hitler, Speer's ministry assumed centralized control over resources and began to dictate to firms "what is produced in the individual firms and how."[45]

This steering system built on organizational antecedents in the Aviation Ministry and on administrative reforms begun by Speer's predecessor, Fritz Todt. The system centered on a number of committees (*Ausschüsse*) that represented the major armaments sectors—tanks, ammunition, aircraft engines, aircraft fuselages, motor vehicles, and so on. So-called production rings supplemented this setup—organizations that united supplier firms for components such as crankshafts and ball bearings. The production rings and the committees were declared "organs of the Ministry" and were endowed with its authority. Engineers and specialists from hundreds of firms staffed its many offices. Though these engineer-officials remained on the payrolls of their firms, Speer expected them to renounce primary allegiance to their employers and put their service at the ministry's disposal.

The moniker that Speer popularized for this organizational setup was "industrial self-responsibility"—*Industrielle Selbstverwaltung*, or ISV. The term refurbished basic ideological conceits about the relationship between state and industry under the Nazi steered economy: namely, that the task of industrial firms was to deliver on the goals set by the regime, and that as long as industry did so "self-responsibly," the regime respected their autonomy.[46] As Speer put it, the system of industrial self-responsibility deserved its name because it was staffed with engineers from industry itself—as opposed to military procurement officers or ministerial bureaucrats, whose unfamiliarity with shop floors had led to problems in the past.

When Speer introduced the administrative reforms to the regional party bosses, he stressed the political implications. The ISV system presented the firms with a chance to assume the initiative lest more coercive measures should become necessary. "Industry has a unique opportunity to send their best people," Speer explained. "Should it pass up this opportunity," he continued, "strict state leadership—which none of us desire—will have to proceed." In the past, the firms had proven reluctant to renounce "self-interest and profit considerations" and clung to "traditional and outdated production methods."

While it was understandable that firms should follow private considerations to some extent, failures in leadership and organization could not be tolerated. Speer deplored that "the leading figures of our industry are unfortunately much too old." The new committees and production rings would therefore empower the engineers within the firms themselves. They now had the authority to override industrialists who lacked technical expertise and to issue recommendations with the force of orders.[47]

Nor was the invocation of a fresh generation of engineer-technocrats pure propaganda. The sprawling ISV system encompassed, according to Speer, around 6,000 members staffing its various committees and subcommittees, production rings and subrings. A glance at the system's directory from 1944 indeed shows a plethora of "Dr.-Ing." and "Dipl.-Ing.," representing engineering degees, in the lists. Of those in charge of the eight main committees (ammunition, artillery, tanks, motor vehicles, rail equipment, airframes, aircraft engines, and aircraft gear), five were diploma engineers and two more were certified toolmakers.[48] Werner, who was forty-eight when he took the helm of the Aircraft Engine Committee in 1942, was on the older side.

The system of "industrial self-responsibility," then, institutionalized the rise of ambitious engineers like Werner into new positions of power. As head of the Committee for Aircraft Engines, William Werner indeed occupied a key position in the entire armaments complex. Aviation was the single most important part of the Nazi war economy, garnering the most voluminous outlays and devouring the most resources. Engines, in turn, were the most expensive and intricate part of the aircraft—bigger and more complex than the standard automobile. Mass-producing aircraft engines, then, was easily the most challenging process in the war of the factories, and offered the automobile engineer Werner a widely expanded field of influence.[49]

Werner's self-stylization as American-credentialed rationalization expert made him one of the most important linking pins in the ISV system. As head of the Committee for Aircraft Engines, he oversaw the various aero-engine producers (BMW, Daimler-Benz, Junkers, and others) as well their far-flung supplier rings. At the same time, Werner remained the leading figure on the Industrial Council, whose membership soon dwindled to an exclusive three—the committee heads of engines, airframes, and aircraft gear. The Industrial Council retained an independent status as rationalization watchdog in the aircraft industry. Werner's most sensitive role, however, was not recorded in any organigram: he became a chief liaison in the all-important relationship between Speer's Munitions Ministry and Milch's Aviation Ministry. Werner reported to Milch on developments at munitions and frequently led tense negotiations with Speer's advisers. As a representative of aviation, vice versa, he participated in the meetings of Speer's "war production cabinet"—Central

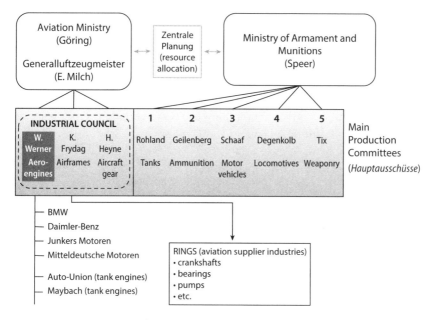

FIGURE 5.3. The German munitions complex, ca. spring 1943.

Planning—where the committees haggled over allocations of raw materials, iron, machine tools, and labor. Milch appears to have had full faith in Werner, whom he singled out as "the best man" on the Industrial Council, and the "pacemaker" in a joint task force with Speer's ministry.[50]

We can reconstruct Werner's activities from the protocols of the so-called GL *Besprechungen*—the weekly meetings chaired by Milch in his capacity as *Generalluftzeugmeister* (or GL), the highest official capacity in the Aviation Ministry. These sources show Werner's activities to be broadly twofold. On the one hand, he improvised fixes to resource and supply shortages. One particularly intractable bottleneck that vexed Werner for the better part of two years was crankshafts, which may serve as an illustration. Crankshafts, which are devices that translate the linear thrust of pistons into circular motion, are crucial parts of any engine. They also had a hold on Werner's imagination ever since he had seen them forged in a single operation at the Rouge. In the summer of 1942, it was clear that crankshaft suppliers could not keep up with their quotas. By year's end, a deficit of 2,600 crankshafts—hence of engines, hence of aircraft—was looming. Meanwhile, at the engine assembly plants, workers sat idle because production could not proceed. Speer's ministry had promised to allocate more tools to the suppliers but failed to follow through. To remedy this situation, Werner came up with a bizarre horse trade: aviation sidestepped munitions and directly "lent" several hundred workers to the Machine Tool Committee so that special-purpose machines for crankshafts could be produced. By the end of the allotted time period, however, the Machine Tool Committee refused to "return" the workers. Soon the crankshaft scarcity was again slowing down the engine assemblers. Since it was intolerable that workers and machines stay idle, Werner hit upon the dubious solution that engines should be assembled without crankshafts and then retrofitted as they became available. The retrofitting, of course, should be set up as flow production.[51]

On the other hand, Werner established himself as a kind of mass production bully toward the firms, whom he accused variously of incompetence, foot-dragging, and dissimulation. At a critical juncture, Werner recalled dressing down the proud heads of the aircraft firms, such as Messerschmidt and Heinkel, telling them, "You are the obstacle to flow production."[52] Werner pressed steel suppliers in the Ruhr to adopt a Ford-style system of one-step forging of crankshafts, but found that "they of course fight tooth and nail against the impositions of an outsider."[53] Less powerful suppliers were dealt with more ruthlessly. Repeatedly, Werner intimidated firm-level engineers; at one occasion he threatened a slow supplier with a court-martial, which, he boasted, "really packed a punch."[54] One telling exchange may showcase the remarkable mix of technical obsession and enforcement mentality that characterized the weekly discussions at the Aviation Ministry:

> VORWALD [reports on visiting a supplier of aircraft engine pumps in Hamburg]: I can only say that the whole place is a terrible dump. Such chaos I've never seen in my life! They work like in prehistoric times, and the whole firm is like that.
>
> WERNER: Hamburg is pointless. It is truly a complete dump. . . . I gave Lehmann a harsh talk. The thing is, the tappet must be fitted with one thousandth millimeter accuracy. Every conical tappet must be fitted. This construction is a complete disaster. I have recommended modifying it in order to make it suitable for actual production. . . . Unfortunately, we have completely diverging systems with different measurements, low numbers of output, etc. Flow production can only be achieved with a standardized engine pump, and we have to get there by all means.[55]

A week later Werner interrupted a discussion about a new production facility for onboard machine guns:

> I infer from the number of machines that this is not planned to be set up as flow production. 400 skilled laborers and 77 vertical milling machines tell me that. The output we require absolutely demands flow production.

At the same meeting, Werner groaned that he had been "preaching refined casting methods and flow production" since assuming his place on the Industrial Council.[56]

Flow and Labor Coercion

"What primarily interests all of German industry today," as Werner had said in his talks, "[is] higher output with fewer skilled workers." These words captured a core problem of the Nazi war economy: the armaments complex confronted a labor shortage both in absolute numbers and in terms of qualification. There were too few workers overall, and there were too few skilled workers. The scissors between arms output and the labor supply had been widening since the mid-Thirties, but during the war it opened to breaking point. As successive military drafts pulled German workers from the shops, men and women from across occupied Europe replaced them, many of whom had been recruited with considerable coercion. By the fall of 1944, more than 7.9 million foreign laborers and POWs—most of them Polish and Soviet, about one-fourth of them women—were registered within the borders of "Greater Germany." They were joined by 400,000 concentration camp inmates who were forced to work on shop floors and construction sites. Taken together, these numbers constituted about one-third of the entire labor force. Without doubt, the Nazi war economy would have collapsed swiftly without the systematic exploitation of forced labor.[57]

While the majority of these "foreign workers" toiled in mining and steel, on roads and construction sites, many of them worked on the shop floors of the armaments industry. Forcing workers into the factories was only the first step, however. The workers arrived on shop floors not only without factory experience but also malnourished and often brutalized. *Within* the factories, the engineers sought ways to integrate these exhausted workers into the production of complex industrial goods, such as aircraft engines. The solution propagated by William Werner and his fellow technocrats was a stark merger of Fordism and various degrees of labor coercion: workers would toil at the lines under sharp policing and ever-present punitive threats. Flow production became a supreme tool to exploit the labor power of the "foreigners" for the Nazi armaments effort.

The technocrats at the Aviation Ministry hoped that flow production would provide a one-step solution to the double issue of skill dilution and worker discipline.[58] Not only did flow setups raise the productivity of workers with few skills. If combined with automated conveyor belts, Werner and his fellow technocrats argued, assembly lines could exert an intrinsic disciplinary power. As Werner explained to Göring in 1943, "assembly-line production according to the American model" had the benefit that "when someone leaves, the entire work comes to a standstill. With such a system I can really compel the foreigners to 100 per cent work."[59] Karl Frydag, the Industrial Council member responsible for airframes, expressed a similar idea. As German skilled workers were lost to the draft, the control of the labor force increasingly had to be shifted to "the production methods themselves—if one uses flow production, the people have to go with it."[60] As Milch expressed the rationale in reference to the BMW 801:

> The manufacture of a high-quality double-row radial engine by unskilled foreigners is possible only when it is being carried out serially on a conveyor-belt, where each person performs only a specific task. It is possible to train foreigners [to perform these tasks] but we cannot turn them into skilled workers.[61]

Shop engineers at the firms themselves arrived at similar conclusions. At Daimler-Benz's aircraft engine plant in Genshagen outside of Berlin, for example, "foreigners" constituted almost two-thirds of the workforce in 1943. These workers, submitted Genshagen's director, had "no inner interest" in their work, hence their labor could only be mobilized by "the furthest possible division of labor."[62] BMW's production engineers expected that "introduction of large series" would "allow deploying the foreigners even better than previously."[63]

How "foreign" and forced labor became a pillar of the armaments effort can be seen at BMW's main facility in Munich-Allach.[64] Allach was one of several new "flow-works" set up in engine production after 1941: others among them were Junkers' Oranienburg works, BMW's Zühlsdorf factory, and the Vienna works overseen by Werner. In the wake of Werner's damning review from March 1941, BMW drew up comprehensive plans to expand the Allach factory for serial production of the 801 engine, complete with flow setups, special-purpose tools, and assembly lines. Over the next three years, Allach grew to be BMW's largest branch. Between 1941 and 1944, the workforce more than tripled, from 5,572 to 17,313; the majority of the influx consisted of "foreigners," whose share of the workforce eventually exceeded two-thirds. Allach exceeded the average ratio of foreign labor employed across all branches of aircraft production, which the Munitions Ministry in October 1943 put at 31 percent.[65] These figures suggest that within the aircraft sector "foreigners" were put to use with greater frequency in the large finishing works, such as Allach, than in the myriad smaller suppliers.

Recruitment of foreigners at Allach followed a sequential pattern characteristic of the Nazi war economy. BMW initially hired workers from Western Europe, most of whom were free contract laborers. Next came POWs and

forced laborers, often from occupied Eastern Europe. Large-scale use of concentration camp labor followed in the final years of the war. In the fall of 1941,
the largest group among BMW's foreigners were free recruits from Italy; a few
months later they were joined by 790 French POWs. Over the course of 1942,
BMW acquired a large number of "Easterners" from the labor deportation
drives in the occupied Soviet territories. In the fall of 1943, Italian POWs arrived along with a contingent of forcibly recruited Czech workers. While the
SS rejected BMW's initial request for concentration camp labor in August 1941,
several months later prisoners from the nearby Dachau camp toiled on
BMW construction sites. By the fall of 1943, 1,924 concentration camp prisoners were also forced to work in the Allach shops; by 1944, that number had
risen to 5,500.

Despite the hopes of production engineers, however, flow production was
no panacea to the mobilization of unskilled labor, whether forcibly recruited
or not. The racial hierarchies dictated by ideology posed a first barrier to the
vision of fully efficient flow production. At Allach, the "foreigners" were divided into various degrees of coercive labor relationships. There were foreigners without contract who were free to switch employers and often did so; other
Westerners held fixed six- or twelve-month contracts; some again were con-
scripted with labor duties. The "Eastern" laborers and French, Soviet, and Italian POWs worked under coercion. The nationalities of those from SS punitive
battalions and concentration camps are not known.[66] On the shop floors, racial, gender, and skill hierarchies intersected to form a stratification in which
German shop engineers, skilled workers, and foremen ruled over the foreigners, who themselves were differentiated. Westerners inhabited more favorable
positions than the "Eastern" workers; French POWs fared better than Soviet
ones. Concentration camp workers fared the worst, suffering inadequate supplies, harsh policing, and punitive violence. Women had to work separately
from men; concentration camp prisoners had to work in workshops isolated
from the remainder of the shop and under SS surveillance. In Allach, for example, the entire facility was crisscrossed with a complex web of restrictions
classifying laborers according to their contract and racial status and keeping
them from moving about.

The second impediment to uninterrupted flow was the shortage of skilled
workers. As Werner and the technocrats at aviation realized full well, even the
most disaggregated production sequence required a core group of skilled
workers to prepare the layouts, fit the machines, supervise operations, and
troubleshoot. Also, unskilled assembly workers required at least a minimal
degree of training. That flow production could not work without skilled workers is evident from the alarm with which production planners responded to
the increasing number of German workers who were drafted off the shop

floors. When a special draft in late 1943 threatened to remove around 60,000 German workers from the aviation industry, Werner and his colleagues on the Industrial Council warned that the effects would be severe. Those drafted, they pointed out, were mostly skilled workers, like toolmakers, fitters, superintendents, and foremen. This would severely affect factories like Allach that already had a "high share of foreigners or female workers," since here the skilled workforce was needed to instruct, train, and supervise the unskilled. Frydag and Werner estimated that the draft would cost 160 planes and 800 engines per month and cause considerable delays in new programs.[67]

To achieve what engineers considered "a good production result" with flow arrangements, it was necessary to create highly coercive conditions. This can be seen in the example of the shop "Hall 7 (concentration camp)" that was set up in 1944 by Henschel—the firm where Werner's colleague on the Industrial Council, Karl Frydag, held responsibility. The shop housed a flow system for aircraft wings and at its peak employed 673 women drawn from the Ravensbrück concentration camp, the majority of them Jews who had only recently been deported from Hungary. They labored twelve to seventeen hours a day under the supervision of German foremen and SS guards. The women slept in quarters adjacent to the shop in poor and cramped conditions, and food was inadequate. Yet under these conditions, the shop floor–cum–concentration camp showed productivity increases that pleased Henschel's production planners: while it took 941 woman-hours to produce one wing in July, by November the figure had fallen to 392. What this meant for the women is clear from one survivor's recollections: "It was the work at the conveyor-belt where the pressure to perform was always increased. If at the beginning the belt came by every three hours, towards the end it came every 40 minutes, leaving practically not a single free moment."[68] As the example shows, only where coercion and control was complete and the threat of violence was ever present could the assembly line achieve its disciplinary strength.[69] Flow production, against the hopes of Werner and the technocrats at aviation, was not an "automatic" enforcer of discipline. On most shop floors, the reality, while hardly more humane, remained messier and more difficult to control.

Fordism and the Nazi Armaments "Miracle"

Germany's armaments complex became more prolific over the course of the war. According to numbers compiled after the war by the US Strategic Bombing Survey (USSBS), German aircraft production shot up from 10,826 in 1940 to 39,807 in 1944, with the biggest gain registered in 1944. Aircraft engines, Werner's home department, registered a similar trajectory, though the biggest

TABLE 5.1. German output of aircraft and aircraft engines, 1939–1944

	1939	1940	1941	1942	1943	1944
All aircraft	8,195	10,826	11,776	15,556	25,527	39,807
Aircraft engines		15,510	22,400	37,000	50,700	54,000

Source: Uziel, "Between Industrial Revolution and Slavery," 293; Overy, *Air War*, 150.

bump came in 1942 and 1943 (see table 5.1). Much of this can be explained as the predictable result of feeding more resources into the armaments complex.[70] Overall, the workforce in firms that answered to the Aviation Ministry more than doubled, from 307,748 in 1940 to 640,448 in 1944; in Werner's department—engines—the increase was even steeper, from 80,353 to over 200,000. But this did not include the numerous suppliers and auxiliary firms; taking those into account, the Aviation Ministry estimated the total number of workers employed in aircraft production at close to two million in 1943.[71] The laborers were also made to work ever-longer hours. At BMW's Allach works, for example, the workweek increased from fifty-four hours in late 1940 to sixty-nine hours in March 1944, peaking intermittently at seventy-two.[72] Aviation benefited from the allocation of new machine tools: between 1942 and 1944, every month around 2,000 new machines were delivered into the aircraft industry.[73] The discrepancy between the stagnating engine numbers and the surprising output peak in aircraft in 1944 throws a light on the regime's ability to effectively move resources into priority areas. The 1944 "Fighter Staff" discontinued four- and two-engine bombers in favor of one-engine fighters. In Speer's own words, "heavy and very heavy aircraft were mostly removed from production" in order to build "a larger number of light aircraft."[74]

Not only overall output increased, however; productivity also rose. According to USSBS data, the most reliable index, labor productivity in German metalworking industries was 48 percent higher in 1944 than in 1939.[75] If we take 1941 as a base year and consider the armaments complex exclusively, the labor productivity index shot up from 100 (1941) to 234 (1944).[76] These results imply a puzzle. How did the Nazi war machine become more efficient amid the mayhem of Allied bombing raids, disintegrating supply chains, and the brutal terror of underground relocations? As we discussed at the outset of this chapter, scholars have discredited a narrative that centers on Speer's putative innovations after 1942. Instead, they emphasize the continuous mobilization of the economy over the entire course of the war. The late peaks amid economic disintegration were due to the coming on line of investments made much earlier, and they owed to the effects of the mass production economies of learning.

The activities of William Werner and his fellow technocrats allow us to disaggregate these findings somewhat. Behind the "automatic" effects of the mass production learning curve stood concrete shop floor actions. Who did the learning plotted by the economists' curve? And what did they learn? Given the large labor turnover and punitive shop environment, it is reasonable to assume that learning took place in particular among the skilled core of the workforce: engineers and foremen learned to exploit unskilled workers more effectively.[77] The performance reports that firms submitted to the Aviation Ministry consistently adduced output and efficiency increases to better production methods and better use of unskilled labor, with flow layouts featuring prominently. At *Mitteldeutsche Motorenwerke*, Werner's home engine maker, the number of "foreigners" peaked in 1942 at over one-third of the workforce; the same year, management reported more output with fewer man-hours as a result of "improving production methods towards best practices."[78] At Junkers and other aircraft assemblers, auditors explained falling labor costs by pointing to improved production methods and the introduction of assembly lines.[79] The aircraft maker Messerschmidt submitted an entire report in 1943 about "productivity increases through flow production."[80] Opel boasted of having "adapted all departments to flow" and increasing deliveries of aircraft components by 250 percent over two years.[81] BMW reported achieving higher output as a result of sharing machine tools across divisions, divulging know-how to license takers, and increasing the use of special-purpose machinery and assembly lines—by implementing, in short, the demands that Werner had first pushed in his critical review of 1941.[82]

The reports must be taken with a grain of salt: the engineers had good reasons to tell the technocrats at the ministry what they wanted to hear. And it is clear that any such rationalization was necessarily hampered by shortages and air raids. Surveying images of the shop floors during war production suggests that firms employed a wide mix of production layouts: some of them featured a classic moving conveyor belt assembly line; others connected rows of machines with carts and trolleys pushed along rails from station to station; all of this was assisted by some old-fashioned bench work.[83] But enough use was made of flow production as a productivity-enhancing, labor-coercive device that the USSBS could summarize its postwar survey of several aviation firms thus: "As a general procedure, all final assembly, major sub-assembly, and sub-assembly was done on continuously moving conveyor lines."[84]

In short, firms were implementing the demands that Werner and the ministry were constantly pressing on them. Werner's hectoring had effects on the shop floors, where the engineers increasingly deployed flow arrangements to mobilize a diverse and inexperienced labor force. The institutional framework that emerged as Werner took charge of Göring's Industrial Council and evolved into Speer's system of "industrial self-responsibility" was effective in bullying industry into "rationalization"—at least to an extent compatible with the generally shortage-prone environment of the Nazi economy.[85]

Ultimately, no degree of learning could alter the war's outcome; too uneven was the distribution of economic potential.[86] While other belligerents harshly curtailed civilian consumption to feed the war machine, the Americans could afford to shield the civilian economy from inroads and still vastly outproduce both allies and opponents.[87] When German aircraft engine output peaked in 1944, it was just approaching the level that the United States had achieved in 1941.[88] Indeed, so prolific was the American war machine that a year after V-J Day, the US government found itself compelled to scrap some 68,000 super-fluous planes—a number that roughly matched Nazi Germany's entire output after Göring gave his Werner-influenced rationalization pep talk in November 1941.[89]

Where the mass production learning experiences did come in handy was *after* the war. Werner, Mayr, Stieler von Heydekampf, Nordhoff, and many other less prominent shop engineers and skilled metalworkers had spent several years assiduously emulating "American" models of production under the hothouse conditions of total war, improvising myriad process innovations along the way. After May 1945, they took this knowledge and put it to use in the backbone industry of the West German economic miracle—the automobile industry. William Werner fled Chemnitz ahead of the approaching Soviet troops. In the 1950s, he reemerged as an executive at the refashioned West German Auto-Union, where he became known as a "rationalization fanatic."[90]

Gaz and the Soviet Production "Miracle"

On November 7, 1941—the same day that Göring erupted in front of staffers in Berlin—the Red Army put on its yearly parade in honor of the October Revolution in Moscow. It was a remarkable display of sangfroid: the Wehrmacht was upon the Soviet capital, and a state of siege had been declared. If Göring had reason to be nervous, the Soviet leadership should have been panicking. All through October, amid looting and riots, factories had been evacuated from Moscow, and the Politburo had decamped to Kuibyshev on the easternmost bend of the Volga. The German invasion had dealt the Soviet economy what should have been a crippling blow: the country had lost more than a third of its grain-producing regions, roughly two-fifths of its population, almost two-thirds of crude steel and coal capacity, and seven-tenths of iron ore deposits. Thousands of industrial plants were lost, and the remainder were hastily dismantled and tied up on eastbound trucks and railcars. Until these factories could be reassembled beyond the Urals, Soviet armaments capacity was reduced by roughly three-fourths. As American observers noted with trepidation in early 1942, if the Red Army was to repel the German onslaught, Soviet industry required nothing "short of a miracle."[91]

And yet, over the course of 1942, something akin to this miracle appeared to transpire. That year Soviet industry increased the output of aircraft by two-thirds over 1941; tank production rose nearly fourfold, and artillery and mortars more than fivefold. For the remainder of the war, the Soviet Union decisively outmatched Germany in the war of the factories in every weapons category except ships and submarines.[92] In contrast to the Soviet economy's wartime performance, evidently, Speer's "production miracle" looks insipid.[93] The official Soviet narrative credited the planning system, which ostensibly allowed for more efficient economic mobilization during the war.[94] But this assessment has always sat uneasily with the chaotic and improvisatory nature of the Soviet economic response to the German invasion. How and why the Soviet economy overperformed in World War II remains one of the great questions of the twentieth century.

Part of the answer is that the Soviet economy, while surprised and overwhelmed by the German attack, was not exactly unprepared for war.[95] Stalin's strategic blunders of 1941 are infamous—he had chosen to ignore mounting evidence that a German attack was imminent, including intelligence that predicted the time and scale of the invasion with precision. And a blanket mobilization plan commensurate to the enormity of the losses sustained in the summer and fall of 1941 did not (and could not) exist. But if Stalin somehow convinced himself that the Germans would not attack in 1941, Stalinist industrialization policies since the First Five-Year Plan had consistently assumed that a large-scale war would eventually arrive. Over the course of the Thirties, the Soviet Union built up a deep armaments capacity that encompassed a host of designated production facilities for planes, tanks, and ammunition. Civilian industry, especially the machine tool, tractor, and automobile factories, adopted various wartime conversion schemes. Evacuation plans anticipating a German invasion were indeed in place; as early as 1934, for example, Leningrad had begun drawing up scenarios for dismantling and shipping off more than one hundred defense-related factories.[96] These preparations surely helped when the Leningrad Kirov works for the vaunted T-34 tank relocated to the Urals in October 1941. In short, while evacuation and conversion happened on an unforeseen scale, existing plans and scenarios helped respond to the calamity unfolding in 1941.[97]

When it came to preparing the economy for war, then, the Soviet Union did not lag behind Nazi Germany.[98] Where the Soviet Union exceeded its enemy was in how ruthlessly it mobilized economic resources *after* the

German attack. Though the invasion had much diminished Soviet steel capacity, what was left of it was relentlessly funneled into armaments production. While the Soviet Union had less steel at its disposal than any of the other belligerents, it built more tanks and aircraft per available unit of steel than all the other belligerents combined.[99] This evidently left next to nothing for nonmilitary uses. The shock to other civilian sectors was equally traumatic. Cotton textile production in 1942 was at 36 percent of its prewar level; meat products at 52; refined sugar at 5. As peasants were drafted into the Red Army, the workforce on the kolkhozy more than halved, with predictable consequences for the food supply.[100] The Soviet Union, then, managed to squeeze out the civilian economy much harder and more quickly than Nazi Germany. It was a contrast in coercive state capacity: by 1943, as Speer's ministry was still busy haranguing regional party bosses about shutting down non-defense-related firms, the Soviet war machine had already gobbled up the last remnants of the civilian sector.

But for our purposes, the salient question is this: How did resource mobilization work at the factory level, where labor power and steel inputs came together to forge enormous quantities of arms? Did the particular way that Soviet industry had indigenized mass production during the Thirties make a difference?[101] The problems facing the Nazi and the Soviet war economies were strikingly similar. In 1941, for the first time since the onset of industrialization, the Soviet factory workforce substantially decreased. By 1942, the Soviet defense sector had lost one-fifth of its prewar workforce (things were worse in other sectors). Punishing workweeks and long hours could make up only part of this loss.[102] Like the Nazi war machine, then, the Soviet armaments industry had to find ways to achieve, in the words of William Werner, "higher output with fewer skilled workers."

How this worked can be illustrated by looking, once more, at Gaz. In the summer and fall of 1941, the city of Gorky, home of Gaz, attained a supreme strategic significance in the Soviet arsenal: located 250 miles east of Moscow, Gorky found itself in relative safety from the front. The city's factories provided a crucial lifeline for the Soviet war effort while industries from Western Russia were evacuated, and hence it played a critically important role in supplying the Red Army in the battle for Moscow in late 1941. Immediately after the German attack, Gaz duly began making various types of bombs, shells, and mortars. But as Moscow scrambled to reshuffle production plans to match the scale of the German attack, Gaz soon received orders for tank engines, spare parts, and various types of ammunition. A separate shop for aircraft engines was set up on factory premises. In July, Moscow dispatched one of the leading tank specialists, Nikolai Astrov, to supervise retooling for light tanks (T-60s).[103]

FIGURE 5.4. Engine block production line at Gaz, 1944. Photo: TsANO.

Over the course of the war, Gaz's production program changed considerably (see table 5.2). Production of trucks was dialed back and supplemented with the assembly of knocked-down Ford-Marmon-Herrington trucks provided by lend-lease. Gaz also produced a number of armored and jeep-style vehicles developed from its own automotive designs of the mid-Thirties. But the factory made its most conspicuous contribution to the Red Army with two light tanks (T-60 and T-70) and a self-propelled piece of artillery (SU-76). The SU-76 was a much heavier vehicle than either of the tanks and indeed looked very much like a tank to untrained eyes—a fact that made it the most propaganda-effective of all of Gaz's wartime contributions.

War conversion was far from smooth. Like other factories across Eurasia during the war, Gaz was asked to do much more with fewer workers. On the one hand, the palette of military matériel expanded drastically—Gaz shops now put out a bewildering assortment of bombs, mines, shells, and other ammunition; vehicles; tank engines and parts; and aircraft supplies. At the same time, Gaz was losing workers. The factory suffered from what the production engineers described as a "severe shortage of labor" even as "the quality of the workforce significantly deteriorated." It was a conundrum that German shop engineers would have recognized: as skilled workers left for the front, a weakened and inexperienced labor force arrived to take their place. Over the course of 1942, more than 8,000 workers were drafted into the Red Army, and another

TABLE 5.2. Production of vehicles and tanks at Gaz, 1941–1945

	T-60	T-70	SU-76	Armored vehicles	Imported trucks, assembled	Trucks and other motor vehicles	Total number of employees present on January 1	Index of output (rubles) (1940 = 100)	Index of labor productivity (1940 = 100)
1941	1,323				221	71,398		100.6	112.8
1942	1,684	3,499		2,485	12,644	23,672		146.2	148.2
1943		3,348	601	1,824	13,891	20,771	39,711	111.7	133.2
1944			4,708	2,950	14,748	26,267	37,357	121.3	151.0
1945			3,824	1,742	5,493	29,749	35,670		
Total	3,007	7,847	9,133	9,001	46,997	171,857			

Source: TsANO archives, f. R-2435, o.9, d. 58; d. 68; d. 69,1.9; d. 78; o.1, d.178, l.149; Gordin, Gor'kovskii Avtomobil'nyi Zavod, 158–59.

7,000 left; meanwhile, less than 13,000 new hires arrived, often directly from the front. "Physically fit, skilled workers with regular living conditions left the factory," Gaz's chief engineer reported. In their stead arrived discharged soldiers, "weakened by sickness and injury," and other newcomers from the countryside. In their majority, these new hires "had not worked in industry nor possessed the necessary skills." They lacked access to adequate housing. The chief engineer, Lifshits, gave a striking image of the factory floor in late 1942:

> A large group of people showed up for work without shoes. Many workers, having no place to lie down in crammed shared apartments, stopped going home altogether and began spending the night in the shops next to the stoves in the common areas. Getting little rest at night, they work poorly during the day and roam the shops dirty and tired, which severely affects work discipline. [When] temperatures dropped sharply, they began lighting camp fires in the shops.

Gaz, Lifshits acknowledged, harbored "a large, highly qualified and experienced collective" of skilled workers and production engineers. But this skilled core struggled to assimilate the many newcomers to the variegated production program. "The number of articles produced exceeds the organizational capacity of the factory," Lifshits lamented. His report concluded with the plea that the factory might return to focusing on truck production, "since armored vehicles and tanks can be produced in many factories" but trucks and spare parts of "our brand" only at Gaz.[104]

Despite these problems, Gaz managed to put out more than 5,000 T-60s and T-70s in 1942, constituting more than half of Soviet light tanks. Gaz's sister plant in Gorky, *Krasnoe Sormovo*, was bringing online T-34s. In light of this output, Wehrmacht officials were "very interested in having these factories destroyed."[105] The Luftwaffe, which had brushed Gorky with air raids before (in November 1941 and February 1942), targeted the city's factories again in June 1943 with a series of destructive attacks. Gaz was hit particularly severely: 5,900 units of machinery and more than ten kilometers of conveyors were smashed; the main assembly shop lay in rubble.[106]

If plant reports from the period can be believed, the engineers at Gaz used the opportunity handed to them by the Luftwaffe to systematically overhaul the entire plant along flow principles. Fully reconstructed by November 1943, Gaz now featured "a radical improvement in factory organization" and better and speedier cooperation between the shops. The task of coordinating the very broad range of products "was solved by way of introducing full flow organization" within the shops, and by connecting the different shops—forge, foundry, press shop, machine shop—with conveyors. Production of the heavy artillery SU-76 began after the plant had been reconstructed. Once flow kicked

FIGURE 5.5. Production of the SU-76 at Gaz, 1944. Photo: TsANO.

in, the engineers boasted, it took Gaz workers 1,693 man-hours to produce a complete SU-76, while it took a sister factory almost twice that number, without the motor. Gaz engineers soon began instructing other factories in the Gorky region in flow production principles.[107]

Even allowing for a measure of self-congratulation, the impression seems warranted that Gaz's engineers managed to harness the unskilled and transient workforce with flow production principles. Soviet skill levels were ranked one to five, with five the lowest; the average skill level of Gaz workers during the war was 4.7. In critical shops, averages were higher, which reflected the skill bifurcation typical of mass production. In the motor shop, for example, 60 percent of workers were in rank three or four, 18 percent in rank two, and 22 percent were highly skilled (rank one). Just like in the German armaments industry, at Gaz a group of highly skilled workers, foremen, and engineers oversaw a largely unskilled, often transient, and frequently malnourished workforce. As the shop engineers concluded, Gaz was able to solve the problem of labor mobilization "only by organizing the overwhelming majority of its production along the method of continuous flow." Flow production allowed the unskilled arrivals to attain the desired norms "within two weeks after joining up."[108]

At the same time, the war ushered in a new phase of Stakhanov-style worker mobilization in the form of the so-called front brigades. As in the 1930s, this

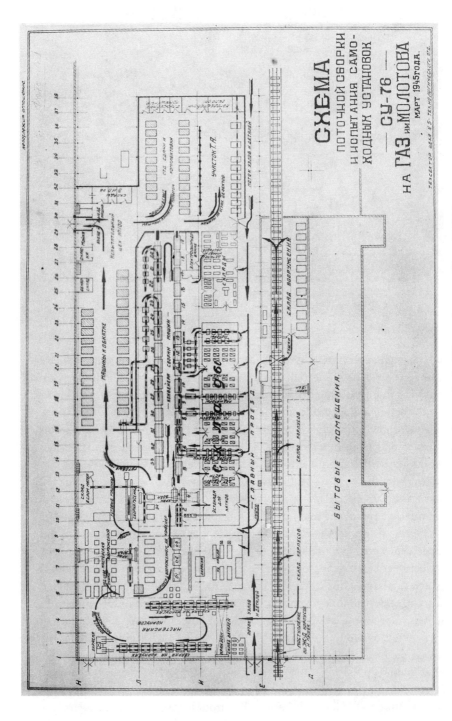

FIGURE 5.6. Flow diagram for the SU-76 at Gaz, 1945. Photo: TsANO.

was a high-propaganda effort orchestrated by cadre workers who enjoyed some level of rank-and-file support. There was a decisive difference, however: unlike the Stakhanovites of 1937, the front brigades did not see themselves in opposition to the engineering and technical staff. The movement still peddled "socialist competition" and overfulfillment of group norms—feats that promised official recognition, monetary rewards, and surplus food rations. Significantly, however, the brigades also espoused the demands of the engineering stratum: they called for treating the machines with care, saving raw materials, and avoiding defective output. They encouraged workers to seek continuous technical instruction after hours, called for close supervision of lower-skilled operatives, and for "strengthening work discipline." By 1943, Gaz reported 661 front brigades with more than 4,600 members—some 11 percent of the workforce.[109] To the extent that these neo-Stakhanovites formed part of the higher-skilled core stratum of mass production—a "new Soviet intelligentsia," as it came to be called—this development eased the tension between the grassroots mobilization of the 1930s and the prerogative of the technical and engineering staff bent on flow production.[110]

Yet it would be misleading to imagine the Gaz shops as a smoothly rationalized operation. While labor turnover declined over the course of the war, it remained substantial. As table 5.3 shows, large numbers of workers defied the threat of draconian sanctions and deserted Gaz, possibly seeking employment in other Gorky factories or drifting to the countryside. New arrivals often could not read or fell into a category factory management designated as "semiliterate."

The unruly reality of the shop floor can be gleaned from other reports. Steel and metal shortages were prevalent in the countryside and food was miserable in the factory, so an illegal trade sprang up. "Petty theft of socialist property" was the result: in 1944, nearly 2,900 workers were temporarily arrested for embezzling steel, metal, and even entire vehicles "to work on the kolkhoz." A foreman from the forge removed a total of 1.5 tons of metal "under false permits" and "brought it to the kolkhoz for agriculture." A superintendent in the wheel shop made two vehicles available to the kolkhoz, where he received "flour, butter, meat, and other foodstuffs" in return. A superintendent on the assembly line diverted an American lend-lease truck to the countryside, "where it worked all summer in exchange for products." Evidently to no avail, "in order to hide this vehicle it was dumped in a river."[111]

Despite these frictions, flow production made a remarkable comeback at Gaz during the war. In the wartime intensification of mass production methods, then, the Nazi and the Soviet regime resembled each other. Both confronted a skills shortage, and both responded by deploying flow production

TABLE 5.3. Reasons for labor turnover at Gaz, 1944

Arrivals	Number by group	Departures	Number by group
From Red Army	2,016	Desertion	2,289
From technical schools	1,462	Sickness or incapacity	1,829
Conscription of civilians	847	Transferred to other enterprises	755
Former Gaz workers returning	614	Drafted into Red Army	517
Transferred from other enterprises	110	Death	398
Other new hires	1,002	Arrests	388
		Family reasons	374
		For educational purposes	270
		Other	141
Total	6,051	Total	6,961

Source: TsANO archives, f.2435, o.9, d.80.

to harness unskilled labor. In both regimes, a highly skilled core group of superintendents and engineers put to work a largely unskilled workforce. Learning by doing was the primary way by which the skilled elite improved the mass production processes in both regimes; the resulting productivity increases were comparable. The shop floors of Gaz and BMW-Allach looked remarkably similar, except for the language of the inspirational banners on the walls.

What, then, explains why the Soviet armaments complex outperformed its German enemy? Evidently, German and Soviet production engineers faced very similar problems and used much the same methods. The decisive difference, it appears, lay not in how the regimes used flow mass production to mobilize an unskilled, exhausted, and brutalized workforce. Both did so pervasively. The difference was, rather, the political economy under which flow production operated. The Soviet command economy was more capable than its German counterpart of enforcing the conditions under which mass production would flourish. More consistently than the Germans, the Soviet Union traded off quantity for quality, production-adequate uniformity for military variety, sheer output for technological improvement. The Germans developed jet engines, but the Soviet Union outproduced them in propeller aircraft. Compared to the other belligerents, the Red Army relied on a limited number of main armaments types in World War II. In the summer of 1943, for example, engineers at the Aviation Ministry in Berlin counted 126 different American military aircraft models; the British even had 235. Germany had 65—"still too many," Milch submitted—and the Soviets 15.[112] Examining these Soviet fighters, German engineers marveled at the radical trade-off in favor of quantity they evinced. Their construction was "exceedingly rough," even "primitive"; they displayed a "strange mix" between "extremely labor-saving production" and "utility."[113] The "unrefined" production that German authorities struggled to foist upon the firms as the war wore on was hardwired into Soviet arms production from the beginning.

The Soviet advantage, then, lay not so much in the "planned" character of its economy than in its "command" character: not in the regime's capacity to efficiently allocate resources but rather in its capacity to ruthlessly mobilize them.[114] The Soviet state was able to uproot people, commandeer resources, and shuffle them across geography and jurisdiction with little chance of meeting organized opposition; it could dictate standards and production programs without having to overcome the kind of local foot-dragging on the firm level that so exasperated William Werner. At the very moment—July 1941—when Milch requested the authority to move resources around industry as he pleased and was thwarted, Soviet war administrators were endowed with precisely this authority in the decree "on the extension of the rights of the Soviet People's Commissars during wartime."[115] Speer grudgingly conceded the difference. "There is one thing that the Bolsheviks have over us," he acknowledged. "They ruthlessly clamp down and punish even the most minimal infractions against the state interest."[116]

Conclusion

Hitler used his last public appearance, in July 1944, to ruminate at length about the place of mass production in the Nazi economic order. Addressing assembled representatives of Speer's system of industrial self-responsibility, Hitler began by returning to the themes he had first elaborated in the 1920s. National Socialism, he rehearsed, was distinct from liberalism (where "the economy was the servant of capital") and from Communism (which crushed the economic initiative of the individual). In contrast, National Socialism harnessed "the individual's creative activity" to a common purpose. Hitler reminded his audience of the goal to acquire "living space" and raise the "standard of living" of the masses. This required the "mass production of goods, a mass production that can only be achieved with genius production methods." By teaching these methods, the war was preparing German industry for the postwar period. "When we win this war, German industry will receive gigantic orders to which only mass production can do justice," Hitler proclaimed. "Oh, but there is nothing that will not have to be produced in masses!"[117]

Hitler's audience did not buy it. One listener later described the speech as "ghostlike": the dictator was weak and unconvincing.[118] In the context of the summer of 1944, when it had become blindingly evident that Germany's industry was unable to thwart the incursions of superior Allied airpower, Hitler failed to persuade the assembled engineers that the industrial system that emerged from the crisis of 1941–1942 was effective, or a harbinger of a future economic order that would conform to Nazi ideology. Implicit in Hitler's speech was the admission that sharp frictions plagued a war-industrial complex that had been built on top of a decentralized landscape of private firms, who often only grudgingly accepted their subservience to the larger demands of a fully mobilized economy. Indeed, in light of the Allies' stark material preponderance, the Nazi ideological discourse about mass production retained a deep ambivalence throughout. Hitler understatedly acknowledged that when it came to mass production, Germany's opponents were "slightly better." In his prolific speechmaking, even Speer himself consistently invoked the idea that Germany's alleged technical weapons superiority would ultimately prevail. "In an increasingly technical war quantity is less and less decisive," Speer asserted, even as his ministry loudly publicized upward-sloping graphs of ever-increasing military output.[119] Outside of the armaments complex, Nazi radicals deplored that total war had enthroned technology and wondered whether a fully mechanized economy was compatible with the "völkisch ideal of life."[120]

For the Soviet Union, by contrast, wartime mass production secured victory. It was hence fully accepted as a specific triumph of the Soviet system, a result of the "technical and economic independence" that the Soviet Union had established since the 1920s.[121] Even before the weapons fell silent, a celebratory discourse took hold that reinterpreted the catastrophes of the war—the German invasion and the massive relocation of factories—as opportunities, boldly seized, for the comprehensive modernization of Soviet industry.[122] Gaz, again, was typical. In March 1945, Gaz production engineers drew up a comprehensive report reviewing the factory's history since its inception. The report narrated the development of mechanized flow production as a learning process in which the factory's engineers gradually weaned themselves off their reliance on the American model and began innovating independently. In the early years, Gaz had to copy Ford's models and American production technology "since we did not have at our disposal a sufficiently strong engineering apparatus for design and production." The 1936 Gaz M-1 still borrowed from American models and was made with American machine tools. Gradually, under Loskutov's tenure as director, Gaz began mass-producing its own designs and using its own equipment. But the push to full independence was achieved only during the war. The factory's main achievement was "applying the most modern methods of automobile technology" to the weaponry—such as the vaunted SU-76—that the war required. Having conquered mass production, Gaz, like Soviet industry at large, was prepared for the challenges of the postwar period.[123] Or so the engineers hoped.

Conclusion

REFASHIONING FORDISM UNDER
AMERICAN HEGEMONY

IN WORLD WAR II, America marshaled its mass production prowess to vanquish its fascist antagonists. By war's end, American global power—the prospect that postliberal insurgents of the interwar years had predicted, feared, and sought to resist—had fully come to pass. Uniquely among the belligerents, the United States emerged strengthened from the war: revving up America's production lines had not required the painful inroads to consumption that had haunted allies and opponents alike. After the war, as a result, mass production received an ideological reformulation in the core vocabulary of American hegemony: democracy, prosperity, consumerism, and economic internationalism. The political architecture, economic organization, and liberal ideological inflection of the US-orchestrated global order determined how automotive mass production would draw on and transform the legacy of the Thirties and Forties. This held true not only among the defeated insurgents; even the ally turned rival, the Soviet Union, remained beholden to the standards set out in the United States. As the global political climate shifted from the antagonisms of the World War to the ostensibly non-zero-sum doctrine of affluence and productivity, however, technology transfers and industrial-oriented development competition resumed, albeit in a new key. Ideological refashioning and political-economic restructuring latched on to strong technological, personal, and political continuities to the Thirties.

American postwar hegemony rested on a "politics of productivity"—the notion that, both at home and abroad, class conflict and distributional struggles could be overcome by forging a consensus around the growth-generating apparatus of mass production and consumption.[1] At home, the politics of consensus became possible because the war had overlaid and transformed the political fissures of the Thirties. The astounding mobilization of productive capacity during the war exorcised the lingering malaise of the Depression, refreshed public confidence in American industry, and firmly fixed organized labor in the political arena.[2] The war routinized and strengthened what Franklin Roosevelt called "the splendid cooperation between the government and industry and labor," giving rise to a political economy that restrained conflict through collective bargaining, state stewardship, and corporate moderation.[3] In the context of global war, these compromises had meshed inseparably with America's sense of mission. In invoking the United States as the "arsenal of democracy," Roosevelt had connected America's production potential to the neo-Wilsonian vision that underpinned the American war effort. By war's end, mass production furnished both an explanation of America's victory and an expression of America's global purpose. Mass production had proved to be "peculiarly an American art"; now it would become "America's gift to the world."[4]

A subtle shift separated these notions from the ideas that Henry Ford had propounded in the 1920s. When Ford died in 1947, the term *Fordism* had all but disappeared from the pages of newspapers and reformers' pamphlets—the term's resurgence in social scientific discourse would not come before the 1980s. In Ford's producerist vision, there had been no room for interest politics, collective bargaining, or the presence of a muscular federal state. In contrast to Henry Ford's open-house stance on international industrial proliferation—welcoming all takers so they could apply the Rouge's lessons at home—now Washington purposely made mass production and the "politics of productivity" an article of export. Productivity remained king, but a new punditry located its source no longer on factory floors but instead in management offices; not in machines but in "human relations."

The Austrian émigré sociologist Peter Drucker encapsulated the new dispensation in his obituary for Henry Ford. Ford-style mass production had "given us a new industrial civilization" with new achievements and new problems, Drucker wrote. Yes, mass production had expanded the horizon of popular prosperity, but it also had created enormous business organizations that now posed society's defining challenge. Tragically, Ford had failed to grasp that the most urgent issues confronting these large institutions were not problems of engineering; they were problems of meaning. How could tens of thousands of employees draw recognition, purpose, and citizenship from working for overweening big businesses? Mass production was therefore "not, fundamentally, a mechanical principle," Drucker said, "but a principle of social organization." Obsessed with "gadgeteering," Ford had failed to realize that the large, mass-producing enterprise required judicious *management*—not the maintenance of machines but the leadership of humans. The task was to finish the job Henry Ford had bequeathed: what Drucker called the "concept of mass production"—Henry Ford's legacy—had to be made whole by the "concept of the corporation."[5]

The new dispensation took root with astonishing rapidity at the Ford Motor Company. In 1945, a twenty-eight-year-old Henry Ford II took over the presidency from his ailing grandfather and lost no time in refashioning the company along what he called "modern organizational lines"—lines, that is, that had been developed at General Motors and popularized by Drucker in his book *Concept of the Corporation*. Henry II, a navy veteran, brought in young, recently decommissioned military officers of his generation—Robert McNamara and the "Whiz Kids"—and hired executives from General Motors to reorganize the company's sprawling domain. Using Drucker's *Concept* loosely as a manual, the new men grafted a managerial collective on top of the old hierarchy of shop superintendents and proceeded to shift the company's center of gravity from the shop floor to the boardroom. Soon college graduates populated management (under the senior Ford, recruitment had been strictly in-house and from the shop floor up). Organizational charts, banned at the company since 1919, now proliferated, delineating lines of authority, divisions, and "profit centers." Rouge foremen and superintendents had to cede control over their shop floor fiefdoms.[6]

The language of mass production changed. *My Life and Work* had portrayed industry as a space of conflict between the champions of production and their enemies among financiers, elite reformers, and organized labor. The book's keywords had been *work, progress, service,* and *production;* in its vocabulary, *capitalist* had a financial—and distinctly pejorative—connotation, notions of *justice* and *distribution* featured prominently, and even *exploitation* made an occasional appearance. Henry II and his executives operated in a discourse that emphasized *human relations* and *free enterprise;* they deployed a corporate newspeak that revolved around *decentralization, performance, incentive, control, policy, planning,* and *responsibility.* The elder Ford had imagined his company as a "productive organization" that brought together labor and machines to produce goods; when his grandson Henry II talked about "the organization," he had in mind the managerial tissue that allowed the company to be governed from the executive office. The new dispensation fundamentally anchored industrial leadership in a functional stratum that the senior Ford had argued mass production could entirely do without: an enlightened managerial elite.

This new managerial ideology, so vividly on display at Ford, infused how America projected and articulated hegemony abroad. It was telling that Marshall Plan programs, rather than funding transfers of technology and engineering know-how, instead sponsored the education of Europeans in American management practices. Human relations, so the thinking went, would more forcefully unleash productivity than technical improvements. As the Marshall-backed European Productivity Agency declared, "projects in the area of technology . . . should be limited" and emphasis put "on improving human relations and changing attitudes." More important than technology was "creating a psychological climate in which productivity will increase."[7] Ironically, the Ford Foundation became a central promoter of this type of entrepreneurial reeducation: having inherited the combined fortunes of Henry and Edsel, the foundation used its ample funds to spread "productivity consciousness" abroad.[8]

Whether such reeducation strategies had much of an impact is open to question. In West Germany, after all, by the mid-Fifties, American productivity officials complained that "positive results in terms of our intent and purpose" were "almost negligible" because both industrialists and workers proved immune to their prescriptions.[9] More decisive were two things: the American-sponsored reconstruction of Western export markets, and ongoing technology transfers—especially from the United States—orchestrated by the firms themselves and supported by the state.[10]

The reconstruction of export markets followed from the grand bargain that America offered to the nations of Western Europe. Europeans pledged to lower tariffs and move toward multilateralism in payments and trade, commit to managed industrial competition, and assume their share of the financial burden of the Western security alliance. In return, the United States would open its own domestic market for imports and provide funds to alleviate the sharp European shortage of dollars. One result of this compromise was that, under the auspices of US hegemony, West Germany experienced the type of export-based growth that Hitler had categorically rejected in the Twenties. The defining constraint of the Weimar economy had been the precarious access to export markets. Now, with America's acquiescence, trade surpluses allowed the West German economy to develop along lines that played to the country's strengths: importing raw materials and exporting high-end manufactures. Crucially, the United States allowed recovery to precede liberalization and tolerated West German import restrictions and capital controls until 1958. By 1960, West Germany commanded close to one-fifth of global manufacturing exports, forcefully breaking free from the balance-of-payments chokehold that had suffocated the Weimar economy three decades earlier.[11]

The emblematic beneficiary of American strategic lenience was the West German automobile industry. Gone was the "struggle for existence" that had embroiled the sector in the 1920s. Exports allowed carmakers to leap out of the limited domestic market and build on the technological learning of the Thirties and Forties. Between 1950 and 1962, America's share of global automobile production sank from over 80 percent to below 50 percent, while West Germany's rose from barely 3 percent to over 15 percent, putting the former insurgent in second place behind the hegemon. That year West Germany exported cars to 141 nations worldwide, slowly chipping away at the mighty

American competition. Even more momentously, thanks to Washington's low-tariff policy, American consumers now began buying German cars: in the early 1960s, the US absorbed close to a quarter of all West German vehicle exports. Volkswagen's role in this surge is difficult to overstate. Beginning in 1955, the erstwhile Nazi white elephant exported more vehicles than it sold at home, and in most years accounted for more than half of all West German car exports.[12] By the late 1950s, as one historian has marveled, "approximately half of West Germany's balance of payments surplus was earned by Volkswagen alone."[13] The Nazis had intended the mammoth Volkswagen works as a harbinger of the continental Fordism by which they meant to challenge America. Now Volkswagen fortified a chastened West Germany that embraced a junior role in the Atlantic alliance in return for an export-fueled *Wirtschaftswunder*.

Volkswagen demonstrates most clearly how the legacies of the antagonistic development competition of the Thirties came to fruition—in ways that the era's postliberals hardly intended—under the *Pax Americana*. Volkswagen's export fixation owed much to Heinrich Nordhoff, who led the firm during its twenty-year postwar period of legendary growth (1948–1968). As we saw in chapter 4, Nordhoff had earned his automotive chops at Opel during the Thirties, where he acted as a skillful broker between the General Motors–owned firm and the Nazi authorities. During the war, he ran Opel's Brandenburg plant that built the bulk of the Wehrmacht's truck fleet. After 1945, Nordhoff, like others of his generation, succeeded in distancing himself from his Nazi past and backed—by all appearances, genuinely—Ludwig Erhard's "social market economy." Yet Nordhoff never seemed able to step out from under the shadow of American preponderance. In language reminiscent of the Thirties, he warned in 1955 that Germany was still "forced to export." The balance of payments still weighed on Nordhoff. "Our economy is so completely dependent on imports," he said, "that it could not survive without exports that procure the necessary means of payment." Keenly aware of the support that the postwar world market architecture received from the United States, he remained wary that exports could be "cut off overnight."[14]

In other ways, too, Volkswagen revived the aspirations of the interwar period.[15] Nordhoff kept the "Beetle" design that Porsche had presented to Hitler in the summer of 1936 and launched it on a two-decade production run, exploiting to the utmost the scale economies of single-type mass flow production. Here, at last, was the German answer to the Model T—a no-nonsense, sturdy, affordable family vehicle that could compete with the Americans in export markets across the world and even penetrate the American market itself. As a state-owned company with no shareholders, Volkswagen was able to reinvest its ample proceeds while lowering prices and raising wages.[16] Like Henry Ford, Nordhoff remained unconvinced that marketing warranted much attention, arguing that "the VW is our most effective advertisement."[17] Reminiscent of Gottl-Ottlilienfeld's Ford-inspired ruminations on "white socialism," Nordhoff presented himself to Volkswagen's workforce as a sternly production-obsessed but otherwise benevolent paterfamilias. He tolerated unions, as long as they renounced adversarial action and accepted his understanding of the works as a production-oriented "community." In his speeches to assembled workers, he lampooned "the obsolete antithesis of capital and labor." Volkswagen's profit-sharing plans, first announced in 1953, caused alarm at the Economics Ministry; Nordhoff justified them by saying that "capital and labor would participate in earnings in absolutely the same way," which, he asserted, was "an injunction of justice."[18]

When it came to technological upgrading, too, Volkswagen resumed the strategies of the Thirties. In 1954, in order "to get a sense of what our factory should look like in about ten years," Nordhoff directed Otto Höhne (whom the German Labor Front had recruited in Chicago in 1939) back to the United States.[19] Höhne encountered American car factories in the grip of "automation."[20] Upon returning, he recommended that Volkswagen adopt the trend and begin connecting individual machines into chains of automated production sequences. By 1958, Nordhoff could boast that in some operations "almost everything proceeds automatically," and add that "the goal is to remove the word 'almost.'"[21] Thanks to exports, Volkswagen in the 1950s was producing, like Ford in the classical era, behind demand, and faced labor shortages. In this environment, increased automation catapulted productivity from a ratio of 6.2 vehicles per worker in 1950 to 20.8 in 1962, even as the workforce tripled.[22] To relieve the main factory, Volkswagen opened a branch in Hannover. Here the America veteran Höhne "realized immense automation projects," according to company reports, before handing the plant's leadership to Joseph Werner—the former Rouge toolmaker who had been Porsche's first American hire in 1937.[23]

Soviet engineers, too, showed up again at American factories. In a first since the Grand Alliance had soured into cold war, American authorities granted Soviet specialists visas to travel to the 1955 machine tool fair in Chicago and visit a few factories along the way. In return, three American engineers traveled to Russia; they were shown around Gaz and the reconstructed tractor factory at Stalingrad. They returned with a revealing report. "At neither place did we find over-all production techniques comparable" to American standards, they recorded; "manufacturing followed procedures approximately ten years old." Soviet industry was operating at the level of production protocols inherited from the war, on tools that were "well-kept" but "old." What the factories had not mastered was the latest Fordist pull toward automation. In consequence, the Soviet Union was "not now geared to provide a standard of living comparable to ours in America." In Moscow, Soviet officials (Gaz's former chief, Ivan Loskutov, among them) sat down with the Americans and asked them for an honest assessment and blunt advice. It was evident that the Soviets "still looked to the US as a leader in modern industry."[24]

The report reflected a basic truth of the Soviet political economy in the 1950s: despite renewed investments in industry, comparative underdevelopment had not disappeared and America remained the benchmark to beat. What had changed was the ideological environment of development competition. Immediately after the war ended, Stalin's jaundiced reading of American intentions led to renewed fears of "capitalist encirclement." Hopes of economic easing at home were dashed; what Stalin imposed instead was a return to the grim development logic of the Thirties. Resources drained from agriculture and consumption once again funded investments in military-industrial reconstruction. By 1950, industrial production had surged even as consumption and grain output languished below prewar levels.[25] In the countryside, the misery of the postwar years recalled the privations of the early Thirties; from 1946 to 1948, in the face of food shortages and famine, grain was again exported in exchange for machinery.[26]

Nikita Khrushchev famously denounced Stalin's crimes; in practice, he also sought to loosen the grip on Soviet citizens of his predecessor's merciless geoeconomics. Khrushchev repurposed Stalin's slogan—"catch up and overtake"—and gave it a Cold War flavor. The recently achieved nuclear parity, Khrushchev reasoned, would keep the imperialist West at bay; war was now avoidable. The time was ripe for "peaceful coexistence" between the socialist and capitalist camps, along with "economic competition with capitalism" on the grounds of living standards and growth rates.[27] Under Khrushchev, military expenditure more narrowly targeted high-end space and missile programs; in the plans, investment for the first time shifted into agriculture and consumer industries.[28] Stalin had justified a politically produced food insecurity, periodically lapsing into famine, as the price for industrial and military power. Khrushchev offered the Soviet people an "anti-famine political contract" that no Kremlin leader after him dared to rescind.[29] Beginning in 1963, the Soviet Union recurrently did what had remained unthinkable under Stalin: it spent hard currency on food imports.[30]

It is the historical experience of food insecurity that makes understandable Khrushchev's 1957 announcement that the Soviet Union would set out to surpass America in the production of meat.[31] Yet such aspirations only betrayed the considerable distance between Khrushchev's concern with basic living standards and American-style consumerism. The disparity could be gauged most readily in the availability of cars—that arch symbol of postwar consumer capitalism in the West. Soviet motor vehicle production had peaked at 211,000 in 1938; that ceiling was broken in 1949, and numbers nudged up toward 500,000 in the late Fifties. This was nowhere near the millions of cars churned out every year by American factories. What was more, the Soviet motor vehicle remained primarily a producer good, with trucks accruing the greatest share of output. Despite the fanfare that surrounded the release of Soviet-designed passenger cars like the Gaz Volga (presented in 1955), it was party officials, state authorities, and public institutions that commandeered the majority of them.[32] The American ideal of individual car ownership remained out of reach. Khrushchev tried to make a virtue out of the contrast, arguing that the Soviet Union would "use cars more rationally than the Americans" and develop "taxi fleets."[33]

It was left to Khrushchev's successors to implement something akin to a Soviet mass automobility. Khrushchev's ouster had many reasons, but among them was the Soviet Union's evident failure under his watch to make much ground in a catch-up process defined in consumerist terms. Consequently, during the Eighth Five-Year Plan (1966–1970), investment in passenger cars more than tripled.[34] The radiant symbol of the new commitment was, once again, an "Auto Giant" on the Volga, built on the basis of a technical assistance agreement with the West. Between 1966 and 1970, in the city of Tolyatti (named after Gramsci's fellow Communist, Palmiro Togliatti), the Vaz facilities (*Volzhskii Avtomobil'nyi Zavod*) took shape under the consultancy of the Italian carmaker Fiat.[35]

With Vaz, the long history of Soviet efforts to import American Fordism came full circle. Much had changed since the heady days of 1929, when Valerii Mezhlauk and Henry Ford traded signatures in Dearborn. Gaz in Nizhnii had taken shape in the context of crash industrialization and had formed a pillar of the Soviet production machine in World War II. For at least two decades after its founding, Gaz predominantly produced trucks. Vaz in Tolyatti, in turn, had an explicit consumer orientation: it was meant to provide the Soviet Union with millions of passenger cars (which eventually it did, though this was not enough to achieve American ownership rates). Yet the stark fact remained that in its development competition with America, the Soviet Union still had to turn to the West and expend enormous sums of foreign exchange on imported technology.

Why the Soviet economy performed so poorly at domestic technological innovation has often been pointed out: an institutional landscape that separated high-end research and development from humdrum industrial production; the inertia of enterprises themselves, which had few reasons to innovate, given that they faced no competition; the systemic bias for output over quality; unresponsive supply chains.[36] From the perspective of comparative political economy, however, it is clear the Soviet Union's subaltern position in the American-dominated global economic order compounded these problems. Though Cold War narratives still convey this impression, the Soviet Union did not in fact build a separate, cordoned-off economic system; rather, like all other nations, it participated in a world economy in which capital and technology were denominated in dollars. Nuclear parity and space race notwithstanding, the Soviet Union confronted America throughout the twentieth century from a position of economic weakness.[37] Excluded, by design, from America's Cold War support system, the Soviet Union failed—unlike West Germany, say—to translate technological imports and industrial upgrading into competitive manufacturing exports. The Soviet Union's principal developmental constraint was the harsh trilemma confronted by all twentieth-century late developers whose industries struggled to compete in world markets: it could not simultaneously sustain investment growth, consumption growth, and a positive balance of payments. Stalin's cruel economic realpolitik had sacrificed the second; his successors eventually surrendered the latter. In hindsight, it appears as no surprise that by the 1980s the Soviet Union succumbed to the same temptation as did import substitution industrializers elsewhere: the "kiss of debt" that came with hard currency loans from the West.[38]

American-style postwar "Fordism", then, was only one pattern in the mottled global legacy left behind by Henry Ford. It was not the least ideological effect of American hegemony that in the 1960s modernization theory could universalize this unique historical arrangement—what Rostow called "high mass-consumption"—as the target of successful development itself. Responding to the crisis of the 1970s and 1980s, social scientists added a next phase: "Post-Fordism" or "post-industrial society" signaled deindustrialization to some and the promise of a "service and information economy" to others. What united these constructs was a thinking in sequential stages, a preoccupation with national patterns of development, and a theory of causation centered on self-generating forces—be it Rostow's "dynamic" process of productive innovation or the shifting dialectics of capital accumulation of the Regulationists. Though this kind of soft Hegelianism occasionally still ensnares historians, twenty-first-century experiences have rendered such narratives unpersuasive. It has become clear that cycles of industrialization and deindustrialization are inseparable from concerted efforts to restructure the global division of labor, that productive dual-use technologies are fiercely contested by states and corporations alike, that investment and disinvestment cannot be dislodged from contests over the terms of globalization, and that capital has no autonomous power outside of the designs and struggles of political actors.

This book has sought to deliver a history of twentieth-century Fordism with these considerations in mind. There is little justification in portraying postwar Fordism as a realization of political and economic tendencies purportedly inherent in complex mass production. Ford's producer populism and the military-industrial states of the 1930s and 1940s were neither teleological antecedents nor aberrations in the unfolding of modern industrial relations. Fordism has operated, and continues to operate, in divergent political and economic arrangements bolstered by differing ideological framings. The two riddles posed by complex mass production—factory discipline and demand management—have found different, usually crisis-prone, temporary, and mixed answers. In times of economic expansion, workers could be persuaded to trade drudgery for high earnings, as in the United States in the 1920s or at Volkswagen in the 1950s. At other junctures, the necessity to earn wages after losing access to subsistence mattered, as it did for the tens of thousands of peasants streaming into the factories of Soviet industrialization. Naked coercion characterized assembly work in the factories of the Nazi aviation complex during World War II. Mass demand, meanwhile, was not intrinsically tied to a state that wielded Keynesian policy tools. Rising farm incomes (that Henry Ford mistook for permanent) bolstered demand in the Model T's heyday. An inflationary state purchasing arms, such as in Nazi Germany, provided its own form of mass demand. For the West German automobile industry, a central strategy of demand management was tapping export markets unlocked by American hegemony.

Whether, how, and where Fordism took hold was the result of fierce conflicts over the global industrial order. From Henry Ford's populist ideology of mass production, interwar postliberals extracted heady promises of political-economic resurgence. During the 1930s, they sought to challenge America by emulating it, using American technology to support military-industrial expansion at home. The Nazi insurgency perished at the hands of its opponents, though its legacies influenced West German industrial development. The insurgent Fordism of the Soviet Union was strong enough to win the largest land war in history, but too weak to challenge American industrial preponderance after World War II. The Cold War predisposed the United States toward a temperate reconstruction policy in Western Europe while keeping the Soviet Union outside of the mechanisms of redollarization, with momentous consequences for Fordism in each.

If there is one clear lesson from this history, it is that development is always relational: it cannot be understood in national terms and without attention to the fundamental power disparities that structure the global economy. Tense and ambivalent global connections are baked into the very logic of development competition: late developers have no choice but to turn, for technology and capital, to those they seek to emulate and challenge. Histories of globalization would do well to imbibe this lesson, lest they continue to mistake as "flows" what have in fact been constantly contested claims on technology, capital, goods, and information within a shifting political architecture of geo-economic relations. In this sense, the type of development competition that spread Fordism through the world in the twentieth century will continue to be with us, shaping a global economic order that is ever contested, never finished.

NOTES

Introduction: Detroit, Capital of the Twentieth Century

1. Benito Mussolini, "La dottrina del fascismo," in *Opera Omnia,* ed. Edoardo Susmel and Duilio Susmel (Firenze, Italy: La Fenice, 1961), 34: 115–38.

2. John Maynard Keynes, "National Self-Sufficiency," *Yale Review* 22, no. 4 (1933): 755–69.

3. Walter Benjamin, "Paris, Hauptstadt des 19. Jahrhunderts" [1935] in *Illuminationen: Ausgewählte Schriften* (Frankfurt: Suhrkamp, 2001), 185–200; Walter Benjamin, "Paris—Capitale du XIXème siècle" [1937] in *Das Passagen-Werk* (Frankfurt: Suhrkamp, 1982), 60–77.

4. Benson Ford Research Center (BFRC), Dearborn, MI, Acc. 285, Box 160.

5. Friedrich von Gottl-Ottlilienfeld, *Fordismus. Über Industrie und technische Vernunft* (Jena, Germany: Fischer, 1926).

6. N. S. Rozenblit, *Fordizm: Amerikanskaia organizatsiia proizvodstva* (Moscow: Ekonomicheskaia Zhizn', 1925).

7. Carl Raushenbush, *Fordism, Ford and the Workers, Ford and the Community* (New York: League for Industrial Democracy, 1937).

8. In Gramsci's words: "Hegemony is born in the factory" (*Quaderno 22: Americanismo e fordismo,* ed. Franco de Felice [Turin, Italy: Einaudi, 1978], 18).

9. The classic Regulationist statement is Michel Aglietta, *A Theory of Capitalist Regulation: The U.S. Experience,* trans. David Fernbach (London: NLB, 1979). For good overviews see Bob Jessop, "Regulation Theories in Retrospect and Prospect," *Economy and Society* 19, no. 2 (1990): 153–216; Bob Jessop, "Fordism and Post-Fordism: A Critical Reformulation," in *Pathways to Regionalism and Industrial Development,* ed. A. J. Scott and M. J. Storper (London: Routledge, 1992), 43–65, reprinted with slight revisions in Bob Jessop and Ngai-Ling Sum, *Beyond the Regulation Approach: Putting Capitalist Economies in Their Place* (Cheltenham, UK: Edward Elgar, 2006), 58–89.

10. Michael J. Piore and Charles F. Sabel, *The Second Industrial Divide: Possibilities for Prosperity* (New York: Basic, 1984).

11. Charles F. Sabel and Johnathan Zeitlin, "Historical Alternatives to Mass Production," *Past and Present* 108, no. 1 (1985): 133–76; Charles F. Sabel and Johnathan Zeitlin, eds., *World of Possibilities: Flexibility and Mass Production in Western Industrialization* (Cambridge, UK: Cambridge University Press, 1997); Philip Scranton, *Endless Novelty: Specialty Production and American Industrialization 1865–1925* (Princeton, NJ: Princeton University Press, 1997).

12. Paul Hirst and Johnathan Zeitlin, "Flexible Specialization versus Post-Fordism: Theory, Evidence, and Policy Implications," *Economy and Society* 20, no. 1 (1991): 1–55.

13. Readers may consult a google ngram view of "Fordism" for confirmation of this claim.

14. Foundational was Charles S. Maier, "Between Taylorism and Technocracy: European Ideologies and the Vision of Industrial Productivity," *Journal of Contemporary History* 5, no. 2 (1970): 27–61. See also Mary Nolan, *Visions of Modernity: American Business and the Modernization of Germany* (New York: Oxford University Press, 1994); Alf Lüdtke, Inge Marßolek, and Adelheid von Saldern, eds., *Amerikanisierung: Traum und Alptraum im Deutschland des zwanzigsten Jahrhunderts* (Stuttgart: Steiner, 1996); Marie-Laure Djelic, *Exporting the American Model: The Post-war Transformation of European Business* (New York: Oxford University Press, 1998); Victoria de Grazia, *Irresistible Empire: America's Advance through Twentieth Century Europe* (Cambridge, MA: Harvard University Press, 2005); Mary Nolan, *The Transatlantic Century: Europe and America, 1890–2010* (New York: Cambridge University Press, 2012); David Ellwood, *The Shock of America: Europe and the Challenge of the Century* (Oxford: Oxford University Press, 2012). For an overview see Philipp Gassert, "The Spectre of Americanization: Western Europe in the American Century," in *The Oxford Handbook of Postwar European History*, ed. Dan Stone (Oxford: Oxford University Press, 2012), 182–200, with further references on the "Americanization" literature.

15. "Command consumption" is de Grazia's term: de Grazia, *Irresistible Empire*, 124–26. On the people's commodities and Nazi consumerism see Wolfgang König, *Volkswagen, Volksempfänger, Volksgemeinschaft. "Volksprodukte" im Dritten Reich: Vom Scheitern einer Nationalsozialistischen Konsumgesellschaft* (Paderborn, Germany: Schöningh, 2004); Shelley Baranowski, *Strength through Joy: Consumerism and Mass Tourism in the Third Reich* (Cambridge, UK: Cambridge University Press, 2004). On Stalinist consumerism see Elena Osokina, *Za fasadom "Stalinskogo izobiliia": raspredelenie i rynok v snabzhenii naseleniia v gody industrializatsii, 1927–41* (Moscow: ROSSPEN, 1998); Amy Randall, *The Soviet Dream World of Retail Trade and Consumption in the 1930s* (Basingstoke, UK: Palgrave Macmillan, 2008).

16. Gassert, "Spectre of Americanization," 190.

17. Robert J. Antonio and Alessandro Bonanno, "A New Global Capitalism? From 'Americanism and Fordism' to 'Americanization-Globalization,'" *American Studies* 41, no. 2/3 (2000): 36.

18. Mira Wilkins and Frank Ernest Hill, *American Business Abroad: Ford on Six Continents*, updated ed. (New York: Cambridge University Press, 2011); Hubert Bonin, Yannick Lung, and Steven Tolliday, eds., *Ford, 1903–2003: The European History*, 2 vols. (Paris: PLAGE, 2003); David Nye, *America's Assembly Line* (Cambridge, MA: MIT Press, 2013), chapter 4; Elizabeth Esch, *The Color Line and the Assembly Line: Managing Race in the Ford Empire* (Berkeley: University of California Press, 2018).

19. Wayne Lewchuk, *American Technology and the British Vehicle Industry* (Cambridge, UK: Cambridge University Press, 1987); James P. Womack, Daniel T. Jones, and Daniel Roos, *The Machine That Changed the World* (New York: Free Press, 1990); Haruhito Shiomi and Kazuo Wada, eds., *Fordism Transformed: The Development of Production Methods in the Automobile Industry* (New York: Oxford University Press, 1995); Robert Boyer et al., eds., *Between Imitation and Innovation: The Transfer and Hybridization of Productive Models in the International Automobile Industry* (New York: Oxford University Press, 1998); Jonathan Zeitlin and Gary Herrigel, eds., *Americanization and Its Limits: Reworking US Technology and Management in Postwar Europe and Japan* (Oxford, UK: Oxford University Press, 2000).

20. The locus classicus is surely Harry Braverman, *Labor and Monopoly Capital: The Degradation of Work in the Twentieth Century* (New York: Monthly Review Press, 1974). See also Wayne

Lewchuck, "Fordist Technology in Britain: The Diffusion of Labour Speed-Up," in *The International Diffusion of Technology*, ed. David Jeremy (Aldershot, UK: Edward Elgar, 1992); Steven Tolliday and Jonathan Zeitlin, eds., *Between Fordism and Flexibility: The Automobile Industry and Its Workers* (New York: St. Martin's, 1992).

21. Jürgen Bönig, *Die Einführung von Fließarbeit in Deutschland bis 1933: Zur Geschichte einer Sozialinnovation* (Münster, Germany: LIT Verlag, 1993).

22. Charles S. Maier, "The Politics of Productivity: Foundations of American International Economic Policy after World War II," in *In Search of Stability: Explorations in Historical Political Economy*, ed. C. S. Maier (Cambridge, UK: Cambridge University Press, 1987), 121–152; Mark Rupert, *Producing Hegemony: The Politics of Mass Production and American Global Power* (Cambridge, UK: Cambridge University Press, 1995).

23. Walt W. Rostow, *The Stages of Economic Growth: A Non-Communist Manifesto* (Cambridge, UK: Cambridge University Press, 1960). In fact, Rostow laid out in miniature the master narrative subsequently followed by Fordism scholarship. The move toward "high mass-consumption," Rostow wrote, began with "Henry Ford's moving assembly line of 1913–14; but it was in the 1920s, and again in the post-war decade, 1946–56, that this stage of growth was pressed to, virtually, its logical conclusion. In the 1950s, Western Europe and Japan appear to have fully entered this phase" (p. 11).

24. In full agreement here with the argument about technology in David Edgerton, *Warfare State: Britain, 1920–1970* (New York: Cambridge University Press, 2006).

25. This section builds on the insights of Adam Tooze: *The Deluge: The Great War, America, and the Making of a New Global Order, 1916–1931* (New York: Viking, 2014).

26. Sven Beckert, "American Danger: US Empire, Eurafrica, and the Territorialization of Capitalism" *American Historical Review* 122, no. 4 (2017): 1137–70.

27. Mariangela Paradisi, "Il commercio estero e la struttura industriale," in *L'economia italiana nel periodo fascista*, ed. Pierluigi Ciocca and Gianni Toniolo (Bologna, Italy: Mulino, 1976), 271–328.

28. Steven Marks, "The Russian Experience with Money, 1914–1924," in *Russian Culture in War and Revolution, 1914–22*, ed. Murray Frame et al. (Bloomington, IN: Slavica, 2014), 2: 142–43; Katherine Siegel, *Loans and Legitimacy: The Evolution of Soviet-American Relations, 1919–1933* (Lexington: University Press of Kentucky, 1996), 100; Oscar Sanchez-Sibony, "Global Money and Bolshevik Authority: The NEP as the First Socialist Project," *Slavic Review* 78, no. 3 (2019): 694–716.

29. "Insurgents" is Tooze's term: Tooze, *Deluge*, 7.

30. Ferdinand Fried, *Autarkie* (Jena, Germany: Diedrichs, 1932); Alberto de Stefani, *Autarchia ed antiautarchia* (Città di Castello, Italy: Unione ArtiGrafiche, 1935); Herbert Backe, *Das Ende des Liberalismus* (Berlin: Reichsnährstand Verlagsanstalt, 1938); H. Kremmler, *Autarkie in der organischen Wirtschaft* (Dresden, Germany: Focken & Oltmans, 1940). See also Eckart Teichert, *Autarkie und Großraumwirtschaft in Deutschland, 1930–39* (Munich: Oldenbourg, 1984); Rolf Petri, *Von der Autarkie zum Wirtschaftswunder: Wirtschaftspolitik und industrieller Wandel in Italien 1935–65* (Tübingen, Germany: Niemeyer, 2001).

31. On the repercussions of the Depression on international trade theory see, e.g., Jacob Viner, "The Doctrine of Comparative Costs," *Weltwirtschaftliches Archiv* 36 (1932): 356–414, and the ensuing discussion in this periodical.

32. Dietmar Petzina, *Autarkiepolitik im "Dritten Reich": Der nationalsozialistische Vierjahres-plan* (Stuttgart: DVA, 1968); Adam Tooze, *The Wages of Destruction: The Making and Breaking of the Nazi Economy* (New York: Viking, 2007), chapters 3 and 7; Luciano Zani, *Fascismo, autar-chia, commercio estero. Felice Guarneri, un tecnocrate al servizio dello "Stato Nuovo"* (Bologna, Italy: Il Mulino, 1988).

33. Jeffry Frieden, *Global Capitalism: Its Rise and Fall in the Twentieth Century* (New York: Norton, 2006), 208.

34. Michael R. Dohan, "The Economic Origins of Soviet Autarky, 1927/28–1934," *Slavic Review* 35, no. 4 (1976): 603–35; Oscar Sanchez-Sibony, "Depression Stalinism: The Great Break Reconsidered," *Kritika: Explorations in Russian and Eurasian History* 15, no. 1 (2014): 23–49; I. P. Bokarev, "Rossiiskaia ekonomika v mirovoi ekonomicheskoi sisteme (konets XIX—30-e gg. XX veka)," in *Ekonomicheskaia istoriia Rossii XIX-XX vv.: Sovremennyi vzgliad*, ed. B.A. Vinogra-dov (Moscow: ROSSPEN, 2000), 433–57, esp. 450–53. Though cf. Stephen Kotkin, *Stalin: The Paradoxes of Power, 1878–1928* (New York: Penguin, 2014), who sees the onset of crash industri-alization determined primarily by the dictator's ideological determination.

35. I. V. Stalin, *Sochineniia* (Moscow: Gosizdat politicheskoi literatury, 1946–52), 7: 354–56 and 13: 171–73; Nikolai A. Voznesenskii, *The Economy of the USSR During World War II* (Wash-ington, DC: Public Affairs, 1948), 41. The 1941 quotes are from "Notes from the Meeting be-tween Comrade Stalin and Economists Concerning Questions in Political Economy, 29 Jan 1941," History and Policy Program Digital Archive, ARAN f. 1705, o.1. d.166, ll.14–26, trans. Ethan Pollock, https://digitalarchive.wilsoncenter.org/document/110984. I owe the reference to Yakov Feygin, "Reforming the Cold War State: Economic Thought, Internationalization, and the Politics of Soviet Reform, 1955–1985" (PhD dissertation, University of Pennsylvania, 2017), 36–37.

36. Traditionally, the literature on Soviet industrialization has assumed that its primary goal was civilian growth. See, e.g., the classic contributions of Maurice Dobb, *Soviet Economic Devel-opment since 1917* (London: Routledge & Kegan Paul, 1948); Alexander Erlich, *The Soviet Indus-trialization Debate* (Cambridge, MA: Harvard University Press, 1960); Eugène Zaleski, *Planning for Economic Growth in the Soviet Union, 1918–1932* (Chapel Hill: University of North Carolina Press, 1971); Alec Nove, *An Economic History of the USSR, 1917–1991* (London: Penguin, 1992); Robert C. Allen, *Farm to Factory: A Reinterpretation of the Soviet Industrial Revolution* (Prince-ton, NJ: Princeton University Press, 2003). For an effective critique of the "growth" assumption see Vladimir Kantorovich, "The Military Origins of Soviet Industrialization," *Comparative Eco-nomic Studies* 57, no. 4 (2015), 669–692. Kantorovich follows a more recent trend among scholars who have stressed the military goals of Stalinist industrialization. See Lennart Samuelson, *Plans for Stalin's War Machine: Tukhachevskii and Military-Economic Planning 1925–1941* (Basingstoke, UK: Palgrave Macmillan, 2000); John Barber and Mark Harrison, eds., *The Soviet Defence In-dustry Complex from Stalin to Khrushchev* (Basingstoke, UK: Palgrave Macmillan, 2000); Mark Harrison, ed., *Guns and Rubles: The Defense Industry in the Stalinist State* (New Haven, CT: Yale University Press, 2008); Vladimir Kantorovich and A. Wein, "What Did the Soviet Rulers Maxi-mize?" *Europe-Asia Studies* 61, no. 1 (2009): 1579–1601; R. W. Davies et al., *The Industrialisation of Soviet Russia: The Soviet Economy and the Approach of War, 1937–1939* (London: Palgrave Macmillan, 2018). This scholarship emphasizes that defense remained a central concern under Stalin, that the Soviet Union indeed built up a formidable military-industrial complex during

the Thirties, and that the regime's crimes make the idea that it prioritized civilian welfare look rather dubious indeed. However, putting the question in terms of either-or priorities misses how the Bolshevik development ideology saw military motives as part of a larger set of goals that included political affirmation, economic independence, and civilizational survival and resurgence.

37. Tooze, *Wages of Destruction*; Benjamin Carter Hett, *The Death of Democracy: Hitler's Rise to Power and the Downfall of the Weimar Republic* (New York: Henry Holt, 2018), esp. pp. 106–114; Brendan Simms, *Hitler: Only the World Was Enough* (New York: Allen Lane, 2019), esp. chapter 7. With few exceptions (e.g., Charles S. Maier, "The Economics of Fascism and Nazism," in Maier, *In Search of Stability*, pp. 70–120), historians of the Nazi economy have shied away from framing their analyses in comparative terms, evidently on the assumption that Nazi economic policy was sui generis. How the Nazi economic system fit into the global Thirties is therefore a question still in search of theoretical framing. For the debates about the nature of the Nazi economic system see Avraham Barkai, *Nazi Economics* (Oxford, UK: Berg, 1990); Ludolf Herbst, *Der Totale Krieg und die Ordnung der Wirtschaft* (Munich, Germany: Oldenbourg, 1982); Richard J. Overy, *War and Economy in the Third Reich* (Oxford, UK: Clarendon Press, 2002); Werner Abelshauser, Jan O. Hesse, and Werner Plumpe, eds., *Wirtschaftsordnung, Staat, und Unternehmen: Neue Forschungen zur Wirtschaftsgeschichte des Nationalsozialismus* (Essen, Germany: Klartext, 2003); Christoph Buchheim, "Unternehmen in Deutschland und NS-Regime 1933–45: Versuch einer Synthese," *Historische Zeitschrift* 282, no. 1 (2006): 351–90; Peter Hayes, "Corporate Freedom of Action in Nazi Germany," *Bulletin of the German Historical Institute* 45 (2009): 29–42, and the ensuing debate in the pages of the *Bulletin*; and most recently Ludolf Herbst, "Gab es ein nationalsozialistisches Wirtschaftssystem?" in *Das Reichswirtschaftsministerium in der NS-Zeit: Wirtschaftsordnung und Verbrechenskomplex*, ed. Albrecht Ritschl (Berlin: De Gruyter, 2016), 611–44.

38. Adolf Hitler, *Reden, Schriften, Anordnungen: Februar 1925 bis Januar 1933*, vol. IIa, ed. Institut für Zeitgeschichte (Munich: Saur, 1995), 14.

39. Hitler, *Reden, Schriften, Anordnungen*, vol. IV/1, 194–96.

40. Theodor Lüddecke, "Amerikanismus als Schlagwort und Tatsache," *Deutsche Rundschau* 56 (August 1930): 214–21.

41. Arsenii Mikhailov, *Sistema Forda* (Moscow: Gosizdat, 1930), 5.

42. Michael Cusumano, *The Japanese Automobile Industry: Technology and Management at Nissan and Toyota* (Cambridge, MA: Harvard University Press, 1985), 1–72; Mira Wilkins, "The Contributions of Foreign Enterprises to Japanese Economic Development," in *Foreign Business in Japan before World War II*, ed. Takeshi Yuzawa and Masaru Udagawa (Tokyo: Tokyo University Press, 1990), 35–57; Mark Mason, *American Multinationals and Japan: The Political Economy of Capital Controls* (Cambridge, MA: Harvard University Press, 1992), 48–99.

43. Pier Angelo Toninelli, "Between Agnelli and Mussolini: Ford's Unsuccessful Attempt to Penetrate the Italian Automobile Market in the Interwar Period," *Enterprise and Society* 10, no. 2 (2009): 335–75; Giuseppe Volpato, "Ford in Italy: Commercial Breakthroughs without Industrial Bridgeheads," in *Ford, 1903–2003: The European History*, vol. 2, 451–56. On Fiat's relationship with the regime see Traute Rafalski, *Italienischer Faschismus in der Weltwirtschaftskrise, 1925–1936* (Opladen, Germany: Westdeutscher Verlag, 1984), 287–340; Valerio Castronovo, *Giovanni Agnelli: la FIAT dal 1899 al 1945* (Turin, Italy: Einaudi, 1977). On Mirafiori and the political

economy of the late Thirties in which it arose see Duccio Bigazzi, *La grande fabbrica: Organiz-zazzione industriale e modello americano alla Fiat dal Lingotto a Mirafiori* (Milan: Feltrinelli, 2000), 72–103; Giuseppe Volpato, "Produzione e mercato: Verso l'automobilismo di massa," in *Mirafiori, 1936–1962*, ed. Carlo Olmo (Turin, Italy: Umberto Allemandi, 1997), 133–50.

44. Mussolini, *Opera Omnia*, 31: 195.

45. Scholars studying the automobile industry have usually approached their subject from the perspective of corporate strategy, industrial relations, and the history of technology. In contrast, the crucial role of states in shaping the fortunes of national automobile sectors, espe-cially in the first half of the twentieth century, is remarkably poorly understood. The lone book that asked explicit questions about the comparative political economy of the mid-century Eu-ropean automobile industry—Simon Reich, *The Fruits of Fascism: Postwar Prosperity in Histori-cal Perspective* (Ithaca, NY: Cornell University Press, 1990)—was unfortunately hamstrung by overstating its case. *Pace* Reich, promoting domestic automobile sectors hardly required a Fas-cist regime or post-Fascist successor state, as the literature on postwar industrial policies across the globe has borne out. See, e.g., Douglas C. Bennett and Kenneth Evan Sharpe, *Transnational Corporations versus the State: The Political Economy of the Mexican Auto Industry* (Princeton: Princeton University Press, 1985); Helen Shapiro, *Engines of Growth: The State and Transnational Auto Companies in Brazil* (Cambridge, UK: Cambridge University Press, 1994); Linsu Kim, *Imitation to Innovation: The Dynamics of Korea's Technological Learning* (Cambridge, MA: Har-vard Business School Press, 1997), esp. chapter 5.

46. These patterns are borne out by the relevant sections in Wilkins and Hill, *Ford on Six Continents*, as well as the essays in Bonin, Lung, and Tolliday, *Ford, 1903–2003: The European History*, vol. 2.

47. Quoted in Talbot Imlay and Martin Horn, *The Politics of Industrial Collaboration during World War II: Ford France, Vichy, and Nazi Germany* (Cambridge, UK: Cambridge University Press, 2014), 17.

48. On the fractious relationship of French auto producers with their American competitors in the interwar period see Imlay and Horn, *Politics of Industrial Collaboration*, 21–49; Patrick Fridenson, "Ford as a Model for French Carmakers," in *Ford, 1903–2003: The European History*, 1: 125–52. See also Yves Cohen, "The Modernization of Production in the French Automobile Industry: A Photographic Essay," *Business History Review* 65, no. 4 (1991), 754–80.

49. Ronald Findlay and Kevin H. O'Rourke, *Power and Plenty: Trade, War, and the World Economy in the Second Millenium* (Princeton, NJ: Princeton University Press, 2007), 365–428; Dietmar Rothermund, "Einleitung: Weltgefälle und Wirtschaftskrise," in *Die Peripherie in der Weltwirtschaftskrise: Afrika, Asien, und Lateinamerika 1929–1939*, ed. Dieter Rothermund (Pader-born, Germany: Schöningh, 1982), 13–36.

50. A fine overview is Frieden, *Global Capitalism*, chapter 9. See also A. J. H. Latham, *The Depression and the Developing World, 1914–1939* (London: Croom Helm, 1981); Rosemary Thorp, ed., *Latin America in the 1930s: The Role of the Periphery in the World Crisis* (Basingstoke, UK: Macmillan, 1984).

51. John B. Condliffe, "Die Industrialisierung der wirtschaftlich rückständigen Länder," *Weltwirtschaftliches Archiv* 37 (1933), 358.

52. See, e.g., Zygmunt Bauman, *Modernity and the Holocaust* (Cambridge, UK: Polity, 1989); Michael Prinz and Rainer Zitelmann, eds., *Nationalsozialismus und Modernisierung* (Darmstadt,

Germany: Wissenschaftliche Buchgesellschaft, 1991); Lawrence Birken, *Hitler as Philosophe: Remnants of the Enlightenment in National Socialism* (Westport, CT: Praeger, 1995); Stephen Kotkin, *Magnetic Mountain: Stalinism as a Civilization* (Berkeley: University of California Press, 1995); James C. Scott, *Seeing Like a State: How Certain Schemes to Improve the Human Condition Have Failed* (New Haven, CT: Yale University Press, 1998); Mark Mazower, *Dark Continent: Europe's Twentieth Century* (New York: Knopf, 1998); Igal Halfin, *From Darkness to Light: Class Consciousness and Salvation in Revolutionary Russia* (Pittsburgh, PA: University of Pittsburgh Press, 2000); Kate Brown, *A Biography of No Place: From Ethnic Borderland to Soviet Heartland* (Cambridge, MA: Harvard University Press, 2005); Jochen Hellbeck, *Revolution on My Mind: Writing a Dairy under Stalin* (Cambridge, MA: Harvard University Press, 2006); Roger Griffin, *Modernism and Fascism: The Sense of a New Beginning under Mussolini and Hitler* (Basingstoke, UK: Palgrave Macmillan, 2007); Peter Fritzsche, *Life and Death in the Third Reich* (Cambridge, MA: Harvard University Press, 2008).

53. Jeffrey Herf, *Reactionary Modernism: Technology, Culture, and Politics in Weimar and the Third Reich* (Cambridge, UK: Cambridge University Press, 1984); Hans Mommsen, "Nationalsozialismus als vorgetäuschte Modernisierung," in *Der Nationalsozialismus und die deutsche Gesellschaft*, ed. H. Mommsen (Reinbek, Germany: Lau, 1991), 405–27. For introductions to the acrimonious debate see Riccardo Bavaj, *Die Ambivalenz der Moderne im Nationalsozialismus: Eine Bilanz der Forschung* (Munich: Oldenbourg, 2003); Mark Roseman, "National Socialism and the End of Modernity," *American Historical Review* 116, no. 3 (2011): 688–701. Anna Krylova has recently argued that Stephen Kotkin's work should be situated in a continuity with Cold War modernization theory: Krylova, "Soviet Modernity: Stephen Kotkin and the Bolshevik Predicament," *Contemporary European History* 23, no. 2 (2014): 167–92. Indeed, there are resemblances between Kotkin's portrayal of Soviet Communism as "a kind of antiworld" (p. 173) and Mommsen's characterization of National Socialism as "dissimulated modernization."

54. Only a selection can be cited here: Stephen Kotkin, "Modern Times: The Soviet Union and the Interwar Conjuncture," *Kritika: Explorations in Russian and Eurasian History* 2, no. 1 (Winter 2001): 111–64; Ruth Ben-Ghiat, *Fascist Modernities: Italy 1922–1945* (Berkeley: University of California Press, 2001); Kiran Klaus Patel, *Soldiers of Labor: Labor Service in Nazi Germany and New Deal America, 1933–45* (Cambridge, UK: Cambridge University Press, 2005); Michael David-Fox, "Multiple Modernities vs. Neo-Traditionalism: On Recent Debates in Russian and Soviet History," *Jahrbücher für Geschichte Osteuropas* 54, no. 4 (2006): 535–55; Wolfgang Schivelbusch, *Three New Deals: Reflections on Roosevelt's America, Mussolini's Italy, and Hitler's Germany, 1933–1939* (New York: Henry Holt, 2006); Michael Geyer and Sheila Fitzpatrick, eds., *Beyond Totalitarianism: Stalinism and Nazism Compared* (New York: Cambridge University Press, 2009); Stephan Plaggenborg, *Ordnung und Gewalt: Kemalismus—Faschismus—Sozialismus* (Munich: Oldenbourg, 2012); Kris Manjapra, *Age of Entanglement: German and Indian Intellectuals across Empire* (Cambridge, MA: Harvard University Press, 2014); Reto Hofmann, *The Fascist Effect: Japan and Italy, 1915–1952* (Ithaca, NY: Cornell University Press, 2015); Kiran Klaus Patel, *The New Deal: A Global History* (Princeton, NJ: Princeton University Press, 2016); Grzegorz Rossoliński-Liebe, *Fascism without Borders: Transnational Connections and Cooperation between Movements and Regimes in Europe from 1918 to 1945* (New York: Berghahn, 2017).

55. Stephen K. Macekura and Erez Manela, eds., *The Development Century: A Global History* (Cambridge, UK: Cambridge University Press, 2018).

56. Greg Grandin, *Fordlandia: The Untold History of Henry Ford's Forgotten Jungle City* (New York: Henry Holt, 2009); Esch, *The Color Line and the Assembly Line*.

57. Instead, historians have left the job to social scientists: Stephan Haggard, *Developmental States* (Cambridge, UK: Cambridge University Press, 2018); Atul Kohli, *State-Directed Development: Political Power and Industrialization in the Global Periphery* (Cambridge, UK: Cambridge University Press, 2004); Alice H. Amsden, *The Rise of "the Rest": Challenges to the West from Late-Industrializing Economies* (Oxford, UK: Oxford University Press, 2001); Peter B. Evans, *Embedded Autonomy: States and Industrial Transformation* (Princeton, NJ: Princeton University Press, 1995); Robert Wade, *Governing the Market: Economic Theory and the Role of Government in East Asian Industrialization* (Princeton, NJ: Princeton University Press, 1990); Chalmers Johnson, *MITI and the Japanese Miracle: The Growth of Industrial Policy, 1925–1975* (Stanford, CA: Stanford University Press, 1982). Though see Amy C. Offner, *Sorting Out the Mixed Economy: The Rise and Fall of Welfare and Developmental States in the Americas* (Princeton, NJ: Princeton University Press, 2019).

58. Charles S. Maier, "Consigning the Twentieth Century to History," *American Historical Review* 105, no. 3 (2000): 807–31.

59. Maier, "Consigning the Twentieth Century to History," 812. The enduring power of such narratives can be discerned, e.g., in the arc of Frieden, *Global Capitalism: Its Fall and Rise in the 20th Century*; the emplotment of Hans-Ulrich Wehler's five-volume *Deutsche Gesellschaftsgeschichte* (Munich: Beck, 1987–2008); also in Piers Brendon, *The Dark Valley: A Panorama of the 1930s* (New York: Knopf, 2000); Zara Steiner, *The Triumph of the Dark: European International History, 1933–39* (Oxford, UK: Oxford University Press, 2011); Heinrich August Winkler, *The Age of Catastrophe: A History of the West, 1914–1945* (New Haven, CT: Yale University Press, 2015); and Ian Kershaw's programmatically titled *To Hell and Back: Europe 1914–1949* (New York: Penguin, 2015).

60. Francis Fukuyama, "The End of History?" *The National Interest* 16 (Summer 1989): 3–18; Eric Hobsbawm, *Age of Extremes: A History of the 20th Century* (New York: Vintage, 1994).

61. On the staying power of modernization theory as metanarrative see Nils Gilman, "Modernization Theory Never Dies," *History of Political Economy* 50, no. S1 (2018): 133–51; Stefan Link, review of *The Age of Catastrophe*, by Heinrich August Winkler, *Journal of Modern History* 89, no. 3 (2017): 669–70.

62. Maier, "Consigning the Twentieth Century to History," 807. Maier argued that no obvious structural narrative mapped onto the twentieth century; he instead proposed a century of "territoriality" spanning roughly from the 1870s to the 1970s.

63. Karl Polanyi, *The Great Transformation: The Political and Economic Origins of Our Time* (Boston: Beacon, 2001 [1944]), 3.

64. Polanyi, *Great Transformation*, 29–31. Polanyi's classic is famous for its account of the rise of nineteenth-century "market society," an unattainable "stark utopia" whose inherent flaws, Polanyi argued, explained the spectacular collapse of the 1930s. But the title referred to his contemporary times—not, as so many readers hastily concluded, to the earlier rise of market society. Polanyi makes the title's intent quite clear in the opening sentences: "Nineteenth-century civilization has collapsed. This book is concerned with the political and economic origins of this event, as well as with the great transformation *which it ushered in*" [emphasis added] (p. 3).

65. Scholarship that explores social, economic, and technological continuities across 1945 includes Werner Abelshauser, "Kriegswirtschaft und Wirtschaftswunder: Deutschlands wirtschaftliche Mobilisierung für den Zweiten Weltkrieg und die Folgen für die Nachkriegszeit," *Vierteljahreshefte für Zeitgeschichte* 47, no. 4 (1999): 503–38; Werner Abelshauser, *Deutsche Wirtschaftsgeschichte seit 1945* (Munich: Beck, 2005); Reich, *The Fruits of Fascism*; Petri, *Von der Autarkie zum Wirtschaftswunder*; Philip Nord, *France's New Deal: From the Thirties to the Postwar Era* (Princeton, NJ: Princeton University Press, 2010); David Edgerton, *Warfare State*; James T. Sparrow, *Warfare State: World War II Americans and the Age of Big Government* (New York: Oxford University Press, 2011); Richard Samuels, *"Rich Nation, Strong Army": National Security and the Technological Transformation of Japan* (Ithaca, NY: Cornell University Press, 1994); Johnson, *MITI and the Japanese Miracle*; Elena Zubkova, *Russia after the War: Hopes, Illusions, and Disappointments* (Armonk, NY: Sharpe, 1998).

Chapter 1: The Populist Roots of Mass Production

1. *Sächsisches Staatsarchiv* (SSAC), Chemnitz, 31050/1046, "Amerikareise Werners 1937"; Hans Mommsen and Manfred Grieger, *Das Volkswagenwerk und seine Arbeiter im Dritten Reich* (Düsseldorf, Germany: Econ, 1996), 167–68; Duccio Bigazzi, *La grande fabbrica: Organizzazzione industriale e modello americano alla Fiat dal Lingotto a Mirafiori* (Milan: Feltrinelli, 2000), 94–95.

2. Ford R. Bryan, *Rouge: Pictured in Its Prime* (Dearborn, MI: Wayne State University Press, 2003), 22–23; Automobile Manufacturers Association, *Automobile Facts and Figures: 1937 Edition* (Detroit: Automobile Manufacturers Association, 1937), 46.

3. SSAC, 31050/1635, Report of the Werner Commission, 1937. The quotes are taken from John H. Van Deventer, *Ford Principles and Practice at River Rouge* (New York: Engineering Magazine Co., 1922), 65, 132, 196; and Hartley W. Barclay, *Ford Production Methods* (New York: Harper, 1936), 93.

4. US Department of Commerce, *Abstract of the Census of Manufactures 1914* (Washington, DC: Government Printing Office, 1917), 26.

5. Census figures put Ohio, Indiana, Illinois, Michigan, and Wisconsin ($8,446,131,000) ahead of New York, Pennsylvania, and New Jersey ($7,343,298,000). Motor vehicles and suppliers combined for $1,506,984,000 in value-added, putting the sector ahead of steel and rolling mill products ($1,496,747,000): US Department of Commerce, *Biennial Census of Manufactures 1937*, vol. 1 (Washington, DC: Government Printing Office, 1939), 20, 34.

6. Automobile Manufacturers Association, *Automobile Facts and Figures: 1937 Edition*, 20, 47–51.

7. Quoted in George Galster, *Driving Detroit: The Quest for Respect in the Motor City* (Philadelphia: University of Pennsylvania Press, 2012), 81.

8. Calculated from US Department of Commerce, *Biennial Census of Manufactures 1937*, vol. 1, 40.

9. See Ronald Edsforth, *Class Conflict and Cultural Consensus: The Making of a Mass Consumer Society in Flint, Michigan* (New Brunswick, NJ: Rutgers University Press, 1987), 91–94.

10. National Automobile Chamber of Commerce, *Automobile Facts and Figures, 1937 edition*, 40; US Federal Trade Commission, *Report on Motor Vehicle Industry* (Washington, DC: Government Printing Office, 1939), 34–36.

11. As highlighted by Edsforth, *Class Conflict.*

12. Noam Maggor, "American Capitalism: From the Atlantic Economy to Domestic Industrialization," in *A Companion to the Gilded Age and Progressive Era*, ed. Christopher McKnight Nichols and Nancy C. Unger (Hoboken, NJ: Wiley-Blackwell, 2017), 205–14. "Second great divergence" is Sven Beckert's phrase: "American Danger: US Empire, Eurafrica, and the Territorialization of Capitalism," *American Historical Review* 122, no. 4 (2017): 1137–70. See also Stefan Link and Noam Maggor, "The United States as a Developing Nation: Revisiting the Peculiarities of American History," *Past and Present* 246, no. 1 (2020): 269–306.

13. Louis Galambos, "The Emerging Organizational Synthesis in Modern American History," *Business History Review* 44, no. 3 (1970): 279–90; Alfred D. Chandler, *Giant Enterprise: Ford, General Motors, and the Automobile Industry* (New York: Harcourt, Brace & World, 1964); Alfred D. Chandler, *The Visible Hand: The Managerial Revolution in American Business* (Cambridge, MA: Harvard University Press, 1977); David Hounshell, *From the American System to Mass Production, 1800–1932* (Baltimore, MD: Johns Hopkins University Press, 1984); Thomas Hughes, *American Genesis: A Century of Invention and Technological Enthusiasm, 1870–1970* (New York: Viking, 1989). For critiques see Philip Scranton, *Endless Novelty: Specialty Production and American Industrialization, 1865–1925* (Princeton, NJ: Princeton University Press, 1997); Robert F. Freeland, *The Struggle for Control of the Modern Corporation: Organizational Change at General Motors, 1924–1970* (New York: Cambridge University Press, 2001).

14. Lawrence Goodwyn, *Democratic Promise: The Populist Movement in America* (New York: Oxford University Press, 1976); David Montgomery, *The Fall of the House of Labor: The Workplace, the State, and American Labor Activism, 1865–1925* (Cambridge, UK: Cambridge University Press, 1987); David Nelson, *Managers and Workers: Origins of the Twentieth-Century Factory System in the United States, 1880–1920* (Madison: University of Wisconsin Press, 1996); Martin Sklar, *The Corporate Reconstruction of American Capitalism, 1890–1916: The Market, the Law, and Politics* (Cambridge, UK: Cambridge University Press, 1988); James Livingston, *Pragmatism and the Political Economy of Cultural Revolution* (Chapel Hill: University of North Carolina Press, 1994); David F. Noble, *America by Design: Science, Technology, and the Rise of Corporate Capitalism* (Oxford, UK: Oxford University Press, 1979); Stephen P. Meyer III, *The Five Dollar Day: Labor Management and Social Control in the Ford Motor Company, 1908–1921* (Albany: State University of New York Press, 1981). See also Link and Maggor, "United States as a Developing Nation," 281–288.

15. As perceptively noted by Gerald Berk, "Corporate Liberalism Reconsidered: A Review Essay," *Journal of Policy History* 3, no. 1 (1991): 70–84. But cf. two works that argue that scientific management, in particular, was a politically situated project with contested impact rather than an all-pervasive expression of capitalist rationality: Sanford M. Jacoby, *Employing Bureaucracy: Managers, Unions, and the Transformation of Work in the 20th Century* (New York: Columbia University Press, 1985); Yehouda Shenhav, *Manufacturing Rationality: The Engineering Foundations of the Managerial Revolution* (Oxford, UK: Oxford University Press, 1999).

16. Donald Finlay Davis, *Conspicuous Production: Automobiles and Elites in Detroit, 1899–1933* (Philadelphia: Temple University Press, 1988), 41–43; James M. Rubenstein, *The Changing US Auto Industry: A Geographical Analysis* (London: Routledge, 1992), 26–28.

17. John B. Rae asserted that "the real explanation comes down to . . . the fortuitous circumstance that a remarkable group of automobile entrepreneurs appeared simultaneously in the

Detroit area" (Rae, "Why Michigan?" in *The Automobile and American Culture*, ed. David L. Lewis and Lawrence Goldstein [Ann Arbor: University of Michigan Press, 1983], 3–5). James Rubenstein called "the location of the North American automotive industry" at the turn of the twentieth century "largely accidental" (Rubenstein, *The Changing US Auto Industry*, 1). Similarly, George S. May, *A Most Unique Machine: The Michigan Origins of the American Automobile Industry* (Madison: University of Wisconsin Press, 1975), 335–344. Galster, *Driving Detroit*, concurs that the rise of Detroit as the Motor City was "accidental" and the result of "innovation and personality" (p. 77).

18. Brian Page and Richard Walker, "From Settlement to Fordism: The Agro-Industrial Revolution in the American Midwest," *Economic Geography* 67, no. 4 (1991): 281–315; Galster, *Driving Detroit*, 71–75; Sten DeGeer, "The North American Manufacturing Belt," *Geografiska Annaler* 9 (1927): 233–359; Davis, *Conspicuous Production*, 43.

19. The quote is from Ford's 1915 testimony before the Walsh Commission. US Senate, *Industrial Relations: Final Report and Testimony of the Commission on Industrial Relations* (Washington, DC: Government Printing Office, 1916), 8: 7634. On producer populism see Daniel Ott, "Producing a Past: McCormick Harvester and Producer Populists in the 1890s," *Agricultural History* 88, no. 1 (2014): 87–119; Alex Gourevitch, *From Slavery to the Cooperative Commonwealth: Labor and Republican Liberty in the Nineteenth Century* (New York: Cambridge University Press, 2015); Noam Maggor, *Brahmin Capitalism: Frontiers of Wealth and Populism in America's First Gilded Age* (Cambridge, MA: Harvard University Press, 2017), esp. chapter 4. On Midwestern populism see Norman Pollack, *The Populist Response to Industrial America: Midwestern Populist Thought* (Cambridge, MA: Harvard University Press, 1962). On Detroit populism see Melvin Holli, *Reform in Detroit: Hazen Pingree and Urban Politics* (New York: Oxford University Press, 1969). See also Stefan Link, "The Charismatic Corporation: Finance, Administration, and Shop Floor Management under Henry Ford," *Business History Review* 92, no. 1 (2018): 91–92.

20. See Gourevitch, *From Slavery*, 127–28.

21. Holli, *Reform in Detroit*, 56, 83. See the anticorporate call-to-arms in Hazen Pingree, *Facts and Opinions; or Dangers That Beset Us* (Detroit: F. B. Dickerson Co., 1895).

22. Allan Nevins and Frank Ernest Hill, *Ford: The Times, the Man, the Company* (New York: Charles Scribner's Sons, 1954), 135.

23. Quoted in Davis, *Conspicuous Production*, 56.

24. Quoted in Davis, 59.

25. Davis, 60–63; Nevins and Hill, *Ford: The Times, the Man, the Company*, 175–180, 211–213.

26. Lawrence H. Seltzer, *A Financial History of the Automobile Industry: A Study of the Ways in Which the Leading American Producers of Automobiles Have Met Their Capital Requirements* (Boston: Houghton Mifflin, 1928), 86–94; Davis, *Conspicuous Production*, 118, 128.

27. *Benson Ford Research Center* (BFRC), Dearborn, MI, Acc. 65, Reminiscences of George Brown, 32; Nevins and Hill, *Ford: The Times, the Man, the Company*, 378; Robert H. Casey, *The Model T: A Centennial History* (Baltimore, MD: Johns Hopkins University Press, 2008), 76.

28. E. D. Kennedy, *The Automobile Industry: The Coming of Capitalism's Favorite Child* (New York: Reynal & Hitchcock, 1941), 316; Rubenstein, *The Changing US Auto Industry*, 41.

29. Henry Ford with Samuel Crowther, *My Life and Work* (Garden City, NY: Doubleday, Page & Co., 1922), 79–80.

30. Ford, *My Life and Work*, 90. For good accounts of the mass production revolution at the Ford Motor Company see Nevins and Hill, *Ford: The Times, the Man, the Company*, 447–80; Hounshell, *From the American System*, 217–61; Lindy Biggs, *The Rational Factory: Architecture, Technology, and Work in America's Age of Mass Production* (Baltimore, MD: Johns Hopkins University Press, 1996), 118–36.

31. Ford, *My Life and Work*, 81; Hounshell, *From the American System*, 239–43.

32. Charles Sorensen with Samuel T. Williamson, *My Forty Years with Ford* (New York: Norton, 1956), 131.

33. A consistent theme in successive descriptions of Ford methods: Horace L. Arnold and Fay L. Faurote, *Ford Methods and the Ford Shops* (New York: Engineering Magazine Company, 1915); Van Deventer, *Ford Principles*; Barclay, *Ford Production Methods*. See also Daniel Raff, "Making Cars and Making Money in the Interwar Automobile Industry: Economies of Scale and Scope and the Manufacturing behind the Marketing," *Business History Review* 65, no. 4 (1991), 729–31.

34. Quoted in Nevins and Hill, *Ford: The Times, the Man, the Company*, 463–64. The increasing sophistication of machine tools required an associated energy revolution: between 1907 and 1927 the electricity consumed in American manufacturing increased tenfold, and by 1939, it had increased by another 40 percent: Cristiano Andrea Ristuccia and Solomos Solomou, "Electricity Diffusion and Trend Acceleration in Inter-War Manufacturing Productivity," Cambridge Working Papers in Economics 0202 (2002), 15, table 8; Bernard C. Beaudreau, *Mass Production, the Stock Market Crash, and the Great Depression: The Macroeconomics of Electrification* (Westport, CT: Greenwood, 1996), 4–28; Warren Devine, "From Shafts to Wires: Historical Perspectives on Electrification," *Journal of Economic History* 43, no. 2 (1983), 347–372; Alexander J. Field, *A Great Leap Forward: 1930s Depression and U.S. Economic Growth* (New Haven, CT: Yale University Press, 2011), 44–47.

35. Arnold and Faurote, *Ford Methods*, 142–150; Biggs, *The Rational Factory*.

36. Arnold and Faurote, 47.

37. Karl Bücher, "Das Gesetz der Massenproduktion," *Zeitschrift für die gesamte Staatswissenschaft* 66, no. 3 (1910): 429–44. To put it in Marxist terms, automotive mass production considerably widened the possibilities for extracting relative surplus value from labor. Regulation Theory, however, argued that a core empirical feature of Fordism was that wage growth closely followed productivity growth, and hence that capital intensity remained relatively stable: Volker Wellhöner, *"Wirtschaftswunder," Weltmarkt, westdeutscher Fordismus: Der Fall Volkswagen* (Münster, Germany: Westfälisches Dampfboot, 1996), 56–57, 134–35; Alain Lipietz, "Behind the Crisis: The Exhaustion of a Regime of Accumulation; A 'Regulation School' Perspective on Some French Empirical Works," *Review of Radical Economics* 18, no. 1–2 (1988): 13–32.

38. SSAC, 31050/1635, Report of the Werner Commission 1937, 12.

39. See, e.g., Hounshell, *From the American System*, 249–53; Nye, *America's Assembly Line*, 33–37.

40. Sorensen, *My Forty Years*, 64–69; Ford R. Bryan, *Henry's Lieutenants* (Detroit: Wayne State University Press, 1993), 213–17, 267.

41. BFRC, Acc. 65, Reminiscences of William C. Klann, 31, 77.

42. BFRC, Acc. 65, Reminiscences of James O'Connor, 16–25.

43. BFRC, Acc. 65, Reminiscences of Arthur Renner, 9.

44. BFRC, Acc. 65, Reminiscences of Alex Lumsden, 11.

45. In fact, Taylorism barely made inroads into Midwestern shops before the 1920s: see the table in Nelson, *Managers and Workers*, 72.

46. Frederick Winslow Taylor, *The Principles of Scientific Management* (New York: Harper & Brothers, 1911), 50–51.

47. Sorensen, *My Forty Years*, 41.

48. Narratives of decline easily miss this. To build mass production, David Montgomery said, "the entrepreneur-engineers of machine-building had to eschew the last remnants of their 19th-century shop culture" (Montgomery, *Fall of the House of Labor*, 213). The Ford Motor Company suggests that abandonment was not a necessity; creative reinvention was possible. This dynamic also explains why many of Ford's skilled mechanics retained a strong allegiance to the company and its founder well into the 1920s. See Link, "Charismatic Corporation."

49. On learning and constant process innovations at the Ford Motor Company see James M. Wilson and Alan McKinlay, "Rethinking the Assembly Line: Organisation, Performance, and Productivity in Ford Motor Company, c. 1908–27," *Business History* 52, no. 5 (2010): 760–78. On learning in mass production more generally see Lutz Budraß, *Flugzeugindustrie und Luftrüstung in Deutschland, 1918–1945* (Düsseldorf, Germany: Droste, 1998), 843–46; Lutz Budraß, Jonas Scherner, and Jochen Streb, "Fixed-Price Contracts, Learning, and Outsourcing: Explaining the Continuous Growth of Output and Labour Productivity in the German Aircraft Industry during the Second World War," *Economic History Review* 63, no. 1 (2010): 107–36; Leonard Rapping, "Learning and World War II Production Functions," *Review of Economics and Statistics* 47, no. 1 (1965): 81–86. On shop suggestion systems and institutional learning see Budraß et al., "Fixed-Price Contracts," 131–32; Allan Nevins and Frank Ernest Hill, *Ford: Expansion and Challenge, 1915–1933* (New York: Charles Scribner's Sons, 1957), 517–18.

50. Bernard A. Weisberger, *The Dream Maker: William C. Durant, Founder of General Motors* (Boston: Little Brown & Co., 1979), chapters 1–3; Edsforth, *Class Conflict*, 39–54.

51. Weisberger, *The Dream Maker*, 94; Seltzer, *Financial History of the Automobile Industry*, 147, 151–54; Kennedy, *Coming of Capitalism's Favorite Child*, 67. A crankshaft translates linear thrust into the circular motion of the wheels; a differential ensures that a vehicle's wheels spin at even speed in a curve.

52. Quoted in Weisberger, *Dream Maker*, 120.

53. The skepticism can be gauged by how the financial press covered the Midwestern automobile industry. See, e.g., "Are Automobiles Tying Up Capitals?" *Wall Street Journal*, July 30, 1907; "Effect Automobile Trade Has on the Money Market," *Wall Street Journal*, October 19, 1907; Franklin Escher, "The Auto and the Bond Market," *Bankers Magazine* 81, no. 4 (1910): 508; "Bond Business Affected by American Extravagances," *Wall Street Journal*, December 31, 1912.

54. Weisberger, *Dream Maker*, chapter 6; Davis, *Conspicuous Production*, 146–48.

55. Seltzer, *Financial History of the Automobile Industry*, 195ff; David Farber, *Everybody Ought to Be Rich: The Life and Times of John J. Raskob, Capitalist* (New York: Oxford University Press, 2013), chapters 6 and 8; Alfred D. Chandler Jr. and Stephen Salsbury, *Pierre S. du Pont and the Making of the Modern Corporation* (New York: Harper & Row, 1971), 455, 478–79. The quote is Chandler's (p. 490).

56. William Greenleaf, *Monopoly on Wheels: Henry Ford and the Selden Automobile Patent* (Detroit: Wayne State University Press, 1961), 114, 227.

57. Greenleaf, *Monopoly on Wheels*, 247–50.

58. Quotes in Meyer, *The Five Dollar Day*, 160–61.

59. John R. Lee, "The So-Called Profit-Sharing System in the Ford Plant," *Annals of the American Academy of Political and Social Science* 65, no. 1 (1916): 308.

60. Meyer, *Five Dollar Day*, 56, 77; Olivier Zunz, *The Changing Face of Inequality: Urbanization, Industrial Development, and Immigrants in Detroit, 1880–1920* (Chicago: University of Chicago Press, 1982), 312.

61. Meyer, *Five Dollar Day*, 161–164; Lee, "Profit-Sharing System."

62. Meyer, *Five Dollar Day*; Clarence Hooker, *Life in the Shadows of the Crystal Palace, 1910–1927: Ford Workers in the Model T Era* (Bowling Green, OH: Bowling Green State University Press, 1997); Daniel M. G. Raff and Lawrence H. Summers, "Did Henry Ford Pay Efficiency Wages?" *Journal of Labor Economics* 5, no. 4 (1987): S57–S86; Daniel M. G. Raff, "Wage Determination Theory and the Five Dollar Day at Ford," *Journal of Economic History* 48, no. 2 (1988): 387–399; Daniel M. G. Raff, "Ford Welfare Capitalism in Its Economic Context," in *Masters to Managers. Historical and Comparative Perspectives on American Employers*, ed. Sanford M. Jacoby (New York: Columbia University Press, 1991), 90–105.

63. Quoted from Ford's testimony before the Walsh Commission: US Senate, *Industrial Relations*, 8: 7627–29.

64. "Gives $10,000,000 to 26,000 Employees," *New York Times*, January 6, 1914.

65. Sorensen, *My Forty Years*, 136–39. For other accounts see Nevins and Hill, *Ford: The Times, the Man, the Company*, 532–534, 647; Meyer, *Five Dollar Day*, 109–10.

66. Meyer, *Five Dollar Day*, 111–12; "Henry Ford Explains Why He Gives Away $10,000,000," *New York Times*, January 11, 1914.

67. Quoted in Meyer, *Five Dollar Day*, 110.

68. The text of the preamble is given in Terence Powderly, *Thirty Years of Labor, 1859–1889* (Columbus, OH: Excelsior, 1889), 128–30.

69. In Powderly's words, the Knights sought "to supersede the wage system by a system of industrial cooperation" (Powderly, *Thirty Years of Labor*, 233). As another member of the Knights put it, transitioning from wage labor to cooperative systems required "changing the *form* of demand from *increase of wages* to *participation in profits*." Quoted in Gourevitch, *From Slavery*, 130 (emphasis in the original).

70. Gourevitch, *From Slavery*, 171. Productive cooperation "implies the virtues of stability, honor, and fraternity," wrote the *Journal of United Labor* in 1884. "There are certain habits, certain attributes of character without cultivation of which there can be no individual progress, hence no social progress. These habits and this character is to make the man an independent being," wrote Henry Sharpe of the Knights of Labor. Quotes in Gourevitch, *From Slavery*, 162–63. See also Leon Fink, *Workingmen's Democracy: The Knights of Labor and American Politics* (Urbana, IL: University of Illinois Press, 1983), 3–17.

71. On the labor republicans' "demanding" stance toward unskilled immigrants see Gourevitch, *From Slavery*, 133–35, 168–71. Leon Fink wrote of the Knights that their "teacherish invocations . . . toward the rank and file" reflected both the "real social distance" between the skilled and the unskilled and "a simultaneous (and sincere) egalitarianism of principle" (Fink, *Workingmen's Democracy*, 14).

72. Quotes from Davis, *Conspicuous Production*, 133; Robert Lacey, *Ford: The Men and the Machine* (Boston: Little Brown & Co.), 120; Nevins and Hill, *Ford: The Times, the Man, the Company*, 536; US Senate, *Industrial Relations*, 8: 7827.

73. Meyer, *Five Dollar Day*, 161–67, 198–99; Sorensen, *My Forty Years*, 145.

74. Link, "Charismatic Corporation."

75. On the suit see Nevins and Hill, *Ford: Expansion and Challenge*, 86–113; M. Todd Henderson, "Everything Old Is New Again: Lessons from Dodge v Ford Motor Company," University of Chicago Law & Economics Olin Working Paper No. 373 (December 2007).

76. BFRC, Ford Legal Department, Supreme Court of Michigan, Dodge v. Ford, vol. II, "Amended Bill of Complaint," 4–9.

77. "Henry Ford Makes Reply to Suit Brought by Dodge Brothers—Says Present Plans Are Only in Line with Past History of Company," *Detroit News*, November 4, 1916.

78. Dodge v. Ford Motor Co., 170 N.W. 668 (Michigan, 1919).

79. Alan Brinkley, *The End of Reform: New Deal Liberalism in Recession and War* (New York: Vintage Books, 1995), chapter 4; Arthur M. Schlesinger Jr., *The Age of Roosevelt: The Crisis of the Old Order, 1919–1933* (Boston: Houghton Mifflin Co., 1957), 67–70, 111; Raff, "Making Cars and Making Money," 751, table 3.

80. Raff, "Making Cars and Making Money"; US Federal Trade Commission, *Report on Motor Vehicle Industry*, 527–31; Norman Beasley, *Knudsen: A Biography* (New York: McGraw-Hill Book Company, 1947), 219–23; Hounshell, *From the American System*, 263–67.

81. See Chandler, *Giant Enterprise*; Arthur J. Kuhn, *GM Passes Ford, 1918–1938: Designing the General Motors Performance-Control System* (University Park: Pennsylvania State University Press, 1986); Richard Tedlow, "The Struggle for Dominance in the Automobile Market: The Early Years of Ford and GM," *Business and Economic History* 17 (1988): 49–62; Raff, "Making Cars and Making Money"; Thomas K. McCraw, *American Business 1920–2000: How It Worked* (Wheeling, IL: Harlan Davidson, 2000), 10–27.

82. Harvard Business School, Baker Library (HBL), Allston, MA, Alfred D. Chandler Papers, Box 33, folder 29, "Interview with Donaldson Brown" (June, 1956), 19.

83. Seltzer, *A Financial History of the Automobile Industry*, 145.

84. I follow Freeland's persuasive reinterpretation of Sloan as a skillful broker of intracorporate politics rather than Chandler's older portrayal of him as primarily an administrative innovator: Freeland, *Struggle for Control*; Alfred D. Chandler, Jr., *Strategy and Structure: Chapters in the History of the American Industrial Enterprise* (Cambridge, MA: MIT Press, 1962), chapter 2.

85. According to one of Ford's accountants: BFRC, Acc. 65, Reminiscences of L. E. Briggs, 22.

86. Link, "Charismatic Corporation."

87. Roland Marchand, *Advertising the American Dream: Making Way for Modernity, 1920–1940* (Berkeley: University of California Press, 1985), chapter 5; Sally H. Clarke, *Trust and Power: Consumers, the Modern Corporation, and the Making of the United States Automobile Market* (New York: Cambridge University Press, 2007).

88. Chandler, *Giant Enterprise*, 97–99, 104–111.

89. General Motors Corporation, *Twenty-Ninth Annual Report: Year Ended December 31, 1937* (New York: General Motors Corporation, 1938), 79; Arthur Pound, *The Turning Wheel: The*

Story of General Motors through Twenty-Five Years 1908–1933 (Garden City, NY: Doubleday, Doran & Co., 1934), 356; US Federal Trade Commission, *Report on Motor Vehicle Industry*, 522.

90. Link, "Charismatic Corporation," 96–98.

91. On "return on investment" (ROI) see Donaldson Brown, "Pricing Policy in Relation to Financial Control: Tuning Up General Motors," in *Alfred P. Sloan: Critical Evaluations in Business and Management*, ed. John C. Wood and Michael C. Wood, vol. 1 (London: Routledge, 2003), 101–9 (originally published in *Management and Administration* 7, no. 3 [1924]: 283–86). See also Freeland, *Struggle for Control*, 43–58. On the significance of ROI for changing standards of profit calculation in the first half of the twentieth century see Jonathan Levy, "Accounting for Profit and the History of Capital," *Critical Historical Studies* 1, no. 2 (2014): 192–203.

92. See the three books published by Henry Ford in collaboration with Samuel Crowther: Ford, *My Life and Work*; Henry Ford with Samuel Crowther, *Today and Tomorrow* (Garden City, NY: Doubleday, Page and Co., 1926); Henry Ford with Samuel Crowther, *Moving Forward* (Garden City, NY: Doubleday, Doran and Co., 1930). See also Samuel Crowther, "Henry Ford: Why I Favor Five Days' Work at Six Days' Pay," *World's Work*, October 1926, 613–16; Henry Ford, "A Rich Man Should Not Have Any Money," *Cosmopolitan*, March 1932, 52–53, 164–65; the Henry Ford's entry on "Mass Production" in *Encyclopedia Britannica*, 13th ed. (1926; reprinted in Steven Tolliday, ed., *The Rise and Fall of Mass Production*, vol. 1 [Cheltenham, UK: Edward Elgar, 1988], 157–63).

93. See, e.g.,the articles in *Management and Administration* 7 (1924), dedicated to the managerial reforms at GM, which are reprinted in Wood and Wood, *Alfred P. Sloan*, vol.1, 101–71. See also Alfred P. Sloan, "The Most Important Thing I Ever Learned about Management," *System: The Magazine of Business* 46 (1924): 140–41, 191; Sloan, "Modern Ideals of Big Business," *World's Work* (October 1926): 695–99; Donaldson Brown, *Centralized Control with Decentralized Responsibilities* (New York: American Management Association, 1927); Alfred P. Sloan, "Getting the Facts Is a Keystone of General Motors Success," *Automotive Industries* 57 (1927): 550–51; Alfred P. Sloan's 1927 speech to journalists, "The Point of View of General Motors," which is reproduced in Pound, *Turning Wheel*, 329–47.

94. On the notion of the "productive organization" see Ford, "Mass Production"; Ford, *My Life and Work*, 193–94; Ford, *Today and Tomorrow*, 14, 150–61.

95. Sloan quoted in Pound, *The Turning Wheel*, 339.

96. Ford, *My Life and Work*, 12; Sloan quoted in Pound, *The Turning Wheel*, 339.

97. Ford, *Moving Forward*, 148; Alfred Sloan with Boyden Sparkes, *Adventures of a White-Collar Man* (New York: Doubleday, Doran & Co., 1941), 145. See David Farber, *Sloan Rules: Alfred P. Sloan and the Triumph of General Motors* (Chicago: University of Chicago Press, 2002), 174–85.

98. Ott, *When Wall Street Met Main Street: The Quest for Investors' Democracy* (Cambridge, MA: Harvard University Press, 2011), 135–40; Meg Jacobs, *Pocketbook Politics: Economic Citizenship in Twentieth-Century America* (Princeton, NJ: Princeton University Press, 2005), 74–81; Brinkley, *End of Reform*, 66–77; William Truant Foster and Waddill Catchings, *Profits* (Cambridge, MA: Riverside Press, 1927).

99. Crowther, "Henry Ford: Why I Favor Five Days' Work"; Ford, *Today and Tomorrow*, 151.

100. Jacobs, *Pocketbook Politics*, 85–86.

101. As one of GM's leading managers put it in retrospect, return on investment was the "final and fundamental measure of industrial efficiency in terms of management's primary

responsibility" (Donaldson Brown, *Some Reminiscences of an Industrialist* [Easton, PA: Hive Publishing Co., 1958], 26). On the logic of capitalization see Eli Cook, *The Pricing of Progress: Economic Indicators and the Capitalization of American Life* (Cambridge, MA: Harvard University Press, 2017).

102. Nevins and Hill, *Ford: Expansion and Challenge*, 529–31.

103. Edsforth, *Class Conflict*, chapters 4–6.

104. Quoted in Steven Watts, *The People's Tycoon: Henry Ford and the American Century* (New York: Vintage, 2006), 459.

105. Ford declined to travel to New York to join Alfred Sloan and other manufacturing executives in a roundtable discussion about defending "free enterprise": BFRC, Acc. 285, Box 2399. In 1940, the National Association of Manufacturers publicly campaigned against New Deal patent reform. In this context, the NAM selected several "Modern Pioneers on the Frontier of American Industry" on whom to bestow a special award. One of the intended awardees was Henry Ford, but he rejected the honor: BFRC, Acc. 285, Box 2362. For the context see Eric S. Hintz, "The 'Monopoly' Hearings, Their Critics, and the Limits of Patent Reform in the New Deal," in *Capital Gains: Business and Politics in Twentieth-Century America*, ed. Richard John and Kim Philips-Fein (Philadelphia: University of Pennsylvania Press, 2017), 61–79. Later that year, Ford abstained when the NAM convened more than 700 businesspeople in the name of "the American business system": BFRC, Acc. 285, Box 2512.

106. BFRC, Acc. 285, Box 1951: Raskob to Ford, January 30, 1936; Campsall to Raskob, February 10, 1936.

107. Farber, *Sloan Rules*, 179–81; BFRC, Acc. 285, Box 2362, "Memorandum [on association membership]," June 29, 1944.

108. In muckraking detail: Max Wallace, *The American Axis: Henry Ford, Charles Lindbergh, and the Rise of the Third Reich* (New York: St. Martin's Press, 2003).

109. Barclay, *Ford Production Methods*, 32.

110. SSAC, 31050/1046, "Amerikareise Werners 1937."

111. BFRC, Acc. 285, Box 2093, Porsche to Ford, July 10, 1937.

Chapter 2: Ford's Bible of the Modern Age

1. Benson Ford Research Center (BFRC), Dearborn, MI, Acc. 285, Box 2031, correspondence between Liebold and Fritz Hailer; Rennie W. Brantz, "German-American Friendship: The Carl Schurz Vereinigung, 1926–1942," *International History Review* 11, no. 2 (1989): 229–51.

2. Albrecht Tyrell, "Gottfried Feder and the NSDAP," in *The Shaping of the Nazi State*, ed. Peter D. Strachura (New York: Barnes & Noble: 1978), 48–87; Avraham Barkai, *Nazi Economics: Ideology, Theory, and Policy* (New Haven, CT: Yale University Press, 1990), chapter 1.

3. Leo P. Ribuffo, "Henry Ford and the International Jew," in *Right Center Left: Essays in American History*, ed. L. P. Ribuffo (New Brunswick, NJ: Rutgers University Press, 1992), 70–105; Stefan Link, "Rethinking the Ford-Nazi Connection," *Bulletin of the German Historical Institute* 49 (2011): 135–50.

4. Gottfried Feder, *Das Programm der NSDAP und seine weltanschaulichen Grundlagen* (Munich: Eher, 1927), 33–34; Gottfried Feder, *Der deutsche Staat auf nationaler und sozialer Grundlage* (Munich: Eher, 1933), 13–20; 59–60.

5. Theodor Lüddecke, "Der neue Wirtschaftsgeist!," in *Industrieller Friede: Ein Symposium*, ed. Jerome Davis and Theodor Lüddecke (Leipzig, Germany: Paul List Verlag, 1928), 45.

6. Peter Berg, *Deutschland und Amerika, 1918–1929: Über das deutsche Amerikabild der zwanziger Jahre* (Lübeck, Germany: Matthiesen, 1963), 99–107; Mary Nolan, *Visions of Modernity: American Business and the Modernization of Germany* (Oxford, UK: Oxford University Press, 1994), 30–57; Philipp Gassert, "'Without Concessions to Marxist or Communist Thought': Fordism in Germany, 1923–1939," in *Transatlantic Images and Perspectives: Germany and America since 1776*, ed. David E. Barclay and Elisabeth Glaser-Schmidt (Cambridge, UK: Cambridge University Press, 1997), 217–42; Christiane Eifert, "Antisemit und Autokönig. Henry Fords Autobiographie und ihre deutsche Rezeption in den 1920er-Jahren," *Zeithistorische Forschungen/Studies in Contemporary History*, online ed. 6, no. 2 (2009), https://zeithistorische-forschungen.de/2-2009; "revelation": Otto Moog, *Drüben steht Amerika* (Braunschweig, Germany: Westermann, 1927), 118; "Ford psychosis"/ "doctrine of salvation" quoted in Nolan, *Visions of Modernity*, 31; "ghastly book" also quoted in Nolan, 35.

7. D. I. Zaslavksii, "Dva Forda: Predislovie k russkomu izdaniiu," in *Segodnia i zavtra* (Leningrad, Russia: Vremia, 1926), 3–14.

8. Yves Guyot, review of *Today and Tomorrow*, by Henry Ford with Samuel Crowther, *Journal des économistes* 85 (October 1926): 145–68; Albert Kinross, review of *My Life and Work*, by Henry Ford with Samuel Crowther, *English Review* 37 (1923): 649–52; José Monteiro Lobato, *How Henry Ford Is Regarded in Brazil* (Rio de Janeiro: O Journal, 1926); *Waga isshō to jigyō: Henrī Fōdo jijoden* [*My Life and Work: The Autobiography of Henry Ford*], trans. Katō Saburō (Tokyo: Henridō, 1927). See Kato's and Nakamura's letters to Ford in BFRC, Acc. 285, Box 252 and Box 464.

9. Highlights from a rich literature: Nolan, *Visions of Modernity*; Egbert Klautke, *Unbegrenzte Möglichkeiten: "Amerikanisierung" in Deutschland und Frankreich, 1900–1933* (Stuttgart: Steiner, 2003); Victoria de Grazia, *Irresistible Empire: America's March through 20th-Century Europe* (Cambridge, MA: Harvard University Press, 2005); Mary Nolan, *The Transatlantic Century: Europe and America, 1890–2010* (New York: Cambridge University Press, 2012); David E. Ellwood, *The Shock of America: Europe and the Challenge of the Century* (Oxford, UK: Oxford University Press, 2012).

10. Paul Rieppel, *Ford-Betriebe und Ford-Methoden* (Berlin: Oldenbourg, 1925), 50.

11. "Absent presence" is Adam Tooze's phrase: Tooze, *The Deluge: The Great War, America, and the Remaking of the Global Order, 1916–1931* (New York: Viking, 2014), 4.

12. Sven Beckert, "American Danger: United States Empire, Eurafrica, and the Territorialization of Global Capitalism, 1870–1950," *American Historical Review* 122, no. 4 (2017): 1137–70. Contemporary warnings about the American menace include Alexander Graf Brockdorff, *Amerikanische Weltherrschaft?* (Berlin: Albrecht, 1929); Lucien Romier, *Qui sera le maître: Europe ou Amérique?* (Paris: Hachette, 1927); Theodor Lüddecke, *Das amerikanische Wirtschaftstempo als Bedrohung Europas* (Leipzig, Germany: List, 1925).

13. See, e.g., Werner Sombart, "Die Wandlungen des Kapitalismus," *Weltwirtschaftliches Archiv* 28 (1928): 243–56; Ferdinand Fried, *Das Ende des Kapitalismus* (Jena, Germany: Diedrichs, 1931).

14. John Maynard Keynes, *The Economic Consequences of the Peace* (New York: Harcourt, Brace, and Howe, 1920); Richard Nicolaus Graf von Coudenhove-Kalergi, *Pan-Europa* (Vienna: Pan-Europa Verlag, 1923).

15. BFRC: Acc. 65, Reminiscences of William Cameron, 157; Acc. 65, Reminiscences of Ernest G. Liebold, 1256; Acc. 285, Box 91, Liebold to Doubleday, September 13, 1922.

16. "Ford Tells How He Foiled Wall Street," *New York Times*, July 23, 1921. In the article, the feat congealed into a piece of company lore, according to which Ford received a solicitous New York banker only to abruptly show him the door after it transpired that the bank intended to install its own treasurer at the company.

17. BFRC, Acc. 285, Box 23, Doubleday to Ford, July 28, 1921.

18. David Farber, *Everybody Ought to Be Rich: The Life and Times of John J. Raskob, Capitalist* (New York: Oxford University Press, 2013), 188–90, 260–61.

19. Henry Ford with Samuel Crowther, *My Life and Work* (Garden City, NY: Doubleday, Page & Co., 1922), 2–3.

20. Ford, *My Life and Work*, 156, 161, 176, 270.

21. Ford, 136, 160–62, 224.

22. Ford, 19, 162, 194. See also p. 75: "No manufacturer can say 'I built this business'—if he has required the help of thousands of men in building it. It is a joint production."

23. Ford, 78–79, 105.

24. Ford, 242–43.

25. Ford, 270, 274. On the politics of producer populism, see Alex Gourevitch, *From Slavery to the Cooperative Commonwealth: Labor and Republican Liberty in the Nineteenth Century* (New York: Cambridge University Press, 2014); Noam Maggor, *Brahmin Capitalism: Frontiers of Wealth and Populism in America's First Gilded Age* (Cambridge, MA: Harvard University Press, 2017).

26. Rexford Tugwell, review of *Today and Tomorrow*, by Henry Ford with Samuel Crowther, *Saturday Review of Literature* 111, no. 2 (August 7, 1926): 17–18; Gustav Faldix, *Henry Ford als Wirtschaftspolitiker* (Munich: Pfeiffer, 1925), 80; Gramsci to Schucht, May 23, 1927, in Antonio Gramsci and Tania Schucht, *Lettere 1926–1935*, ed. Aldo Natoli and Chiara Daniele (Turin, Italy: Einaudi, 1997), 105; Zaslavskii, "Dva Forda," 11.

27. Lobato, *How Henry Ford Is Regarded in Brazil*, 9–10.

28. Harold James, *The German Slump: Politics and Economics, 1924–1936* (Oxford, UK: Oxford University Press, 1986), 114–23, 138; Albrecht Ritschl, *Deutschlands Krise und Konjunktur, 1924–1934: Binnenkonjunktur, Auslandsverschuldung und Reparationsproblem zwischen Dawes-Plan und Transfersperre* (Berlin: Akademie, 2002), 19; Stephen Gross, *Export Empire: German Soft Power in Southeastern Europe, 1890–1945* (Cambridge, UK: Cambridge University Press, 2015), chapter 4.

29. Charles S. Maier, "Between Taylorism and Technocracy: European Ideologies and the Vision of Industrial Productivity," *Journal of Contemporary History* 5, no. 2 (1970): 27–61; Nolan, *Visions of Modernity*, esp. 30–82; Carl Köttgen, *Das wirtschaftliche Amerika* (Berlin: VDI, 1925), 48; Fritz Tarnow, *Warum arm sein?* (Berlin: Allgemeiner Deutscher Gewerkschaftsbund, 1928).

30. Gassert, "'Without Concessions to Marxist or Communist Thought'"; Lüddecke, "Der neue Wirtschaftsgeist!," 45; Rieppel, *Ford-Betriebe*, 44.

31. Ford, *My Life and Work*, 164.

32. For a sense of the outpouring of antiliberal and anticapitalist literature from the global right during the Twenties, readers may consult the international bibliography in Gaëtan Pirou et al., eds., *La crisi del capitalismo* (Florence: G. C. Sansoni, 1933), 153–98. See also Reto

Hoffmann, *The Fascist Effect: Japan and Italy, 1915–1952* (Ithaca, NY: Cornell University Press, 2015); Zeev Sternhell, *Neither Right nor Left: Fascist Ideology in France*, trans. David Maisel (Berkeley: University of California Press, 1986). For the German context see Udi Greenberg, "Revolution from the Right: Against Equality," in *The Cambridge History of Modern European Thought*, ed. Peter Gordon and Warren Breckman (Cambridge, UK: Cambridge University Press, 2019), 233–58.

33. Ford, *My Life and Work*, 177–83.

34. Allan Nevins and Frank Ernest Hill, *Ford: Expansion and Challenge, 1915–1933* (New York: Charles Scribner's Sons, 1957), 305 ff.; David L. Hammes, *Harvesting Gold: Thomas Edison's Experiment to Re-Invent American Money* (Silver City, NM: Richard Mahler, 2012); "Ford Sees Wealth in Muscle Shoals," *New York Times*, December 6, 1921.

35. "Ford Sees Wealth in Muscle Shoals," *New York Times*.

36. Feder, *Der deutsche Staat*, 131–33, 194.

37. Thorstein Veblen, *The Engineers and the Price System* (New York: B. W. Huebsch, 1921); C. H. Douglas, *Economic Democracy* (London: Palmer, 1920); C. H. Douglas, *Social Credit* (London: Eyre and Spottiswoode, 1924). On Douglas's anti-Semitism and the politics of the Alberta Social Credit party in the 1930s see Bob Hesketh, *Major Douglas and Alberta Social Credit* (Toronto: University of Toronto Press, 1997).

38. Tooze, *Deluge*, 353–73; Niall Ferguson, "Constraints and Room for Manoeuvre in the German Inflation of the Early 1920s," *Economic History Review* 49, no. 4 (1996): 653–66; Barry Eichengreen, *Golden Fetters: The Gold Standard and the Great Depression, 1919–1939* (New York: Oxford University Press, 1995), chapter 1; Werner Link, *Die amerikanische Stabilisierungspolitik in Deutschland, 1921–32* (Düsseldorf, Germany: Droste, 1970).

39. BFRC, Acc. 285, Box 137, Irvine to Liebold, March 15, 1923.

40. Friedrich von Gottl-Ottlilienfeld, *Fordismus: Über Industrie und technische Vernunft* (Jena, Germany: Fischer, 1926), 80. In the view of engineer Paul Rieppel, Ford's methods were "tantamount to Prussian-German Socialism"(*Ford-Betriebe*, 51). The French engineer André Fourgeaud called Ford "the vanguard of a new socialism" (quoted in Klautke, *Unbegrenzte Möglichkeiten*, 226).

41. Christoph Werth, *Sozialismus und Nation: Die deutsche Ideologiedebatte zwischen 1918 und 1945* (Opladen, Germany: Westdeutscher Verlag, 1996); Walter Rathenau, *Die neue Wirtschaft* (Berlin: Fischer, 1919); Oswald Spengler, *Preußentum und Sozialismus* (Munich: Beck, 1920); Wichard von Moellendorff, *Konservativer Sozialismus* (Hamburg: Hanseatischer Verlag, 1932); Werner Sombart, *A New Social Philosophy*, trans. Karl F. Geiser (Princeton, NJ: Princeton University Press, 1937 [originally published in 1934 as *Deutscher Sozialismus*]), 146. For the currency of "socialism" among French fascists see Zeev Sternhell, *Neither Right nor Left*. See also Griffin, *Modernism and Fascism: The Sense of a New Beginning under Mussolini and Hitler*.

42. Gottl-Ottlilienfeld dedicated a series of essays to Fordism: "Fordismus? Von Frederick W. Taylor zu Henry Ford" (1924); "Industrie im Geiste Henry Fords" (1925); and the encyclopedia entry "Fordismus und Fordisation" (1925). They are collected in Gottl-Ottlilienfeld, *Fordismus: Über Industrie und Technische Vernunft*, from which the quotes in this section are taken.

43. Osamu Yanagisawa, "The Impact of German Economic Thought on Japanese Economists before World War II," in *The German Historical School: The Historical and Ethical Approach*

to Economics, ed. Yuichi Shionova (London: Routledge, 2001), 173–87; Janis Mimura, *Planning for Empire: Reform Bureaucrats and the Japanese Wartime State* (Ithaca, NY: Cornell University Press, 2011), 114–16.

44. On Weimar economic debates, including Gottl's role in them, see Hauke Janssen, *Nationalökonomie und Nationalsozialismus: Die deutsche Volkswirtschaftslehre in den dreißiger Jahren* (Marburg, Germany: Metropolis, 2000), 20–75.

45. These and the following quotes are from Gottl-Ottlilienfeld, *Fordismus,* 3–40.

46. Lüddecke, *Das amerikanische Wirtschaftstempo.*

47. Lüddecke, 6, 47.

48. Lüddecke, 49, 106.

49. Lüddecke, 29, 64–65.

50. See Friedrich von Gottl-Ottlilienfeld, *Vom Sinn der Rationalisierung* (Jena, Germany: Fischer, 1929); Tilla Siegel and Thomas von Freyberg, *Industrielle Rationalisierung unter dem Nationalsozialismus* (Frankfurt: Campus, 1991), 77–89; Janssen, *Nationalökonomie,* 81–82.

51. See https://www.catalogus-professorum-halensis.de/lueddecketheodor.html. I thank Alex Korb for pointing me to this information.

52. The pictured copy was retrieved by US military personnel from Hitler's private Munich residence in 1945 and was later in possession of John K. Lattimer, a former medical examiner at the Nuremberg trials and collector of Nazi paraphernalia. It is now in French private possession. This information was conveyed to me by the auction house that produced the image (communication via Sandra Funck). An inventory of the library of the Berlin Reichs Chancellory, which was retrieved by American soldiers in 1945, included only the third Ford-Crowther installment, *Moving Forward.* Philipp Gassert and Daniel S. Mattern, *The Hitler Library: A Bibliography* (Westport, CT: Greenwood, 2001), 485.

53. See Hess's memo from April 9, 1924: "Hitler's thoughts are primarily oriented towards better production methods and increased output. Here he points primarily to Ford, who delivers an excellent car for a few hundred dollars, so that the broad masses are able to buy an automobile." Rudolf Hess, *Briefe, 1908–1933,* ed. Wolf Rüdiger Hess (Munich: Langen Müller, 1987), 319. See also pp. 324, 339.

54. Adolf Hitler, *Mein Kampf* (Munich: Zentralverlag der NSDAP, 1938), reprint of the 1927 edition, 730.

55. As Adam Tooze put it pithily, in his "Second Book" Hitler expressed the view that "Fordism . . . required Lebensraum" (Tooze, *The Wages of Destruction: The Making and Breaking of the Nazi Economy* [New York: Viking, 2007], 10).

56. Quoted in Philipp Gassert, *Amerika im Dritten Reich: Ideologie, Propaganda, und Volksmeinung, 1933–1945* (Stuttgart: Steiner, 1997), 89, footnote 7.

57. Adolf Hitler, *Reden, Schriften, Anordnungen. Februar 1925 bis Januar 1933,* vol. IIa, ed. Institut für Zeitgeschichte (Munich: Saur, 1995), 84.

58. Hitler, *Reden, Schriften, Anordnungen,* vol. II/2, 615.

59. Hitler, vol. IIa, 84, 123. See Gassert, *Amerika im Dritten Reich,* 88–94; Tooze, *Wages of Destruction,* 10–11.

60. In a pamphlet from February 1926, Hitler lauded Ford's independence from the "Jewish" American stock market: Hitler, *Reden, Schriften, Anordnungen,* vol. I, 292. On March 30, 1926, Hitler addressed a gathering of Nazi party members in Munich and delivered "remarks that dealt

in detail with the working conditions in Ford's factories," according to the police report of his speech: Hitler, vol. I, 361–62. On April 1, 1926, Hitler repeated these points in a speech to party members and compared the German auto industry unfavorably to Ford: Hitler, vol. I, 368.

61. Hitler, *Reden, Schriften, Anordnungen*, vol. IV/1, 194–95.

62. See Ludolf Herbst, *Der Totale Krieg und die Ordnung der Wirtschaft* (Munich: Oldenbourg, 1982), 84–92; Rainer Zitelmann, *Hitler: Selbstverständnis eines Revolutionärs*, 5th rev. ed. (Reinbek, Germany: Lau, 2017 [1987]), 401–5.

63. In early 1933, after being released from Turi, Gramsci's fellow Communist Athos Lisa penned a memoir of the conversations among the prisoners. Lisa's text is reproduced in Perry Anderson, *The Antinomies of Antonio Gramsci: With a New Preface* (London: Verso, 2017), 156–75, here 172.

64. Gramsci and Schucht, *Lettere, 1926–1935*, 105; Antonio Gramsci, *Quaderno 22: Americanismo e fordismo*, ed. Franco de Felice (Turin, Italy: G. Einaudi, 1978), 21; Antonio Gramsci, *Amerika und Europa*, ed. Thomas Barfuss (Hamburg: Argument, 2007), 21; Alastair Davidson, *Antonio Gramsci: Towards an Intellectual Biography* (London: Merlin, 1977), 246.

65. On the affirmative Ford reception of German Social Democrats see Nolan, *Visions of Modernity*, 50–54, 63–67. See also Leon Trotsky, "Culture and Socialism" (February 1926), reprinted in Trotsky, *Problems of Everyday Life* (New York: Monad, 1973), 227–49, here 243.

66. Peter D. Thomas, *The Gramscian Moment: Philosophy, Hegemony, and Marxism* (Leiden, Netherlands: Brill, 2009), 115; Giuseppe Vacca, "Gramsci Studies since 1989," *Journal of Modern Italian Studies* 16, no. 2 (2011), 188.

67. On the reception of Gramsci's *Prison Notebooks* among the New Left see Anderson, *Antinomies of Antonio Gramsci: With a New Preface*, 1–28. Anderson notes (p. 1) that "the first extensive translation" from the notebooks "into any language" came in the classic *Selections from the Prison Notebooks of Antonio Gramsci*, ed. Quintin Hoare and Geoffrey Nowell-Smith (New York: International Publishers, 1971). *Selections* (pp. 279–320) includes much of notebook 22. See also Eric Hobsbawm, ed., *Gramsci in Europa e in America* (Rome: Sagittari Laterza, 1995).

68. Giorgio Baratta, "Americanismo e fordismo," in *Le parole di Gramsci: Per un lessico dei Quaderni del Carcere*, ed. Fabio Frosini and Guido Liguori (Rome: Carocci, 2004), 18.

69. Craig Brandist, "The Cultural and Linguistic Dimensions of Hegemony: Aspects of Gramsci's Debt to Early Soviet Cultural Policy," *Journal of Romance Studies* 12, no. 3 (2012), 25.

70. Gramsci and Schucht, *Lettere, 1926–1935*.

71. Robert C. Allen, *Farm to Factory: A Reinterpretation of the Soviet Industrial Revolution* (Princeton, NJ: Princeton University Press, 2003), 48; Maurice Dobb, *Soviet Economic Development since 1917* (London: Routledge & Kegan Paul, 1948), 161; Andrei Markevich and Mark Harrison, "Great War, Civil War, and Recovery: Russia's National Income, 1913 to 1928," *Journal of Economic History* 71, no. 3 (2011): 680, 688; Mark R. Beissinger, *Scientific Management, Socialist Discipline, and Soviet Power* (Cambridge, MA: Harvard University Press, 1988), chapter 2.

72. Trotsky, "Culture and Socialism," 236.

73. Nikolai Bukharin, "Problema kul'tury v epokhu rabochei revoliutsii," *Pravda*, October 11, 1922; Hans Rogger, "*Amerikanizm* and the Economic Development of Russia," *Comparative Studies in Society and History* 23, no. 3 (1981): 384. A sure guide to early Soviet Americanism is Alan M. Ball, *Imagining America: Influence and Images in Twentieth-Century Russia* (New York: Rowman & Littlefield, 2003), esp. chapter 1.

74. Trotsky, "Culture and Socialism," 241.

75. Quoted in Rogger, "*Amerikanizm*," 385.

76. Sheila Fitzpatrick, "The Soft Line in Culture and Its Enemies, 1922–1927," *Slavic Review* 33, no. 2 (1974): 267–87; John Biggart, "Bukharin and the Origins of the 'Proletarian Culture' Debate," *Soviet Studies* 39, no. 2 (1987): 229–46; John Biggart, "Bukharin's Theory of Cultural Revolution," in *The Ideas of Nikolai Bukharin*, ed. Anthony Kemp-Welch (Oxford, UK: Clarendon Press, 1992), 131–58; Trotsky, "Culture and Socialism."

77. Gastev quoted in Kendall E. Bailes, "Alexei Gastev and the Soviet Controversy over Taylorism, 1918–24," *Soviet Studies* 29, no. 3 (1977): 377–78.

78. Peter Fritzsche and Jochen Hellbeck, "The New Man in Stalinist Russia and Nazi Germany," in *Beyond Totalitarianism: Stalinism and Nazism Compared*, ed. Michael Geyer and Sheila Fitzpatrick (Cambridge, UK: Cambridge University Press, 2009), esp. 315–17.

79. Gramsci, *Quaderno 22: Americanismo e fordismo*, 60–63, 71–76, 85–86.

80. Gramsci, 41–48.

81. Gramsci, 62–63, 71–75; Trotsky, *Problems of Everyday Life*, 29.

82. David Priestland describes this contradiction in terms of a tension between "elitist" and "populist" tenets in Bolshevik ideology (Priestland, *Stalinism and the Politics of Ideological Mobilization: Ideas, Power, and Terror in Inter-war Russia* [Oxford, UK: Oxford University Press, 2007]).

83. Quoted in Stephen Kotkin, *Stalin: The Paradoxes of Power, 1878–1928* (New York: Penguin, 2015), 517.

84. On the decline of the "bourgeois" technical intelligentsia and the emergence of a "proletarian" one during the 1930s see Kendall E. Bailes, "The Politics of Technology: Stalin and Technocratic Thinking among Soviet Engineers," *American Historical Review* 79, no. 2 (1974): 445–69; Kendall E. Bailes, *Technology and Society under Lenin and Stalin: Origins of the Soviet Technical Intelligentsia, 1917–1941* (Princeton, NJ: Princeton University Press, 1978); Beissinger, *Scientific Management*, 1–156; Sheila Fitzpatrick, *Education and Social Mobility in the Soviet Union, 1921–1934* (Cambridge, UK: Cambridge University Press, 1979). See also Sheila Fitzpatrick, "Cultural Revolution as Class War," in *The Cultural Front: Power and Culture in Revolutionary Russia*, ed. S. Fitzpatrick (Ithaca, NY: Cornell University Press, 1992), 115–48; Loren Graham, *The Ghost of the Executed Engineer: Technology and the Fall of the Soviet Union* (Cambridge, MA: Harvard University Press, 1993).

85. N. S. Lavrov, *Genri Ford i ego proizvodstvo* (Leningrad: Vremia, 1925). In 1917, after the February Revolution, Lavrov had written to Henry Ford expressing the hope that his ideas would help rebuild a "renewed Russia" (BFRC, Acc. 1, Box 173).

86. Bukharin as quoted in Bailes, "Alexei Gastev," 387.

87. O. A. Ermanskii, *Legenda o Forde* (Moscow: Gosizdat, 1925); O. A. Ermanskii, *Teoriia i praktika ratsionalizatsii* (Moscow: Gosizdat, 1927); Beissinger, *Scientific Management*, 94–99.

88. Arsenii Mikhailov, *Sistema Forda* (Moscow: Gosizdat, 1930).

89. Bailes, "Alexei Gastev"; Lewis H. Siegelbaum, "Soviet Norm Determination in Theory and Practice, 1917–1941," *Soviet Studies* 36, no. 1 (1984): 45–68; Beissinger, *Scientific Management*, 35–43, 71–73; Judith A. Merkle, *Management and Ideology: The Legacy of the International Scientific Management Movement* (Berkeley: University of California Press, 1980), 105–109.

90. Beissinger, *Scientific Management*, 56, 87–89; Bailes, "Alexei Gastev," 386, 390.

91. O. A. Ermanskii, *Theorie und Praxis der Rationalisierung* (Vienna: Verlag für Literatur und Politik, 1928), vi.

92. Henry Ford, *Moia zhizn', moi dostizheniia* (Leningrad: Vremia, 1924); Ford, *Segodnia i zavtra* (Leningrad: Vremia, 1926); Ford, *Segodnia i zavtra* (Moscow: Gosizdat, 1926); Ford, *Segodnia i zavtra* (Moscow: Gostekhizdat, 1926). Information on the various editions and their circulation can be gleaned from the advertisements in the back matter of Ford, *Segodnia* (Vremia edition), and from Mikhailov, *Sistema Forda*, 139.

93. N. S. Lavrov, "Predislovie," in Ford, *Moia zhizn'*, 3–8. For similar arguments see Aleksei K. Gastev, "Marks i Ford" [1927], in A. K. Gastev, *Kak nado rabotat': Prakticheskoe vvedenie v nauku organizatsii truda* (Moscow: Ekonomika, 1972), 311–15.

94. Iakob Walkher, *Ford ili Marks* (Moscow: Profintern, 1925); German edition: Jakob Walcher, *Ford oder Marx: Die praktische Lösung der sozialen Frage* (Berlin: Neuer Deutscher Verlag, 1925), 55.

95. I. V. Rabchinskii, "Vvodnaia stat'ia," in Ford, *Segodnia i zavtra* (Moscow: Gostekhizdat, 1926), 3–8. Rabchinskii had published major works on Taylorism and scientific management: *O sisteme Teilora* (Moscow: Gostekhizdat, 1921); *Promkapital i novaia shkola NOT v Amerike* (Moscow: Gostekhizdat, 1922). See also his *Printsipy Forda* (Moscow: Gostekhizdat, 1925).

96. O. A. Ermanskii, "Predislovie," in N. S. Rozenblit, *Fordizm: Amerikanskaia organizatsiia proizvodsto* (Moscow: Ekonomicheskaia Zhizn', 1925), 5–13. Ermanskii expanded on these themes in his comprehensive takedown *Legenda o Forde*.

97. Rozenblit, *Fordizm*, 73–78.

98. Mikhailov, *Sistema Forda*, 87–89.

99. Mikhailov, 122.

100. Gastev, "K perepiske s Fordom" [1928], in *Kak nado rabotat'*, 306–7.

101. Trotsky, "Culture and Socialism," 241–44.

102. Gastev, "Remeslo i sovremennaia industriia" [1925], in *Kak nado rabotat'*, 171–77.

103. Mikhailov, *Sistema Forda*, 90, 104.

104. Quotes in Beissinger, *Scientific Management*, 105–9.

105. N. S. Lavrov, *Fordizm: Uchenie o proizvodstve veshchei* (Leningrad: n. p., 1928); Mikhailov, *Sistema Forda*, 140.

106. *Rossiiskii gosudarstvennyi arkhiv ekonomiki* (RGAE), Moscow, f.7620, o.1, d.13.

107. Beissinger, *Scientific Management*, 101.

108. David R. Shearer, "The Language and Politics of Socialist Rationalization. Productivity, Industrial Relations, and the Social Origins of Stalinism at the End of NEP," *Cahiers du Monde Russe et Soviétique* 32, no. 4 (1991): 581–608. Shearer, *Industry, State, and Society in Stalin's Russia, 1926–1934* (Ithaca, NY: Cornell University Press, 1996), chapters 3–5. Sheila Fitzpatrick, "Ordzhonikidze's Takeover of Vesenkha: A Case Study in Soviet Bureaucratic Politics," *Soviet Studies* 37, no. 2 (1985): 153–72. On the ideological horizon of the Stalinist modernizers see also Andrea Graziosi, "'Building the First System of State Industry in History.' Piatakov's VSNKh and the Crisis of the NEP, 1923–1926," *Cahiers du Monde Russe et Soviétique* 32, no. 4 (1991): 539–80; Shearer, *Industry, State, and Society in Stalin's Russia*, 77–85, 115–17, 239; Arkadii Rozengol'ts, "Ispol'zuem preimushchestva sotsialisticheskogo stroitel'stva," in *Promyshlennost': Sbornik statei po materialam TsKK VKP(b)-NK RKI*, ed. A. Rozengol'ts (Moscow: Gosizdat, 1930), 5–16.

109. Rozengol'ts, "Ispol'zuem preimushchestva."

110. N. Osinskii, *Avtomobilizatsiia SSSR: Stat'i, ocherki, rechi* (Moscow: Gosizdat, 1930), 5–23.

111. Rozengol'ts, "Ispol'zuem preimushchestva," 14–15.

112. Mikhailov, *Sistema Forda*, 5.

113. Aleksei Gastev, "Fordism," in *Bol'shaia sovetskaia entsiklopediia*, vol. 58 (Moscow: Gosudarstvennyi Institut "Sovetskaia Entsiklopediia", 1936).

114. N. Beliaev, *Genri Ford* (Moscow: Zhurnal'no-gazetnoe Ob"edinenie, 1935), 7.

115. Louis Lochner, *Henry Ford: America's Don Quixote* (New York: International Publishers, 1925); Russian: Luis Lokhner, *Genri Ford i ego "korabl' mira"* (Leningrad: Vremia, 1925); Frank Mäckbach and Otto Kienzle, eds., *Fließarbeit. Beiträge zu ihrer Einführung* (Berlin: VDI Verlag, 1926); Russian: F. Mekkbakh and A. Kintsle, *Rabota nepreryvnym proizvodstvennym potokom* (Moscow: Promizdat, 1927); Mikhailov, *Sistema Forda*, 142.

116. O. A. Ermanskii, *Nauchnaia organizatsiia truda i proizvodstva i sistema Teilora* (Moscow: Gosizdat, 1923); German: O. A. Ermanskii, *Wissenschaftliche Betriebsorganisation und Taylor-System* (Berlin: Karl Dietz Verlag, 1925); Ermanskii, *Teoriia i praktika ratsionalizatsii*; German: Ermanskii, *Theorie und Praxis der Rationalisierung*.

117. Klautke, *Unbegrenzte Möglichkeiten*, 226; Yanagisawa, "The Impact of German Economic Thought on Japanese Economists."

118. Irene Margarete Witte, *Taylor, Gilbreth, Ford: Gegenwartsfragen der amerikanischen und europäischen Arbeitswissenschaft* (Munich: Oldenbourg, 1925); Russian: I. M. Vitte, *Amerika—Germaniia: Teilor, Dzhil'bret, Ford* (Leningrad: Vremia, 1926); Hilda Weiss, *Abbe und Ford: Kapitalistische Utopien* (Berlin: Prager, 1927); Russian: G. Veis, *Abbe i Ford. Kapitalisticheskie utopii* (Moscow: Gosizdat, 1928).

119. Gramsci, *Quaderno 22: Americanismo e fordismo*, 18.

120. Lüddecke, "Amerikanismus als Schlagwort und Tatsache," 215.

121. Quoted in Rogger, "*Amerikanizm*," 385. The words that Soviets used to describe Americanism—*delovitost', delochestvo*—derived from *delo*, "the deed."

122. Lüddecke, "Amerikanismus als Schlagwort und Tatsache," 221.

123. Gramsci, *Quaderno 22: Americanismo e fordismo*, 41–42.

Chapter 3: The Soviet Auto Giant

1. V. I. Lenin, "How We Should Reorganize the Workers and Peasants Inspectorate," quoted in Sarah Davies and James Harris, *Stalin's World: Dictating the Soviet Order* (New Haven, CT: Yale University Press, 2014), 22.

2. Alice Amsden, *The Rise of "the Rest": Challenges to the West from Late-Industrializing Economies* (Oxford, UK: Oxford University Press, 2001), 64.

3. Benson Ford Research Center (BFRC), Dearborn, MI, Acc. 38, Box 80, Camerana to Sorensen, September 28, 1936; Duccio Bigazzi, *La grande fabbrica. Organizzazione industriale e modelo americano alla Fiat dal Lingotto a Mirafiori* (Milan: Feltrinelli, 2000), 73–75.

4. BFRC, Acc. 38, Box 80, Sorensen to Camerana, October 2, 1936.

5. *Rossiiskii gosudarstvennyi arkhiv ekonomiki* (RGAE), Moscow, f. 7622, o. 3, d. 68; Aleksandr Bek, "Takova dolzhnost' (vospominaniia Dybetsa)" *Novyi mir* 7 (1969): 106–68.

6. See the reference book on foreign technical agreements in RGAE, f. 7620, o. 1, d. 776; S. S. Khromov, ed., *Industrializatsiia sovetskogo soiuza: Novye dokumenty, novye fakty, novye podkhody*, 2 vols. (Moscow: RAN, 1999), 2: 254.

7. For a list of agreements reflecting the status of early 1930 see Saul Bron, *Soviet Economic Development and American Business* (New York: Liveright, 1930), 144–46.

8. Sonia Melnikova-Raich, "The Problem with Two 'Unknowns': How an American Architect and a Soviet Negotiator Jump-Started the Industrialization of Russia, Part I: Albert Kahn," *Journal of the Society for Industrial Archeology* 36, no. 2 (2010): 57–80. Melnikova-Raich estimates that by 1932 "several hundred plants and factories in twenty-one cities" in the Soviet Union had been based on Albert Kahn's designs (p. 75).

9. Technology transfers are side notes in the classic works of E. H. Carr and R. W. Davies, *Foundations of a Planned Economy, 1926–1929* (New York: Macmillan, 1971); Davies, *The Soviet Economy in Turmoil, 1929–1930* (Cambridge, MA: Harvard University Press, 1989); Davies, *Crisis and Progress in the Soviet Economy, 1931–33* (Basingstoke, UK: Macmillan, 1996); Alec Nove, *An Economic History of the USSR, 1917–1991* (London: Penguin, 1992); and R. W. Davies, Mark Harrison, and S. G. Wheatcroft, eds., *The Economic Transformation of the Soviet Union, 1913–1945* (Cambridge, UK: Cambridge University Press, 1994).

10. See, in particular, Antony C. Sutton, *Western Technology and Soviet Economic Development*, 3 vols. (Stanford, CA: Hoover Institution, 1968–1973). Sutton obsessively detailed the Soviet dependency on Western technological imports, which he interpreted as a characteristic failure of the Communist system rather than as a standard feature of catch-up development. Comprehensively surveying Soviet production processes, machinery, and equipment, Sutton noted that "in all cases [but two] a Western precursor was found" (vol. 2, p. 329, footnote 1). While this certainly points to the lack of Soviet innovation capacity, as Sutton emphasized, it also demonstrates the Soviet skill at adopting and indigenizing foreign technology—a point that Sutton acknowledged. "In the light of the history of technical transfers, the Soviet choice of Western techniques has been superb. . . . The Soviet system has institutional procedures enabling the rapid, usually successful transfer of Western technology at a low cost and in a relatively efficient manner. . . . Since about 1920 the Soviets have conducted a thorough and continuing worldwide dragnet of technical advances. They have probably acquired or tried to acquire one of every article made in the West" (vol. 2, pp. 291–93). See also George D. Holliday, *Technology Transfer to the USSR, 1928–1937 and 1966–1975: The Role of Western Technology in Soviet Economic Development* (Boulder, CO.: Westview Press, 1979); Philipp Hanson, *Trade and Technology in Soviet-Western Relations* (New York: Columbia University Press, 1981); Bruce Parrott, ed., *Trade, Technology, and Soviet-American Relations* (Bloomington: Indiana University Press, 1985).

11. Foundational was Kendall E. Bailes, "The American Connection: Ideology and the Transfer of American Technology to the Soviet Union, 1917–1941," *Comparative Studies in Society and History* 23, no. 3 (1981): 421–48. See also Kurt Schultz, "The American Factor in Soviet Industrialization: Fordism and the First Five-Year Plan, 1928–1932" (PhD dissertation, Ohio State University, 1992); Shpotov, "Uchastie amerikanskikh promyshlennykh kompanii v sovetskoi industrializatsii, 1928–1933," *Ekonomicheskaia istoriia: Ezhegodnik* (2005): 172–96; and the important articles by historian of architecture Sonia Melnikova-Raich, "The Problem with Two 'Unknowns,' Part I," and "Part II: Saul Bron," *Journal of the Society for Industrial Archeology* 37, no. 1/2 (2011): 5–28. On various aspects of the Ford-Russia connection in the 1920s and 1930s see Mira Wilkins and Frank Ernest Hill, *American Business Abroad: Ford on Six Continents*, updated ed. (New York: Cambridge University Press, 2011), chapter 10; Christine White, "Ford in Russia: In Pursuit of the Chimerical Market," *Business History* 28, no. 4 (1986): 77–104; Boris

Shpotov, "Ford in Russia, from 1909 to World War II," in *Ford, 1903–2003: The European History*, ed. Hubert Bonin, Yannick Lung, and Steven Tolliday (Paris: PLAGE, 2003), 2: 514–18. The construction period of Gaz (1930–1931), under the auspices of the Cleveland engineering firm Austin, is explored in Shpotov, "Bisnesmeny i biurokraty: Amerikanskaia tekhnicheskaia po-moshch' v stroitel'stve Nizhegorodskogo avtozavoda, 1929–1931 gg.," *Ekonomicheskaia istoriia: Ezhegodnik* (2002): 191–232; Kurt Schultz, "Building the 'Soviet Detroit': The Construction of the Nizhnii-Novgorod Automobile Factory, 1927–1932," *Slavic Review* 49, no. 2 (1990): 200–12; and Richard Austin, *Building Utopia: Erecting Russia's First Modern City, 1930* (Kent, OH: Kent State University Press, 2004). On the Ford Motor Company's *Fordson* tractor see Dana D. Dal-rymple, "The American Tractor Comes to Soviet Agriculture: The Transfer of a Technology," *Technology and Culture* 5, no. 2 (1964): 191–214; and Yves Cohen, "The Soviet Fordson: Between the Politics of Stalin and the Philosophy of Ford, 1924–1932," in *Ford, 1903–2003: The European History*. See also the *histoire croisée* presented in David Greenstein, "Assembling *Fordizm*: The Production of Automobiles, Americans, and Bolsheviks in Detroit and Early Soviet Russia," *Comparative Studies in Society and History* 56, no. 2 (2014): 259–89.

12. Amsden, *The Rise of "the Rest"*; Chalmers Johnson, *MITI and the Japanese Miracle: The Growth of Industrial Policy, 1925–1975* (Stanford, CA: Stanford University Press, 1982); Richard Samuels, *"Rich Nation, Strong Army": National Security and the Technological Transformation of Japan* (Ithaca, NY: Cornell University Press, 1994) speaks of "indigenization, nurturance, and diffusion" (chapter 2). See also Kevin O'Rourke and Jeffrey Williamson, eds., *The Spread of Modern Industry to the Periphery since 1871* (Oxford, UK: Oxford University Press, 2017).

13. For example, Schultz, "American Factor"; Lewis Siegelbaum, *Cars for Comrades: The Life of the Soviet Automobile* (Ithaca, NY: Cornell University Press, 2008).

14. As perceptively argued by Johnson, *MITI and the Japanese Miracle*, 21–22.

15. On the history of Gaz see Siegelbaum, *Cars for Comrades*, chapter 2, and the useful com-pany histories of Polina Aleshina et. al., *Gor'kovskii Avtomobil'nyi: Ocherk istorii zavoda* (Mos-cow: Profizdat, 1964); V. Ia. Dobrokhotov, *Gor'kovskii Avtomobil'nyi* (Moscow: Mysl', 1981); and A. A. Gordin, *Gor'kovskii Avtomobil'nyi Zavod: Istoriia i sovremennost' 1932–2012* (Nizhnii Novgorod: Kvarts, 2012).

16. Robert C. Allen, *Farm to Factory: A Reinterpretation of the Soviet Industrial Revolution* (Princeton, NJ: Princeton University Press, 2003); Andrei Markevich and Steven Nafziger, "State and Market in Russian Industrialization, 1870–2010," in *Spread of Modern Industry*, ed. O'Rourke and Williamson, esp. 33–37, 43–47; Davies, Harrison, and Wheatcroft, *Economic Transformation of the Soviet Union*; Mark Harrison, "Foundations of the Soviet Command Economy 1917–1941," in *The Cambridge History of Communism, Vol. 1: World Revolution and So-cialism in One Country*, ed. Silvio Pons and Stephen Smith (Cambridge, UK: Cambridge Uni-versity Press, 2017), 327–47; Anton Cheremukhin et al., "Was Stalin Necessary for Russia's Economic Development?" NBER Working Paper No. 19425 (September 2013).

17. On the connections between industrialization, collectivization, and famine I follow Terry Martin, "The 1932–33 Ukrainian Terror: New Documentation on Surveillance and the Thought Process of Stalin," in *Famine-Genocide in Ukraine, 1932–1933. Western Archives, Testimonies and New Research*, ed. Wsevolod W. Isajiw (Toronto: Ukranian Canadian Research and Documenta-tion Center, 2003), 97–114; and Andrea Graziosi, "Les famines soviétiques de 1931–1933 et le Holodomor ukrainien. Une nouvelle interprétation est-elle possible et quelles en seraient les

conséquences?" *Cahiers du monde russe et soviétique* 46, no. 3 (2005): 453–72. For a recent summary of the ongoing debate see Sergei Nefedov and Michael Ellman, "The Soviet Famine of 1931–1934: Genocide, a Result of Poor Harvests, or the Outcome of a Conflict between the State and the Peasants?" *Europe-Asia Studies* 71, no. 6 (2019): 1048–65.

18. On Bolshevik millenarianism see Halfin, *From Darkness to Light: Class Consciousness and Salvation in Revolutionary Russia*; Yuri Slezkine, *The House of Government: A Saga of the Russian Revolution* (Princeton, NJ: Princeton University Press, 2017).

19. On how comparative underdevelopment spurred Japanese catch-up efforts see Samuels, *"Rich Nation, Strong Army."* As Chalmers Johnson summarized, "The goals of the developmental state were invariably derived from comparisons with external reference economies" (*MITI and the Japanese Miracle*, 24).

20. Trotsky quoted in Richard Day, *Leon Trotsky and the Politics of Economic Isolation* (Cambridge, UK: Cambridge University Press, 1973), 155.

21. Michael Dohan, "Soviet Foreign Trade in the NEP Economy and Soviet Industrialization Strategy," (PhD dissertation, Massachusetts Institute of Technology, 1969), 53–58; Michael Dohan, "The Economic Origins of Soviet Autarky, 1927/28–1934," *Slavic Review* 35, no. 4 (1976): 633–34.

22. James Harris, "Encircled by Enemies: Stalin's Perceptions of the Capitalist World, 1918–1941," *Journal of Strategic Studies* 30, no. 3 (2007): 513–45.

23. Quoted in Maurice Dobb, *Soviet Economic Development since 1917* (London: Routledge & Kegan Paul: 1948), 192.

24. On the international pressure that contributed to the end of NEP see Jon Jacobson, *When the Soviet Union Entered World Politics* (Berkeley: University of California Press, 1994), 233–56; Robert Lewis, "Foreign Economic Relations," in *Economic Transformation of the Soviet Union*, ed. Davies, Harrison, and Wheatcroft, 202–6.

25. David Shearer, *Industry, State, and Society in Stalin's Russia, 1926–1934* (Ithaca, NY: Cornell University Press, 2006), chapter 5.

26. Dohan, "Economic Origins," 612–13; Oscar Sanchez-Sibony, *Red Globalization: The Political Economy of the Soviet Cold War from Stalin to Khrushchev* (Cambridge, UK: Cambridge University Press, 2014), 42–43; Shearer, *Industry, State, and Society*, 77–85, 96; Paul Gregory, *The Political Economy of Stalinism: Evidence from the Soviet Secret Archives* (Cambridge, UK: Cambridge University Press, 2004), chapter 2; Jeffrey J. Rossman, *Worker Resistance under Stalin: Class and Revolution on the Shop Floor* (Cambridge, MA: Harvard University Press, 2005), 3–6; Elena Osokina, *Zoloto dlia industrializatsii: TORGSIN* (Moscow: ROSSPEN, 2009).

27. Dohan, "Economic Origins."

28. Lars Lih, Oleg Naumov, and Oleg Khlevniuk, eds., *Stalin's Letters to Molotov* (New Haven, CT: Yale University Press, 1995), 205. Avtozavod refers to Gaz. Cheliabzavod is a reference to the tractor plant in Cheliabinsk, then under construction; the plant would become "Tankograd," one of the primary forges of Soviet tanks. See Lennart Samuelson, *Tankograd: The Formation of a Soviet Company Town: Cheliabinsk, 1900–1950s* (London: Palgrave, 2011).

29. Shearer, *Industry, State, and Society*, 77–85, 115–17, 239.

30. Siegelbaum, *Cars for Comrades*, 11–15. See also N. Osinskii, *Avtomobilizatsiia SSSR: Stat'i, ocherki, rechi* (Moscow: Gozisdat, 1930), 8–10; Adrian Streather, *Bernar Nahum: A Pioneer of Turkey's Automotive Industry* (Eden, SD: Nettleberry, 2011), 45; Joel Wolfe, *Autos and Progress:*

The Brazilian Search for Modernity (New York: Oxford University Press, 2010), 44; Michael Cusumano, *The Japanese Automobile Industry: Technology and Management at Nissan and Toyota* (Cambridge, MA: Harvard University Asia Center, 1985), 385; Stefan Tetzlaff, "The Motorisation of the 'Moffusil': Automobile Traffic and Social Change in Rural and Small-Town India, c. 1915–1940," (PhD dissertation, University of Göttingen, 2015), 288, table 2.

31. For struggles within the economic administration see Shearer, *Industry, State, and Society*; for interregional rivalries see James R. Harris, *The Great Urals: Regionalism and the Evolution of the Soviet System* (Ithaca, NY: Cornell University Press, 1999).

32. Eugène Zaleski, *Planning for Economic Growth in the Soviet Union, 1918–1932* (Chapel Hill: University of North Carolina Press, 1971), 50–73; Osinskii, *Avtomobilizatsiia SSSR*, 13.

33. Osinskii features as a Bolshevik leftist par excellence in Yuri Slezkine, *The House of Government*. His commitment to the party left is evident from an intervention in October 1927, when Osinskii objected to the expulsion of Trotsky and Zinoviev from the Central Committee by invoking "a necessary minimum of intra-party democracy." Quoted in Khromov, *Industrializatsiia*, 1: 191–92. For a sample of Osinskii's various activities see also Hassan Malik, *Bankers and Bolsheviks: International Finance and the Russian Revolution* (Princeton, NJ: Princeton University Press, 2018), 187–90; N. Osinskii, *Mirovoi selskokhoziastvennyi krisis* (Moscow, 1923); Osinskii, *Ocherki mirovogo selskokhoziastvennogo rynka* (Moscow, 1925); V. V. Obolensky-Ossinsky (N. Osinksii), "Social Economic Planning in the USSR: The Premises, Nature, and Forms of Social Economic Planning," *Annals of Collective Economy* 7, no. 3 (1931); Obolensky-Ossinsky, "Planning in the Soviet Union," *Foreign Affairs* (April 1935).

34. On the debate see Siegelbaum, *Cars for Comrades*, 37–39; Schultz, "American Factor," 107–8.

35. Osinskii, *Avtomobilizatsiia SSSR*, 5–23.

36. "Rabotniki Gosplana i VSNKh o predlozheniakh t. Osinskogo," in N. Osinskii, *Amerikanskaia avtomobil' ili rossiiskaia telega* (Moscow: Pravda, 1927), 63–70.

37. Osinskii, *Avtomobilizatsiia SSSR*, 24–27.

38. The following paragraphs draw from Osinskii, *Avtomobilizatsiia SSSR*, 108–12; Shpotov, "Ford in Russia, from 1909 to World War II"; Siegelbaum, *Cars for Comrades*, 16–19; Schultz, "American Factor," 109–17.

39. Osinskii, *Amerikanskaia avtomobil' ili rossiiskaia telega*, 67.

40. Osinskii, *Avtomobilizatsiia SSSR*, 112; Charles Sorensen with Samuel T. Williamson, *My Forty Years with Ford* (New York: Norton, 1956), 182. A draft of the contract proposed by Sorensen is in BFRC, Acc. 572, Box 24.

41. Schultz, "American Factor," 114; Siegelbaum, *Cars for Comrades*, 17.

42. On *Vato*'s administrative structure see RGAE, f. 7620, o.1, d.1.

43. Quoted in Day, *Leon Trotsky*, 133.

44. NEP concessions are understudied. Sutton, *Western Technology and Soviet Economic Development*, vol. 1, delivers a comprehensive overview of NEP concessions but does not clarify how they fit into the shifting strategies of Soviet economic policy. Some information on concessions can be gleaned from Bailes, "American Connection,"; Carr and Davies, *Foundations of a Planned Economy*, 1: 716–18; Katherine Siegel, *Loans and Legitimacy: The Evolution of Soviet-American Relations, 1919–1933* (Lexington: University Press of Kentucky, 1996), chapter 7; Andy Williams, *Trading with the Bolsheviks. The Politics of East-West Trade, 1920–39* (Manchester, UK:

Manchester University Press, 1992), 10–11. See also Cyrus Veeser, "A Forgotten Instrument of Global Capitalism? International Concessions, 1870–1930," *International History Review* 35, no. 5 (2013): 1136–55. As chairman of the Main Concession Committee, Trotsky argued in 1926 that concessions should be subordinated to the larger Soviet industrialization strategy. See Khromov, *Industrializatsiia*, 2: 208–20.

45. Quoted in Kendall E. Bailes, *Technology and Society under Lenin and Stalin: Origins of the Soviet Technical Intelligentsia, 1917–1941* (Princeton, NJ: Princeton University Press, 1978), 343.

46. Sutton, *Western Technology*, 1: 99; Osinskii, *Avtomobilizatsiia SSSR*, 84.

47. "Dogovor s Fordom," in Osinskii, *Avtomobilizatsiia SSSR*, 82–86.

48. Oskinskii, *Avtomobilizatsiia SSSR*, 111–12.

49. Bailes, "American Connection." On other major industrial projects of the First Plan see Anne Rassweiler, *The Generation of Power: The History of Dneprostroi* (New York: Oxford University Press, 1988); Kotkin, *Magnetic Mountain: Stalinism as a Civilization*; Jean-Paul Depretto, "Un grand chantier du premier plan quinquennal soviétique: Kuznetskstroï," *Genèses* 39, no. 2 (2000): 5–26.

50. These numbers are cited in Elena Osokina, *Our Daily Bread: Socialist Distribution and the Art of Survival in Stalin's Russia, 1927–1941*, ed. Kate Transchel (Armonk, NY: Sharpe, 2001), 127.

51. BFRC, Acc. 572, Box 17, folder 11.14, "Agreement" (between Ford Motor Company and *Vesenkha*), May 31,1929; Osinskii, "Dogovor s Fordom."

52. See Shpotov, "Biznesmeny i biurokraty," 193–94. A representative example is the 1931 agreement between Nitrogen Engineering Corporation and the Soviet chemical industry, reprinted in Sutton, *Western Technology*, 2: 352–62. The 1930 agreement for a large-scale Moscow ball-bearing plant with Fiat-RIV (Italy) features the same elements of technology transfer: Fiat Archives (FAT), Turin, Italy, Fondo URSS; Sutton, *Western Technology*, 2: 145–46.

53. In the negotiations, Mezhlauk broached the issue of royalties, but Sorensen waved him off, writing to Mezhlauk: "We shall be glad to permit the use . . . of all licenses, patents, etc. . . . without additional compensation other than your agreement to purchase our products as stipulated" (BFRC, Acc. 6, Box 275: Mezhlauk to Edsel Ford, May 6, 1929; Sorensen to Mezhlauk, May 17, 1929; Sorensen to Edsel Ford, May 20, 1929). The favorable nature of the Ford contract can be gauged by putting its terms in comparison. Under the 1931 contract cited above, Nitrogen Engineering charged the Soviet side "the actual cost" of preparing drawings, plans, and blueprints, plus 100 percent overhead. Per the 1929 agreement, in contrast, the Ford Motor Company charged "actual cost" plus 10 percent overhead. In terms of royalties, the Soviet chemical industry was to pay Nitrogen Engineering Corporation $400,000 over four years "for the rights and technical services to be rendered." No such clause was included in the Ford contract.

54. BFRC, Acc. 531, Box 1, Fitzgerald (Ford accounting) to Malychevitch (Autostroy), November 11, 1929.

55. BFRC, Acc. 531, Box 1, "Instructions covering equipment to be sold to Amtorg Trading Corporation for Autostroy," April 27, 1931.

56. BFRC, Acc. 38, Box 67, Sorensen to Perry, December 6, 1929. Similar requests are Sorensen to Perry, May 16, 1930, and Sorensen to Perry, August 27, 1931.

57. BFRC, Acc. 531, Box 1, "List of Ford Motor Company purchase orders covering machinery and equipment purchased for the Amtorg Trading Corporation [1931]"; Fitzgerald to Malychevitch, November 11, 1929.

58. BFRC, Acc. 65, Box 66, Reminiscences of Charles Sorensen, folder "Amtorg."

59. Quoted in Gordin, *Gor'kovskii Avtomobil'nyi Zavod*, 20.

60. RGAE, f.7620, o.1, d.1, l.56.

61. L. Mertts et. al., "GAZ i Ford," *Planovoe Khoziaistvo* 6–7 (1932): 258–59.

62. RGAE, f.7297, o.38, d. 20, ll.91–96, Lomanov to Bogdanov, March 8, 1934.

63. "Technical dragnet" is Sutton's term: Sutton, *Western Technology*, 2: 291.

64. I am drawing on Everett Rogers, *Diffusion of Innovations* (New York: Free Press, 1962); Nathan Rosenberg, "Economic Development and the Transfer of Technology: Some Historical Perspectives," *Technology and Culture* 11, no. 4 (1970): 553–56, 568–70; Amsden, *The Rise of "the Rest,"* 51–64; David Edgerton, *The Shock of the Old: Technology and Global History since 1900* (New York: Oxford University Press, 2007).

65. *Tsentral'nyi arkhiv Nizhegorodskoi oblasti* (TsANO), Nizhnii Novgorod, f.2431, o.2, d.6, ll.7–8; 57–59; TsANO, f.2431, op.4, d.2, l.1.

66. See, e.g., BFRC, Acc. 285, Box 1298, Dybets to Henry Ford, January 28, 1931.

67. BFRC, Acc. 199, Box 37: "Badge No. Arrangement" and "Combined Chart"; "List of Ford Men with Autostroy," March 18, 1930; BFRC, Acc. 531, Box 1, "Departmental Communication—Subject: Students Autostroy," May 21, 1930.

68. These and the following citations are from Dybets's reports to *Vesenkha* from January 1930, TsANO, f. 2431, o.2, d.10.

69. TsANO, f. 2431, o.2, d.10, l.52.

70. TsANO, f. 2431, o.2, d.10, ll. 21–22; Schultz, "Building the Soviet Detroit"; Austin, *Building Utopia*.

71. See the various reports in TsANO f. 2431, o.1, d.15; RGAE, f.7297, op.24, dd. 60, 61,105.

72. Quoted from Dybets's December 1930 report to Ordzhonikidze, TsANO, f. 2431, o.4, d.11a, l.21.

73. See Lomanov's 1933 report in RGAE, f.7297, o.24. d.71.

74. TsANO, f. 2431, o.4, d.11a, ll.35–42; Shpotov, "Uchastie," 184.

75. TsANO, f.2431, o.4, d.14, ll.137–39, Mertts to Dybets, November 25, 1930.

76. Shpotov lists more than one hundred American firms whose tools and equipment formed part of the Nizhnii machine park: Shpotov, "Uchastie," 194–96. Documentation in the Ford archives suggests that the number was even higher: BFRC, Acc. 531, Box 1, "List of Ford Motor Company Purchase Orders."

77. BFRC, Acc. 390, Box 87, Ford Motor Company to Amtorg, April 7, 1931; BFRC, Acc. 531, Box 1, "Instructions covering equipment to be sold to Amtorg Trading Corporation for Autostroy," April 27, 1931, and "List of Ford Motor Company Purchase Orders"; BFRC, Acc. 199, Box 2, "Draft of General Plan for handling orders received from Amtorg," April 3, 1931.

78. BFRC, Acc. 199, Box 2, Amtorg Trading Corp., "Standard Sheets and Instructions for Ordering and Manufacturing Tools and Equipment," March 1931; BFRC, Acc. 531, Box 1, "Comments [on] tools which were made here for Amtorg," February 10, 1932. The tussle is covered in Boris Shpotov, "Pereplatil-li sovetskii soiuz kompanii Forda? K voprosu o tsene industrializatsii," *Ekonomicheskaia istoriia: Ezhegodnik* (2004): 160–80.

79. BFRC, Acc. 65, Reminiscences of Frank Bennett, 117–18.

80. See BFRC, Acc. 531, Box 1, Oleinikoff to Sorensen, February 10, 1932, and the surrounding correspondence.

81. RGAE, f.7620, o.1, d.802, l.149.

82. Z. K. Zvezdin and N. I. Kuprianova, eds., *Istoriia industrializatsii Nizhegorodskogo-Gor'kovskogo kraia, 1926–1941* (Gorky: Volgo-Viatskoe Knizhnoe Izdatel'stvo, 1968), 183–87; RGAE, f.7620, o.1, d.774, ll.1–15.

83. Nelson Lichtenstein, *Walter Reuther: The Most Dangerous Man in Detroit* (Urbana: University of Illinois Press, 1995), chapter 3.

84. See Robert Robinson's memoir, *Black on Red: My Forty-Four Years inside the Soviet Union* (New York: Acropolis, 1988).

85. The fate of these workers is explored in striking fashion in Tim Tzouliadis, *The Forsaken: An American Tragedy in Stalin's Russia* (New York: Penguin, 2008). See also Andrea Graziosi, "Foreign Workers in Soviet Russia, 1920–40: Their Experience and Their Legacy," *International Labor and Working-Class History* 33 (1988): 38–59.

86. RGAE, f.7620, o.1, d.756, ll.45–47, Protocol of *Vato* board meeting, December 5, 1930.

87. RGAE, f.7620, o.1, d.774, ll.1–15. On Grondon, see Tzouliadis, *The Forsaken*, 44–45, 100.

88. BFRC, Acc. 65, Reminiscences of Frank Bennett, 128–29, 133.

89. Graziosi, "Foreign Workers," 45.

90. Quoted in Schultz, "American Factor," 147.

91. BFRC, Acc. 390, Box 87, Schram to Falland, June 30, 1932.

92. Quoted in Schultz, "American Factor," 214.

93. RGAE, f.7620, o.1, d.768, ll.3–7.

94. RGAE, f.7620, o.1, d.756, l.47.

95. See the December 1933 NKTP report on foreign technical assistance in RGAE, f. 7297, o.38, d.289, ll.65–74, quoted in Khromov, *Industrializatsiia*, 2: 260. These points are echoed in RGAE, f. 7297, o.38, d.203, l.81–82, M. Kaganovich to Ezhov, January 9, 1934.

96. RGAE, f. 7297, o.38, d.129, l.120.

97. RGAE, f. 7620, o.1, d.701, l.47.

98. RGAE, f.7620, o.1, d.785, l.33.

99. BFRC, Acc. 818, Box 1. On Lipgart see Siegelbaum, *Cars for Comrades*, 54–55.

100. TsMAMLS, f.86, o.1, Kriger files; RGAE, f.7622, o.2, d.52.

101. RGAE, f. 7297, o.38, d.129, ll.313ff.

102. On the effect of the global Depression on exporters of primary goods see Dietmar Rothermund, "Einleitung: Weltgefälle und Wirtschaftskrise," in *Die Peripherie in der Weltwirtschaftskrise: Afrika, Asien, und Lateinamerika 1929–1939*, 13–36; Jeffry A. Frieden, *Global Capitalism: Its Fall and Rise in the Twentieth Century* (New York: Norton, 2006), 221–23.

103. The squeeze on the terms of trade was quick and devastating. According to Michael Dohan's calculations, had 1929 price levels prevailed in 1931, actual Soviet trade would have earned a surplus of 277 million rubles. In fact, the year ended with a trade deficit of 294 million rubles. See Michael Dohan and Edward Hewett, *Two Studies in Soviet Terms of Trade, 1918–1970* (Bloomington: International Development and Research Center, Indiana University, 1973), 51, table 7.

104. Dohan, "Economic Origins."

105. On the campaign against Soviet dumping, see Schultz, "American Factor," chapter 6.

106. In 1933, officials calculated that more than 18 million convertible rubles had been paid to Western engineers and specialists. Overall, 65 million convertible rubles had been spent on

170 foreign technical assistance agreements concluded between 1921 and 1933. This sum represented outlays for consulting, licenses, patents, and *komandirovki* only; it did not include "hundreds of millions of rubles" for imports of machinery. See "Spravka INO NKTP o privlechenii inostrannoi tekhnicheskoi pomoshchi," in Khromov, *Industrializatsiia,* 2: 260–65.

107. Khromov, 2: 252–54; RGAE, f. 7297, o.38, d.67, ll.126ff; f. 7297, o.38, d.376, ll.15–19.

108. Dohan, "Economic Origins," 616, table 4.

109. RGAE, f. 7622, o.1, d.1, l.86, Gutap board meeting, October 14, 1933.

110. RGAE, f. 7297, o.38, d.129, l.50.

111. RGAE, f. 7297, o.38, d.203, l.224, Piatakov to Mezhlauk, October 16, 1935.

112. Stalin to Ordzhonikidze, September 9, 1931, quoted in *The Stalin-Kaganovich Correspondence, 1931–36,* ed. R. W. Davies et al. (New Haven, CT: Yale University Press, 2003), 375.

113. It is the paramount issue in the reports that Kaganovich sent to Stalin in August and September 1931: Davies et al., *Stalin-Kaganovich Correspondence,* 49–103. See Oscar Sanchez-Sibony, "Depression Stalinism: The Great Break Reconsidered," *Kritika* 15, no. 1 (2014): 44.

114. Davies et al., *Stalin-Kaganovich Correspondence,* 66.

115. Davies et al., 63.

116. RGAE, f.7620, o.1, d.786, l.139, Dybets to *Vato* board, September 23, 1931.

117. BFRC, Acc. 199, Box 1: "Amtorg agreement dated May 31st, 1929"; Amtorg to Ford Motor Company, November 22, 1934.

118. BFRC, Acc. 199, Box 1, "Agreement" (between Ford Motor Company and NKTP), March 14, 1935.

119. BFRC, Acc. 199, Box 1, Sorensen to Wibel, April 18, 1935.

120. As Sorensen directed: "Wibel: Model B is the same as Model A. Let them have the prints" (BFRC, Acc. 390, Box 87, Wibel to Sorensen, October 22, 1935). See also Grosny to Wibel, June 27, 1935, Grosny to Sorensen, October 17, 1935, and the surrounding correspondence in BFRC, Acc. 390, Box 87.

121. BFRC, Acc. 390, Box 87, Wibel to Sorensen, January 31, 1936.

122. BFRC, Acc. 390, Box 87, Buell to Wibel, November 10, 1936.

123. BFRC, Acc. 390, Box 87, Morgan Construction Company to Ford Motor Company, October 19, 1936, and following correspondence.

124. "The Russians are not on our payroll but come in as observers. They are allowed to go about where they wish and have their own interpreters and their own guides to go after them. Our people try to help them whenever they are able to" (BFRC, Acc. 390, Box 87, Buell to Wibel, April 27, 1937).

125. BFRC, Acc. 38, Box 80: Boyeff to Sorensen, March 11, 1936; Gnau to Boyeff, March 16, 1936.

126. BFRC, Acc. 65, Box 66, Reminiscences of Charles Sorensen, folder "Amtorg"; "Soviet Official to Study U.S. Food Devices," *New York Times,* August 12, 1936.

127. BFRC, Acc. 65, Box 66, Reminiscences of Charles Sorensen, folder "Amtorg."

128. Melnikova-Raich, "The Problem with Two 'Unknowns,' Part II," 19–20.

129. Zvezdin and Kuprianova, *Istoriia industrializatsii,* 296.

130. Dobrokhotov, *Gor'kovskii Avtomobil'nyi,* 39–40.

131. See the "Survey on production at Gaz in 1932" in TsANO, f. 2435, o.2, d.6.

132. See the Gaz labor force census in TsANO, f. 2435, o.2, d. 26, ll.26–27.

133. Rossman, *Worker Resistance under Stalin*.

134. Zvezdin and Kuprianova, *Istoriia industrializatsii*, 325.

135. Dobrokhotov, *Gor'kovskii Avtomobil'nyi*, 41.

136. Zvezdin and Kuprianova, *Istoriia industrializatsii*, 298.

137. Lewis H. Siegelbaum, *Stakhanovism and the Politics of Productivity in the USSR, 1935–1941* (Cambridge, UK: Cambridge University Press, 1988), 158–61.

138. See the report on the Gutap branch conference in Khar'kov, February/ March 1936, in RGAE, f. 7622, o.1, d.58, ll. 1–63.

139. RGAE, f. 7622, o.1, d.58, ll.33–37.

140. Siegelbaum, *Stakhanovism and the Politics of Productivity*, 86.

141. Factory meetings like this one took place across industries in early 1937 and scapegoated directors and technical management: Sheila Fitzpatrick, "Workers against Bosses: The Impact of the Great Purges on Labor-Management Relations," in *Making Workers Soviet: Power, Class, and Identity*, ed. Lewis Siegelbaum and Ronald Suny (Ithaca, NY: Cornell University Press, 1994). The quotes that follow are from RGAE, f. 7622, o.1, d.97, ll.2–14.

142. Zvezdin and Kuprianova, *Istoriia industrializatsii*, 546; TsANO, f. 2435, o.1, d. 171. Arrests and executions: "Zhertvy politicheskogo terrora v SSSR," http://lists.memo.ru/index2.htm.

143. See Loskutov's report for 1938 in TsANO, f. 2435, o.1, d. 169.

144. TsANO, f. 2435, o.1, d.169, l.105.

145. TsANO, f. 2435, o.1, d. 180, ll.1–8a.

146. A. V. Mitrofanova, *Industrializatsiia SSSR, 1938–1941: Dokumenty i materialy* (Moscow: Nauka, 1973), 68.

147. TsANO, f. 2435, o.1, d.177, l.38.

148. Siegelbaum, Stakhanovism and the Politics of Productivity, chapter 7.

149. TsANO, f. 2435, o.1, d.178, l.92.

150. Quoted in Bigazzi, *La grande fabbrica*, 74.

Chapter 4: Nazi *Fordismus*

1. *Sächsisches Staatsarchiv* (SSAC), Chemnitz, 31050/1046: Bruhn to Werner, October 21, 1937; Werner to Bruhn, October 24, 1937.

2. *Unternehmensarchiv Volkswagen* (UVW), Wolfsburg: Rückwanderer Akten, 174/1590; 69/166; 69/168, interview with J. Werner, February 21, 1961; Henry Nelson, *Small Wonder: The Amazing Story of the Volkswagen* (Boston: Little, Brown and Company, 1967), 54–55; Hans Mommsen and Manfred Grieger, *Das Volkswagenwerk und seine Arbeiter im Dritten Reich* (Düsseldorf, Germany: Econ, 1996), 407–8.

3. Mira Wilkins, *The History of Foreign Investment in the United States, 1914–1945* (Cambridge, MA: Harvard University Press, 2004), 117–18, 238–47; Kathryn Steen, *The American Synthetic Organic Chemicals Industry: War and Politics, 1910–1930* (Chapel Hill: University of North Carolina Press, 2014).

4. Harold James, *The German Slump: Politics and Economics, 1924–1936* (New York: Clarendon Press, 1986), 387–413; Albrecht Ritschl, *Deutschlands Krise und Konjunktur 1924–1934: Binnenkonjunktur, Auslandsverschuldung und Reparationsproblem zwischen Dawes-Plan und Transfersperre* (Berlin: Akademie, 2002), 177–88.

5. Ralf Banken, "Die wirtschaftspolitische Achillesferse des 'Dritten Reiches': Das Reichswirtschaftsministerium und die NS-Außenwirtschaftspolitik 1933–39," in *Das Reichswirtschaftsministerium in der NS-Zeit: Wirtschaftsordnung und Verbrechenskomplex*, ed. Albrecht Ritschl (Berlin: De Gruyter, 2016), 111–232. On Nazi export promotion schemes, see Michael Ebi, *Export um jeden Preis: Die deutsche Exportförderung von 1932–1938* (Stuttgart: Steiner, 2004); Stephen Gross, *Export Empire: German Soft Power in Southeastern Europe, 1890–1945* (Cambridge, UK: Cambridge University Press, 2015), 184–197. For a concise overview over the "New Plan" see Adam Tooze, *The Wages of Destruction: The Making and Breaking of the Nazi Economy* (New York: Viking, 2007), 91–96.

6. "Steered market economy" is the term of Christoph Buchheim and Jonas Scherner, "Anmerkungen zum Wirtschaftssystem des 'Dritten Reiches,'" in *Wirtschaftsordnung, Staat und Unternehmen: Neuere Forschungen zur Wirtschaftsgeschichte des Nationalsozialismus*, ed. Werner Abelshauser, Jan O. Hesse, and Werner Plumpe (Essen, Germany: Klartext, 2003), 81–97. For highlights in this recent literature see Johannes Bähr and Ralf Banken, eds., *Wirtschaftssteuerung durch Recht im Nationalsozialismus. Studien zur Entwicklung des Wirtschaftsrechts im Interventionsstaat des 'Dritten Reichs'* (Frankfurt: Klostermann, 2006); Christoph Buchheim, ed., *German Industry in the Nazi Period* (Stuttgart: Steiner, 2008); Jonas Scherner, *Die Logik der Industriepolitik im Dritten Reich: Die Investitionen in die Autarkie- und Rüstungsindustrie und ihre staatliche Förderung* (Stuttgart: Steiner, 2008); Dieter Ziegler, "'A Regulated Market Economy': New Perspectives on the Nature of the Economic Order of the Third Reich, 1933–39," in *Business in the Age of Extremes: Essays in Modern German and Austrian Economic History*, ed. Hartmut Berghoff, Jürgen Kocka, and Dieter Ziegler (Washington, DC: German Historical Institute, 2013), 139–52; Alexander Donges, *Die Vereinigten Stahlwerke AG im Nationalsozialismus: Konzernpolitik zwischen Marktwirtschaft und Staatswirtschaft* (Paderborn, Germany: Schöningh, 2014). For a dissenting perspective that stresses limits to business autonomy cf. Peter Hayes, "Corporate Freedom of Action in Nazi Germany," *Bulletin of the German Historical Institute* 45 (2009): 29–42, along with the rejoinder by Christoph Buchheim and Jonas Scherner, "Corporate Freedom of Action in Nazi Germany: A Response to Peter Hayes" in the same publication (43–50).

7. Quoted from Wilhelm Treue, "Hitlers Denkschrift zum Vierjahresplan 1936," *Vierteljahreshefte für Zeitgeschichte* 3, no.2 (1955): 208–9.

8. *Bundesarchiv* (BAL), Berlin-Lichterfelde, R43 II/547, fol. 143ff.; Albert Pietzsch, "Wirtschaftslenkung durch den Staat," June 1938.

9. See Scherner, *Die Logik*, 278–84. As Göring clarified in 1942: "It has always been my stance that the state should only participate meaningfully in industrial enterprises if the demands put on them exceeds the abilities of private business" (quoted in Scherner, *Die Logik*, 281). On the expropriation of the aircraft manufacturer Junkers see Lutz Budraß, *Flugzeugindustrie und Luftrüstung in Deutschland 1918–1945* (Düsseldorf, Germany: Droste, 1998), 320–35. On the state-run iron and steel complex Reichswerke Hermann Göring see Richard Overy, *War and Economy in the Third Reich* (Oxford, UK: Clarendon Press, 1994), 144–74.

10. BAL, R43 II/1465, fol. 92, "Berichtigung zur Aufzeichnung betreffed Mr. Mooney, General Motors Corporation," April 13, 1934.

11. BAL, NS 6/231, fol. 89, "Betrifft: Wirtschaftliche Betätigung von ausländischem Kapital in Deutschland," November 19, 1938.

12. Mira Wilkins, *The Maturing of Multinational Enterprise: American Business Abroad from 1914 to 1970* (Cambridge, MA: Harvard University Press, 1974), 185–86.

13. Rainer Karlsch and Raymond G. Stokes, *Faktor Öl: Die Mineralölwirtschaft in Deutschland 1859–1974* (Munich: Beck, 2003), 195–96.

14. Edwin Black, *IBM and the Holocaust: The Strategic Alliance between Nazi Germany and America's Most Powerful Corporation* (Washington, DC: Dialog, 2009), 122–23; Lars Heide, "Between Parent and 'Child': IBM and Its German Subsidiary, 1910–1945," in *European Business, Dictatorship, and Personal Risk 1920–1945*, ed. Christopher Kobrak and Per Hansen (New York: Berghahn Books, 2004), 160–61; Mira Wilkins, "Multinationals and Dictatorship: Europe in the 1930s and Early 1940s," in *European Business, Dictatorship, and Personal Risk*, 32–33.

15. Henry Ashby Turner, *General Motors and the Nazis: The Struggle for Control of Opel, Europe's Biggest Carmaker* (New Haven, CT: Yale University Press, 2005), 41–42.

16. Benson Ford Research Center (BFRC), Dearborn, MI, Acc. 38, Box 37, "Memo covering the plan to execute orders from the government," December 7, 1937.

17. Gerhard Kümmel, *Transnationale Wirtschaftskooperation und der Nationalstaat: Deutsch-amerikanische Unternehmensbeziehungen in den dreißiger Jahren* (Stuttgart: Steiner, 1995), 103–40; Wilkins, "Multinationals and Dictatorship," 22–38; Turner, *General Motors and the Nazis*, 10–12; Simon Reich, *Research Findings about Ford-Werke under the Nazi Regime* (Dearborn, MI: Ford Motor Company, 2001), 24–25.

18. Wilkins, *Maturing of Multinational Enterprise*, 186–89.

19. Black, *IBM and the Holocaust*; Reinhold Billstein et. al., *Working for the Enemy: Ford, General Motors, and Forced Labor in Germany during the Second World War* (New York: Berghahn Books, 2000).

20. Turner, *General Motors and the Nazis*; Reich, *Research Findings*.

21. Tooze, *Wages of Destruction*, 133–34.

22. Pier Angelo Toninelli, "Between Agnelli and Mussolini: Ford's Unsuccessful Attempt to Penetrate the Italian Automobile Market in the Interwar Period," *Enterprise and Society* 10, no. 2 (2009): 335–75.

23. Talbot Imlay and Martin Horn, *The Politics of Industrial Collaboration during World War II: Ford France, Vichy and Nazi Germany* (Cambridge, UK: Cambridge University Press, 2014), chapter 1. The General Motors assembly plant in Denmark similarly faced import restrictions resulting from "exchange stringencies": General Motors Corporation, *The War Effort of the Overseas Division* (New York: General Motors Overseas Operations, 1944), 80.

24. Michael Cusumano, *The Japanese Automobile Industry: Technology and Management at Nissan and Toyota* (Cambridge, MA: Harvard University Press, 1985), 113, 116–22.; Mark Mason, *American Multinationals and Japan: The Political Economy of Capital Controls* (Cambridge, MA: Harvard University Press, 1992), 60–93; Masaru Udagawa, "The Prewar Japanese Automobile Industry and American Manufacturers," *Japanese Yearbook of Business History* 2 (1985): 81–99. See also Mira Wilkins and Frank E. Hill, *American Business Abroad: Ford on Six Continents* (New York: Cambridge University Press, 2011), 254–56; J. Scott Mathews, "Nippon Ford," *Michigan Historical Review* 22, no. 2 (1996).

25. Udagawa, "Prewar Japanese Automobile Industry," 87; General Motors Corporation, *War Effort*, 88–91.

26. A succinct recent overview is Stephan Haggard, *Developmental States* (Cambridge, UK: Cambridge University Press, 2018). For the core building blocks of this literature see Chalmers

Johnson, *MITI and the Japanese Miracle: The Growth of Industrial Policy, 1925–1975* (Stanford, CA: Stanford University Press, 1982); Peter B. Evans, *Embedded Autonomy: States and Industrial Transformation* (Princeton, NJ: Princeton University Press, 1995); Robert Wade, *Governing the Market: Economic Theory and the Role of Government in East Asian Industrialization* (Princeton, NJ: Princeton University Press, 1990); Alice Amsden, *The Rise of "the Rest": Challenges to the West from Late-Industrializing Economies* (Oxford, UK: Oxford University Press, 2001); Atul Kohli, *State-Directed Development: Political Power and Industrialization in the Global Periphery* (Cambridge, UK: Cambridge University Press, 2004). On developmental states and technology transfers see Sanjay Lall, "Technological Capabilities and Industrialization," *World Development* 20, no. 2 (1992): 165–86; John Cantwell and Yanli Zhang, "The Co-evolution of International Business Connections and Domestic Technological Capabilities: Lessons from the Japanese Catch-Up Experience," *Transnational Corporations* 25, no. 2 (2009): 37–68.

27. Georg Schlesinger, *Der Daseinskampf der deutschen Automobil-Industrie* (Berlin: RDA, 1925).

28. Reiner Flik, *Von Ford lernen? Automobilbau und Motorisierung in Deutschland bis 1933* (Cologne: Böhlau, 2001), 34–35, 57, 146; Heidrun Edelmann, *Vom Luxusgut zum Gebrauchsgegenstand: Die Geschichte der Verbreitung von Personenkraftwagen in Deutschland* (Frankfurt: VDA, 1989), 146.

29. Magnus Tessner, *Die deutsche Automobilindustrie im Strukturwandel von 1919 bis 1938* (Cologne: Botermann, 1994), 82–83; Flik, *Von Ford lernen?*, 221–36; quote on p. 239.

30. Fred Ledermann, *Fehlrationalisierung—der Irrweg der deutschen Automobilindustrie seit der Stabilisierung der Mark* (Stuttgart: Pöschel, 1933).

31. Flik, *Von Ford lernen?*, 168–69; Edelmann, *Vom Luxusgut*, 140–50.

32. James Foreman-Peck, "The American Challenge of the Twenties: Multinationals and the European Motor Industry," *Journal of Economic History* 42, no. 4 (1982): 865–81; Stephen Tolliday, "Transplanting the American Model? US Automobile Companies and the Transfer of Technology and Management to Britain, France, and Germany, 1928–1962," in *Americanization and Its Limits: Reworking US Technology and Management in Post-War Europe and Japan*, ed. Jonathan Zeitlin and Gary Herrigel (Oxford, UK: Oxford University Press, 2000), 79–93.

33. Flik, *Von Ford lernen?*, 160–61.

34. Louis Betz, *Das Volksauto: Rettung oder Untergang der deutschen Automobilindustrie?* (Stuttgart: Petri, 1931), 31, 64, 71–94.

35. BAL, R43 II/748: Allmers to Hitler, January 31, 1933; Lammers to Allmers, February 3, 1933. Max Domarus, *Hitler: Reden und Proklamationen, 1932–1945* (Neustadt an der Aisch, Germany: VDS, 1962), 1: 266; Bernhard Rieger, *The People's Car: A Global History of the Volkswagen Beetle* (Cambridge, MA: Harvard University Press, 2013), 47; Edelmann, *Vom Luxusgut*, 174.

36. Richard Overy, "Cars, Roads, and Economic Recovery in Germany, 1932–8," *Economic History Review* 28, no. 3 (1975): 466–83; Flik, *Von Ford lernen?*, 60; Edelmann, *Vom Luxusgut*, 160–65.

37. Dorothee Hochstetter, *Motorisierung und 'Volksgemeinschaft': Das Nationalsozialistische Kraftfahrkorps (NSKK), 1931–1945* (Munich: Oldenbourg, 2005).

38. Uwe Day, *Silberpfeil und Hakenkreuz: Autorennsport im Nationalsozialismus* (Berlin: Bebra, 2005).

39. See, e.g., the description of the 1936 and 1937 exhibitions in BAL, R43 II/749.

40. Domarus, *Hitler: Reden und Proklamationen*, 1: 370; Rieger, *People's Car*, 57–58.

41. Mommsen and Grieger, *Volkswagenwerk*, 375–76.

42. See Mommsen and Grieger, *Das Volkswagenwerk*; Wolfgang König, *Volkswagen, Volksempfänger, Volksgemeinschaft: "Volksprodukte" im Dritten Reich; Vom Scheitern einer nationalsozialistischen Konsumgesellschaft* (Paderborn: Schöningh, 2004); Rieger, *People's Car*, chapter 2. Tooze called the Volkswagen "a disastrous flop" (*Wages of Destruction*, 156).

43. Quoted in Rieger, *People's Car*, 59.

44. Mommsen and Grieger, *Das Volkswagenwerk*, 60–70, 119.

45. This according to Herbert Quint, *Porsche: der Weg eines Zeitalters* (Stuttgart: Steingrüben, 1951), 144–49. I was not able to locate evidence for a Soviet invitation of Porsche in the files of the *Vato* foreign bureau.

46. See the internal memo of the Association of Auto Manufacturers, February 5, 1936, in BAL R43 II/753; Mommsen and Grieger, *Das Volkswagenwerk*, 71–79.

47. Turner, *General Motors and the Nazis*, 4–10; Kümmel, *Transnationale Wirtschaftskooperation*, 105–11; Daniel Wren, "James D. Mooney and General Motors' Multinational Operations, 1922–1940," *Business History Review* 87, no. 3 (2013): 515–43; Jacob Anbinder, "Selling the World: Public Relations and the Global Expansion of General Motors, 1922–1940," *Business History Review* 92, no. 3 (2018): 483–507.

48. Quoted in Kümmel, *Transnationale Wirtschaftskooperation*, 122.

49. Black, *IBM and the Holocaust*, 232; Reich, *Research Findings*, 7, footnote 25. Diplomatic history buffs will be familiar with Heinrich Albert as the "minister without portfolio": in August 1915, when Albert served as a German commercial attaché in Washington, he negligently left a briefcase containing sensitive intelligence on a New York tram, causing a scandal and further straining already tense relations between Germany and the USA. On Albert's career see Johannes Reiling, *Deutschland, Safe for Democracy? Deutsch-amerikanische Beziehungen aus dem Tätigkeitsbereich Heinrich F. Alberts, kaiserlicher Geheimrat in Amerika, erster Staatssekretär der Reichskanzlei der Weimarer Republik, Reichsminister, Betreuer der Ford-Gesellschaften im Herrschaftsgebiet des Dritten Reiches, 1914 bis 1945* (Stuttgart: Steiner, 1997).

50. See Keppler's personal file in BAL, R43 II/1602. Keppler's multifarious activities in the economic administration during the Thirties have not been systematically reconstructed. But see Henry Ashby Turner, *German Big Business and the Rise of Hitler* (New York: Oxford University Press, 1985), 238–46; Peter Hayes, *Industry and Ideology: IG Farben in the Nazi Era* (Cambridge, UK: Cambridge University Press, 1987), 144–51; and Tooze, *Wages of Destruction*, 131–34, 214. I have also benefited from Tobias Bütow, "Der 'Freundeskreis Himmler': Ein Netzwerk im Spannungsfeld zwischen Wirtschaft, Politik und staatlicher Administration" (Diploma thesis, Free University Berlin, 2004), esp. 22–37.

51. Yale Sterling Library (YSL-GM), New Haven, CT, MS 1799, Box 1, doc 10669–70, Mooney to Sloan, April 28, 1936.

52. National Archives and Records Administration (NARA), College Park, MD, RG 165, Entry 179, Box 745, "Interrogation of Wilhelm Keppler," September 14, 1945.

53. *Staatsarchiv* (SAH), Hamburg, 622–1/153 C7/1, Krogmann to von der Goltz, November 4, 1932 (copy).

54. Mommsen and Grieger, *Das Volkswagenwerk*, 62–63; König, *Volkswagen*, 160–61; BAL, R43 II/753, fol. 8ff.

55. BAL: R43 II/ 748, fol. 234–36; R43 II/1465, fol. 88–91.

56. BAL, R43 II/1465, fol. 92, "Berichtigung zur Aufzeichnung betreffed Mr. Mooney, General Motors Corporation," April 13, 1934.

57. YSL-GM, Ms 1799, Box 1, doc 682–84; Turner, *General Motors*, 32–34.

58. Turner, *General Motors*, 7–9; BAL, R43II/1465, fol. 135, Mooney to Hitler, May 21, 1934.

59. Heinrich Albert, memorandum, June 1934, BFRC, Acc. 572, Box 16.

60. SAH, 622–1/153, C23a/13, "Niederschrift über den Plan, in Hamburg eine Automobil-Fabrik zu errichten," July 18, 1934.

61. BFRC: Acc. 64, Box 1, Henry Ford to Wilhelm II, April 15, 1929; Acc. 285, Box 1346, Liebold to Louis Ferdinand, December 27, 1929; Louis Ferdinand to Liebold, February 2, 1930; Acc. 23, Box 6, Louis Ferdinand to Liebold, March 21, 1933. Prinz Louis Ferdinand von Preussen, *Als Kaiserenkel durch die Welt* (Berlin: Argon Verlag, 1952), 261.

62. BFRC, Acc. 572, Box 16: Louis Ferdinand to Gnau, April 3, 1934; Louis Ferdinand to Liebold, April 26, 1934.

63. SAH, 622–1/153, C15 II 5, Krogmann diaries, entry July 17, 1934: "I relayed to the gentlemen the Führer's agreement."

64. BFRC, Acc. 572, Box 16: Sorensen to Wirtz, August 2, 1934; Sorensen to Perry, August 22, 1934; Sorensen to Perry, August 27, 1934; Sorensen to Perry, September 24, 1934.

65. BFRC, Acc. 285, Box 1766, Keppler to Louis Ferdinand, September 8, 1934; SAH, 622–1/153, C23a/13, "Niederschrift über die Besprechung bei dem Wirtschaftsbeauftragten des Führers, Pg. Keppler, am 25. Oktober 1934."

66. BFRC, Acc. 572, Box 16, Sorensen to Perry, September 24, 1934.

67. SAH, 622–1/153: C23a/13, "Niederschrift über die Entwicklung und den augenblicklichen Stand der Ford-Angelegenheit," October 18, 1934; "Niederschrift über die Besprechung bei dem Wirtschaftsbeauftragten des Führers, Pg. Keppler, am 25. Oktober 1934"; C15 II 5, Krogmann diaries, entry October 18, 1934.

68. YSL-GM, Box 15, doc 19065–70, Evans to Mooney, November 16, 1934; Turner, *General Motors*, 35–36.

69. BFRC, Acc. 38, Box 28, Albert to Sorensen, December 14, 1934.

70. BFRC, Acc. 6, Box 227, Louis Ferdinand to Edsel Ford, January 3, 1935.

71. "Compromise" was Mooney's term: YSL-GM, Box 1, doc 1067–70, Mooney to Sloan, April 28, 1938.

72. YSL-GM, Box 15: Fleischer to Keppler, December 18, 1934; Keppler to Fleischer, December 22, 1934.

73. YSL-GM, Box 15: Keppler to Fleischer, January 3, 1935; Fleischer to Keppler, January 15, 1935; Keppler to Fleischer, January 30, 1935; Paetsch to Fleischer, February 26, 1935. Opel's treasurer Rudolf Fleischer ran the layouts of the new factory by General Thomas of the army procurement office. The office in return "commended the construction of the factory in Brandenburg and the production of trucks there" (YSL-GM, Box 15: Fleischer to Thomas, February 19, 1935; Paetsch to Fleischer, February 26, 1935).

74. YSL-GM, Box 3, doc 1599–1601.

75. BFRC, Acc. 38, Box 33, Albert to Sorensen, January 20, 1936.

76. On the mobilizational dynamic of "working towards" under Nazism see Ian Kershaw, "'Working Towards the Führer': Reflections on the Nature of Hitler's Dictatorship," *Contemporary European History* 2, no. 2 (1993): 103–18.

77. YSL-GM, Box 15, folder 19073–19366, Fleischer to Evans, April 4,1935; Turner, *General Motors*, 42; YSL-GM, Box 1, doc 1071–73, Howard to Mooney, March 10, 1937.

78. Quoted in Turner, *General Motors*, 72. See also the effusive letter of thanks in YSL-GM, Box 2, doc 1193, Howard to Thomas, June 17, 1938.

79. YSL-GM, Box 4, doc 3730–39, Osborn to Howard, August 28, 1937.

80. Turner, *General Motors*, 72–73, 81, 87–88; YSL-GM, Box 2, doc 1189–91, "Memo concerning the visit of Mr. Knudsen to Field Marshall Göring," September 18, 1938. According to Turner, Göring spontaneously arranged the meeting upon learning that Knudsen was visiting Berlin (*General Motors*, 81). Göring's initiative came in the context of deliberations at the Aviation Ministry about how to rope Opel into the Ju-88 bomber program (Budraß, *Flugzeugindustrie*, 561).

81. This is evident from manifold examples in the GM documentation at Yale's Sterling Library, not all of which are reflected in Turner's account. In January 1937, Opel established a liaison office in Berlin with the task of "conversing with the individual ministries in relation to the Four Year Plan, that is, about raw material questions etc." (YSL-GM, Box 44, doc 61896). The office eventually produced a detailed "organization plan of all ministries, government authorities, and other relations, which are of any importance for our business." The office emphasized the centrality of network politics in the Nazi political economy: "A considerable amount of time, effort, and money is spent in Berlin for meetings, 'Bierabende,' or other social gatherings, in other words, social life plays an important part in the business life of the capital of the Reich. . . . Our company should not leave out a single one of these events because they give opportunity to meet people who are important for our business" (YSL-GM, Box 44, doc 61859ff., Wahlert to Fleischer, February 10, 1938). Mooney cultivated his relationship with Hjalmar Schacht until the latter fell from grace with the regime: YSL-GM, Box 15, folder 19426–98, Mooney to Schacht, April 6, 1933; YSL-GM, Box 1, doc 1067–70, Mooney to Sloan, April 28, 1936; YSL-GM, Box 4, Mooney to Sloan, October 6, 1936, which gives a detailed report on a recent meeting with Schacht. In 1939, Mooney, Osborn, and Howard appealed to the chancellery for inclusion on Hitler's list of guests of honor at the September Nuremberg Party Rally: YSL-GM, Box 2, doc 1179, Osborn to Mooney, August 2, 1939. (The rally was canceled after the German invasion of Poland.)

82. Turner, *General Motors*, 49–84. Turner spends two chapters detailing Howard's and Osborn's struggles with the *Gauleiter* in 1938 but neglects to explore how GM's executives built up remarkably close relationships in Berlin over the entire period between 1934 and 1940. Only in light of these connections, however, does it become fully comprehensible why Mooney thought he was qualified to play diplomatic broker between Roosevelt and Hitler in 1940. For Mooney's vain efforts, see *General Motors*, chapter 7.

83. Osborn to Howard, February 9, 1939, quoted in Turner, *General Motors*, 73.

84. BFRC, Acc. 38, Box 28, Albert to Sorensen, April 16, 1935.

85. BFRC: Acc. 38, Box 33, Albert to Sorensen, January 20, 1936; Acc. 6, Box 230, Albert to Edsel Ford, August 17, 1936.

86. BFRC, Acc. 6, Box 230, Albert to Edsel Ford, March 9, 1936.

87. BFRC, Acc. 38. Box 28, Diefenbach to Roberge, September 12, 1935.

88. BFRC, Acc. 285, Box 2415, Louis Voss to Henry and Edsel Ford, December 29, 1938.

89. BFRC, Acc. 38, Box 38, "Memo concerning the Stoewer Werke Stettin," enclosed in Albert to Sorensen, January 3, 1936.

90. BFRC, Acc. 6, Box 230, Albert to Edsel Ford, March 9, 1936.

91. BFRC Acc. 38, Box 38, Albert to Sorensen, July 20, 1936; Sorensen to Albert, July 29, 1936; Reich, *Research Findings*, 21, footnote 117.

92. BFRC, Acc. 38, Box 28, Sorensen to Albert, August 12, 1936.

93. Kümmel, *Transnationale Wirtschaftskooperation*, 126, 133.

94. As GM's executive Osborn said in 1938, "The overall financial interests of the company could best be protected by a continuation of investing our profits and cash in plants and equipment" (YSL-GM, Box 4, doc 3725–29, Osborn to Howard, August 26, 1938).

95. See Sorensen's marginalia on Albert to Sorensen, December 6, 1935, in BFRC, Acc. 38, Box 28.

96. Tolliday, "Transplanting the American Model," 79–80, 87–90.

97. BFRC, Acc. 572, Box 26, Sorensen to Louis Ferdinand, July 12, 1934.

98. YSL-GM, Box 4, Mooney to Sloan, October 6, 1936.

99. Quoted in Turner, *General Motors*, 27.

100. Kümmel, *Transnationale Wirtschaftskooperation*, 126–35; BFRC, Ford-Werke Database (FWDb) FMC 0006505–08, Manager's report to directors, third quarter 1938; BFRC, FWDb, FMC 0005974, USSBS Report on German Vehicles Industry.

101. Reich, *Research Findings*, 26–27; BFRC, Acc. 38, Box 37, "Memo covering the plan to execute orders from the government," December 7, 1937.

102. See Opel's annual reports, 1933–1942, YSL-GM, Box 40.

103. YSL-GM, Box 3, doc 2640–2708, "Opel under General Motors Management: A Review and Outlook" (March 1940).

104. YSL-GM, Box 44, doc 61694.

105. YSL-GM, Box 1, doc 1071–73, Howard to Mooney, March 10, 1937; Box 9, doc 9261–63, "Capital Appropriations Request for Project #158."

106. Günter Neliba, *Die Opel-Werke im Konzern von General Motors (1929–1948) in Rüsselsheim und Brandenburg: Produktion für Aufrüstung und Krieg ab 1935 unter nationalsozialistischer Herrschaft* (Frankfurt: Brandes & Apsel, 2000), 107; BFRC, FWDb, FMC 0005974, USSBS Report on German Vehicles Industry.

107. This, in any case, was Osborn's impression, according to whom the Nazi authorities had communicated that they wished to maintain "the closest possible type of relationship between Opel and the German Government on the one hand and the GM Corporation on the other hand" (YSL-GM, Box 1, doc 719–42, Osborn to Mooney, November 22, 1939).

108. YSL-GM, Box 3, folder 2640–2708, "Opel under General Motors Management: A Review and Outlook."

109. YSL-GM, Box 15, folder 18333–18539, "Report über Rationalisierungsmassnahmen," January 16, 1942.

110. See the handwritten remark by Craig on BFRC, Acc. 38, Box 28, Albert to Perry, August 6, 1935: "My understanding is that we carry the charge on our books as accounts receivable which we hope to collect in the future."

111. BFRC, Acc. 38, Box 28, Albert to Ministry of National Economy, March 29, 1935 (copy).

112. BFRC, Acc. 712, Box 5, various items from folder "Machinery for Cologne," e.g.: "Imports against raw material agreements," 1938; Streit to Fenske, July 12, 1939; Streit to Fenske, January 13,

1939; "Machinery to be imported against 1939 raw material agreements," September 22, 1939. See Kümmel, *Transnationale Wirtschaftskooperation*, 136–37.

113. YSL-GM, Box 14, doc 17120–32, Schneider to Heydekampf, March 14, 1936.

114. YSL-GM, Box 31, doc 43291, Guthrie to Osborn, January 12, 1937.

115. This episode is reconstructed from Otto Dyckhoff's files in YSL-GM, Box 22, folder 30718–31035.

116. This aligns with the learning process identified in Ralf Richter and Jochen Streb, "Catching Up and Falling Behind: Knowledge Spillover from American to German Machine Toolmakers," *Journal of Economic History* 71, no. 4 (2011); and Cristiano Andrea Ristuccia and Adam Tooze, "Machine Tools and Mass Production: Germany and the United States, 1929–44," *Economic History Review* 66, no. 4 (2013): 953–74.

117. YSL-GM, Box 15, doc 19073ff.: Fleischer to Evans, March 6, 1935; Evans to Fleischer, April 5, 1935.

118. YSL-GM, Box 28, doc 39923ff., Heydekampf files; Box 40, Opel annual reports.

119. Heidrun Edelmann, "Heinrich Nordhoff: Ein deutscher Manager in der Automobilindustrie," in *Deutsche Unternehmer zwischen Kiregswirtschaft und Wiederaufbau: Studien zur Erfahrungsbildung von Industrie-Eliten*, ed. Paul Erker and Toni Pierenkemper (Munich: Oldenbourg, 1999), 19–52; YSL-GM, Box 9, doc 9278–98, Osborn to Mooney, March 26, 1940.

120. YSL-GM, Box 40, Opel annual reports; Box 41, folder "Richtlinien."

121. Constanze Werner, *Kriegswirtschaft und Zwangsarbeit bei BMW* (Munich: Oldenbourg 2006), 115–16, 270–78.

122. See the interview with Gerd Stieler von Heydekampf: "Wankel war der Zucker im Kaffee," *Der Spiegel*, March 17, 1969, 78–86.

123. Edelmann, "Heinrich Nordhoff."

124. Mommsen and Grieger, *Das Volkswagenwerk*, 104–7.

125. YSL-GM, Box 15, doc 19073–366: *Aktennotiz* by Fleischer, September 5, 1936; Fleischer to Lammers, September 9, 1936; "Notes on a meeting between Keppler, Mooney, Howard, Palmer, Fleischer at the Reichskanzlei, September 22, 1936."

126. YSL-GM, Box 4, doc 3730–39, Osborn to Howard, August 28, 1937.

127. UVW, 69/8, Memo of DAF Amt Reisen, Wandern, Urlaub, "Die Verwirklichung des Volkswagens," April 1937; Rüdiger Hachtmann, *Das Wirtschaftsimperium der Deutschen Arbeitsfront, 1933–1945* (Göttingen, Germany: Wallstein, 2012), 501–7; Mommsen and Grieger, *Das Volkswagenwerk*, 128–32.

128. UVW, 67/185/1, Ferdinand Porsche, "Denkschrift zum Deutschen Volkswagen," May 1934; Mommsen and Grieger, *Das Volkswagenwerk*, 80–81.

129. A very similar proposition was already laid out by Porsche's fellow automotive engineer Louis Betz in his 1931 pamphlet *Das Volksauto*, which appears to have influenced Porsche's 1934 memo: Betz, *Das Volksauto*, 71ff. For another cooperative merger proposal see the memo drawn up by the Chamber of Commerce in 1934: BAL R43 II/753, IHK Berlin to Hitler, June 7, 1934.

130. "Mr. Dyckhoff has been taken from Opel and employed by the VW crowd" (YSL-GM, Box 4, doc 3730–39, Osborn to Howard, August 28, 1937).

131. BFRC, Acc. 285, Box 2093: Steppacher to Liebold, June 21, 1937; Liebold to Steppacher, June 29, 1937.

132. UVW 69/168, Jakob Werlin: "Gedanken zur Entstehung des VWW," 1951; "Auszug aus den Erinnerungen," 1964.

133. BFRC, Acc. 285, Box 2093: Ford to Werlin and Porsche, July 6, 1937; Porsche to Ford, July 10, 1937.

134. Information on the first Volkswagen recruits in 1937 can be reconstructed from various sources in UVW: Personal Files "Rückwanderer"; Joseph Werner interview, 69/168; Fritz Kuntze file, 373/5/5; and from NARA RG 319, Entry 47, Box 464, FBI report, "Labor recruiting campaign conducted in United States by German Volkswagen Werke," June 26, 1944.

135. UVW, 69/166, 69/168, interviews with Joseph Werner, 1961.

136. Mommsen and Grieger, *Das Volkswagenwerk*, 250–257.

137. UVW 373/5/5, Fritz Kuntze file; UVW Z204, Kuntze dairy.

138. The FBI reconstructed this list of Volkswagen returnees based on Hapag-Lloyd passenger registries: NARA RG 319, Entry 47, Box 464, FBI report, "Labor recruiting campaign conducted in United States by German Volkswagen Werke," June 26, 1944. On Volkswagen's pilot plant and vocational shop in Braunschweig see Mommsen and Grieger, *Das Volkswagenwerk*, 227–242.

139. NARA, RG 319, Entry 47, Box 464, FBI report, "Labor recruiting campaign conducted in US by German Labor Front," April 14, 1944; "Memorandum on organized repatriation of German workers from the United States," December 19, 1938, and "Memorandum by State Secretary [Weizsäcker]," January 13, 1939, in *Documents on German Foreign Policy, 1918–1945: From the Archives of the German Foreign Ministry*, series D (1937–1945) (Washington, DC: Government Printing Office, 1949), 2: 657–73.

140. Mommsen and Grieger, *Das Volkswagenwerk*, 317–18, 368–73.

141. Of the 1937 hires, only Reinhold Ficht returned to the United States. Of the 1939 hires, at least seven (Rumpf, Ruf, Neuse, Fritzke, Mayr, Eckhardt, and Seichter) returned: NARA, RG 319, Entry 47, Box 464, FBI report, "Labor recruiting campaign conducted in United States by German Volkswagen Werke," June 26, 1944.

142. Mommsen and Grieger, 1032.

143. NARA, RG 165, Entry 179C, Box 669, "Detailed Interrogation Report on Personalities of Volkswagenwerk," June 17, 1945; Mommsen and Grieger, *Das Volkswagenwerk*, 664, 806–8, 869–71, 920–22, 1028.

144. BFRC, FWDb, FMC 0005979, "USSBS Intelligence Report—German Motor Industry."

145. NARA RG 243, Entry 6, Box 708, Report of Th. Targa, May 22, 1945.

146. NARA, RG 165, Entry 179C, Box 669, "Detailed Interrogation Report on Personalities of Volkswagenwerk," June 17, 1945.

147. UVW: 373/5/5, Fritz Kuntze files; 174/159/1, Otto Höhne files; 69/166, Joseph Werner interview; 69/168, Joseph Werner interview, Ghislaine Kaes interview.

148. *New York Times*, November 25, 1938. For more background on the Cross of the German Eagle see Stefan Link, "Rethinking the Ford-Nazi Connection," *Bulletin of the German Historical Institute* 49 (2011): 135–50.

149. "Thomas J. Watson Is Decorated by Hitler for Work in Bettering Economic Relations," *New York Times*, July 2, 1937; Black, *IBM and the Holocaust*, 134; Neliba, *Die Opel-Werke*, 81–82.

150. Overy, "Cars, Roads, and Economic Recovery"; Kümmel, *Transnationale Wirtschaftskooperation*, 110; YSL-GM, Box 3, folder 2640–2708, "Opel under General Motors Management: A Review and Outlook."

151. On Japan see Mason, *American Multinationals and Japan*, esp. pp. 48–99. On Brazil see Shapiro, *Engines of Growth: The State and Transnational Auto Companies in Brazil.* On South Korea see Kim, *Imitation to Innovation: The Dynamics of Korea's Technological Learning,* esp. chapter 5; Alice Amsden, *Asia's Next Giant: South Korea and Late Industrialization* (New York: Oxford University Press, 1989), esp. chapter 7. On China see Wan-Wen Chu, "How the Chinese Government Promoted a Global Automobile Industry," *Industrial and Corporate Change* 20, no. 5 (2011): 1235–76.

152. Avraham Barkai quoted in Stephen Gross, "The Nazi Economy," in *A Companion to Nazi Germany*, ed. Shelley Baranowski et al. (Hoboken, NJ: Wiley and Blackwell, 2018), 269.

Chapter 5: War of the Factories

1. *Bundesarchiv* (BAL), Berlin-Lichterfelde, R3112/99, "Bericht über die Sitzung beim Herrn Reichsmarschall am 7.11.1941." On the context of the meeting see Rolf-Dieter Müller, "Die Mobilisierung der deutschen Wirtschaft für Hitlers Kriegführung," in *Das deutsche Reich und der Zweite Weltkrieg: Organisation und Mobilisierung des deutschen Machtbereichs*, vol. 5/1, ed. Bernhard R. Kroener, Rolf-Dieter Müller, and Hans Umbreit (Stuttgart: DVA, 1988), 610–15.

2. Müller, "Die Mobilisierung," 638–41; Chris Bellamy, *Absolute War: Soviet Russia in the Second World War* (New York: Vintage Books, 2008), 278, 303–4.

3. Jeffrey Fear, "War of the Factories," in *The Cambridge History of the Second World War*, vol. 3, ed. Michael Geyer and Adam Tooze (Cambridge, UK: Cambridge University Press, 2015), 94–121.

4. Müller, "Die Mobilisierung," 630, 634. As Müller summarizes the situation: "There was no chance to compensate for the immense losses on the Eastern front and prevail in the armaments race with the enemy powers. . . . Germany's situation was hopeless."

5. BAL, NS 6/336, fol. 82–84, "Besprechung vom 7.11.1941 über den Einsatz von Sowjetrussen"; Ulrich Herbert, *Hitler's Foreign Workers: Enforced Foreign Labor in Germany under the Third Reich* (Cambridge, UK: Cambridge University Press, 1997), 147–50.

6. German Federal Archives, Military Archives (BA-MA), Freiburg, RW 19/295, Erlass "Vereinfachung und Leistungssteigerung unserer Rüstungsindustrie," December 3, 1941.

7. Long-standing rivalries between the powerful proprietors of automobile and aircraft firms hardly abated during the war. For example, Daimler-Benz resented having to produce an Opel-designed truck: Heidrun Edelmann, "Heinrich Nordhoff: Ein deutscher Manager in der Automobilindustrie," in *Deutsche Unternehmer zwischen Kriegswirtschaft und Wiederaufbau: Studien zur Erfahrungsbildung von Industrie-Eliten*, ed. Paul Erker and Toni Pierenkemper (Munich: Oldenbourg, 1999), 33, footnote 84. Aircraft firm Heinkel resisted having to produce a Junkers design: Paul Erker, "Die Luftfahrtindustrie im Spannungsfeld von technologischem Wandel und politischem Umbruch," in *Deutsche Unternehmer*, 237.

8. As Speer put it in a speech to armaments workers on June 5, 1943: BAL, R3/1547.

9. To name only the prominent case studies used in this chapter: Hans Mommsen and Manfred Grieger, *Das Volkswagenwerk und seine Arbeiter im Dritten Reich* (Düsseldorf, Germany: Econ, 1996); Constanze Werner, *Kriegswirtschaft und Zwangsarbeit bei BMW* (Munich: Oldenbourg, 2006); Martin Kukowski and Rudolf Boch, *Kriegswirtschaft und Arbeitseinsatz bei der Auto-Union AG Chemnitz im Zweiten Weltkrieg* (Stuttgart: Steiner, 2014); Peter Kohl and Peter Bessel, *Auto-Union und Junkers: Geschichte der Mitteldeutschen Motorenwerke* (Stuttgart: Franz Steiner, 2003); Neil Gregor, *Daimler-Benz in the Third Reich* (New Haven, CT: Yale University Press, 1998).

10. Speer actively popularized this narrative in his long postwar career as interpreter of the Nazi system (released from prison in 1966, he died in 1981). See Magnus Brechtken, *Albert Speer: Eine deutsche Karriere* (Munich: Siedler, 2017).

11. See Lutz Budraß, *Flugzeugindustrie und Luftrüstung in Deutschland 1918–1945* (Düsseldorf, Germany: Droste, 1998), 834–46; Adam Tooze, "No Room for Miracles. German Industrial Output in World War II Reassessed," *Geschichte und Gesellschaft* 31, no. 3 (2005): 439–64; Jonas Scherner and Jochen Streb, "Das Ende eines Mythos? Albert Speer und das so genannte Rüstungswunder," *Vierteljahresschrift für Sozial- und Wirtschaftsgeschichte* 93, no. 2 (2006): 172–96; Adam Tooze, *The Wages of Destruction: The Making and Breaking of the Nazi Economy* (New York: Viking, 2007), 429–52, 552–89; Lutz Budraß, Jonas Scherner, and Jochen Streb, "Fixed-Price Contracts, Learning, and Outsourcing: Explaining the Continuous Growth of Output and Labor Productivity in the German Aircraft Industry during the Second World War," *Economic History Review* 63, no. 1 (2010): 107–136; Jonas Scherner, "'Armament in Depth' or 'Armament in Breadth'? German Investment Pattern and Rearmament during the Nazi Period," *Economic History Review* 66, no. 2 (2013): 497–517.

12. Streb and Scherner, "Das Ende eines Mythos?," 193; Budraß, *Flugzeugindustrie und Luftrüstung*, 846.

13. Hironori Sasada, *The Evolution of the Japanese Developmental State: Institutions Locked In by Ideas* (London: Routledge, 2013), 82–84; Satoshi Sasaki, "The Rationalization of Production Management Systems in Japan during World War II," in *World War II and the Transformation of Business Systems*, ed. Jun Sakudō and Takao Shiba (Tokyo: University of Tokyo Press, 1994), 30–54.

14. Mark Wilson, *Destructive Creation: American Business and the Winning of World War II* (Philadelphia: University of Pennsylvania Press, 2016), 63–80 and chapter 4; David Edgerton, *Warfare State: Britain, 1920–1970* (Cambridge, UK: Cambridge University Press), 77.

15. Klaus Segbers, *Die Sowjetunion im Zweiten Weltkrieg: Die Mobilisierung von Verwaltung, Wirtschaft und Gesellschaft im "Großen Vaterländischen Krieg," 1941–1943* (Munich: Oldenbourg, 1987), 89ff., 285ff.; Mark Harrison, *Soviet Planning for Peace and War, 1938–1945* (Cambridge: Cambridge University Press, 1985), chapter 2.

16. Werner Abelshauser, "Modernisierung oder institutionelle Revolution? Koordinaten einer Ortsbestimmung des 'Dritten Reiches' in der deutschen Wirtschaftsgeschichte des 20. Jahrhunderts," in *Wirtschaftsordnung, Staat, und Unternehmen: Neue Forschungen zur Wirtschaftsgeschichte des Nationalsozialismus*, ed. Werner Abelshauser, Jan O. Hesse, and Werner Plumpe (Essen, Germany: Klartext, 2003), 33–34.

17. Information on Werner's career can be gleaned from the files on his 1938 honorary doctorate in engineering, in *Sächsisches Staatsarchiv* (SSAC), Chemnitz, 31050/5873. See also Kukowski and Boch, *Kriegswirtschaft und Arbeitseinsatz bei der Auto-Union AG*, 67–68.

18. See Werner's correspondence (1933–1941) with the Society of Automotive Engineers in SSAC, 31050/749.

19. SSAC, 31030/5873.

20. Kukowski and Boch, *Kriegswirtschaft*, 67–68. Werner's name does not appear in the central party registry, which is retained in the federal archives in Berlin. However, at least one correspondent addressed Werner as "Pg." (party comrade): SSAC, 31050/789, fol. 36, Böttger to Werner, October 24, 1942.

21. Werner urged his colleagues "to set aside their differences and work together to solve the problem of Volkswagen as quickly as possible" in a meeting of the association on October 29, 1936, as quoted in Yale Sterling Library (YSL-GM), New Haven, CT, Box 15, folder 18333ff., RDA circular, November 4, 1936.

22. SSAC: 31050/1042; 31050/316.

23. Paul Erker, *Industrie-Eliten in der NS-Zeit: Anpassungsbereitschaft und Eigeninteresse von Unternehmen in der Rüstungs- und Kriegswirtschaft, 1936–1945* (Passau, Germany: Wissenschaftsverlag, 1993); Gerhard Hirschfeld and Tobias Jersak, eds., *Karrieren im Nationalsozialismus: Funktionseliten zwischen Mitwirkung und Distanz* (Frankfurt: Campus Verlag, 2004); Karl-Heinz Ludwig, *Technik und Ingenieure im Dritten Reich* (Düsseldorf, Germany: Droste, 1974).

24. Götz Aly and Susanne Heim, *Architects of Annihilation: Auschwitz and the Logic of Destruction* (Princeton, NJ: Princeton University Press, 2002).

25. Mommsen and Grieger, *Das Volkswagenwerk und seine Arbeiter*, assembles extensive evidence that Porsche supported Nazi occupation policies and vigorously took advantage of the wartime forced-labor system. Incongruously, the authors nevertheless describe Porsche as "apolitical." For a critique along these lines see Mary Nolan, review of *Das Volkswagenwerk und seine Arbeiter*, by Mommsen and Grieger, *International Labor and Working-Class History* 55 (Spring 1999): 149–54. On von Braun see Rainer Esfeld, *Mondsüchtig: Wernher von Braun und die Geburt der Raumfahrt aus dem Geist der Barbarei* (Hamburg: Rowohlt, 1996).

26. SSAC, 31050/1635, Report of the Werner Commission, 1937.

27. SSAC, 31050/5878, "Handakte Dr. Werners zur Rationalisierung der Automobilindustrie 1938–1939." A version of this talk is reproduced in William Werner, "Wir brauchen Sonder-Werkzeugmaschinen!," *Werkstattstechnik und Werksleiter* 36 (1942): 337–43.

28. BA-MA, RL 3/1702, Werner and Bruhn to Koppenberg, November 5, 1940, which cites the Werner memorandum from 1939: "Of about 1700kg of material allotted to the forge for the Junkers Jumo 211 aircraft engine only about 200kg end up as parts in the engine—ca. 540kg = 32% of the material is wasted in the forge; ca. 960kg = 56% of the material end up as scraps in the machine shop!"

29. Daniel Uziel, *Arming the Luftwaffe: The German Aviation Industry in World War II* (Jefferson, NC: McFarland & Company, 2012), 27–28; Charles Sorensen with Samuel T. Williamson, *My Forty Years with Ford* (New York: Norton, 1956), 289 ff.; Reich, *The Fruits of Fascism: Postwar Prosperity in Historical Perspective*, 83–84; Jonathan Zeitlin, "Flexibility and Mass Production at War: Aircraft Manufacture in Britain, the United States, and Germany, 1939–1945," *Technology and Culture* 36, no. 1 (1994): 46–79.

30. BA-MA, RL 3/1702, Werner and Bruhn to Koppenberg, November 5, 1940.

31. Budraß, *Flugzeugindustrie und Luftrüstung in Deutschland*, 705.

32. Budraß, 545–49, 705.

33. Budraß, 713–38.

34. Werner, *Kriegswirtschaft und Zwangsarbeit bei BMW*, 70.

35. BA-MA, RL 3/52, fol. 311–14.

36. Public Records Office (PRO), National Archives, Kew, FO 1078.95, "Bericht über den Stand der Flugmotoren-Fertigung im BMW-Konzern," March 1941.

37. YSL-GM, Box 15, folder 18333ff., note by Lüer, July 15, 1941.

38. Mommsen and Grieger, *Das Volkswagenwerk*, 456.

39. BA-MA, RW 19/1503, fol. 170–82, "Bericht über die Aufgaben des Industrierats," December 12, 1941. Quotes in Budraß, *Flugzeugindustrie*, 711.

40. SSAC, 31050/789, fol. 1 and 139–46; Hans-Joachim Braun, "Aero-Engine Production in the Third Reich," *History of Technology* 14 (1992): 7–8.

41. Budraß, *Flugzeugindustrie*, 715–24. Quotes are from the protocol of a June 26, 1941, meeting of the procurement agencies with Milch: reproduced in Georg Thomas and Wolfgang Birkenfeld, *Geschichte der deutschen Wehr- und Rüstungswirtschaft, 1918–1943/45* (Boppard am Rhein, Germany: Boldt, 1966), 448–51.

42. BA-MA, RW 19/177, fol. 280–86.

43. Werner, *Kriegswirtschaft*, 87.

44. According to Hitler's decree of April 18, 1942, BAL, R3/1547.

45. Gregor Janssen, *Das Ministerium Speer: Deutschlands Rüstung im Krieg* (Frankfurt: Ullstein, 1968), 43–47.

46. See the 1944 memoranda by Hans Kehrl, "Problematische Fragen der industriellen Selbstverantwortung" and "Die Grundlagen der deutschen Wirtschaftslenkung," in BAL, R3/1550, fol. 4963–65 and 4969–75.

47. BAL, R3/1547, "1. Gauleiterrede," February 24, 1942, fol. 35ff.

48. BAL, R3/1381, "Die Selbstverantwortungs- und Selbstverwaltungsorgane der Rüstungswirtschaft" (1944).

49. Braun, "Aero-Engine Production in the Third Reich," 1.

50. BA-MA, RL3/17, GL meeting, November 10, 1942. See also, RL 3/17, GL meeting, November 17, 1942, where Milch assured Werner: "You have my full backing to do what you want. You do not need to heed anyone else."

51. BA-MA: RL 3/15, GL meeting, August 18, 1942; RL 3/17, GL meeting, December 21, 1942; RL 3/17, GL meeting, June 15, 1943.

52. BA-MA, RL 3/18, GL meeting, February 16, 1943.

53. BA-MA, RL 3/21, GL meeting, June 22, 1943.

54. BA-MA, RL 3/21, GL meeting, June 15, 1943.

55. BA-MA, RL 3/16, GL meeting, November 3, 1942.

56. BA-MA, RL 3/17, GL meeting, November 10, 1942.

57. Ulrich Herbert, "Einleitung," in *Europa und der "Reichseinsatz": Ausländische Zivilarbeiter, Kriegsgefangene und KZ-Häftlinge in Deutschland, 1938–1945*, ed. U. Herbert (Essen, Germany: Klartext, 1991), 7–8. The literature on foreign and forced labor during the war is extensive. For overviews see Herbert, *Hitler's Foreign Workers*; Mark Spoerer, *Zwangsarbeit unter dem Hakenkreuz: Ausländische Zivilarbeiter, Kriegsgefangene und Häftlinge im Deutschen Reich und im besetzten Europa, 1939–1945* (Munich: DVA, 2001).

58. On foreign labor and labor coercion in the aviation industry, see Budraß, *Flugzeugindustrie*, 767–88; Uziel, "Between Industrial Revolution and Slavery."

59. Quoted in Hachtmann, "Fordism and Unfree Labor," 502.

60. BA-MA, RL 3/19, GL meeting, March 2 1943; quoted in Gregor, *Daimler-Benz in the Third Reich*, 122.

61. GL meeting, March 31, 1944; quoted in Uziel, "Between Industrial Revolution and Slavery," 291.

62. Quoted in Gregor, *Daimler-Benz*, 123.

63. Quoted in Werner, *Kriegswirtschaft*, 163.

64. The following is based on Werner, *Kriegswirtschaft*, 168–216.

65. BA-MA, RL3/2310, "Gesamtüberblick." This percentage was on par with other branches of the armaments industries, though the ratio of foreigners was considerably higher in construction (45.5 percent), coal and steel (54 percent), and roads and fortifications built under the Organisation Todt (85 percent).

66. Werner, *Kriegswirtschaft*, 64, 187, 196.

67. BA-MA, RL3/2310, Industrierat to Milch, November 10, 1943; Frydag to Milch, November 18, 1943; Werner to Milch, November 19, 1943.

68. After Lutz Budraß and Manfred Grieger, "Die Moral der Effizienz: Die Beschäftigung von KZ-Häftlingen am Beispiel des Volkswagenwerks und der Henschel-Flugzeug-Werke," *Jahrbuch für Wirtschaftsgeschichte* 34, no. 2 (1993): 121–23, 126–32.

69. A point made forcefully by Budraß and Grieger, "Die Moral der Effizienz," 130–31.

70. See for the following Budraß, *Flugzeugindustrie*, 818–46; Adam Tooze, "No Room for Miracles"; Budraß, Scherner, and Streb, "Fixed-Price Contracts."

71. Budraß, *Flugzeugindustrie*, 832–33.

72. Werner, *Kriegswirtschaft*, 205.

73. Budraß, *Flugzeugindustrie*, 829.

74. "Rechenschaftsbericht Speers vom 27. Januar 1945," reprinted in Janssen, *Das Ministerium Speer*, 325–42, here 336.

75. Tooze, "No Room for Miracles", 457.

76. Scherner and Streb, "Das Ende eines Mythos?," 191.

77. Budraß, Scherner, and Streb, "Fixed-Price Contracts," 131.

78. Kohl and Bessel, *Auto-Union und Junkers*, 171.

79. Budraß, Scherner, and Streb, "Fixed-Price Contracts," 131.

80. Quoted in Uziel, "Between Industrial Revolution and Slavery," 298, footnote 52.

81. YSL-GM, Box 15, folder 18333ff., "Bericht über Rationalisierungsmassnahmen," January 16, 1942.

82. Werner, *Kriegswirtschaft*, 145–68.

83. See, e.g., the images in Werner, *Kriegswirtschaft*, 150, 154, 164, 183, 207, 223, 241, 272, 300; Kohl and Bessel, *Auto-Union und Junkers*, 60, 66; Uziel, *Arming the Luftwaffe*, 39, 45, 115, 129, 181.

84. Quoted in Uziel, "Between Industrial Revolution and Slavery," 287.

85. As suggested at this chapter's outset, to say that the late-war boom was "the result of an inevitable development" and would have happened "even without Speer" (Streb and Scherner, "Das Ende eines Mythos?," 193) seems to overstate the case. Did the Milch-Speer reforms, which were implemented by technocrats like Werner, really make no difference? Would output and productivity increases equally have occurred if the entire system of arms supervision, the "self-responsibility of industry," had simply packed up and shut down in 1942? This seems

implausible. The focus of research should move on from Speer to a more detailed analysis of how the political economy of total war worked on the mesolevel.

86. This conclusion is widely accepted: Richard Overy, *Why the Allies Won* (New York: Norton, 1995); Mark Harrison, ed., *The Economics of World War II: Six Great Powers in International Comparison* (Cambridge, UK: Cambridge University Press, 1998); Tooze, *Wages of Destruction*.

87. On the deliberate American effort to protect the civilian economy see Wilson, *Destructive Creation*, 147–48.

88. American engine output in 1941 was 58,181, and 256,912 in 1944: Overy, *The Air War*, 150.

89. Wilson, *Destructive Creation*, 257.

90. "Kleinwagen-Odyssee," *Der Spiegel*, February 12, 1958, 22.

91. Bellamy, *Absolute War*, 287–92, 303–4; Harrison, *Soviet Planning for Peace and War*, 51, 64; quote from Klaus Segbers, *Die Sowjetunion im Zweiten Weltkrieg*, 37.

92. Harrison, *Soviet Planning for Peace and War*, 118; Mark Harrison, "The Economics of World War II: An Overview," in *The Economics of World War II*, 15–16.

93. A point made by Tooze, *Wages of Destruction*, 671–85, and echoed by Jonas Scherner, "Die Grenzen der Informationsbeschaffung, -transfer und -verarbeitung in der deutschen Wehr- und Kriegswirtschaftsverwaltung im Dritten Reich," *Jahrbuch für Wirtschaftsgeschichte* 56, no. 1 (2015): 134.

94. See, e.g., Nikolai A. Voznesenskii, *The Economy of the USSR during World War II* (Washington, DC: Public Affairs, 1947).

95. On Soviet rearmament and mobilization planning see Walter S. Dunn, *The Soviet Economy and the Red Army 1930–1945* (Westport, CT: Greenwood 1995); Lennart Samuelson, *Plans for Stalin's War Machine: Tukhachevskii and Military-Economic Planning 1925–1941* (Basingstoke, UK: Macmillan, 2000); Nikolai Simonov, "*Mobpodgotovka*: Mobilization Planning in Interwar Industry," in *The Soviet Defense-Industry Complex from Stalin to Khrushchev*, ed. John Barber and Mark Harrison (Basingstoke, UK: Macmillan, 2000), 205–22; Mark Harrison, ed., *Guns and Rubles: The Defense Industry in the Stalinist State* (New Haven, CT: Yale University Press, 2008).

96. R.W. Davies, "Planning for Mobilization: The 1930s," in *Guns and Rubles*, 146.

97. As argued by Lennart Samuelson, *Tankograd: The Formation of a Soviet Company Town: Cheliabinsk, 1900–1950s* (London: Palgrave, 2011), chapters 6 and 7.

98. R. W. Davies and Mark Harrison, "Defence Spending and Defence Industry in the 1930s," in *Soviet Defense-Industry Complex*, 70–98; Scherner, "'Armament in Depth' or 'Armament in Breadth'?"

99. Harrison, *Soviet Planning in Peace and War*, 128; Samuelson, *Tankograd*, 193–95.

100. Harrison, *Soviet Planning in Peace and War*, 131, 138; Mark Harrison, *Accounting for War: Soviet Production, Employment, and the Defence Burden, 1940–1945* (Cambridge, UK: Cambridge University Press, 1996), 67–73.

101. See Mark Harrison, "Wartime Mobilization: A German Comparison," in *The Soviet Defense-Industry Complex*, 99–117.

102. Harrison, *Soviet Planning*, 82ff.; Harrison, *Accounting for War*, 121ff.

103. *Tsentral'nyi arkhiv Nizhegorodskoi oblasti* (TsANO), Nizhnii Novgorod, f. 2435, o.9, d. 46; A. A. Gordin, *Gor'kovskii Avtomobil'nyi Zavod: Istoriia i sovremennost'*, *1932–2012* (Nizhnii Novgorod: Kvarts, 2012), 110.

104. Lifshits's report is in TsANO, f. 2435, o.9, d.58.

105. BA-MA, RL3/51, fol.1259–61, "Überblick über die entscheidenden Angriffsziele in der S.U.," June 4, 1943.

106. Gordin, *Gor'kovskii Avtomobil'nyi Zavod*, 143.

107. TsANO, f.2435: o.1, d.178, l.149f.; o.9. d.68, *otchetnyi doklad* 1943; o.9, d.78, *ob"iasnitel'naia zapiska* 1944; o.9, d.87, l.1.

108. TsANO, f. 2435, o.1, d.178, l. 149.

109. TsANO, f. 2435, o.7, d.26; Gordin, *Gor'kovskii Avtomobil'nyi Zavod*, 117.

110. On Stakhanovism's post-Purge shedding of grassroots radicalism and record chasing, and its realignment with the goals of factory management see Lewis Siegelbaum, *Stakhanovism and the Politics of Productivity in the USSR, 1935–1941* (Cambridge, UK: Cambridge University Press, 1988), chapter 7; "new Soviet intelligentsia" (p. 275).

111. TsANO, f. 2435, o.9, d. 87, ll.40ff.

112. BA-MA, RL 3/24, GL meeting, August 24, 1943, fol. 64.

113. Budraß, *Flugzeugindustrie*, 818ff.

114. On the crucial distinction see David Shearer, *Industry, State, and Society in Stalin's Russia, 1926–1934* (Ithaca, NY: Cornell University Press, 1996), 96ff.; see also Harrison, "Wartime Mobilization."

115. Harrison, *Soviet Planning for Peace and War*, 89.

116. BAL, R3/1547, "1. Gauleiterrede," February 24, 1942, fol. 49–50.

117. The speech is reproduced in Hildegard von Kotze and Helmut Krausnick, eds., *"Es spricht der Führer": 7 exemplarische Hitler-Reden* (Gütersloh, Germany: Siegbert Mohn, 1966), 329–68.

118. Hans Kehrl, *Krisenmanager im Dritten Reich: 6 Jahre Frieden, 6 Jahre Krieg. Erinnerungen* (Düsseldorf, Germany: Droste, 1973), 393.

119. As stated by Speer in a speech to Labor Front representatives, August 4, 1942: BAL, R3/1547.

120. Ludolf Herbst, *Der Totale Krieg und die Ordnung der Wirtschaft* (Munich: Oldenbourg, 1982), 320.

121. Voznesenskii, *Economy of the USSR*, 92.

122. Segbers, *Die Sowjetunion im Zweiten Weltkrieg*, 285–89.

123. "Organizatsiia potochnogo proizvodstva na GAZ imena Molotova v dni Velikoi Otechestvennoi Voiny," in TsANO, f. 2435, o.1, d.178.

Conclusion: Refashioning Fordism under American Hegemony

1. Charles S. Maier, "The Politics of Productivity: Foundations of American International Economic Policy after World War II," in *In Search of Stability: Explorations in Historical Political Economy*, ed. C. S. Maier (Cambridge, UK: Cambridge University Press, 1987), 121–152; Mark Rupert, *Producing Hegemony: The Politics of Mass Production and American Global Power* (Cambridge, UK: Cambridge University Press, 1995).

2. James T. Sparrow, *Warfare State: World War II Americans and the Age of Big Government* (New York: Oxford University Press, 2011). On the unions' acceptance of the tripartite compromises between government, business, and labor see Nelson Lichtenstein, *Labor's War at Home: The CIO during World War II* (Cambridge, UK: Cambridge University Press, 1982); Rupert, *Producing Hegemony*, chapter 5.

3. Roosevelt's "Arsenal of Democracy" fireside chat of December 1940 can be found at https://en.wikisource.org/wiki/Roosevelt%27s_Fireside_Chat,_29_December_1940.

4. Christy Borth, *Masters of Mass Production* (New York: Bobbs-Merrill, 1945), 13–15. See also Eric Larrabee, "The Doctrine of Mass Production," in *American Perspectives: The National Self-Image in the Twentieth Century*, ed. Robert Ernest Spiller and Eric Larrabee (Cambridge, MA: Harvard University Press, 1961), 178–94.

5. Peter Drucker, "Henry Ford: Success and Failure," *Harper's Magazine* 195 (June 1947): 1–8. Drucker's *Concept of the Corporation* (New York: John Day, 1946) was based on a study of GM's managerial organization during the war. In it, Drucker set out to explore what he called "the relationship between the big-business corporation and a free industrial society" (p. viii). On Drucker see Nils Gilman, "The Prophet of Post-Fordism: Peter Drucker and the Legitimation of the Corporation," in *American Capitalism: Social Thought and Political Economy in the Twentieth Century*, ed. Nelson Lichtenstein (Philadelphia: University of Pennsylvania Press, 2006), 109–31; Christian Olaf Christiansen, *Progressive Business: An Intellectual History of the Role of Business in American Society* (Oxford, UK: Oxford University Press, 2015), 75–83.

6. On the managerial overhaul see Allan Nevins and Frank Ernest Hill, *Ford: Decline and Rebirth, 1933–1962* (New York: Scribner's, 1962), 317–45; David Hounshell, "Ford Automates: Technology and Organization in Theory and Practice," *Business and Economic History* 24, no. 1 (1995): 59–71. Hounshell notes that Nevins and Hill neglected "how difficult applying the General Motors model to Ford proved to be" and "provide little or no indication of the struggle waged within Ford" (p. 60) in the phase of reorganization. See also the material in BFRC, Acc. 881, Box 5, folder "Organization and Administration—Reorganization," where Henry II invokes Drucker's inspiration: "At that time a book had just been published by a fellow called Drucker on General Motors' organization. I was very anxious that [Ford] should become a line and staff organization and divisionalized, rather than having a purely centralized organization."

7. Quoted in Christian Kleinschmidt, *Der produktive Blick: Wahrnehmung amerikanischer und japanischer Management- und Produktionsmethoden durch deutsche Unternehmer 1950–1985* (Berlin: Akademie, 2002), 64–65. The same ideology infused American productivity missions in Japan: Jennifer M. Miller, *Cold War Democracy: The United States and Japan* (Cambridge, MA: Harvard University Press, 2019), 227–43.

8. Giuliana Gemelli, "American Influence on European Management Education: The Role of the Ford Foundation," in *Management Education and Competitiveness: Europe, Japan, and the United States*, ed. Rolv Petter Amdam (London: Routledge, 1996), 38–68; Miller, *Cold War Democracy*, 266–70.

9. Quoted in Henry B. Wend, "'But the German Manufacturer Doesn't Want Our Advice': West German Labor and Business and the Limits of American Technical Assistance, 1950–54," in *Catching Up with America: Productivity Missions and the Diffusion of American Economic and Technological Influence after the Second World War*, ed. Dominique Barjot (Paris: Presses de

L'Université de Paris-Sorbonne, 2002), 133. On the ambiguous impact of Marshall Plan productivity initiatives see also Jacqueline McGlade, "Americanization: Ideology or Process? The Case of the United States Technical Assistance and Productivity Programme," in *Americanization and Its Limits: Reworking US Technology and Management in Post-war Europe and Japan*, ed. Jonathan Zeitlin and Gary Herrigel (Oxford, UK: Oxford University Press, 2000), 53–75. Also cf. Volker Berghahn, *The Americanization of West German Industry 1945–1973* (Cambridge, UK: Cambridge University Press, 1986), 250–59.

10. Reinhard Neebe, "Technologietransfer und Außenhandel in den Anfängen der Bundesrepublik Deutschland," *Vierteljahreshefte für Sozial- und Wirtschaftsgeschichte* 76, no. 1 (1989): 49–75.

11. Charles S. Maier, "The Two Postwar Eras and the Conditions for Stability in Twentieth-Century Western Europe," in *In Search of Stability*, 153–84; Adam Tooze, "Reassessing the Moral Economy of Post-war Reconstruction: The Terms of the West German Settlement in 1952," *Past and Present* (2011), Supplement 6, 47–70; Volker Wellhöner, *"Wirtschaftswunder," Weltmarkt, westdeutscher Fordismus: Der Fall Volkswagen* (Münster, Germany: Westfälisches Dampfboot, 1996), 21–39, 62–67; Christoph Buchheim, *Westdeutschland und die Weltwirtschaft 1945–1958* (Munich: Oldenbourg, 1990), chapter 4; Tony Judt, *Postwar: A History of Europe since 1945* (New York: Penguin, 2005), 326.

12. Wellhöner, *"Wirtschaftwunder,"* 77–87; Heidrun Edelmann, *Heinz Nordhoff und Volkswagen: Ein deutscher Unternehmer im amerikanischen Jahrhundert* (Göttingen, Germany: Vandenhoek und Ruprecht, 2003), 192.

13. Werner Abelshauser, "Two Kinds of Fordism: On the Differing Roles of the Automobile Industry in the Development of the Two German States," in *Fordism Transformed: The Development of Production Methods in the Automobile Industry*, ed. Haruhito Shiomi and Kazuo Wada (New York: Oxford University Press, 1995), 279.

14. As Nordhoff put it in his inaugural lecture on "Industrial and Economic Leadership" at the Technical University of Bern on November 29, 1955: Heinrich Nordhoff, *Reden und Aufsätze: Zeugnisse einer Ära* (Düsseldorf, Germany: Econ, 1992), 172–73.

15. For perspectives on postwar Volkswagen and various assessments of the Nazi legacy see Reich, *The Fruits of Fascism: Postwar Prosperity in Historical Perspective*, chapter 5; Steven Tolliday, "Enterprise and State in the West German Wirtschaftswunder: Volkswagen and the Automobile Industry, 1939–62," *Business History Review* 69, no. 3 (1995): 273–330; Abelshauser, "Two Kinds of Fordism"; Edelmann, *Heinz Nordhoff*; Bernhard Rieger, *The People's Car: A Global History of the Volkswagen Beetle* (Cambridge, MA: Harvard University Press, 2013), chapters 3 and 4.

16. Tolliday, "Enterprise and State," 327–45. When the Economics Ministry insisted on a sale of Volkswagen stock in 1961, Nordhoff justified a Beetle price increase by pointing to the new burden of dividends: Reich, *Fruits of Fascism*, 195.

17. Quoted in Edelmann, *Heinz Nordhoff*, 193.

18. Edelmann, 155–62.

19. Quoted in Wellhöner, *"Wirtschaftswunder,"* 111.

20. On automation see David Noble, *Forces of Production: A Social History of Automation* (New York: Knopf, 1984); David Hounshell, "Automation, Transfer Machinery, and Mass Production in the U.S. Automobile Industry in the Post-World War Era," *Enterprise and Society* 1, no. 1 (2000): 100–38.

21. Quoted in Wellhöner, *"Wirtschaftswunder,"* 123.

22. Wellhöner, 131.

23. UVW, 174/1590/1, Höhne file; 69/166, interviews with Höhne and Werner.

24. BFRC, Acc. 662, "Report on Russian Engineering and Automation, December 1955"; another version of the report can be found in Acc. 1660, Box 140.

25. For a compelling overview of the incipient Cold War from a Soviet perspective see Vladimir A. Pechatnov, "The Soviet Union and the World, 1944–1953," in *The Cambridge History of the Cold War*, ed. Melvyn P. Leffler and Odd Arne Westad (New York: Cambridge University Press, 2012), 90–111. On the return to the Stalinist development logic see Philip Hanson, *The Rise and Fall of the Soviet Economy: An Economic History of the USSR Since 1945* (London: Longman, 2003), 25–26, 30–42; Oscar Sanchez-Sibony, *Red Globalization: The Political Economy of the Soviet Cold War from Stalin to Khrushchev* (Cambridge, UK: Cambridge University Press, 2014), 73–74.

26. To be precise, in 1947, at the height of the famine, grain exports declined but did not cease: Michael Ellman, "The 1947 Soviet Famine and the Entitlement Approach to Famines," *Cambridge Journal of Economics* 24, no. 5 (2000): 603–30. On the famine and the enduring misery in the countryside see also Elena Zubkova, *Russia after the War: Hopes, Illusions, and Disappointments, 1945–1957*, trans. Hugh Ragsdale (Armonk, NY: Sharpe, 1998), 40–50, 59–67.

27. James G. Richter, *Khrushchev's Double Bind: International Pressures and Domestic Coalition Politics* (Baltimore: Johns Hopkins University Press, 1994), 77–81, 88–89; see also Yakov Feygin, "Reforming the Cold War State: Economic Thought, Internationalization, and the Politics of Soviet Reform, 1955–1985" (PhD dissertation, University of Pennsylvania, 2017), 37–38, 59–60.

28. Hanson, *Rise and Fall of the Soviet Economy*, 48–52.

29. Ellman, "1947 Soviet Famine," 620. Hanson cites estimates that put per capita consumption growth for the entire Stalin period (1928–1953) at as low as 3.7 percent and compares them with 44.6 percent consumption growth under Khrushchev (1953–1964): Hanson, *Rise and Fall of the Soviet Economy*, 65.

30. Hanson, *Rise and Fall of the Soviet Economy*, 34, 85, 122.

31. Anatolii Strelianyi, "Khrushchev and the Countryside," in *Nikita Khrushchev*, ed. William Taubman, Sergei Khrushchev, and Abbott Gleason (New Haven, CT: Yale University Press, 2000), 114.

32. Lewis Siegelbaum, *Cars for Comrades: The Life of the Soviet Automobile* (Ithaca, NY: Cornell University Press, 2008), 218–19.

33. Quoted in Siegelbaum, *Cars for Comrades*, 225.

34. George Holliday, *Technology Transfer to the USSR, 1928–1937 and 1966–1975* (Boulder, CO: Westview, 1974), 140.

35. On VAZ see Holliday, *Technology Transfer to the USSR*, 137–54; Siegelbaum, *Cars for Comrades*, chapter 3.

36. For concise summaries see Philip Hanson, *Trade and Technology in Soviet-Western Relations* (New York: Columbia University Press, 1981), 49–80; Charles Feinstein, "Technical Progress and Technology Transfer in a Centrally Planned Economy: The Experience of the USSR, 1917–87," in *Chinese Technology Transfer in the 1990s: Current Experience, Historical Problems and International Perspectives*, ed. Charles Feinstein and Christopher Howe (Cheltenham, UK: Edward Elgar, 1997), 62–81.

37. These are the core arguments of Sanchez-Sibony, *Red Globalization*.

38. Stephen Kotkin, "Kiss of Debt: The East Bloc Goes Borrowing," in *The Shock of the Global: The 1970s in Perspective*, ed. Niall Ferguson, Charles S. Maier, Erez Manela, and Daniel Sargent (Cambridge, MA: Harvard University Press, 2010), 80–93.

BIBLIOGRAPHY

Archival Materials
German Archives

BAL	*Bundesarchiv* Berlin-Lichterfelde
NS 6	NSDAP *Parteikanzlei*
R 3	*Reichsministerium für Rüstung und Kriegsproduktion* (Speer)
R 43 II	*Reichskanzlei, 1933–1945*
BA-MA	*Bundesarchiv-Militärarchiv, Freiburg i. Br.*
RL 3	*Generalluftzeugmeister* (Milch)
SAH	*Staatsarchiv* Hamburg
622–1/153	*Nachlass Krogmann*
SSAC	*Sächsisches Staatsarchiv* Chemnitz
31050	Auto-Union AG
UVW	*Unternehmensarchiv Volkswagen*, Wolfsburg
67/185	*Akte* Daimler-Benz
69/8	*Akte Volkswagensparerprozess*
69/166–68	Interviews for *Small Wonder*
69/178	*Fließarbeit im VWW 1943*
69/219	*Akte Popp* (BMW)
453/1	*Gezuvor*

Personal Files/*Bestand Rückwanderer*

Italian Archives

FAT	Fiat Archives, Turin
Fondo URSS	

Russian Archives

RGAE	*Rossiiskii gosudarstvennyi arkhiv ekonomiki*, Moscow
Fond 7260	*Vato, 1929–1932*

Fond 7297   NKTP

Fond 7622   Gutap

TsANO   *Tsentral'nyi arkhiv nizhegorodskoi oblasti*, Nizhnii Novgorod

Fond 2431   *Avtostroi*

Fond 2435   Gaz

TsMAMLS   *Tsentral'nyi moskovskii arkhiv-muzei lichnykh sobranii*, Moscow

Fond 86   Kriger files

UK Archives

PRO   Public Records Office, National Archives, Kew

FO   Foreign Office records

US Archives

BFRC   Benson Ford Research Center, Dearborn, MI

Acc. 1   Henry Ford personal papers

Acc. 6   Edsel B. Ford office papers

Acc. 38   Charles Sorensen papers

Acc. 64   Liebold papers

Acc. 65   Oral history project

Acc. 199   Russian Students Series

Acc. 285   Henry Ford office papers (Ernst Liebold)

Acc. 390   Accounting (Wibel)

Acc. 531   Amtorg

Acc. 572   Nevins and Hill research papers

Acc. 712   Foreign purchasing records

Acc. 818   Amtorg

FWDb   Ford-Werke database

HBL   Harvard Business School, Baker Library, Allston, MA
Alfred D. Chandler Papers

NARA   National Archives and Records Administration, College Park, MD

RG 165   Military Intelligence Division

RG 242   Captured German records

RG 243   United States Strategic Bombing Survey

RG 319   Federal Bureau of Investigation

YSL-GM   Yale Sterling Library, New Haven, CT

MS 1799   General Motors files

Printed Primary Sources

Arnold, Lucien, and Fay Faurote. *Ford Methods and the Ford Shops*. New York: Engineering Magazine Company, 1915.

Automobile Manufacturers Association. *Automobile Facts and Figures: 1937 Edition*. Detroit: Automobile Manufacturers Association, 1937.

Backe, Herbert. *Das Ende des Liberalismus*. Berlin: Reichsnährstand Verlagsanstalt, 1938.

Barclay, Hartley W. *Ford Production Methods*. New York: Harper, 1936.

Beasley, Norman. *Knudsen, A Biography*. New York: McGraw-Hill, 1947.

Bek, Aleksandr. "Takova dolzhnost' (vospominaniia Dybetsa)." *Novyi mir* 7 (1969): 106–68.

Beliaev, N. *Genri Ford*. Moscow: Zhurnal'no-gazetnoe ob"edinenie, 1935.

Benjamin, Walter. "Paris—Capitale du XIXème siècle." In *Das Passagen-Werk*, 60–77. Frankfurt: Suhrkamp, 1982.

———. "Paris, Hauptstadt des 19. Jahrhunderts." In *Illuminationen: Ausgewählte Schriften*, 185–200. Frankfurt: Suhrkamp, 2001.

Betz, Louis. *Das Volksauto: Rettung oder Untergang der deutschen Automobilindustrie?* Stuttgart: Petri, 1931.

Borth, Christy. *Masters of Mass Production*. New York: Bobbs-Merrill, 1945.

Brockdorff, Alexander Graf. *Amerikanische Weltherrschaft?* Berlin: Albrecht, 1929.

Bron, Saul. *Soviet Economic Development and American Business*. New York: Liveright, 1930.

Brown, Donaldson. *Centralized Control with Decentralized Responsibilities*. New York: American Management Association, 1927.

———. "Pricing Policy in Relation to Financial Control: Tuning Up General Motors." *Management Administration* 7, no. 3 (1924): 283–86.

———. *Some Reminiscences of an Industrialist*. Easton, PA: Hive Publishing Co., 1958.

Bücher, Karl. "Das Gesetz der Massenproduktion." *Zeitschrift für die gesamte Staatswissenschaft* 66, no. 3 (1910): 429–44.

Condliffe, John B. "Die Industrialisierung der wirtschaftlich rückständigen Länder." *Weltwirtschaftliches Archiv* 37 (1933): 335–59.

Coudenhove-Kalergi, Richard Nicolaus Graf von. *Pan-Europa*. Vienna: Pan-Europa Verlag, 1923.

Davies, R. W., Oleg Khlevniuk, E. A. Rees, Liudmila P. Kosheleva, and Larisa A. Rogovaya, eds. *The Stalin-Kaganovich Correspondence, 1931–36*. New Haven, CT: Yale University Press, 2003.

DeGeer, Sten. "The American Manufacturing Belt." *Geografisker Annaler* 9 (1927): 233–359.

De Stefani, Alberto. *Autarchia ed antiautarchia*. Città di Castello, Italy: Unione ArtiGrafiche, 1935.

Documents on German Foreign Policy, 1918–1945: From the Archives of the German Foreign Ministry, Series D (1937–1945). 13 vols. Washington, DC: Government Printing Office, 1949–64.

Dodge v. Ford Motor Co., 170 N.W. 668 (Michigan State Court, 1919).

Domarus, Max. *Hitler: Reden und Proklamationen, 1932–1945*. 2 vols. Neustadt an der Aisch, Germany: VDS, 1962–63.

Douglas, C. H. *Economic Democracy*. London: Palmer, 1920.

———. *Social Credit*. London: Eyre and Spottiswoode, 1924.

Drucker, Peter F. *Concept of the Corporation*. New York: John Day, 1946.

———. "Henry Ford: Success and Failure." *Harper's Magazine* (June 1947): 1–8.

Ermanskii, Osip A. *Legenda o Forde*. Moscow: Gosizdat, 1925.

———. *Nauchnaia organizatsiia truda i proizvodstva i sistema Teilora*. Moscow: Gosizdat, 1923.

———. "Predislovie." In *Fordizm: Amerikanskaia organizatsiia proizvodstva*, edited by N. S. Rozenblit, 5–13. Moscow: Ekonomicheskaia Zhizn', 1925.

———. *Teoriia i praktika ratsionalizatsii*. Moscow: Gosizdat, 1927.

———. *Theorie und Praxis der Rationalisierung*. Vienna: Verlag f. Literatur und Politik, 1928.

———. *Wissenschaftliche Betriebsorganisation und Taylor-System*. Berlin: Karl Dietz, 1925.

Faldix, Gustav. *Henry Ford als Wirtschaftspolitiker*. Munich: Pfeiffer, 1925.

Feder, Gottfried. *Das Programm der NSDAP und seine weltanschaulichen Grundlagen*. Munich: Eher, 1927.

———. *Der deutsche Staat auf nationaler und sozialer Grundlage*. Munich: Eher, 1933.

Ford, Genri. *Moia zhizn', moi dostizheniia*. Leningrad: Vremia, 1924.

———. *Segodnia i zavtra*. Moscow: Gostekhizdat, 1926.

Ford, Henry. "Mass Production." In *Encyclopedia Britannica*, 13th edition (1926). (Text written by William J. Cameron but published under the name of Henry Ford.) Reprinted in *The Rise and Fall of Mass Production*, vol. 1, edited by Steven Tolliday, 157–63. Cheltenham, UK: Edward Elgar, 1988.

Ford, Henry. "A Rich Man Should Not Have Any Money." *Cosmopolitan* (March 1932): 52–53, 164–65.

Ford, Henry. *Waga isshō to jigyō: Henrī Fōdo jijoden* [*My Life and Work: The Autobiography of Henry Ford*], translated by Katō Saburō. Tokyo: Henridō, 1927.

Ford, Henry, with Samuel Crowther. *Moving Forward*. Garden City, NY: Doubleday, Doran & Company, 1930.

———. *My Life and Work*. Garden City, NY: Doubleday, Page & Co., 1922.

———. *Today and Tomorrow*. Garden City, NY: Doubleday, Page & Co., 1926.

———. "Why I Favor Five Days' Work at Six Days' Pay." *World's Work* (October 1926): 613–16.

Foster, William, and Waddill Catchings. *Profits*. Cambridge, MA: Riverside, 1925.

Fried, Ferdinand. *Autarkie*. Jena, Germany: Diedrichs, 1932.

———. *Das Ende des Kapitalismus*. Jena, Germany: Diedrichs, 1931.

Gastev, Aleksei. "Fordism." In *Bol'shaia sovetskaia entsiklopediia*, vol. 58. Moscow: Gosudarstvennyi Institut Sovetskaia Entsiklopediia, 1936.

———. *Kak nado rabotat': Prakticheskoe vvedenie v nauku organizatsii truda*. Moscow: Ekonomika, 1972 [1928].

General Motors Corporation. *Twenty-Ninth Annual Report: Year Ended December 31, 1937*. New York: General Motors Corporation, 1938.

———. *The War Effort of the Overseas Division*. New York: General Motors Overseas Operations, 1944.

Gottl-Ottlilienfeld, Friedrich von. *Fordismus: Über Industrie und Technische Vernunft*. Jena, Germany: Fischer, 1926.

———. *Vom Sinn der Rationalisierung*. Jena, Germany: Fischer, 1929.

Gramsci, Antonio. *Amerika und Europa*, edited by Thomas Barfuss. Hamburg: Argument, 2007.

———. *Quaderno 22: Americanismo e fordismo*, edited by Franco de Felice. Turin, Italy: Einaudi, 1978.

———. *Selections from the Prison Notebooks*, edited by Quintin Hoare and Geoffrey Nowell-Smith. New York: International Publishers, 1971.

Gramsci, Antonio, and Tania Schucht. *Lettere, 1926–1935*, edited by Aldo Natoli and Chiara Daniele. Turin, Italy: Einaudi, 1997.

Guyot, Yves. Review of *Today and Tomorrow*, by Henry Ford with Samuel Crowther. *Journal des économistes* 85 (1926): 145–68.

Hess, Rudolf. *Briefe, 1908–1933*, edited by Wolf Rüdiger Hess. Munich: Langen Müller, 1987.

Hitler, Adolf. *Mein Kampf*. Munich: Zentralverlag der NSDAP, 1938. Reprint of the 1927 edition.

———. *Reden, Schriften, Anordnungen: Februar 1925 bis Januar 1933*, edited by Institut für Zeitgeschichte. 12 vols. Munich: Saur, 1992ff.

Kehrl, Hans. *Krisenmanager im Dritten Reich: 6 Jahre Frieden, 6 Jahre Krieg; Erinnerungen*. Düsseldorf, Germany: Droste, 1973.

Kennedy, E. D. *The Automobile Industry: The Coming of Capitalism's Favorite Child*. New York: Reynal & Hitchcock, 1941.

Keynes, John Maynard. *The Economic Consequences of the Peace*. New York: Harcourt, Brace, and Howe, 1920.

———. "National Self-Sufficiency." *Yale Review* 22, no. 4 (1933): 755–69.

Khromov, S. S., ed. *Industrializatsiia sovetskogo soiuza: Novye dokumenty, novye fakty, novye podkhody*. 2 vols. Moscow: RAN, 1999.

Kinross, Albert. Review of *My Life and Work*, by Henry Ford with Samuel Crowther. *English Review* 37 (1923): 649–52.

Köttgen, Carl. *Das wirtschaftliche Amerika*. Berlin: VDI Verlag, 1925.

Kotze, Hildegard von, and Helmut Krausnick, eds. *"Es spricht der Führer": 7 exemplarische Hitler-Reden*. Gütersloh, Germany: Mohn, 1966.

Kremmler, H. *Autarkie in der organischen Wirtschaft*. Dresden, Germany: Focken & Oltmans, 1940.

Lavrov, N. S. *Fordizm: Uchenie o proizvodstve veshchei*. Leningrad: n. p., 1928.

———. *Genri Ford i ego proizvodstvo*. Leningrad: Vremia, 1925.

Ledermann, Fred. *Fehlrationalisierung: Der Irrweg der deutschen Automobilindustrie seit der Stabilisierung der Mark*. Stuttgart: Pöschel, 1933.

Lee, John R. "The So-Called Profit-Sharing System in the Ford Plant." *Annals of the American Academy of Political and Social Science* 65, no. 1 (1916): 297–310.

Lih, Lars, Oleg Naumov, and Oleg Khlevniuk, eds. *Stalin's Letters to Molotov*. New Haven, CT: Yale University Press, 1995.

Lobato, José Monteiro. *How Henry Ford Is Regarded in Brazil*. Rio de Janeiro: O Journal, 1926.

Lochner, Louis. *Henry Ford: America's Don Quixote*. New York: International Publishers, 1925. (Published in Russian as Luis Lokhner, *Genri Ford i ego "korabl' mira"* [Leningrad: Vremia, 1925].)

Lüddecke, Theodor. "Amerikanismus als Schlagwort und Tatsache." *Deutsche Rundschau* 56 (March 1930): 214–21.

———. *Das amerikanische Wirtschaftstempo als Bedrohung Europas*. Leipzig, Germany: Paul List, 1925.

———. "Der neue Wirtschaftsgeist!" In *Industrieller Friede: Ein Symposium*, edited by Jerome Davis and Theodor Lüddecke, 9–61. Leipzig, Germany: Paul List, 1928.

Mäckbach, Frank, and Otto Kienzle, eds. *Fliessarbeit. Beiträge zu ihrer Einführung*. Berlin: VDI Verlag, 1926. (Published in Russian as F. Mekkbakh and A. Kintsle, *Rabota nepreryvnym proizvodstvennym potokom* [Moscow: Promizdat, 1927].)

Mertts, L., et al. "GAZ i Ford." *Planovoe khoziaistvo* 6–7 (1932): 258–59.

Mikhailov, Arsenii. *Sistema Forda*. Moscow: Gosizdat, 1930.

Mitrofanova, A. V., ed. *Industrializatsiia SSSR, 1938–1941: Dokumenty i materialy*. Moscow: Nauka, 1973.

Moellendorff, Wichard von. *Konservativer Sozialismus*. Hamburg: Hanseatischer Verlag, 1932.

Moog, Otto. *Drüben steht Amerika*. Braunschweig, Germany: Westermann, 1927.

Mussolini, Benito. *Opera Omnia*, edited by Edoardo Susmel and Duilio Susmel. 36 vols. Florence: La Fenice, 1951–1980.

Nelson, Walter Henry. *Small Wonder: The Amazing Story of the Volkswagen*. Boston: Little, Brown and Co., 1967.

Nordhoff, Heinrich. *Reden und Aufsätze: Zeugnisse einer Ära*. Düsseldorf, Germany: Econ, 1992.

Obolensky-Ossinsky, V. V. [Nikolai Osinskii]. "Planning in the Soviet Union." *Foreign Affairs*, April 1935.

———. "Social Economic Planning in the USSR: The Premises, Nature, and Forms of Social Economic Planning." *Annals of Collective Economy* 7, no. 3 (1931).

Osinskii, Nikolai. *Amerikanskaia avtomobil' ili rossiiskaia telega*. Moscow: Pravda, 1927.

———. *Avtomobilizatsiia SSSR: Stat'i, ocherki, rechi*. Moscow: Gosizdat, 1930.

———. *Mirovoi selskokhoziaistvennyi krizis*. Moscow, 1923.

———. *Ocherki mirovogo selskokhoziaistvennogo rynka*. Moscow, 1925.

Pingree, Hazen S. *Facts and Opinions; or Dangers That Beset Us*. Detroit: F. B. Dickerson Co., 1895.

Pirou, Gaëtan, Werner Sombart, E. F. M. Durbin, E. M. Patterson, and Ugo Spirito, eds. *La crisi del capitalismo*. Florence: G. C. Sansoni, 1933.

Polanyi, Karl. *The Great Transformation: The Political and Economic Origins of Our Time*. Boston: Beacon, 2001. (First published by Farrar & Reinhart, New York, 1944.)

Powderly, Terence. *Thirty Years of Labor, 1859–1889*. Columbus, OH: Excelsior, 1889.

Pound, Arthur. *The Turning Wheel: The Story of General Motors through Twenty-Five Years, 1908–1933*. Garden City, NY: Doubleday, Doran & Co., 1934.

Preussen, Prinz Louis Ferdinand von. *Als Kaiserenkel durch die Welt*. Berlin: Argon, 1952.

Quint, Herbert. *Porsche: Der Weg eines Zeitalters*. Stuttgart: Steingrüben, 1951.

Rabchinskii, L. V. *O sisteme Teilora*. Moscow: Gostekhizdat, 1921.

———. *Printsipy Forda*. Moscow: Gostekhizdat, 1925.

———. *Promkapital i novaia shkola NOT v Amerike*. Moscow: Gostekhizdat, 1922.

Rathenau, Walther. *Die neue Wirtschaft*. Berlin: Fischer, 1919.

Raushenbush, Carl. *Fordism, Ford and the Workers, Ford and the Community*. New York: League for Industrial Democracy, 1937.

Rieppel, Paul. *Ford-Betriebe und Ford-Methoden*. Berlin: Oldenbourg, 1925.

Robinson, Robert. *Black on Red: My Forty-Four Years inside the Soviet Union*. New York: Acropolis, 1988.

Romier, Lucien. *Qui sera le maître: Europe ou Amérique?* Paris: Hachette, 1927.

Rostow, Walt W. *The Stages of Economic Growth: A Non-Communist Manifesto*. Cambridge, UK: Cambridge University Press, 1960.

Rozenblit, N. S. *Fordizm: Amerikanskaia organizatsiia proizvodstva.* Moscow: Ekonomicheskaia Zhizn', 1925.

Rozengol'ts, Arkadii, ed. *Promyshlennost': Sbornik statei po materialam TsKK VKP(b)-NK RKI.* Moscow: Gosizdat, 1930.

Schlesinger, Georg. *Der Daseinskampf der deutschen Automobil-Industrie.* Berlin: RDA, 1925.

Seltzer, Lawrence H. *A Financial History of the Automobile Industry: A Study of the Ways in Which the Leading American Producers of Automobiles Have Met Their Capital Requirements.* Boston: Houghton Mifflin, 1928.

Sloan, Alfred P. "Getting the Facts Is a Keystone of General Motors' Success." *Automotive Industries* 57 (1927): 550–51.

———. "Modern Ideals of Big Business." *World's Work* (October 1926): 695–99.

———. "The Most Important Thing I Ever Learned about Management." *System: The Magazine of Business* 46 (1924): 140–41, 191.

———. *My Years with General Motors,* edited by John McDonald with Catherine Stevens. Garden City, NY: Doubleday, 1963.

Sloan, Alfred P., with Boyden Sparkes. *Adventures of a White-Collar Man.* New York: Doubleday, Doran & Co., 1941.

Sombart, Werner. "Die Wandlungen des Kapitalismus." *Weltwirtschaftliches Archiv* 28 (1928): 243–56.

———. *A New Social Philosophy,* translated by Karl F. Geiser. Princeton, NJ: Princeton University Press, 1937. (First published as *Deutscher Sozialismus* [Berlin: Buchholz & Weisswange, 1934].)

Sorensen, Charles, with Samuel T. Williamson. *My Forty Years with Ford.* New York: Norton, 1956.

Spengler, Oswald. *Preußentum und Sozialismus.* Munich: Beck, 1920.

Stalin, I. V. *Sochineniia.* 13 vols. Moscow: Gosizdat politicheskoi literatury, 1946–1952.

Tarnow, Fritz. *Warum arm sein?* Berlin: Allgemeiner Deutscher Gewerkschaftsbund, 1928.

Taylor, Frederick Winslow. *The Principles of Scientific Management.* New York: Harper & Brothers, 1911.

Trotsky, Leon. *Problems of Everyday Life: Creating the Foundations for a New Society in Revolutionary Russia.* New York: Monad, 1973.

Tugwell, Rexford. Review of *Today and Tomorrow,* by Henry Ford with Samuel Crowther. *Saturday Review of Literature* 111, no. 2 (1926): 17–18.

US Department of Commerce. *Abstract of the Census of Manufacturers 1914.* Washington, DC: Government Printing Office, 1917.

———. *Biennial Census of Manufactures 1937,* vol. 1. Washington, DC: US Government Printing Office, 1939.

US Federal Trade Commission. *Report on Motor Vehicle Industry.* Washington, DC: Government Printing Office, 1939.

US Senate. *Industrial Relations: Final Report and Testimony of the Commission on Industrial Relations.* 11 vols. Washington, DC: Government Printing Office, 1916.

Van Deventer, John H. *Ford Principles and Practice at River Rouge.* New York: Engineering Magazine Co., 1922.

Veblen, Thorstein. *The Engineers and the Price System.* New York: B. W. Huebsch, 1921.

Viner, Jacob. "The Doctrine of Comparative Costs." *Weltwirtschaftliches Archiv* 36 (1932): 356–414.

Voznesenskii, Nikolai A. *The Economy of the USSR during World War II.* Washington, DC: Public Affairs, 1947.

Walcher, Jakob. *Ford oder Marx. Die praktische Lösung der sozialen Frage.* Berlin: Neuer Deutscher Verlag, 1925. (Published in Russian as Iakob Walkher, *Ford ili Marks* [Moscow: Profintern, 1925].)

Weiss, Hilda P. *Abbe und Ford: Kapitalistische Utopien.* Berlin: Prager, 1927. (Published in Russian as Gilda Veis, *Abbe i Ford: Kapitalicheskie utopii* [Moscow: Gosizdat, 1928].)

Werner, William. "Wir brauchen Sonder-Werkzeugmaschinen!," *Werkstatttechnik und Werksleiter* 36 (1942): 337–43.

Witte, Irene Margarete. *Taylor, Gilbreth, Ford. Gegenwartsfragen der amerikanischen und europäischen Arbeitswissenschaft.* Munich: Oldenbourg, 1925. (Published in Russian as I. M. Vitte, *Amerika—Germaniia: Teilor, Dzhil'bret, Ford* [Leningrad: Vremia, 1926].)

Zaslavskii, D. I. "Dva Forda: Predislovie k russkomu izdaniiu." In *Segodnia i zavtra,* 3–14. Leningrad: Vremia, 1926.

Zvezdin, Z. K., and N. I. Kuprianova, eds. *Istoriia industrializatsii Nizhegorodskogo-Gor'kovskogo kraia, 1926–1941.* Gorky: Volgo-viatskoe knizhnoe izdatel'stvo, 1968.

Secondary Literature

Abelshauser, Werner. *Deutsche Wirtschaftsgeschichte seit 1945.* Munich: Beck, 2005.

———. "Kriegswirtschaft und Wirtschaftswunder: Deutschlands wirtschaftliche Mobilisierung für den Zweiten Weltkrieg und die Folgen für die Nachkriegszeit." *Vierteljahreshefte für Zeitgeschichte* 47, no. 4 (1999): 503–38.

———. "Modernisierung oder institutionelle Revolution? Koordinaten einer Ortsbestimmung des 'Dritten Reiches' in der deutschen Wirtschaftsgeschichte." In *Wirtschaftsordnung, Staat und Unternehmen: Neue Forschungen zur Wirtschaftsgeschichte des Nationalsozialismus,* edited by Werner Abelshauser, Jan-Ottmar Hesse, and Werner Plumpe, 33–38. Essen, Germany: Klartext, 2003.

———. "Two Kinds of Fordism: On the Differing Roles of the Automobile Industry in the Development of the Two German States." In *Fordism Transformed: The Development of Production Methods in the Automobile Industry,* edited by Haruhito Shiomi and Kazuo Wada, 269–96. New York: Oxford University Press, 1995.

Aglietta, Michael. *A Theory of Capitalist Regulation: The US Experience,* translated by David Fernbach. London: NLB, 1979.

Aleshina, Polina, et al. *Gor'kovskii Avtomobil'nyi: Ocherk istorii zavoda.* Moscow: Profizdat, 1964.

Allen, Robert C. *Farm to Factory: A Reinterpretation of the Soviet Industrial Revolution.* Princeton, NJ: Princeton University Press, 2003.

Aly, Götz, and Susanne Heim. *Architects of Annihilation: Auschwitz and the Logic of Destruction.* Princeton, NJ: Princeton University Press, 2002.

Amsden, Alice. *Asia's Next Giant: South Korea and Late Industrialization.* New York: Oxford University Press, 1989.

———. *The Rise of "the Rest": Challenges to the West from Late-Industrializing Economies.* Oxford, UK: Oxford University Press, 2001.

Anbinder, Jacob. "Selling the World: Public Relations and the Global Expansion of General Motors, 1922–1940." *Business History Review* 92, no. 3 (2018): 483–507.

Anderson, Perry. *The Antinomies of Antonio Gramsci: With a New Preface.* London: Verso, 2017.

Antonio, Robert J., and Alessandro Bonanno. "A New Global Capitalism? From 'Americanism and Fordism' to 'Americanization-Globalization.'" *American Studies* 41, no. 2/3 (2000).

Austin, Richard C. *Building Utopia: Erecting Russia's First Modern City, 1930.* Kent, OH: Kent State University Press, 2004.

Bähr, Johannes, and Ralf Banken, eds. *Wirtschaftssteuerung durch Recht im Nationalsozialismus: Studien zur Entwicklung des Wirtschaftsrechts im Interventionsstaat des "Dritten Reiches."* Frankfurt: Klostermann, 2006.

Bailes, Kendall E. "Alexei Gastev and the Soviet Controversy over Taylorism, 1918–24." *Soviet Studies* 29, no. 3 (1977): 373–94.

———. "The American Connection: Ideology and the Transfer of American Technology to the Soviet Union, 1917–1941." *Comparative Studies in Society and History* 23, no. 3 (1981): 421–48.

———. "The Politics of Technology: Stalin and Technocratic Thinking among Soviet Engineers." *American Historical Review* 79, no. 2 (1974): 445–69.

———. *Technology and Society under Lenin and Stalin: Origins of the Soviet Technical Intelligentsia, 1917–1941.* Princeton, NJ: Princeton University Press, 1978.

Ball, Alan M. *Imagining America: Influence and Images in Twentieth-Century Russia.* New York: Rowman & Littlefield, 2003.

Banken, Ralf. "Die wirtschaftspolitische Achillesferse des 'Dritten Reiches': Das Reichswirtschaftsministerium und die NS-Außenwirtschaftspolitik, 1933–39." In *Das Reichswirtschaftsministerium in der NS-Zeit: Wirtschaftsordnung und Verbrechenskomplex*, edited by Albrecht Ritschl, 111–232. Berlin: De Gruyter, 2016.

Baranowski, Shelly. *Strength through Joy: Consumerism and Mass Tourism in the Third Reich.* Cambridge, UK: Cambridge University Press, 2007.

Baratta, Giorgio. "Americanismo e fordismo." In *Le parole di Gramsci: Per un lessico dei Quaderni del Carcere*, edited by Fabio Frosini and Guido Liguori, 15–34. Rome: Carocci, 2004.

Barkai, Avraham. *Nazi Economics: Ideology, Theory, and Policy.* New Haven, CT: Yale University Press, 1990.

Bauman, Zygmunt. *Modernity and the Holocaust.* Cambridge, UK: Polity, 1989.

Bavaj, Riccardo. *Die Ambivalenz der Moderne im Nationalsozialismus: Eine Bilanz der Forschung.* Munich: Oldenbourg, 2003.

Beaudreau, Bernard C. *Mass Production, the Stock Market Crash, and the Great Depression: The Macroeconomics of Electrification.* Westport, CT: Greenwood, 1996.

Beckert, Sven. "American Danger: US Empire, Eurafrica, and the Territorialization of Capitalism." *American Historical Review* 122, no. 4 (2017): 1137–70.

Beissinger, Mark R. *Scientific Management, Socialist Discipline, and Soviet Power.* Cambridge, MA: Harvard University Press, 1988.

Bellamy, Chris. *Absolute War: Soviet Russia in the Second World War.* New York: Vintage, 2008.

Ben-Ghiat, Ruth. *Fascist Modernities: Italy 1922–1945.* Berkeley: University of California Press, 2001.

Bennett, Douglas C., and Kenneth Evan Sharpe. *Transnational Corporations versus the State: The Political Economy of the Mexican Auto Industry.* Princeton, NJ: Princeton University Press, 1985.

Bera, Matt. *Lobbying Hitler: Industrial Associations between Democracy and Dictatorship.* New York: Berghahn Books, 2016.

Berg, Peter. *Deutschland und Amerika, 1918–1929: Über das deutsche Amerikabild der zwanziger Jahre*. Lübeck, Germany: Matthiesen, 1963.

Berghahn, Volker. *The Americanisation of West German Industry, 1945–1973*. Cambridge, UK: Cambridge University Press, 1986.

Berk, Gerald. "Corporate Liberalism Reconsidered: A Review Essay." *Journal of Policy History* 3, no. 1 (1991): 70–84.

Bigazzi, Duccio. *La grande fabbrica: Organizzazione industriale e modello americano alla Fiat dal Lingotto a Mirafiori*. Milan: Feltrinelli, 2000.

Biggart, John. "Bukharin and the Origins of the 'Proletarian Culture' Debate." *Soviet Studies* 39, no. 2 (1987): 229–46.

———. "Bukharin's Theory of Cultural Revolution." In *The Ideas of Nikolai Bukharin*, edited by Anthony Kemp-Welch, 131–58. Oxford, UK: Clarendon Press, 1992.

Biggs, Lindy. *The Rational Factory: Architecture, Technology, and Work in America's Age of Mass Production*. Baltimore: Johns Hopkins University Press, 1996.

Billstein, Reinhold, Karola Fings, and Anita Kugler. *Working for the Enemy: Ford, General Motors, and Forced Labor in Germany during the Second World War*. New York: Berghahn Books, 2000.

Black, Edwin. *IBM and the Holocaust: The Strategic Alliance between Nazi Germany and America's Most Powerful Corporation*. Washington, DC: Dialog, 2009.

Bokarev, I. P. "Rossiiskaia ekonomika v mirovoi ekonomicheskoi sisteme (konets XIX—30-e gg. XX veka)." In *Ekonomicheskaia istoriia Rossii XIX-XX vv.: Sovremennyi vzgliad*, edited by B. A. Vinogradov, 433–57. Moscow: ROSSPEN, 2000.

Bönig, Jürgen. *Die Einführung von Fließarbeit in Deutschland bis 1933: Zur Geschichte einer Sozialinnovation*. Münster, Germany: LIT Verlag, 1993.

Bonin, Hubert, Yannick Lung, and Steven Tolliday, eds. *Ford, 1903–2003: The European History*. 2 vols. Paris: PLAGE, 2003.

Boyer, Robert, et al., eds. *Between Imitation and Innovation: The Transfer and Hybridization of Productive Models in the International Automobile Industry*. New York: Oxford University Press, 1998.

Brandist, Craig. "The Cultural and Linguistic Dimensions of Hegemony: Aspects of Gramsci's Debt to Early Soviet Cultural Policy." *Journal of Romance Studies* 12, no. 3 (2012): 24–43.

Brantz, Rennie W. "German-American Friendship: The Carl Schurz Vereinigung, 1926–1942." *International History Review* 11, no. 2 (1989): 229–51.

Braun, Hans-Joachim. "Aero-Engine Production in the Third Reich." *History of Technology* 14 (1992): 1–15.

Braverman, Harry. *Labor and Monopoly Capital: The Degradation of Work in the Twentieth Century*. New York: Monthly Review Press, 1974.

Brechtken, Magnus. *Albert Speer: Eine deutsche Karriere*. Munich: Siedler, 2017.

Brendon, Piers. *The Dark Valley: A Panorama of the 1930s*. New York: Knopf, 2000.

Brinkley, Alan. *The End of Reform: New Deal Liberalism in Recession and War*. New York: Vintage, 1995.

Brown, Kate. *A Biography of No Place: From Ethnic Borderland to Soviet Heartland*. Cambridge, MA: Harvard University Press, 2005.

Bryan, Ford R. *Henry's Lieutenants*. Detroit: Wayne State University Press, 1993.

———. *Rouge: Pictured in Its Prime*. Dearborn, MI: Wayne State University Press, 2003.

Buchheim, Christoph. *German Industry in the Nazi Period*. Stuttgart: Steiner, 2008.

———. "Unternehmen in Deutschland und NS-Regime, 1933–45: Versuch einer Synthese." *Historische Zeitschrift* 282, no. 1 (2006): 351–90.

———. *Westdeutschland und die Weltwirtschaft, 1945–1958*. Munich: Oldenbourg, 1990.

Buchheim, Christoph, and Jonas Scherner. "Anmerkungen zum Wirtschaftssystem des 'Dritten Reiches.'" In *Wirtschaftsordnung, Staat und Unternehmen: Neuere Forschungen zur Wirtschaftsgeschichte des Nationalsozialismus,* edited by Werner Abelshauser, Jan-Otmar Hesse, and Werner Plumpe, 81–97. Essen, Germany: Klartext, 2003.

———. "Corporate Freedom of Action in Nazi Germany: A Response to Peter Hayes." *Bulletin of the German Historical Institute* 45 (2009): 29–42.

Budraß, Lutz. *Flugzeugindustrie und Luftrüstung in Deutschland 1918–1945*. Düsseldorf, Germany: Droste, 1998.

Budraß, Lutz, and Manfred Grieger. "Die Moral der Effizienz: Die Beschäftigung von KZ-Häftlingen am Beispiel des Volkswagenwerks und der Henschel-Flugzeug-Werke." *Jahrbuch für Wirtschaftsgeschichte* 34, no. 2 (1993): 89–136.

Budraß, Lutz, Jonas Scherner, and Jochen Streb. "Fixed-Price Contracts, Learning, and Outsourcing: Explaining the Continuous Growth of Output and Labor Productivity in the German Aircraft Industry during the Second World War." *Economic History Review* 63, no. 1 (2009): 107–36.

Bütow, Tobias. "Der 'Freundeskreis Himmler': Ein Netzwerk im Spannungsfeld zwischen Wirtschaft, Politik und staatlicher Administration." Diploma thesis, Free University Berlin, 2004.

Cantwell, John, and Yanli Zhang. "The Co-evolution of International Business Connections and Domestic Technological Capabilities: Lessons from the Japanese Catch-Up Experience." *Transnational Corporations* 25, no. 2 (2009): 37–68.

Carr, Edward H., and R. W. Davies. *Foundations of a Planned Economy, 1926–1929*. New York: Macmillan, 1971.

Casey, Robert H. *The Model T: A Centennial History*. Baltimore: John Hopkins University Press, 2008.

Castronovo, Valerio. *Giovanni Agnelli: La FIAT dal 1899 al 1945*. Turin, Italy: Einaudi, 1977.

Centeno, Miguel, Atul Kohli, Deborah J. Yashar, and Dinsha Mistree, eds. *States in the Developing World*. Cambridge, UK: Cambridge University Press, 2017.

Chandler, Jr., Alfred D. *Giant Enterprise: Ford, General Motors, and the Automobile Industry*. New York: Harcourt, Brace & World, 1964.

———. *Strategy and Structure: Chapters in the History of the American Industrial Enterprise*. Cambridge, MA: MIT Press, 1962.

———. *The Visible Hand: The Managerial Revolution in American Business*. Cambridge, MA: Harvard University Press, 1977.

Chandler, Jr., Alfred D., and Stephen Salsbury. *Pierre S. Du Pont and the Making of the Modern Corporation*. New York: Harper & Row, 1971.

Cheremukhin, Anton, Mikhail Golosov, Sergei Guriev, and Aleh Tsyvinski. "Was Stalin Necessary for Russia's Economic Development?" NBER Working Paper No. 19425, Cambridge, MA, September 2013.

Christiansen, Christian Olaf. *Progressive Business: An Intellectual History of the Role of Business in American Society*. Oxford, UK: Oxford University Press, 2015.

Ciocca, Pierluigi, and Gianni Toniolo, eds. *L'economia italiana nel periodo fascista*. Bologna, Italy: Mulino, 1976.

Clarke, Sally H. *Trust and Power: Consumers, the Modern Corporation, and the Making of the United States Automobile Market*. New York: Cambridge University Press, 2007.

Cohen, Yves. "The Modernization of Production in the French Automobile Industry: A Photographic Essay." *Business History Review* 65, no. 4 (1991): 754–80.

———. "The Soviet Fordson: Between the Politics of Stalin and the Philosophy of Ford, 1924–1932." In *Ford, 1903–2003: The European History*, vol. 2, edited by Hubert Bonin, Yannick Lung, and Steven Tolliday, 531–553. Paris: PLAGE, 2003.

Cook, Eli. *The Pricing of Progress: Economic Indicators and the Capitalization of American Life*. Cambridge, MA: Harvard University Press, 2017.

Cusumano, Michael. *The Japanese Automobile Industry: Technology and Management at Nissan and Toyota*. Cambridge, MA: Harvard University Press, 1985.

Dalrymple, Dana D. "The American Tractor Comes to Soviet Agriculture: The Transfer of a Technology." *Technology and Culture* 5, no. 2 (1964): 191–214.

David-Fox, Michael. "Multiple Modernities vs. Neo-traditionalism: On Recent Debates in Russian and Soviet History." *Jahrbücher für Geschichte Osteuropas* 54, no. 4 (2006): 535–55.

Davidson, Alistair. *Antonio Gramsci: Towards an Intellectual Biography*. London: Merlin, 1977.

Davies, R. W. *Crisis and Progress in the Soviet Economy, 1931–33*. Basingstoke, UK: Macmillan, 1996.

———. "Planning for Mobilization: The 1930s." In *Guns and Rubles: The Defense Industry in the Stalinist State*, edited by Mark Harrison, 118–55. New Haven, CT: Yale University Press, 2008.

———. *The Soviet Economy in Turmoil, 1929–1930*. Cambridge, MA: Harvard University Press, 1989.

Davies, R. W., and Mark Harrison. "Defence Spending and Defence Industry in the 1930s." In *The Soviet Defence-Industry Complex from Stalin to Khrushchev*, edited by John Barber and Mark Harrison, 70–98. Basingstoke, UK: Palgrave Macmillan, 2000.

Davies, R. W., Mark Harrison, Oleg Khlevniuk, and Steven G. Wheatcroft. *The Industrialization of Soviet Russia: The Soviet Economy and the Approach of War, 1937–39*. London: Palgrave Macmillan, 2018.

Davies, R. W., Mark Harrison, and Steven G. Wheatcroft, eds. *The Economic Transformation of the Soviet Union, 1913–1945*. Cambridge, UK: Cambridge University Press, 1994.

Davies, Sarah, and James Harris. *Stalin's World: Dictating the Soviet Order*. New Haven, CT: Yale University Press, 2014.

Davis, Donald Finlay. *Conspicuous Production: Automobiles and Elites in Detroit, 1899–1933*. Philadelphia: Temple University Press, 1988.

Day, Richard B. *Leon Trotsky and the Politics of Economic Isolation*. Cambridge, UK: Cambridge University Press, 1973.

Day, Uwe. *Silberpfeil und Hakenkreuz: Autorennsport im Nationalsozialismus*. Berlin: Bebra, 2005.

de Grazia, Victoria. *Irresistible Empire: America's Advance through Twentieth Century Europe*. Cambridge, MA: Harvard University Press, 2005.

Depretto, Jean-Paul. "Un grand chantier du premier plan quinquennal soviétique: Kuznetsk-stroï." *Genèses* 39, no. 2 (2000): 5–26.

Devine, Jr., Warren D. "From Shafts to Wires: Historical Perspectives on Electrification." *Journal of Economic History* 43, no. 2 (1983): 347–72.

Djelic, Marie-Laure. *Exporting the American Model: The Post-war Transformation of European Business*. New York: Oxford University Press, 1998.

Dobb, Maurice. *Soviet Economic Development since 1917*. London: Routledge & Kegan Paul, 1948.

Dobrokhotov, V. I. *Gor'kovskii Avtomobil'nyi*. Moscow: Mysl', 1981.

Dohan, Michael. "The Economic Origins of Soviet Autarky, 1927/28–1934." *Slavic Review* 35, no. 4 (1976): 603–35.

———. "Soviet Foreign Trade in the NEP Economy and Soviet Industrialization Strategy." PhD dissertation, Massachusetts Institute of Technology, 1969.

Dohan, Michael, and Edward Hewett. *Two Studies in Soviet Terms of Trade, 1918–1970*. Bloomington: International Development and Research Center, Indiana University, 1973.

Donges, Alexander. *Die Vereinigten Stahlwerke AG im Nationalsozialismus: Konzernpolitik zwischen Marktwirtschaft und Staatswirtschaft*. Paderborn, Germany: Schöningh, 2014.

Dunn, Walter S. *The Soviet Economy and the Red Army 1930–1945*. Westport, CT: Greenwood, 1995.

Ebi, Michael. *Export um jeden Preis: Die deutsche Exportförderung von 1932–1938*. Stuttgart: Steiner, 2004.

Edelmann, Heidrun. "Heinrich Nordhoff: Ein deutscher Manager in der Automobilindustrie." In *Deutsche Unternehmer zwischen Kriegswirtschaft und Wiederaufbau: Studien zur Erfahrungsbildung von Industrie-Eliten*, edited by Paul Erker and Toni Pierenkemper, 19–52. Munich: Oldenbourg, 1999.

———. *Heinz Nordhoff und Volkswagen: Ein deutscher Unternehmer im amerikanischen Jahrhundert*. Göttingen, Germany: Vandenhoek und Ruprecht, 2003.

———. *Vom Luxusgut zum Gebrauchsgegenstand: Die Geschichte der Verbreitung von Personenkraftwagen in Deutschland*. Frankfurt: VDA, 1989.

Edgerton, David. *The Shock of the Old: Technology and Global History since 1900*. New York: Oxford University Press, 2007.

———. *Warfare State: Britain, 1920–1970*. New York: Cambridge University Press, 2006.

Edsforth, Ronald. *Class Conflict and Cultural Consensus: The Making of a Mass Consumer Society in Flint, Michigan*. New Brunswick, NJ: Rutgers University Press, 1987.

Eichengreen, Barry. *Golden Fetters: The Gold Standard and the Great Depression, 1919–1939*. New York: Oxford University Press, 1995.

Eifert, Christiane. "Antisemit und Autokönig: Henry Fords Autobiographie und ihre deutsche Rezeption in den 1920er-Jahren." *Zeithistorische Forschungen* 2 (2009): 209–29.

Ellman, Michael. "The 1947 Soviet Famine and the Entitlement Approach to Famines." *Cambridge Journal of Economics* 24, no. 5 (2000): 603–30.

Ellwood, David. *The Shock of America: Europe and the Challenge of the Century*. Oxford, UK: Oxford University Press, 2012.

Erker, Paul. "Ernst Heinkel: Die Luftfahrtindustrie im Spannungsfeld von technologischem Wandel und politischem Umbruch." In *Deutsche Unternehmer zwischen Kriegswirtschaft und*

Wiederaufbau: Studien zur Erfahrungsbildung von Industrie-Eliten, edited by Paul Erker and Toni Pierenkemper, 217–90. Munich: Oldenbourg, 1999.

———. *Industrie-Eliten in der NS-Zeit: Anpassungsbereitschaft und Eigeninteresse von Unternehmen in der Rüstungs- und Kriegswirtschaft, 1936–1945*. Passau, Germany: Wissenschaftsverlag, 1994.

Erlich, Alexander. *The Soviet Industrialization Debate*. Cambridge, MA: Harvard University Press, 1960.

Esch, Elizabeth. *The Color Line and the Assembly Line: Managing Race in the Ford Empire*. Berkeley: University of California Press, 2018.

Esfeld, Rainer. *Mondsüchtig: Wernher von Braun und die Geburt der Raumfahrt aus dem Geist der Barbarei*. Hamburg: Rowohlt, 1996.

Evans, Peter B. *Embedded Autonomy: States and Industrial Transformation*. Princeton, NJ: Princeton University Press, 1995.

Farber, David. *Everybody Ought to Be Rich: The Life and Times of John J. Raskob, Capitalist*. New York: Oxford University Press, 2013.

———. *Sloan Rules: Alfred P. Sloan and the Triumph of General Motors*. Chicago: University of Chicago Press, 2002.

Fear, Jeffrey. "War of the Factories." In *The Cambridge History of the Second World War*, vol. 3, edited by Michael Geyer and Adam Tooze, 94–121. Cambridge, UK: Cambridge University Press, 2015.

Feinstein, Charles. "Technical Progress and Technology Transfer in a Centrally Planned Economy: The experience of the USSR, 1917–87." In *Chinese Technology Transfer in the 1990s: Current Experience, Historical Problems and International Perspectives*, edited by Charles Feinstein and Christopher Howe, 62–81. Cheltenham, UK: Edward Elgar, 1997.

Ferguson, Niall. "Constraints and Room for Manoeuvre in the German Inflation of the Early 1920s." *Economic History Review* 49, no. 4 (1996): 635–66.

Feygin, Yakov. "Reforming the Cold War State: Economic Thought, Internationalization, and the Politics of Soviet Reform, 1955–1985." PhD dissertation, University of Pennsylvania, 2017.

Field, Alexander J. *A Great Leap Forward: 1930s Depression and US Economic Growth*. New Haven, CT: Yale University Press, 2011.

Findlay, Ronald, and Kevin H. O'Rourke. *Power and Plenty: Trade, War, and the World Economy in the Second Millennium*. Princeton, NJ: Princeton University Press, 2007.

Fink, Leon. *Workingmen's Democracy: The Knights of Labor and American Politics*. Urbana: University of Illinois Press, 1983.

Fitzpatrick, Sheila. "Cultural Revolution as Class War." In *The Cultural Front: Power and Culture in Revolutionary Russia*, edited by Sheila Fitzpatrick, 115–48. Ithaca, NY: Cornell University Press, 1992.

———. *Education and Social Mobility in the Soviet Union, 1921–1934*. Cambridge, UK: Cambridge University Press, 1979.

———. "Ordzhonikidze's Takeover of Vesenkha: A Case Study in Soviet Bureaucratic Politics." *Soviet Studies* 37, no. 2 (1985): 153–72.

———. "The Soft Line in Culture and Its Enemies, 1922–1927." *Slavic Review* 33, no. 2 (1974): 267–87.

———. "Workers against Bosses: The Impact of the Great Purges on Labor-Management Relations." In *Making Workers Soviet: Power, Class, and Identity*, edited by Lewis H. Siegelbaum and Ronald G. Suny, 311–40. Ithaca, NY: Cornell University Press, 1994.

Flik, Reiner. *Von Ford lernen? Automobilbau und Motorisierung in Deutschland bis 1933*. Cologne: Böhlau, 2001.

Foreman-Peck, James. "The American Challenge of the Twenties: Multinationals and the European Motor Industry." *Journal of Economic History* 42, no. 4 (1982): 865–81.

Freeland, Robert F. *The Struggle for Control of the Modern Corporation: Organizational Change at General Motors, 1924–1970*. New York: Cambridge University Press, 2001.

Frei, Norbert. "Die Wirtschaft des 'Dritten Reiches.' Überlegungen zu einem Perspektivenwechsel." In *Unternehmen im Nationalsozialismus: Zur Historisierung einer Forschungskonjunktur*, edited by Norbert Frei and Tim Schanetzky, 9–24. Göttingen, Germany: Wallstein, 2010.

Fridenson, Patrick. "Ford as a Model for French Carmakers." In *Ford, 1903–2003: The European Story*, vol. 1, edited by Hubert Bonin, Yannick Lung, and Steven Tolliday, 125–52. Paris: PLAGE, 2003.

Frieden, Jeffry. *Global Capitalism: Its Fall and Rise in the Twentieth Century*. New York: Norton, 2006.

Fritzsche, Peter. "Nazi Modern." *Modernism/Modernity* 3, no. 1 (1996): 1–22.

Fritzsche, Peter, and Jochen Hellbeck. "The New Man in Stalinist Russia and Nazi Germany." In *Beyond Totalitarianism: Stalinism and Nazism Compared*, edited by Michael Geyer and Sheila Fitzpatrick, 302–44. Cambridge, UK: Cambridge University Press, 2009.

Fukuyama, Francis. "The End of History?" *National Interest* 16 (1989): 3–18.

Galambos, Louis. "The Emerging Organizational Synthesis in Modern American History." *Business History Review* 44, no. 3 (1970): 279–90.

Galster, George. *Driving Detroit: The Quest for Respect in the Motor City*. Philadelphia: University of Pennsylvania Press, 2012.

Gassert, Philipp. *Amerika im Dritten Reich: Ideologie, Propaganda, und Volksmeinung, 1933–1945*. Stuttgart: Franz Steiner, 1997.

———. "The Spectre of Americanization: Western Europe in the American Century." In *The Oxford Handbook of Postwar European History*, edited by Dan Stone, 182–200. Oxford, UK: Oxford University Press, 2012.

———. "'Without Concessions to Marxist or Communist Thought': Fordism in Germany, 1923–1939." In *Transatlantic Images and Perspectives: Germany and America since 1776*, edited by David E. Barclay and Elisabeth Glaser-Schmidt, 217–42. Cambridge, UK: Cambridge University Press, 1997.

Gassert, Philipp, and Daniel S. Mattern. *The Hitler Library: A Bibliography*. Westport, CT: Greenwood, 2001.

Gemelli, Giuliana. "American Influence on European Management Education: The Role of the Ford Foundation." In *Management Education and Competitiveness: Europe, Japan, and the United States*, edited by Rolv Petter Amdam, 38–68. London: Routledge, 1996.

Geyer, Michael, and Sheila Fitzpatrick, eds. *Beyond Totalitarianism: Stalinism and Nazism Compared*. Cambridge, UK: Cambridge University Press, 2009.

Gilman, Nils. *Mandarins of the Future: Modernization Theory in Cold War America*. Baltimore: Johns Hopkins University Press, 2003.

Gilman, Nils. "Modernization Theory Never Dies." *History of Political Economy* 50, no. S1 (2018): 133–51.

———. "The Prophet of Post-Fordism: Peter Drucker and the Legitimation of the Corporation." In *American Capitalism: Social Thought and Political Economy in the Twentieth Century*, edited by Nelson Lichtenstein, 109–31. Philadelphia: University of Pennsylvania Press, 2006.

Goodwyn, Lawrence. *Democratic Promise: The Populist Movement in America.* New York: Oxford University Press, 1976.

Gordin, A. A. *Gor'kovskii Avtomobil'nyi Zavod: Istoriia i sovremennost', 1932–2012.* Nizhnii Novgorod: Kvarts, 2012.

Gourevitch, Alex. *From Slavery to the Cooperative Commonwealth: Labor and Republican Liberty in the Nineteenth Century.* New York: Cambridge University Press, 2015.

Graham, Loren. *The Ghost of the Executed Engineer: Technology and the Fall of the Soviet Union.* Cambridge, MA: Harvard University Press, 1993.

Grandin, Greg. *Fordlandia: The Rise and Fall of Henry Ford's Forgotten Jungle City.* New York: Metropolitan Books, 2009.

Graziosi, Andrea. "'Building the First System of State Industry in History.' Piatakov's VSNKh and the Crisis of the NEP, 1923–1926." *Cahiers du Monde Russe et Soviétique* 32, no. 4 (1991): 539–80.

———. "Foreign Workers in Soviet Russia, 1920–40: Their Experience and Their Legacy." *International Labor and Working-Class History* 33 (1988): 38–59.

———. "Les famines soviétiques de 1931–1933 et le Holodomor ukrainien. Une nouvelle interprétation est-elle possible et quelles en seraient les conséquences?" *Cahiers du monde russe et soviétique* 46, no. 3 (2005): 453–72.

Greenberg, Udi. "Revolution from the Right: Against Equality." In *The Cambridge History of Modern European Thought*, edited by Peter Gordon and Warren Breckman, 233–58. Cambridge, UK: Cambridge University Press, 2019.

Greenleaf, William. *Monopoly on Wheels: Henry Ford and the Selden Automobile Patent.* Detroit: Wayne State University Press, 1961.

Greenstein, David E. "Assembling Fordizm: The Production of Automobiles, Americans, and Bolsheviks in Detroit and Early Soviet Russia." *Comparative Studies in Society and History* 56, no. 2 (2014): 259–89.

Gregor, Neil. *Daimler-Benz in the Third Reich.* New Haven, CT: Yale University Press, 1998.

Gregory, Paul. *The Political Economy of Stalinism: Evidence from the Soviet Secret Archives.* Cambridge, UK: Cambridge University Press, 2004.

Griffin, Roger. *Modernism and Fascism: The Sense of a New Beginning under Mussolini and Hitler.* Basingstoke, UK: Palgrave Macmillan, 2007.

Gross, Stephen. *Export Empire: German Soft Power in Southeastern Europe, 1890–1945.* Cambridge, UK: Cambridge University Press, 2015.

———. "The Nazi Economy." In *A Companion to Nazi Germany*, edited by Shelley Baranowski, Armin Nolzen, and Claus-Christian Szejnmann, 263–79. Hoboken, NJ: Wiley Blackwell, 2018.

Hachtmann, Rüdiger. *Das Wirtschaftsimperium der Deutschen Arbeitsfront, 1933–1945.* Göttingen, Germany: Wallstein, 2012.

———. "Fordism and Unfree Labor: Aspects of the Work Deployment of Concentration Camp Prisoners in German Industry between 1941 and 1944." *International Review of Social History* 55, no. 3 (2010): 485–513.

Haggard, Stephan. *Developmental States.* Cambridge, UK: Cambridge University Press, 2018.

Halfin, Igal. *From Darkness to Light: Class Consciousness and Salvation in Revolutionary Russia.* Pittsburgh, PA: University of Pittsburgh Press, 2000.

Hammes, David L. *Harvesting Gold: Thomas Edison's Experiment to Re-invent American Money.* Silver City, NM: Richard Mahler, 2012.

Hanson, Philip. *The Rise and Fall of the Soviet Economy: An Economic History of the USSR since 1945.* London: Longman, 2003.

———. *Trade and Technology in Soviet-Western Relations.* New York: Columbia University Press, 1981.

Harris, James. "Encircled by Enemies: Stalin's Perceptions of the Capitalist World, 1918–1941." *Journal of Strategic Studies* 30, no. 3 (2007): 513–45.

———. *The Great Urals: Regionalism and Evolution of the Soviet System.* Ithaca, NY: Cornell University Press, 1999.

Harrison, Mark. *Accounting for War: Soviet Production, Employment, and the Defence Burden, 1940–1945.* Cambridge, UK: Cambridge University Press, 1996.

———, ed. *The Economics of World War II: Six Great Powers in International Comparison.* Cambridge, UK: Cambridge University Press, 1998.

———. "Foundations of the Soviet Command Economy, 1917 to 1941." In *The Cambridge History of Communism, Vol. 1: World Revolution and Socialism in One Country*, edited by Silvio Pons and Stephen Smith, 327–47. Cambridge, UK: Cambridge University Press, 2017.

———, ed. *Guns and Rubles: The Defense Industry in the Stalinist State.* New Haven, CT: Yale University Press, 2008.

———. "Resource Mobilization for World War II: The U.S.A., U.K., U.S.S.R., and Germany, 1938–1945." *Economic History Review* 41, no. 2 (1988): 171–92.

———. *Soviet Planning for Peace and War, 1938–1945.* Cambridge, UK: Cambridge University Press, 1985.

———. "Wartime Mobilization: A German Comparison." In *The Soviet Defence-Industry Complex from Stalin to Khrushchev*, edited by John Barber and Mark Harrison, 99–117. Basingstoke, UK: Macmillan, 2000.

Hartley, K. "The Learning Curve and Its Application to the Aircraft Industry." *Journal of Industrial Economics* 13, no. 2 (1965): 122–28.

Hayes, Peter. "Corporate Freedom of Action in Nazi Germany." *Bulletin of the German Historical Institute* 45 (2009): 29–42.

———. *Industry and Ideology: IG Farben in the Nazi Era.* Cambridge, UK: Cambridge University Press, 1987.

Heide, Lars. "Between Parent and 'Child': IBM and Its German Subsidiary, 1910–1945." In *European Business, Dictatorship, and Personal Risk, 1920–1945*, edited by Christopher Kobrak and Per Hansen, 149–73. New York: Berghahn Books, 2004.

Hellbeck, Jochen. *Revolution on My Mind: Writing a Dairy under Stalin.* Cambridge, MA: Harvard University Press, 2006.

Henderson, M. Todd. "Everything Old Is New Again: Lessons from Dodge v. Ford Motor Company." Law & Economics Olin Working Paper No. 373, University of Chicago, December 2007.

Herbert, Ulrich. *Hitler's Foreign Workers: Enforced Foreign Labor in Germany under the Third Reich.* Cambridge, UK: Cambridge University Press, 1997.

Herbst, Ludolf. *Der totale Krieg und die Ordnung der Wirtschaft*. Munich: Oldenbourg, 1982.

———."Gab es ein nationalsozialistisches Wirtschaftssystem?" In *Das Reichswirtschaftsministerium in der NS-Zeit: Wirtschaftsordnung und Verbrechenskomplex*, edited by Albrecht Ritschl, 611–34. Berlin: De Gruyter, 2016.

Herf, Jeffrey. *Reactionary Modernism: Technology, Culture, and Politics in Weimar and the Third Reich*. Cambridge, UK: Cambridge University Press, 1984.

Hesketh, Bob. *Major Douglas and Alberta Social Credit*. Toronto: University of Toronto Press, 1997.

Hett, Benjamin C. *The Death of Democracy: Hitler's Rise to Power and the Downfall of the Weimar Republic*. New York: Henry Holt, 2018.

Hirschfeld, Gerhard, and Tobias Jersak, eds. *Karrieren im Nationalsozialismus: Funktionseliten zwischen Mitwirkung und Distanz*. Frankfurt: Campus, 2004.

Hirst, Paul, and Jonathan Zeitlin. "Flexible Specialization vs. Post-Fordism: Theory, Evidence, and Policy Implications." *Economy and Society* 20, no. 1 (1991): 1–55.

Hobsbawm, Eric. *Age of Extremes: A History of the 20th Century*. New York: Vintage, 1994.

———, ed. *Gramsci in Europa e in America*. Rome: Sagittari Laterza, 1995.

Hochstetter, Dorothee. *Motorisierung und "Volksgemeinschaft": Das Nationalsozialistische Kraftfahrkorps (NSKK), 1931–1945*. Munich: Oldenbourg, 2005.

Hofmann, Reto. *The Fascist Effect: Japan and Italy, 1915–1952*. Ithaca, NY: Cornell University Press, 2015.

Holli, Melvin. *Reform in Detroit: Hazen Pingree and Urban Politics*. New York: Oxford University Press, 1969.

Holliday, George. *Technology Transfer to the USSR: 1928–1937 and 1966–1975*. Boulder, CO.: Westview, 1974.

Hooker, Clarence. *Life in the Shadows of the Crystal Palace, 1910–1927: Ford Workers in the Model T Era*. Bowling Green, OH: Bowling Green State University Popular Press, 1997.

Hounshell, David. "Automation, Transfer Machinery, and Mass Production in the U.S. Automobile Industry in the Post-World War Era." *Enterprise and Society* 1, no. 1 (2000): 100–38.

———. "Ford Automates: Technology and Organization in Theory and Practice." *Business and Economic History* 24, no. 1 (1995): 59–71.

———. *From the American System to Mass Production, 1800–1932*. Baltimore: Johns Hopkins University Press, 1984.

Hughes, Thomas P. *American Genesis: A Century of Invention and Technological Enthusiasm, 1870–1970*. New York: Viking, 1989.

Imlay, Talbot, and Martin Horn. *The Politics of Industrial Collaboration during World War II: Ford France, Vichy and Nazi Germany*. Cambridge, UK: Cambridge University Press, 2014.

Jacobs, Meg. *Pocketbook Politics: Economic Citizenship in Twentieth-Century America*. Princeton, NJ: Princeton University Press, 2005.

Jacobson, Jon. *When the Soviet Union Entered World Politics*. Berkeley: University of California Press, 1994.

Jacoby, Sanford M. *Employing Bureaucracy: Managers, Unions, and the Transformation of Work in American Industry, 1900–1945*. New York: Columbia University Press, 1985.

James, Harold. *The End of Globalization: Lessons from the Great Depression*. Cambridge, MA: Harvard University Press, 2001.

———. *The German Slump: Politics and Economics, 1924–1936*. Oxford, UK: Oxford University Press, 1986.

Janssen, Gregor. *Das Ministerium Speer. Deutschlands Rüstung im Krieg*. Frankfurt: Ullstein, 1968.

Janssen, Hauke. *Nationalökonomie und Nationalsozialismus: Die deutsche Volkswirtschaftslehre in den dreißiger Jahren*. Marburg, Germany: Metropolis, 2000.

Jessop, Bob. "Fordism and Post-Fordism: A Critical Reformulation." In *Pathways to Regionalism and Industrial Development*, edited by A. J. Scott and M. J. Storper, 58–89. London: Routledge, 1992. (Reprinted with slight revisions in *Beyond the Regulation Approach: Putting Capitalist Economies in Their Place*, edited by Bob Jessop and Ngai-Ling Sum, 43–65. Cheltenham, UK: Edward Elgar, 2006.)

———. "Regulation Theories in Retrospect and Prospect." *Economy and Society* 19, no. 2 (1990): 153–216.

Johnson, Chalmers. *MITI and the Japanese Miracle: The Growth of Industrial Policy, 1925–1975*. Stanford, CA: Stanford University Press, 1982.

Judt, Tony. *Postwar: A History of Europe since 1945*. New York: Penguin, 2005.

Kantorovich, Vladimir. "The Military Origins of Soviet Industrialization." *Comparative Economic Studies* 57, no. 4 (2015): 669–92.

Kantorovich, Vladimir, and A. Wein. "What Did the Soviet Rulers Maximize?" *Europe-Asia Studies* 61, no. 1 (2009): 1579–1601.

Karlsch, Rainer, and Raymond G. Stokes. *Faktor Öl: Die Mineralölwirtschaft in Deutschland 1859–1974*. Munich: Beck, 2003.

Kershaw, Ian. *To Hell and Back: Europe 1914–1949*. New York: Penguin, 2015.

———. "'Working Towards the Führer'. Reflections on the Nature of Hitler's Dictatorship." *Contemporary European History* 2, no. 2 (1993): 103–18.

Kim, Linsu. *Imitation to Innovation: The Dynamics of Korea's Technological Learning*. Cambridge, MA: Harvard Business School Press, 1997.

Klautke, Egbert. *Unbegrenzte Möglichkeiten: "Amerikanisierung" in Deutschland und Frankreich, 1900–1933*. Stuttgart: Steiner, 2003.

Kleinschmidt, Christian. *Der produktive Blick: Wahrnehmung amerikanischer und japanischer Management- und Produktionsmethoden durch deutsche Unternehmer, 1950–1985*. Berlin: Akademie, 2002.

Kohl, Peter, and Peter Bessel. *Auto-Union und Junkers: Geschichte der Mitteldeutschen Motorenwerke*. Stuttgart: Steiner, 2003.

Kohli, Atul. *State-Directed Development: Political Power and Industrialization in the Global Periphery*. Cambridge, UK: Cambridge University Press, 2004.

König, Wolfgang. *Volkswagen, Volksempfänger, Volksgemeinschaft: "Volksprodukte" im Dritten Reich; Vom Scheitern einer nationalsozialistischen Konsumgesellschaft*. Paderborn, Germany: Schöningh, 2004.

Kotkin, Stephen. "Kiss of Debt: The East Bloc Goes Borrowing." In *The Shock of the Global: The 1970s in Perspective*, edited by Niall Ferguson, Charles S. Maier, Erez Manela, and Daniel Sargent, 80–93. Cambridge, MA: Harvard University Press, 2010.

———. *Magnetic Mountain: Stalinism as a Civilization*. Berkeley: University of California Press, 1995.

Kotkin, Stephen. "Modern Times: The Soviet Union and the Interwar Conjuncture." *Kritika: Explorations in Russian and Eurasian History* 2, no. 1 (2001): 111–64.

———. *Stalin: The Paradoxes of Power, 1878–1928*. New York: Penguin, 2015.

Krylova, Anna. "Soviet Modernity: Stephen Kotkin and the Bolshevik Predicament." *Contemporary European History* 23, no. 2 (2014): 167–92.

Kuhn, Arthur J. *GM Passes Ford, 1918–1938: Designing the General Motors Performance-Control System*. University Park: Pennsylvania State University Press, 1986.

Kukowski, Martin, and Rudolf Boch. *Kriegswirtschaft und Arbeitseinsatz bei der Auto-Union AG Chemnitz im Zweiten Weltkrieg*. Stuttgart: Steiner, 2014.

Kümmel, Gerhard. *Transnationale Wirtschaftskooperation und der Nationalstaat: Deutsch-amerikanische Unternehmensbeziehungen in den dreißiger Jahren*. Stuttgart: Steiner, 1995.

Lacey, Robert. *Ford: The Men and the Machine*. Boston: Little Brown & Co., 1986.

Lall, Sanjay. "Technological Capabilities and Industrialization." *World Development* 20, no. 2 (1992): 165 86.

Larrabee, Eric. "The Doctrine of Mass Production." In *American Perspectives: The National Self-Image in the Twentieth Century*, edited by Robert Ernest Spiller and Eric Larrabee, 178–94. Cambridge, MA: Harvard University Press, 1961.

Latham, A. J. H. *The Depression and the Developing World 1914–1939*. London: Croom Helm, 1981.

Lennart, Samuelson. *Plans for Stalin's War Machine: Tukhachevskii and Military-Economic Planning 1925–1941*. Basingstoke, UK: Palgrave Macmillan, 2000.

Levy, Jonathan. "Accounting for Profit and the History of Capital." *Critical Historical Studies* 1, no. 2 (2014): 171–214.

Lewchuk, Wayne. *American Technology and the British Vehicle Industry*. Cambridge, UK: Cambridge University Press, 1987.

———. "Fordist Technology in Britain: The Diffusion of Labour Speed-Up." In *The Transfer of International Technology: Europe, Japan, and the USA in the Twentieth Century*, edited by David Jeremy. Aldershot, UK: Edward Elgar, 1992.

Lewis, Robert. "Foreign Economic Relations." In *The Economic Transformation of the Soviet Union, 1913–1945*, edited by R. W. Davies, Mark Harrison, and Steven G. Wheatcroft, 198–215. Cambridge, UK: Cambridge University Press, 1994.

Lichtenstein, Nelson. *Labor's War at Home: The CIO during World War II*. Cambridge, UK: Cambridge University Press, 1982.

———. *Walter Reuther: The Most Dangerous Man in Detroit*. Urbana: University of Illinois Press, 1995.

Link, Stefan. "The Charismatic Corporation: Finance, Administration, and Shop Floor Management under Henry Ford." *Business History Review* 92, no. 1 (2018): 85–115.

———. "How Might 21st-Century De-globalization Unfold? Some Historical Reflections." *New Global Studies* 12, no. 3 (2018): 343–65.

———. "Rethinking the Ford-Nazi Connection." *Bulletin of the German Historical Institute* 49 (2011): 135–50.

———. Review of *The Age of Catastrophe: A History of the West, 1914–1945*, by Heinrich August Winkler. *Journal of Modern History* 89, no. 3 (2017): 669–70.

Link, Stefan, and Noam Maggor. "The United States as a Developing Nation: Revisiting the Peculiarities of American History," *Past and Present* 246, no. 1 (2020): 269–306.

Link, Werner. *Die amerikanische Stabilisierungspolitik in Deutschland, 1921–32*. Düsseldorf, Germany: Droste, 1970.

Lipietz, Alain. "Behind the Crisis: The Exhaustion of a Regime of Accumulation; A 'Regulation School' Perspective on Some French Empirical Works." *Review of Radical Economics* 18, no. 1–2 (1988): 13–32.

Livingston, James. *Pragmatism and the Political Economy of Cultural Revolution, 1850–1940*. Chapel Hill: University of North Carolina Press, 1994.

Lüdtke, Alf, Inge Marßolek, and Adelheid von Saldern, eds. *Amerikanisierung: Traum und Alptraum im Deutschland des zwanzigsten Jahrhunderts*. Stuttgart: Steiner, 1996.

Ludwig, Karl-Heinz. *Technik und Ingenieure im Dritten Reich*. Düsseldorf, Germany: Droste, 1974.

Macekura, Stephen K., and Erez Manela, eds. *The Development Century: A Global History*. Cambridge, UK: Cambridge University Press, 2018.

Maggor, Noam. "American Capitalism: From the Atlantic Economy to Domestic Industrialization." In *A Companion to the Gilded Age and Progressive Era*, edited by Christopher McKnight Nichols and Nancy C. Unger, 205–214. Hoboken, NJ: Wiley-Blackwell, 2017.

———. *Brahmin Capitalism: Frontiers of Wealth and Populism in America's First Gilded Age*. Cambridge, MA: Harvard University Press, 2017.

Maier, Charles S. "Between Taylorism and Technocracy: European Ideologies and the Vision of Industrial Productivity." *Journal of Contemporary History* 5, no. 2 (1970): 27–61.

———. "Consigning the Twentieth Century to History." *American Historical Review* 105, no. 3 (2000): 807–31.

———. "The Economics of Fascism and Nazism." In *In Search of Stability: Explorations in Historical Political Economy*, edited by C. S. Maier, 70–120. Cambridge, UK: Cambridge University Press, 1987.

———. "The Politics of Productivity: Foundations of American International Economic Policy after World War II." In *In Search of Stability: Explorations in Historical Political Economy*, edited by C. S. Maier, 121–52. Cambridge, UK: Cambridge University Press, 1987.

———. "The Two Postwar Eras and the Conditions for Stability in Twentieth-Century Western Europe." In *In Search of Stability: Explorations in Historical Political Economy*, edited by C. S. Maier, 15–84. Cambridge, UK: Cambridge University Press, 1987.

Malik, Hassan. *Bankers & Bolsheviks: International Finance and the Russian Revolution*. Princeton, NJ: Princeton University Press, 2018.

Manjapra, Kris. *Age of Entanglement: German and Indian Intellectuals across Empire*. Cambridge, MA: Harvard University Press, 2014.

Marchand, Roland. *Advertising the American Dream: Making Way for Modernity, 1920–1940*. Berkeley: University of California Press, 1985.

Markevich, Andrei, and Mark Harrison. "Great War, Civil War, and Recovery: Russia's National Income, 1913 to 1928." *Journal of Economic History* 71, no. 3 (2011): 672–703.

Markevich, Andrei, and Steven Nafziger. "State and Market in Russian Industrialization, 1870–2010." In *The Spread of Modern Industry to the Periphery since 1871*, edited by Kevin H. O'Rourke and Jeffrey G. Williamson, 33–62. Oxford, UK: Oxford University Press, 2017.

Marks, Steven G. "The Russian Experience with Money, 1914–1924." In *Russian Culture in War and Revolution, 1914–22*, vol. 2, edited by Murray Frame, B. I. Kolonitskii, Steven G. Marks, and Melissa K. Stockdale, 121–50. Bloomington, IN: Slavica, 2014.

Martin, Terry. "The 1932–33 Ukrainian Terror: New Documentation on Surveillance and the Thought Process of Stalin." In *Famine-Genocide in Ukraine, 1932–1933: Western Archives, Testimonies and New Research*, edited by Wsevolod W. Isajiw, 97–114. Toronto: Ukrainian-Canadian Research and Documentation Center, 2003.

Mason, Mark. *American Multinationals and Japan: The Political Economy of Capital Controls.* Cambridge, MA: Harvard University Press, 1992.

Matthews, J. Scott. "Nippon Ford." *Michigan Historical Review* 22, no. 2 (1996): 83–102.

May, George S. *A Most Unique Machine: The Michigan Origins of the American Automobile Industry.* Madison: University of Wisconsin Press, 1975.

Mazower, Mark. *Dark Continent: Europe's Twentieth Century.* New York: Knopf, 1998.

McCraw, Thomas K. *American Business, 1920–2000: How It Worked.* Wheeling, IL: Harlan Davidson, 2000.

McGlade, Jacqueline. "Americanization: Ideology or Process? The Case of the United States Technical Assistance and Productivity Programme." In *Americanization and Its Limits: Reworking US Technology and Management in Post-war Europe and Japan*, edited by Jonathan Zeitlin and Gary Herrigel, 53–75. Oxford, UK: Oxford University Press, 2000.

Melnikova-Raich, Sonia. "The Problem with Two 'Unknowns': How an American Architect and a Soviet Negotiator Jump-Started the Industrialization of Russia. Part I: Albert Kahn." *Journal of the Society for Industrial Archeology* 36, no. 2 (2010): 57–80.

———. "The Problem with Two 'Unknowns': How an American Architect and a Soviet Negotiator Jump-Started the Industrialization of Russia. Part II: Saul Bron." *Journal of the Society for Industrial Archeology* 37, no. 1/2 (2011): 5–28.

Merkle, Judith A. *Management and Ideology: The Legacy of the International Scientific Management Movement.* Berkeley: University of California Press, 1980.

Meyer, Stephen P. *The Five Dollar Day: Labor Management and Social Control in the Ford Motor Company, 1908–1921.* Albany: State University of New York Press, 1981.

Miller, Jennifer M. *Cold War Democracy: The United States and Japan.* Cambridge, MA: Harvard University Press, 2019.

Mimura, Janis. *Planning for Empire: Reform Bureaucrats and the Japanese Wartime State.* Ithaca, NY: Cornell University Press, 2011.

Mommsen, Hans. "Nationalsozialismus als vorgetäuschte Modernisierung." In *Der Nationalsozialismus und die deutsche Gesellschaft*, edited by Hans Mommsen, 405–27. Reinbek, Germany: Lau, 1991.

Mommsen, Hans, and Manfred Grieger. *Das Volkswagenwerk und seine Arbeiter im Dritten Reich.* Düsseldorf, Germany: Econ, 1996.

Montgomery, David. *The Fall of the House of Labor: The Workplace, the State, and American Labor Activism, 1865–1925.* Cambridge, UK: Cambridge University Press, 1987.

Müller, Rolf-Dieter. "Die Mobilisierung der deutschen Wirtschaft für Hitlers Kriegführung." In *Das deutsche Reich und der Zweite Weltkrieg: Organisation und Mobilisierung des deutschen Machtbereichs*, vol. 5/1, edited by Bernhard R. Kroener, Rolf-Dieter Müller, and Hans Umbreit, 349–689. Stuttgart: DVA, 1988.

Neebe, Reinhard. "Technologietransfer und Außenhandel in den Anfängen der Bundesrepublik Deutschland." *Vierteljahreshefte für Sozial- und Wirtschaftsgeschichte* 76, no. 1 (1989): 49–75.

Nefedov, Sergei, and Michael Ellman, "The Soviet Famine of 1931–1934: Genocide, a Result of Poor Harvests, or the Outcome of a Conflict between the State and the Peasants?" *Europe-Asia Studies* 71, no. 6 (2019): 1048–65.

Neliba, Günter. *Die Opel-Werke im Konzern von General Motors (1929–1948) in Rüsselsheim und Brandenburg: Produktion für Aufrüstung und Krieg ab 1935 unter nationalsozialistischer Herrschaft.* Frankfurt: Brandes & Apsel, 2000.

Nelson, Daniel. *Managers and Workers: Origins of the Twentieth-Century Factory System in the United States, 1880–1920.* Madison: University of Wisconsin Press, 1996.

Nevins, Allan, and Frank Ernest Hill. *Ford: Decline and Rebirth, 1933–1962.* New York: Charles Scribner's Sons, 1962.

———. *Ford: Expansion and Challenge, 1915–1933.* New York: Charles Scribner's Sons, 1957.

———. *Ford: The Times, the Man, the Company.* New York: Charles Scribner's Sons, 1954.

Noble, David F. *America by Design: Science, Technology, and the Rise of Corporate Capitalism.* Oxford, UK: Oxford University Press, 1979.

———. *Forces of Production: A Social History of Automation.* New York: Knopf, 1984.

Nolan, Mary. Review of *Das Volkswagenwerk und seine Arbeiter,* by Hans Mommsen and Manfred Grieger. *International Labor and Working-Class History* 55 (Spring 1999): 149–54.

———. *The Transatlantic Century: Europe and America, 1890–2010.* New York: Cambridge University Press, 2012.

———. *Visions of Modernity: American Business and the Modernization of Germany.* Oxford, UK: Oxford University Press, 1994.

Nord, Philip. *France's New Deal: From the Thirties to the Postwar Era.* Princeton, NJ: Princeton University Press, 2010.

Nove, Alec. *An Economic History of the USSR, 1917–1991.* London: Penguin, 1992.

Nye, David. *America's Assembly Line,* Cambridge, MA: MIT Press, 2013.

Offner, Amy C. *Sorting Out the Mixed Economy: The Rise and Fall of Welfare and Developmental States in the Americas.* Princeton, NJ: Princeton University Press, 2019.

O'Rourke, Kevin, and Jeffrey Williamson, eds. *The Spread of Modern Industry to the Periphery since 1871.* Oxford, UK: Oxford University Press, 2017.

Ortolano, Guy. "The Typicalities of the English? Walt Rostow, the Stages of Economic Growth, and Modern British History." *Modern Intellectual History* 12, no. 3 (2015): 657–84.

Osokina, Elena. *Our Daily Bread: Socialist Distribution and the Art of Survival in Stalin's Russia, 1927–1941,* edited by Kate Transchel. Armonk, NY: Sharpe, 2001.

———. *Za fasadom "Stalinskogo izobiliia": Raspredelenie i rynok v snabzhenii naseleniia v gody industrializatsii, 1927–41.* Moscow: ROSSPEN, 1999.

———. *Zoloto dlia industrializatsii: TORGSIN.* Moscow: ROSSPEN, 2009.

Ott, Daniel. "Producing a Past: McCormick Harvester and Producer Populists in the 1890s." *Agricultural History* 88, no. 1 (2014): 87–119.

Ott, Julia C. *When Wall Street Met Main Street: The Quest for an Investors' Democracy.* Cambridge, MA: Harvard University Press, 2011.

Overy, Richard J. *The Air War, 1939–1945.* Washington, DC: Potomac, 2005.

Overy, Richard J. "Cars, Roads, and Economic Recovery in Germany, 1932–8." *Economic History Review* 28, no. 3 (1975): 466–83.

———. *War and Economy in the Third Reich*. Oxford, UK: Clarendon Press, 1994.

———. *Why the Allies Won*. New York: Norton, 1995.

Page, Brian, and Richard Walker. "From Settlement to Fordism: The Agro-Industrial Revolution in the American Midwest." *Economic Geography* 67, no. 4 (1991): 281–315.

Paradisi, Mariangela. "Il commercio estero e la struttura industriale." In *L'economia italiana nel periodo fascista*, edited by Pierluigi Ciocca and Gianni Toniolo, 271–328. Bologna, Italy: Mulino, 1976.

Parrott, Bruce, ed. *Trade, Technology, and Soviet-American Relations*. Bloomington: Indiana University Press, 1985.

Patel, Kiran K. *The New Deal: A Global History*. Princeton, NJ: Princeton University Press, 2016.

———. *Soldiers of Labor: Labor Service in Nazi Germany and New Deal America, 1933–45*. Cambridge, UK: Cambridge University Press, 2005.

Pechatnov, Vladimir A. "The Soviet Union and the World, 1944–1953." In *The Cambridge History of the Cold War*, vol. 1, edited by Melvyn P. Leffler and Odd Arne Westad, 90–111. New York: Cambridge University Press, 2012.

Petri, Rolf. *Von der Autarkie zum Wirtschaftswunder: Wirtschaftspolitik und industrieller Wandel in Italien, 1935–65*. Tübingen, Germany: Niemeyer, 2001.

Petzina, Dietmar. *Autarkiepolitik im "Dritten Reich": Der nationalsozialistische Vierjahresplan*. Stuttgart: DVA, 1968.

Piore, Michael J., and Sabel, Charles F. *The Second Industrial Divide: Possibilities for Prosperity*. New York: Basic, 1984.

Plaggenborg, Stephan. *Ordnung und Gewalt: Kemalismus—Faschismus—Sozialismus*. Munich: Oldenbourg, 2012.

Pollack, Norman. *The Populist Response to Industrial America: Midwestern Populist Thought*. Cambridge, MA: Harvard University Press, 1962.

Rae, John B. "Why Michigan?" In *The Automobile and American Culture*, edited by David L. Lewis and Lawrence Goldstein, 1–9. Ann Arbor: University of Michigan Press, 1983.

Rafalski, Traute. *Italienischer Faschismus in der Weltwirtschaftskrise, 1925–1936*. Opladen, Germany: Westdeutscher Verlag, 1984.

Raff, Daniel M. G. "Ford Welfare Capitalism in Its Economic Context." *Masters to Managers: Historical and Comparative Perspectives on American Employers*, edited by Sanford M. Jacoby, 90–110. New York: Columbia University Press, 1991.

———. "Making Cars and Making Money in the Interwar Automobile Industry: Economies of Scale and Scope and the Manufacturing behind the Marketing." *Business History Review* 65, no 4 (1991): 721–53.

———. "Wage Determination Theory and the Five Dollar Day at Ford." *Journal of Economic History* 48, no. 2 (1988): 387–99.

Raff, Daniel M. G., and Lawrence H. Summers. "Did Henry Ford Pay Efficiency Wages?" *Journal of Labor Economics* 5, no. 4 (1987): S57–S86.

Randall, Amy. *The Soviet Dream World of Retail Trade and Consumption in the 1930s*. Basingstoke, UK: Palgrave Macmillan, 2008.

Rapping, Leonard. "Learning and World War II Production Functions." *Review of Economics and Statistics* 47, no. 1 (1965): 81–86.

Rassweiler, Anne D. *The Generation of Power: The History of Dneprostroi*. New York: Oxford University Press, 1988.

Reich, Simon. *The Fruits of Fascism: Postwar Prosperity in Historical Perspective*. Ithaca, NY: Cornell University Press, 1990.

———. *Research Findings about Ford-Werke under the Nazi Regime*. Dearborn, MI: Ford Motor Company, 2001.

Reiling, Johannes. *Deutschland, Safe for Democracy? Deutsch-amerikanische Beziehungen aus dem Tätigkeitsbereich Heinrich F. Alberts, kaiserlicher Geheimrat in Amerika, erster Staatssekretär der Reichskanzlei der Weimarer Republik, Reichsminister, Betreuer der Ford-Gesellschaften im Herrschaftsgebiet des Dritten Reiches, 1914–1945*. Stuttgart: Steiner, 1997.

Ribuffo, Leo P. "Henry Ford and the International Jew." In Leo P. Ribuffo, *Right Center Left: Essays in American History*, 135–50. New Brunswick, NJ: Rutgers University Press, 1992.

Richter, James G. *Khrushchev's Double Bind: International Pressures and Domestic Coalition Politics*. Baltimore: Johns Hopkins University Press, 1994.

Richter, Ralf, and Jochen Streb. "Catching-Up and Falling Behind: Knowledge Spillover from American to German Machine Toolmakers." *Journal of Economic History* 71, no. 4 (2011): 1006–31.

Rieger, Bernhard. *The People's Car: A Global History of the Volkswagen Beetle*. Cambridge, MA: Harvard University Press, 2013.

Ristuccia, Andrea, and Solomos Solomou. "Electricity Diffusion and Trend Acceleration in Inter-war Manufacturing Productivity." Cambridge Working Papers in Economics 0202, 2002.

Ristuccia, Andrea, and Adam Tooze. "Machine Tools and Mass Production: Germany and the United States, 1929–44." *Economic History Review* 66, no. 4 (2013): 953–74.

Ritschl, Albrecht. *Deutschlands Krise und Konjunktur, 1924–1934: Binnenkonjunktur, Auslandsverschuldung und Reparationsproblem zwischen Dawes-Plan und Transfersperre*. Berlin: Akademie, 2002.

Rogers, Everett. *Diffusion of Innovations*. New York: Free Press, 1962.

Rogger, Hans. "*Amerikanizm* and the Economic Development of Russia." *Comparative Studies in Society and History* 23, no. 3 (1981): 382–420.

Roseman, Mark. "National Socialism and the End of Modernity." *American Historical Review* 116, no. 3 (2011): 688–701.

Rosenberg, Nathan. "Economic Development and the Transfer of Technology: Some Historical Perspectives." *Technology and Culture* 11, no. 4 (1970): 550–75.

Rossman, Jeffrey J. *Worker Resistance under Stalin: Class and Revolution on the Shop Floor*. Cambridge, MA: Harvard University Press, 2005.

Rossoliński-Liebe, Grzegorz. *Fascism without Borders: Transnational Connections and Cooperation between Movements and Regimes in Europe from 1918 to 1945*. New York: Berghahn, 2017.

Rothermund, Dietmar, ed. *Die Peripherie in der Weltwirtschaftskrise: Afrika, Asien und Lateinamerika, 1929–1939*. Paderborn, Germany: Schöningh, 1982.

Rubenstein, James M. *The Changing US Auto Industry: A Geographical Analysis*. London: Routledge, 1992.

Rupert, Mark. *Producing Hegemony: The Politics of Mass Production and American Global Power*. New York: Cambridge University Press, 1995.

Sabel, Charles F., and Jonathan Zeitlin. "Historical Alternatives to Mass Production: Politics, Markets and Technology in Nineteenth Century Industrialization." *Past and Present* 108, no. 1 (1985): 133–76.

———, eds. *World of Possibilities. Flexibility and Mass Production in Western Industrialization*. Cambridge, UK: Cambridge University Press, 1997.

Samuels, Richard. *"Rich Nation, Strong Army": National Security and the Technological Transformation of Japan*. Ithaca, NY: Cornell University Press, 1994.

Samuelson, Lennart. *Tankograd: The Formation of a Soviet Company Town; Cheliabinsk, 1900–1950s*. London: Palgrave, 2011.

Sanchez-Sibony, Oscar. "Depression Stalinism: The Great Break Reconsidered." *Kritika: Explorations in Russian and Eurasian History* 15, no. 1 (2014): 23–49.

———. "Global Money and Bolshevik Authority: The NEP as the First Socialist Project," *Slavic Review* 78, no. 3 (2019): 694–716.

———. *Red Globalization: The Political Economy of the Soviet Cold War from Stalin to Khrushchev*. Cambridge, UK: Cambridge University Press, 2014.

Sasada, Hironori. *The Evolution of the Japanese Developmental State: Institutions Locked In by Ideas*. London: Routledge, 2013.

Sasaki, Satoshi. "The Rationalization of Production Management Systems in Japan during World War II." In *World War II and the Transformation of Business Systems*, edited by Jun Sakudō and Takao Shiba, 30–54. Tokyo: University of Tokyo Press, 1994.

Scherner, Jonas. "'Armament in Depth' or 'Armament in Breadth'? German Investment Pattern and Rearmament during the Nazi Period." *Economic History Review* 66, no. 2 (2013): 497–517.

———. "Die Grenzen der Informationsbeschaffung, -transfer und -verarbeitung in der deutschen Wehr- und Kriegswirtschaftsverwaltung im Dritten Reich." *Jahrbuch für Wirtschaftsgeschichte* 56, no. 1 (2015): 99–135.

———. *Die Logik der Industriepolitik im Dritten Reich: Die Investitionen in die Autarkie- und Rüstungsindustrie und ihre staatliche Förderung*. Stuttgart: Steiner, 2008.

Scherner, Jonas, and Jochen Streb. "Das Ende eines Mythos? Albert Speer und das sogenannte Rüstungswunder." *Vierteljahresschrift für Sozial- und Wirtschaftsgeschichte* 93, no. 2 (2006): 172–96.

Schivelbusch, Wolfgang. *Three New Deals: Reflections on Roosevelt's America, Mussolini's Italy, and Hitler's Germany, 1933–1939*. New York: Henry Holt, 2006.

Schlesinger, Jr., Arthur M. *The Age of Roosevelt: The Crisis of the Old Order, 1919–1933*. Boston: Houghton Mifflin, 1957.

Schultz, Kurt S. "The American Factor in Soviet Industrialization: Fordism and the First Five-Year Plan, 1928–1932." PhD dissertation, Ohio State University, 1992.

———. "Building the 'Soviet Detroit': The Construction of the Nizhnii-Novgorod Automobile Factory, 1927–1932." *Slavic Review* 49, no. 2 (1990): 200–212.

Scott, James C. *Seeing Like a State: How Certain Schemes to Improve the Human Condition Have Failed*. New Haven, CT: Yale University Press, 1998.

Scranton, Philip. *Endless Novelty: Specialty Production and American Industrialization 1865–1925*. Princeton, NJ: Princeton University Press, 1997.

Segbers, Klaus. *Die Sowjetunion im Zweiten Weltkrieg: Die Mobilisierung von Verwaltung, Wirtschaft und Gesellschaft im "Großen Vaterländischen Krieg," 1941–1943*. Munich: Oldenbourg, 1987.

Shapiro, Helen. *Engines of Growth: The State and Transnational Auto Companies in Brazil*. Cambridge, UK: Cambridge University Press, 1994.

Shearer, David R. *Industry, State, and Society in Stalin's Russia, 1926–1934*. Ithaca, NY: Cornell University Press, 1996.

———. "The Language and Politics of Socialist Rationalization. Productivity, Industrial Relations, and the Social Origins of Stalinism at the End of NEP." *Cahiers du monde russe et soviétique* 32, no. 4 (1991): 581–608.

Shenhav, Yehouda. *Manufacturing Rationality: The Engineering Foundations of the Managerial Revolution*. Oxford, UK: Oxford University Press, 1999.

Shiomi, Haruhito, and Kazuo Wada, eds. *Fordism Transformed: The Development of Production Methods in the Automobile Industry*. New York: Oxford University Press, 1995.

Shpotov, Boris. "Bisnesmeny i biurokraty: Amerikanskaia tekhnicheskaia pomoshch' v stroitel'stve nizhegorodskogo avtozavoda, 1929–1931 gg." *Ekonomicheskaia istoriia: Ezhegodnik* (2002): 191–232.

———. "Ford in Russia, from 1909 to World War II." In *Ford, 1903–2003: The European History*, vol. 2, edited by Hubert Bonin, Yannick Lung, and Steven Tolliday, 514–20. Paris: PLAGE, 2003.

———. "Pereplatil-li sovetskii soiuz kompanii Forda? K voprosu o tsene industrializatsii." *Ekonomicheskaia istoriia: Ezhegodnik* (2004): 160–80.

———. "Uchastie amerikanskikh promyshlennykh kompanii v sovetskoi industrializatsii, 1928–1933." *Ekonomicheskaia istoriia: Ezhegodnik* (2005): 172–96.

Siegel, Katherine A. S. *Loans and Legitimacy: The Evolution of Soviet-American Relations, 1919–1933*. Lexington: University Press of Kentucky, 1996.

Siegel, Tilla, and Thomas von Freyberg. *Industrielle Rationalisierung unter dem Nationalsozialismus*. Frankfurt: Campus, 1991.

Siegelbaum, Lewis H. *Cars for Comrades: The Life of the Soviet Automobile*. Ithaca, NY: Cornell University Press, 2008.

———. "Soviet Norm Determination in Theory and Practice, 1917–1941." *Soviet Studies* 36, no. 1 (1984): 45–68.

———. *Stakhanovism and the Politics of Productivity in the USSR, 1935–1941*. Cambridge, UK: Cambridge University Press, 1988.

Simms, Brendan. *Hitler: Only the World Was Enough*. New York: Allen Lane, 2019.

Simonov, Nikolai. "*Mobpodgotovka*: Mobilization Planning in Interwar Industry." In *The Soviet Defence-Industry Complex from Stalin to Khrushchev*, edited by John Barber and Mark Harrison, 205–222. Basingstoke, UK: Macmillan, 2000.

Sklar, Martin J. *The Corporate Reconstruction of American Capitalism, 1890–1916: The Market, the Law, and Politics*. Cambridge, UK: Cambridge University Press, 1988.

Slezkine, Yuri. *The House of Government: A Saga of the Russian Revolution*. Princeton, NJ: Princeton University Press, 2017.

Sparrow, James T. *Warfare State: World War II Americans and the Age of Big Government*. New York: Oxford University Press, 2011.

Spoerer, Mark. *Zwangsarbeit unter dem Hakenkreuz: Ausländische Zivilarbeiter, Kriegsgefangene und Häftlinge im Deutschen Reich und im besetzten Europa, 1939–1945*. Munich: DVA, 2001.

Steen, Kathryn. *The American Synthetic Organic Chemicals Industry: War and Politics, 1910–1930*. Chapel Hill: University of North Carolina Press, 2014.

Steiner, Zara. *The Triumph of the Dark: European International History, 1933–39*. Oxford, UK: Oxford University Press, 2011.

Sternhell, Zeev. *Neither Right nor Left: Fascist Ideology in France*, translated by David Maisel. Berkeley: University of California Press, 1986.

Streather, Adrian. *Bernar Nahum: A Pioneer of Turkey's Automotive Industry*. Eden, SD: Nettleberry, 2011.

Strelianyi, Anatolii. "Khrushchev and the Countryside." In *Nikita Khrushchev*, edited by William Taubman, Sergei Khrushchev, and Abbott Gleason, 113–37. New Haven, CT: Yale University Press, 2000.

Sutton, Antony C. *Western Technology and Soviet Development*. 3 vols. Stanford, CA: Hoover Institution, 1968–1973.

Tedlow, Richard S. "The Struggle for Dominance in the Automobile Market: The Early Years of Ford and GM." *Business and Economic History* 17 (1988): 49–62.

Teichert, Eckart. *Autarkie und Großraumwirtschaft in Deutschland, 1930–1939: Außenwirtschaftspolitische Konzeptionen zwischen Wirtschaftskrise und Zweitem Weltkrieg*. Munich: Oldenbourg, 1984.

Tessner, Magnus. *Die deutsche Automobilindustrie im Strukturwandel von 1919 bis 1938*. Cologne: Botermann, 1994.

Tetzlaff, Stefan. "The Motorisation of the 'Moffusil': Automobile Traffic and Social Change in Rural and Small-Town India, c. 1915–1940." PhD dissertation, University of Göttingen, 2015.

Thomas, Peter D. *The Gramscian Moment: Philosophy, Hegemony, and Marxism*. Leiden, Netherlands: Brill, 2009.

Thorp, Rosemary, ed. *Latin America in the 1930s: The Role of the Periphery in the World Crisis*. Basingstoke, UK: Macmillan, 1984.

Tolliday, Steven. "Enterprise and State in the West German Wirtschaftswunder: Volkswagen and the Automobile Industry, 1939–62." *Business History Review* 69, no. 3 (1995): 273–330.

———, ed. *The Rise and Fall of Mass Production*. 2 vols. Cheltenham, UK: Edward Elgar, 1998.

———. "Transplanting the American Model? US Automobile Companies and the Transfer of Technology and Management to Britain, France, and Germany, 1928–1962." In *Americanization and Its Limits: Reworking US Technology and Management in Post-war Europe and Japan*, edited by Jonathan Zeitlin and Gary Herrigel, 76–119. Oxford, UK: Oxford University Press, 2000.

Tolliday, Steven, and Jonathan Zeitlin, eds. *Between Fordism and Flexibility: The Automobile Industry and Its Workers*. New York: St. Martin's, 1992.

Toninelli, Pier A. "Between Agnelli and Mussolini: Ford's Unsuccessful Attempt to Penetrate the Italian Automobile Market in the Interwar Period." *Enterprise and Society* 10, no. 2 (2009): 335–75.

Tooze, Adam. *The Deluge: The Great War, America, and the Making of a New Global Order, 1916–1931*. New York: Viking, 2014.

———. "No Room for Miracles. German Industrial Output in World War II Reassessed." *Geschichte und Gesellschaft* 31, no. 3 (2005): 439–64.

———. "Reassessing the Moral Economy of Post-war Reconstruction: The Terms of the West German Settlement in 1952." *Past and Present* (2011), Supplement 6, 47–70.

———. *The Wages of Destruction: The Making and Breaking of the Nazi Economy*. New York: Viking, 2007.

Treue, Wilhelm. "Hitlers Denkschrift zum Vierjahresplan 1936." *Vierteljahreshefte für Zeitgeschichte* 3, no.2 (1955): 206–10.

Turner, Henry Ashby. *General Motors and the Nazis: The Struggle for Control of Opel, Europe's Biggest Carmaker*. New Haven, CT: Yale University Press, 2005.

———. *German Big Business and the Rise of Hitler*. New York: Oxford University Press, 1985.

Tyrell, Albrecht. "Gottfried Feder and the NSDAP." In *The Shaping of the Nazi State*, edited by Peter D. Strachura, 48–87. New York: Barnes & Noble, 1978.

Tzouliadis, Tim. *The Forsaken: An American Tragedy in Stalin's Russia*. New York: Penguin, 2008.

Udagawa, Masaru. "The Prewar Japanese Automobile Industry and American Manufacturers." *Japanese Yearbook of Business History* 2 (1986): 81–99.

Uziel, Daniel. *Arming the Luftwaffe: The German Aviation Industry in World War II*. Jefferson, NC: McFarland, 2012.

———. "Between Industrial Revolution and Slavery: Mass Production in the German Aviation Industry in World War II." *History and Technology* 22, no. 3 (2006): 277–300.

Vacca, Giuseppe. "Gramsci Studies since 1989." *Journal of Modern Italian Studies* 16, no. 2 (2011): 179–94.

Veeser, Cyrus. "A Forgotten Instrument of Global Capitalism? International Concessions, 1870–1930." *International History Review* 35, no. 5 (2013): 1136–55.

Volpato, Giuseppe. "Ford in Italy: Commercial Breakthroughs without Industrial Bridgeheads." In *Ford, 1903–2003: The European History*, vol. 2, edited by Hubert Bonin, Yannick Lung, and Steven Tolliday, 451–477. Paris: PLAGE, 2003.

———. "Produzione e mercato: Verso l'automobilismo di massa." In *Mirafiori, 1936–1962*, edited by Carlo Olmo, 133–150. Turin, Italy: Umberto Allemandi, 1997.

Wade, Robert. *Governing the Market: Economic Theory and the Role of Government in East Asian Industrialization*. Princeton, NJ: Princeton University Press, 1990.

Wallace, Max. *The American Axis: Henry Ford, Charles Lindbergh, and the Rise of the Third Reich*. New York: St. Martin's, 2003.

Watts, Steven. *The People's Tycoon: Henry Ford and the American Century*. New York: Vintage, 2006.

Wehler, Hans-Ulrich. *Deutsche Gesellschaftsgeschichte*. 5 vols. Munich: Beck, 1987–2008.

Weisberger, Bernard A. *The Dream Maker: William C. Durant, Founder of General Motors*. Boston: Little, Brown & Co., 1979.

Wellhöner, Volker. *"Wirtschaftswunder," Weltmarkt, westdeutscher Fordismus: Der Fall Volkswagen*. Münster, Germany: Westfälisches Dampfboot, 1996.

Wend, Henry B. "'But the German Manufacturer Doesn't Want Our Advice': West German Labor and Business and the Limits of American Technical Assistance, 1950–54." In *Catching Up with America: Productivity Missions and the Diffusion of American Economic and Technological Influence after the Second World War*, edited by Dominique Barjot. Paris: Presses de L'Université de Paris-Sorbonne, 2002.

Werner, Constanze. *Kriegswirtschaft und Zwangsarbeit bei BMW*. Munich: Oldenbourg, 2006.

Werth, Christoph. *Sozialismus und Nation: Die deutsche Ideologiedebatte zwischen 1918 und 1945*. Opladen, Germany: Westdeutscher Verlag, 1996.

White, Christine. "Ford in Russia: In Pursuit of the Chimerical Market." *Business History* 28, no. 4 (1986): 77–104.

Wilkins, Mira. "The Contributions of Foreign Enterprises to Japanese Economic Development." In *Foreign Business in Japan before World War II*, edited by Takeshi Yuzawa and Masaru Udagawa, 35–57. Tokyo: University of Tokyo Press, 1990.

———. *The History of Foreign Investment in the United States, 1914–1945.* Cambridge, MA: Harvard University Press, 2004.

———. *The Maturing of Multinational Enterprise: American Business Abroad from 1914 to 1970.* Cambridge, MA: Harvard University Press, 1974.

———. "Multinationals and Dictatorship: Europe in the 1930s and Early 1940s." In *European Business, Dictatorship, and Political Risk, 1920–1945*, edited by Christopher Kobrak and Per Hansen, 22–38. New York: Berghahn Books, 2004.

Wilkins, Mira, and Frank E. Hill. *American Business Abroad: Ford on Six Continents.* New edition with a new introduction by Mira Wilkins. Cambridge: Cambridge University Press, 2011. (First published in 1964 by Wayne State University Press, Detroit.)

Williams, Andy J. *Trading with the Bolsheviks. The Politics of East-West Trade, 1920–39.* Manchester, UK: Manchester University Press, 1992.

Wilson, James M., and Alan McKinlay. "Rethinking the Assembly Line: Organisation, Performance, and Productivity in Ford Motor Company, c. 1908–27." *Business History* 52, no. 5 (2010): 760–78.

Wilson, Mark. *Destructive Creation: American Business and the Winning of World War II.* Philadelphia: University of Pennsylvania Press, 2016.

Winkler, Heinrich A. *The Age of Catastrophe. A History of the West, 1914–1945.* New Haven, CT: Yale University Press, 2015.

Wolfe, Joel. *Autos and Progress: The Brazilian Search for Modernity.* New York: Oxford University Press, 2010.

Womack, James P., Daniel T. Jones, and Daniel Roos. *The Machine That Changed the World.* New York: Free Press, 1990.

Wood, John C., and Michael C. Wood, eds. *Alfred P. Sloan: Critical Evaluations in Business and Management.* 2 vols. London: Routledge, 2003.

Wren, Daniel. "James D. Mooney and General Motors' Multinational Operations, 1922–1940." *Business History Review* 87, no. 3 (2013): 515–43.

Yanagisawa, Osamu. "The Impact of German Economic Thought on Japanese Economists before World War II." In *The German Historical School: The Historical and Ethical Approach to Economics*, edited by Yuichi Shionova, 173–87. London: Routledge, 2001.

Zaleski, Eugène. *Planning for Economic Growth in the Soviet Union, 1918–1932.* Chapel Hill: University of North Carolina Press, 1971.

Zani, Luciano. *Fascismo, autarchia, commercio estero: Felice Guarneri, un tecnocrate al servizio dello "Stato Nuovo."* Bologna, Italy: Il Mulino, 1988.

Zeitlin, Jonathan. "Flexibility and Mass Production at War: Aircraft Manufacture in Britain, the United States, and Germany, 1939–1945." *Technology and Culture* 36, no. 1 (1994): 46–79.

Zeitlin, Jonathan, and Gary Herrigel, eds. *Americanization and Its Limits: Reworking US Technology and Management in Postwar Europe and Japan.* Oxford, UK: Oxford University Press, 2000.

Ziegler, Dieter. "'A Regulated Market Economy': New Perspectives on the Nature of the Economic Order of the Third Reich, 1933–39." In *Business in the Age of Extremes: Essays in Modern German and Austrian Economic History*, edited by Hartmut Berghoff, Jurgen Kocka, and Dieter Ziegler, 139–52. Washington, DC: German Historical Institute, 2013.

Zitelmann, Rainer. *Hitler: Selbstverständnis eines Revolutionärs*. 5th rev. ed. Reinbek, Germany: Lau, 2017. (First published in 1987.)

Zubkova, Elena. *Russia after the War: Hopes, Illusions, and Disappointments*, translated by Hugh Ragsdale. Armonk, NY: Sharpe, 1998.

Zunz, Olivier. *The Changing Face of Inequality: Urbanization, Industrial Development, and Immigrants in Detroit, 1880–1920*. Chicago: University of Chicago Press, 1982.

ACKNOWLEDGMENTS

Researching and writing this book has been a longer and more arduous climb
than I naively anticipated when I first strapped on my boots. The journey
turned out to be full of obstacles and rife with detours; often the path I scouted
led me to the foot of a rockface or the edge of a precipice. More than once
turning back seemed attractive. I only made it thanks to those who tendered
moral and logistical support, gave advice, encouragement, and directions, offered shelter, company, and sustenance.

My colleagues at Dartmouth supported me on the agonizing final stretch.
Thanks to Ron Edsforth, Steve Ericson, Max Fraser, Udi Greenberg, Douglas
Haynes, Ed Miller, Jennifer Miller, and Bethany Moreton for sharing reflec-
tions and criticisms. I am grateful to Doug Irwin for our discussions of eco-
nomic history over lunch sandwiches. Timothy Rosenkoetter encouraged me
to master Peer Pressure and has been patient with my efforts. Bob Bonner,
Leslie Butler, Pamela Crossley, Peggy Darrow, Carl Estabrook, Cecilia Ga-
poschkin, Rashauna Johnson, Darrin McMahon, Paul Musselwhite, Annelise
Orleck, Gail Patten, Naaborko Sackeyfio-Lenoch and Derrick White made the
History department a haven of unusual collegiality.

Thanks to Mario Daniels, Colleen Dunlavy, Kristy Ironside, and John Krige,
who generously gave their time to read and comment on the manuscript. A
conversation with Oscar Sanchez-Sibony in a *stolovaia* in Moscow pointed me
in the direction of a Soviet economic history that I intuited had to exist; thanks
to him, I was able to uncover it. Anna Krylova pleaded that any attempt to
exorcise modernization theory was hampered by leaning on the notion of the
"illiberal"—this was a key insight, for which I thank her; the book is much
better for it. Mary Nolan offered a perceptive and generous critique of the
project that helped me finish it. Gabrielle Clark listened to my plaints and
confusions and invariably offered clear-sighted responses that led to solutions.
At several forks in the road Kiran Patel gave characteristically hard-nosed ap-
praisals on the state of the project: his feedback helped me push forward and
avoid distractions. A special note of thanks goes out to Noam Maggor, who
even in the badlands of this journey urged me to trust my intuitions. Quite
simply, without Noam's intellectual encouragement and moral support this

book would not have seen the light of day. Thanks, Noam—let's continue this. Some conversations spark a thought that lingers; possibly without knowing it, a number of scholars have contributed to the book in this way: David Sicilia in Toledo, Ohio; Youssef Cassis, Simon Jackson, Nathan Marcus, and Aidan Regan in Florence; Manfred Grieger and Jan Logemann in Göttingen; Mark Harrison in Hanover, New Hampshire; Sarah Ehlers and Alex Korb in Berlin. (In his inimitable way Alex also reminded me that there was more to life.)

My early work germinated at Harvard among an inspirational group of historians. I came to understand the stakes of economic history thanks to working and debating with Charles Maier, Sven Beckert and Niall Ferguson; Christine Desan, Terry Martin, and Peter Gordon taught me much that has stood the test of time. I want to thank Tariq Ali, Johanna Conterio, Eli Cook, Ian Klaus, Vanessa Ogle, Jennifer Yum Park, Maya Peterson, Caitlin Rosenthal, Rainer Schultz, Heidi Tworek, and Jeremy Yellen for their irreverence. With characteristic generosity, Misha Akulov and Hassan Malik helped me find my feet in Russia. Molly Chow and Ethan Seidman imparted wisdom and resilience. A later stint at Harvard introduced me to Martin Gireaudeaux, Nicolas Barreyre, Tracy Newman, and Paul Kershaw.

I thank the many institutions that have supported my research, including the Center for European Studies, the Davis Center for Russian and Eurasian Studies, the Charles Warren Center for American Studies, and the Weatherhead Center for International Affairs at Harvard; the Benson Ford Research Center in Dearborn, Michigan; the German Historical Institute in Washington, DC; the German Historical Institute in Moscow; the European University Institute in Florence, Italy; and Dartmouth College, whose Burke Grant and generous leave policy allowed me to finish this book. Among the many archivists whose patience I have taxed I want to give especial thanks to Linda Skolarus at the Benson Ford Research Center; Galina Deminova at the Central Regional Archives in Nizhnii Novgorod; and Ulrike Gutzmann at the Volkswagen archive in Wolfsburg. A group of stellar research assistants helped me pull the manuscript together: Sandra Funck, Noah Grass, Sam Neff, and Rine Uhm.

I doubt Clio is an extrovert; I imagine her spending countless hours secluded in communion with books. I'd like to believe she still prefers this analog virtual sociability to its newer digital modes. Hence an emphatic note of thanks to all the historians and social scientists with whose work I have spent so many hours, provoked, inspired, enthused, amused, bored, appalled, delighted, irritated, awed—all of you contributed intellectual rivulets that have issued into this book.

Gaby—I said I wouldn't do this, but without you nothing would have worked out. Thank you. And thank you for the beautiful wonder you have brought into our lives. This book is dedicated to you and Solène, with love.

INDEX

Agnelli, Giovanni, 130

agriculture, 10, 64; in Midwest, 24, 27; in Soviet Union, 94–95, 99, 203, 213

aircraft industry: BMW, 181–82, 184; and Fordism, 180–81; Junkers, 180, 181; in Nazi Germany, 86–88, 134, 135, 167, 183, 192–95, 216, 265n58; in Soviet Union, 116, 196–97, 204

Albert, Heinrich (Ford AG), 146, 149–50, 152, 153, 155–57, 161, 256n49

Allach (BMW plant), 190–92, 193, 204

Ambi-Budd, 158

Americanism: "Americanism and Fordism" (*see* Gramsci, Antonio); in Soviet Union, 75–77, 81, 87–88

Americanization, 5–6

AMO. *See* Moscow Automobile Society

Amsden, Alice, 90

anti-Semitism, 62, 63, 64, 69, 238n37; Henry Ford and, 52, 64

assembly lines, 2–3, 5, 7, 30, 53, 61, 110, 168, 172, 173; at Fiat Mirafiori, 130; at Ford Highland Park, 30–31, 34, 80; Fordism and, 6; at Ford River Rouge, 22; at Gaz (Gorky Automobile Factory), 115, 119, 120, 123–26, 128, 129–30, 203; at GM Pontiac plant, 20; Gramsci on, 4; postliberals on, 61, 69; at Opel Brandenburg plant, 159; Regulation School on, 4; speedup of, 49; at Volkswagen, 167; in war production in Germany, 189, 190, 192, 194; in Weimar automobile industry, 141. *See also* conveyors; flow production; Fordism; mass production

Austin (construction firm), 106–7

autarky, 9–11, 25, 71–72

Auto Giant. *See* Gaz (Gorky Automobile Factory)

automation, of manufacturing, 160, 212–13

automobile industry, 13, 224n45; and aircraft industry, 181; development and, 15, 98–100, 133, 170–71; elites and, 29, 36; in France, 14, 137–38; in Germany (–1933), 12, 139–40; in Germany (1933–45), 133, 148, 152–53, 170, 181; in Germany (1945–), 163, 195, 210, 216; Hitler on, 70; in Italy, 14, 137; in Japan, 13, 138; mergers in, 138, 140–41, 164; in Midwest, 24–25, 27, 32, 35–37, 229n17; Midwest mechanics and, 35, 36; and "people's car," 139, 141–42; in Soviet Union, 98, 100, 104, 118, 122; in United States, 14, 25, 43, 109, 181; *See also* Fiat; Ford AG (Cologne); Ford Motor Company; Gaz (Gorky Automobile Factory); General Motors (GM); Opel AG; Volkswagen

Automobile Manufacturing Enterprise Law (Japan, 1936), 13

Automotive Association. *See* Reich Association of the German Automobile Industry (RDA)

Autostroy, 106, 107, 110–15, 116–17

Auto-Union, 20, 50, 131, 140, 143, 145, 174, 177–78, 182, 187, 195

Aviation Ministry (Nazi Germany), 154, 172–74, 180–89, 191–94, 204, 258n80. *See also* Göring, Hermann

Avtostroi, 91, 104, 106–7, 109–11, 116

A NOTE ON THE TYPE

This book has been composed in Arno, an Old-style serif typeface in the classic Venetian tradition, designed by Robert Slimbach at Adobe.